Access to Criminal Justice

Access to Criminal Justice

Edited by

Richard Young

and

David Wall

Foreword by The Right Hon. Sir Thomas Bingham

BLACKSTONE
PRESS LIMITED

First published in Great Britain 1996 by Blackstone Press Limited, 9–15 Aldine Street, London W12 8AW. Telephone: 0181-740 1173

ISBN: 1 85431 502 1

British Library Cataloguing in Publication Data
A CIP catalogue record for this book is available from the British Library.

Typeset by Montage Studios Limited, Tonbridge, Kent
Printed by Livesey Ltd, Shrewsbury, Shropshire

Foreword

There are a number of compelling reasons why this book should command the attention of all who are concerned about state-funded legal aid for criminal suspects and defendants.

First, the book appears at a time when soaring costs have provoked an unprecedented level of debate about the merits and demerits of existing arrangements and the form which future arrangements should take. How, if resources are limited, are the demands of criminal and civil legal aid to be balanced? How is money best spent to ensure sound advice for the suspect at the outset, thorough preparation of his defence and effective representation? How can managerial efficiency and budgetary economy best be allied with an improved quality of service? These are fundamental questions which the contributors to this book confront and seek to answer.

Secondly, the book is founded on the findings of much detailed research, here made accessible to a wider public. In a field where so many interests and sensitivities are engaged — governmental, professional, libertarian, ethnic — it is almost inevitable that slogans take the place of argument and assertions pass as fact. Here is a valuable antidote, a serious professional examination of these important public issues.

Thirdly, the book describes and appraises the procedures now followed as they actually work out in practice: the filling in of applications by solicitors, the consideration of applications by clerks in magistrates' courts and the review of refusals by legal aid committees. Any sound proposals for reform must be founded on a clear understanding of what really happens now, into which this book provides a clear insight.

Fourthly, the book does not approach these issues simply from the viewpoint of the practising lawyer or legal administrator in England and Wales. It draws on experience in Scotland, Ireland, Australia and elsewhere, and it applies to the issues the critical methods of disciplines other than the law, so deepening and enriching the quality of discussion.

Foreword

Fifthly, the book does not shrink from posing fundmental, almost philosophical, questions. What is the purpose of granting criminal legal aid? Is that purpose achieved? Should more attention, and more money, be concentrated on alternatives to criminal prosecution?

No one will agree with all the views which contributors express in this book, but no careful reader can fail to be informed, provoked to serious thought and, as a result, enlightened.

The Right Hon. Sir Thomas Bingham
Royal Courts of Justice
11 January 1996

Contents

Contents

Contents

Preface

The theme of this collection is access to justice in the criminal process. The main focus is on how this might (or might not) be achieved through legal aid. The agenda for debate concerning legal aid has usually been set by the legal profession and the Government. In consequence, argument has tended to revolve around the scope of the scheme and the issue of remuneration. More recently, the Government has taken an interest in ensuring that the standards of service provided under legal aid are of a prescribed quality. In 1995 it issued a Green Paper, *Legal Aid — Targeting Need*, which set out a radical programme of reform for the legal aid scheme. A White Paper is planned for the spring of 1996, with November of that year identified as the earliest possible date for legislation. The legal aid debate has continued, however, to be largely atheoretical and based on the defence of vested interests rather than a body of empirical evidence.

This book represents an attempt to place the legal aid debate within a broader intellectual and inter-disciplinary context which embraces both theoretical insights and empirical evidence. It brings together the work of writers and researchers prominent in this field of study. All of the chapters were written especially for this book. Our initial assumption was that a proper analysis of legal aid would require the application of a range of conceptual tools. We therefore have sought to include in this collection a variety of different perspectives on the legal aid scheme. It is for the reader to judge how successful we have been in achieving both this objective and the related aim of organising the material into a coherent whole. Many of the chapters examine the implications of the 1995 Green Paper, but the book is not intended as a reaction to that document.

We acknowledge all the help given to us in bringing this book to fruition. We thank all the contributors for their hard work and for being so responsive to the many comments made on their chapters. We are also grateful to Alistair MacQueen and Heather Saward of Blackstone Press for their encouragement and support at all stages. On a personal note, Richard Young thanks Hannah,

Preface

Solange and Arun for helping him preserve his sanity at a difficult time, and David Wall expresses his gratitude for the support he receives in all his endeavours from Helen, Harrison and Sophie, and from his colleagues at the University of Leeds. Thanks are also due to Andrew Francis and Trish Barton, postgraduate students at the Universities of Birmingham and Leeds, respectively, who proof-read the manuscript in its entirety. In keeping with the quality-assured spirit of the times, we asked Professor John Bell at the University of Leeds to act as this book's informal referee, a task which he undertook with a degree of commitment and rigour which we had no right to expect. It hardly needs saying that the views of individual chapter authors are not necessarily shared by us, as editors, or by other contributors, and that responsibility for any defects in the editing of this collection remains ours alone. The law in this book is accurate up to October 1995.

Richard Young, Birmingham
David Wall, Leeds
January 1996

List of Contributors

Andrew Ashworth is Edmund-Davies Professor of Criminal Law and Criminal Justice at King's College, London.

Lee Bridges is Principal Research Fellow in the School of Law at the University of Warwick and a member of the Lord Chancellor's Advisory Committee on Legal Education and Conduct.

Mel Cousins is a Barrister and a freelance researcher. He is also visiting lecturer at a number of higher educational institutions in Ireland.

Adam Crawford is a Lecturer in Criminology and a deputy director of the Centre for Criminal Justice Studies at the University of Leeds.

Paul Fenn is the Norwich Union Professor of Insurance Studies, Nottingham University.

Tamara Goriely is a Barrister and a Lecturer in Law at the University of East London.

Alastair Gray is a Research Associate and Senior Visiting Fellow at the Centre for Socio-Legal Studies, University of Oxford, and a part-time Senior Lecturer in Health Economics at the London School of Hygiene and Tropical Medicine.

Karen Kerner is a freelance researcher and cultural anthropologist who specialises in the study of complex systems. She has been an honourary Senior Research Fellow at the University of Strathclyde since 1983.

Francis Regan is a social scientist and a Lecturer in Legal Studies at Flinders University, Adelaide, Australia.

List of Contributors

Neil Rickman is the Foundation Fund Lecturer in Economics at the University of Surrey.

Elaine Samuel is a Research Fellow at the Centre for Social Welfare Research and part-time Lecturer in Social Policy at the University of Edinburgh.

Andrew Sanders is Deputy Director of the Centre for Criminological Research, University of Oxford and a Fellow of Pembroke College, Oxford.

Hilary Sommerlad is a solicitor and a Lecturer in Law at Leeds Metropolitan University.

David Wall is a Lecturer in Criminal Justice and a deputy director of the Centre for Criminal Justice Studies, University of Leeds.

Adrian Wood is a solicitor and a Senior Lecturer in Law at Leeds Metropolitan University.

Richard Young is Senior Lecturer in Law at the University of Birmingham.

1

Criminal Justice, Legal Aid, and the Defence of Liberty

Richard Young and David Wall[*]

At a time when the legal aid system in England and Wales is facing a major overhaul, this book considers the meaning of criminal justice and how access to it might be obtained through state-funded defence lawyers. It aims to take the reader beyond the hitherto narrow debate over legal aid by demonstrating its theoretical importance in defending liberty and achieving justice. By drawing upon empirical research findings, it also explores the reasons why lawyers of legally-aided clients have failed, by and large, to turn this theory into a practical reality.

This chapter provides an overview of the issues surrounding legal aid and also introduces the chapters which form the rest of this book. The chapter is divided into six parts. The first provides a sketch of the criminal legal aid schemes and their development. The second develops the themes of 'access to criminal justice' and 'the defence of liberty', while the third looks at the role of legal aid in society. The administration of legal aid and cost control are the subjects of the fourth and fifth parts of this chapter respectively. The final part discusses some of the impacts of the reform of legal aid and related criminal justice processes.

I CRIMINAL LEGAL AID IN ENGLAND AND WALES

There is a tendency to refer to criminal legal aid[1] as if it were a distinct and unitary entity. In fact there are four quite different, but overlapping,

---

[*] The authors are indebted to John Baldwin and David Feldman for their many perceptive comments on an earlier draft of this chapter.
[1] Unless specified otherwise, references in this book to legal aid should be taken as meaning the legal aid system in England and Wales.

types of publicly-funded schemes available for those suspected or accused of crime.[2]

First, there is the police station duty solicitor scheme. Suspects detained in the police station following arrest have a right under s. 58 of the Police and Criminal Evidence Act 1984 to consult a solicitor in private at any time. To make this right effective a national police station duty solicitor scheme was instituted. Suspects can request to see either their own lawyer or the solicitor on duty. Solicitors or their representatives are entitled to be present at interrogation if the client requests this, and may interrupt the interview in order to give further advice. All work under the duty solicitor scheme is paid for at an hourly rate at no cost to the suspect. No means test is applied, and there are no limitations as to the kind of alleged offence in respect of which advice is sought. In the legal aid year 1994–95 (running from 1 April to 31 March), 663,224 suspects were assisted under this scheme.[3]

The second type of legal aid is the 'green form' scheme, which can be used to give initial advice to those not in detention at the police station. The scheme tends to be used by solicitors to cover the costs of carrying out an initial interview with a defendant and making an application for full criminal legal aid. An initial limit of two hours' work applies, although this can be extended by obtaining authorisation from a legal aid area committee. Bureaucratic control of this scheme is minimal — all the solicitor needs to do is administer a simple means test. The scheme does not cover representation in court. In 1994–95, 397,169 green form bills in respect of criminal matters were paid by the Legal Aid Board.[4]

The third type of scheme is criminal legal aid. In relation to proceedings in the magistrates' courts, approximately 480,000 'acts of assistance'[5] were performed by defence lawyers in 1994–95 under this head.[6] Criminal legal aid covers the costs of preparing a case and representation in court. Applicants for criminal legal aid are subject both to a means test and to a merits test. The merits test states that legal aid may be granted where it appears desirable in the interests of justice to do so. The magistrates' courts apply these two tests based on information contained in the application form as submitted by the defendant's solicitor. Refusals can be 'appealed' to an area committee of the

---

[2] We do not deal here with the Assistance by Way of Representation (ABWOR) Scheme which is of minor significance in the criminal sphere. It covers persons who are subject to an application for a warrant of further detention in the police station or for an extension of such a warrant (Police and Criminal Evidence Act 1984, ss. 43–44).

[3] See Legal Aid Board, *Annual Report 1994–95*, HC 526, London: HMSO, 1995, p. 40.

[4] *Ibid.*, p. 85.

[5] This is a term used by the Legal Aid Board. The number of acts of assistance differs from the number of persons assisted since some such acts help more than one person.

[6] Legal Aid Board, *op. cit.*, p. 4.

Legal Aid Board. In June 1993, a new system of payment for solicitors acting under a criminal legal aid certificate was introduced under which most cases now attract a fixed or standard fee rather than being paid for at an hourly rate.

The last type of legally-aided service available is the court-based duty solicitor scheme, which acts as a safety net to catch some of those who arrive at court unrepresented. No means test is applied, but the scheme is subject to a number of restrictions. A duty solicitor may not provide representation in committal proceedings or on a not guilty plea, or, save in exceptional circumstances, offer advice or representation in connection with a non-imprisonable offence. These rules prevent duty solicitors acting in the most complex or serious proceedings and also in relatively trivial cases. In the former, a grant of criminal legal aid will usually be made, while in the latter the defendant will be left unrepresented, although the court clerk may offer some assistance in the courtroom itself. A total of 261,360 defendants were assisted under this scheme in 1994–95.[7]

The Legal Aid Board, created by the Legal Aid Act 1988, pays the bills in respect of both types of duty solicitor scheme and the green form scheme. It also pays criminal legal aid bills, but only for proceedings in the magistrates' courts. In the higher courts the Lord Chancellor's Department bears this responsibility. Many important changes have been introduced to the legal aid scheme since 1988, including the introduction of standard fees and franchising in criminal legal aid. The Government's 1995 Green Paper, *Legal Aid – Targeting Need*, set out a more radical programme of reform, including a capped budget, block contracting, and the restriction of legal aid work to franchised firms.[8]

The legal aid scheme is clearly undergoing a major transformation. In order to assess this fundamental shift, it is important to have a sense of historical perspective. We need to understand the forces that have shaped the legal aid scheme in order to evaluate the Government's reform programme and its likely effects. In her chapter, Tamara Goriely charts the development of the various legal aid schemes. She draws attention to the fact that legal aid is a relative newcomer to the criminal justice scene. Whereas the police and prosecution functions were professionalised during the nineteenth century, it was not until the 1960s that legal representation for defendants became the norm in jury trial, and not until the 1970s that significant numbers of defendants in the magistrates' courts were represented under legal aid.

---

[7] *Ibid.*, p. 77.
[8] Lord Chancellor's Department, *Legal Aid – Targeting Need: The future of publicly funded help in solving legal problems and disputes in England and Wales*, Cm 2854, London: HMSO, 1995 (hereinafter, the Green Paper).

Goriely's chronological analysis of legal aid draws attention to the complex factors at work in its growth. Social reformers lobbied for representation to be made available to the poor, as did many lawyers, although whether the latter were motivated more by self-interest than by a principled concern for the plight of the unrepresented is a moot point. Historical accidents also played their part, and the patchwork nature of the various legal aid schemes and their administration are testimony to the *ad hoc* way in which criminal legal aid developed.

The factor identified by Goriely as most important, is the bureaucratic needs of the courts. For many years the courts and government were agreed that legal aid was a dangerous innovation which was bound to lead to more contested cases and to more defendants escaping justice through being helped to establish false defences. Once it was recognised that defence lawyers actually facilitated speedier court proceedings (often by negotiating a guilty plea), grants of legal aid were made much more freely. The result, however, has been an emphasis on legal services which will help the courts in their work: advocacy at trial and representation in preliminary proceedings. Much less stress has been placed on police station work and early evidence gathering. As McConville et al. have noted,[9] the skewed way in which the legal aid scheme developed is one of the key factors underlying the current emphasis in criminal defence work on representation in court at the expense of proper preparation of the defence case beforehand.

Goriely concludes by noting that the Government's concern to clamp down on the spiralling costs of legal aid has led to a new emphasis, as expressed in the 1995 Green Paper, on strategic planning. The Government has dressed up its proposals in the language of access to justice and 'quality assurance' as much as cost control. But Goriely notes that history illustrates that defendants' interests are rarely given primacy when it comes to legal aid. Her final observation, that one cannot measure quality without first considering what legal aid is meant to achieve, leads us into a discussion of the intimate relationship between legal aid and access to criminal justice.

II ACCESS TO CRIMINAL JUSTICE AND THE DEFENCE OF LIBERTY

The term 'criminal justice' is rarely questioned. It is not a self-explanatory term, however, and tends to mean different things to different people. Usually it is taken to mean the various institutions and practices which are concerned

---

[9] McConville, M., Hodgson, J., Bridges, L. and Pavlovic, A., *Standing Accused: The Organisation and Practices of Criminal Defence Lawyers in Britain*, Oxford: Clarendon Press, 1994, pp. 277–8.

with the phenomenon of crime. In the context of a discussion about access, it is more appropriate to focus on the normative implications of employing the word 'justice'. As Lacey observes, this 'marks the fact that the practices which form the subject-matter of criminal justice aspire to moral and political legitimacy, and do so in terms of certain values'.[10]

One of the main issues developed in the chapters that follow this introduction is the question of whether and to what extent those who are suspected or accused of crime are able to obtain justice within the criminal process. Care is needed on this point. Unless the criteria by which procedures and outcomes are adjudged 'just' and 'unjust' are spelt out, the use of such terminology can obscure more than it enlightens. There is not the space here to review the immense literature on 'justice' as a generalisable ideal, or to develop a fully rounded theory of 'criminal justice'.[11] Rather, we will develop some elementary notes about a just criminal process of particular relevance to this book.

One purpose of the criminal process is to arrive at an authoritative conclusion as to whether a person is guilty of a criminal offence. Those conclusions would be neither authoritative nor just if they were shown to be unreliable. Justice consists, in part, of a fair distribution of goods and burdens throughout society, although what amounts to a fair distribution will clearly differ according to one's philosophical and political standpoints.[12] In a liberal democracy such as the UK, few would dispute that when innocent people are punished for crimes they did not commit the burden of punishment has been distributed in an unjust manner, particularly as those responsible for the crime will thereby have escaped detection. One mark of a just criminal process is thus its ability to produce just outcomes by distinguishing the guilty from the innocent.

The fact-finding procedures in the criminal courts of this country are rooted in the adversarial theory of justice. According to this theory, truth emerges through a battle in which the prosecution's and defence's competing versions of events are put forward and tested before an impartial adjudicator. That such a contest enables the court to discern the truth presupposes that the two sides have access to roughly equivalent resources and expertise, or that the prosecution will behave in a way which negates the need for 'equality of arms'. Otherwise, what emerges in court may reflect no more than that one side had the time and money to construct a case and that the other did not. In this setting, faced with the might of the state as represented by the police and by prosecution lawyers, it is apparent that the individual defendant requires expert assistance.

---

[10] Lacey, N., 'Making Sense of Criminal Justice', in Lacey, N. (ed.), *Criminal Justice*, Oxford: OUP, 1994, p. 4.

[11] Some pointers are provided in *ibid.*, pp. 24–34.

[12] Compare utilitarianism with Rawlsian justice and Nozick's minimal state, for example: Freeman, M.D.A., *Lloyd's Introduction to Jurisprudence*, London, Sweet & Maxwell, 1994, pp. 356–73.

For defendants of modest means, the state must either fund their representation or perpetuate injustice.

Access to justice seems, therefore, to imply access to legal aid and lawyers.[13] Another argument which supports this conclusion is that it would be contrary to the liberal due process principle of equality were legal aid to be denied to the poor.[14] To do so would place those of modest means in an unequal position with the rich. Thus denying legal aid would not only create the potential for an absolute wrong in the form of a miscarriage of justice, it would also create a relative sense of injustice between different groups in society. Furthermore, such a denial would run contrary to an element of the ideal of the rule of law — that all subjects are entitled to the equal protection of law.

These liberal arguments in favour of legal aid provide the starting point for Andrew Ashworth's chapter. Ashworth explores the extent to which they are reflected in the law, looking first at the European Convention on Human Rights and then at the English common law position. Ashworth finds that neither international human rights law nor domestic law currently gives sufficient weight to the arguments in favour of an automatic right to legal aid for all defendants who lack the means to purchase legal services. Lastly, he observes that the state spends far more on the police and the Crown Prosecution Service than it does on legal aid. Cuts to the legal aid scheme (whether to scope or to eligibility levels) are, as he puts it, a matter of political preference and not of 'financial necessity'. It is, in short, because the Government lacks a genuine commitment to equal access to justice that the scope of legal aid remains so restrictive.

It is possible for the state to resist these traditional liberal lines of argument by invoking radical free-market philosophy such as that developed by Hayek[15] and Nozick.[16] From this standpoint any attempt by the state to interfere with the workings of the free market is unjustified.

For Hayek, no one can ever know enough about the workings of the economy to know whether interference in the market will do more harm than good.[17] The provision of legal aid and other forms of social welfare, for example, may improve an individual's material position in the short term at the unacceptable cost of so discouraging the virtues of thrift and hard work as to do long-term

---

[13] It implies a good deal more than this of course: Smith, R., 'Current Trends', in Smith, R. (ed.), *Shaping the Future: New Directions in Legal Services*, London: Legal Action Group, 1995, pp. 11–13. See, more generally, Sarat, A., 'Access to Justice: Citizen Participation and the American Legal Order', in Lipson, L. and Wheeler, S. (eds), *Law and the Social Sciences*, New York: Russell Sage Foundation, 1986, p. 519.

[14] See Sanders, A. and Young, R., *Criminal Justice*, London: Butterworths, 1994, p. 17.

[15] Hayek, F. A., *Law, Legislation and Liberty*, London: Routledge & Kegan Paul, 1981.

[16] Nozick, R., *Anarchy, State and Utopia*, Oxford: Basil Blackwell, 1974.

[17] Hayek, *op. cit.*, pp. 8–54.

damage to the economy. It is, however, a defensible and rational position to regard the theoretical risk of long-term damage to the economy posed by the provision of legal aid as outweighed by the immediate and practical goal of defending the security and liberty of an accused person.

The resources needed to fund a legal aid scheme must be raised through taxation, and Nozick would object that raising money in this way involves an infringement of individual liberty to do as one pleases with one's own property. Taxation of previously acquired property is tantamount to retrospective legislation; taxation legislation imposes a form of forced labour (or slavery) for the ends of another.[18] Nozick's objection assumes that the mechanism of the market is fair and beyond challenge. Feldman demonstrates, however, that when the state redistributes wealth through taxation it is not so much interfering with property rights as 'giving effect to the essential conditions for allowing people to enjoy property rights at all'.[19] The market is comprised of a number of socially determined rules, and it is open to society to amend those rules in order to achieve a democratically approved goal, such as making provision for a legal aid scheme.

Another problem with the free-market position is that it seems to assume that to be accused of crime is one of life's vicissitudes for which we should all make advance provision. In reality, by making an accusation of crime, the state bears a responsibility for putting people in a position where they need legal aid. In other words, the state itself creates the initial infringement of liberty and legal aid is made available so as to redress the balance disturbed by this action. It might be argued, however, that the initial infringement of liberty is that of the crime itself and that, as defendants have brought their plight upon themselves, they have no valid claim on public funds. This line of thinking, no doubt, is what makes the legal aid scheme so vulnerable to cost-cutting. But it suffers from the fatal flaw of assuming that defendants are guilty. Because mistakes are bound to be made by the police and prosecution agencies[20] (and indeed have been made in cases which resulted in seemingly clear-cut convictions and long sentences),[21] defendants are entitled to be presumed innocent unless and until proven guilty.

The presumption of innocence is important to arguments about legal aid in another way too. This presumption exists not merely because of the factual problem of distinguishing the guilty from the innocent, but because of the

---

[18] Nozick, *op. cit.*, p. 180.

[19] Feldman, D., *Civil Liberties and Human Rights in England and Wales*, Oxford: Clarendon Press, 1993, p. 16.

[20] See Zuckerman, A.A.S., 'Miscarriages of Justice — A Root Treatment', *Criminal Law Review*, 1992, p. 323.

[21] As in the case of Stefan Kiszco, released after serving 16 years in prison for a murder which he could not have committed: Sanders and Young, *op. cit.*, p. 185.

normative issue of how the state ought to behave in its relations with individuals. The adversarial model assumes that the state is trying to prove a case against one of its citizens. It is therefore particularly important that guarantees are provided against the state abusing its investigative and prosecution powers and that infringements of the civil liberties of defendants are kept to a justified minimum.[22] Criminal justice is about correct and fair procedures as well as correct and fair outcomes. This is, in part, why public funds are made available for lawyers to give advice and assistance in the police station as well as representation in court. Lawyers are needed not only to defend clients against the possibility of losing their liberty on conviction, but to minimise the deprivations of liberty involved in the pre-trial process and to provide a check on abuse of public power by officials of the state.

We have argued that criminal legal aid plays an important part in defending liberty. An alternative perspective is provided by Francis Regan in his chapter in this book. He develops the intriguing counter-proposition that the current priority afforded to criminal legal aid within developed societies is a positive threat to liberty. At a time when the welfare state is being dismantled, such priority may entail that civil legal aid will be allowed to wither on the vine unless new ways of defending its achievements are found. Regan's approach is to examine the effect of legal aid in promoting citizenship by making effective the civil right to justice and equal treatment before the law.

He accepts that legal aid is needed to fund representation in criminal matters in order to defend liberty, but argues that this far from exhausts the ways in which legal aid promotes citizenship. Most problems with a legal element that citizens experience do not need the involvement of the courts (or lawyers), but people still need to know their rights in order to assess whether they should or could institute formal legal proceedings, or should or could resolve their problems privately, by self-help, negotiation, mediation, and so forth. Through legal advice, training programmes and self-help education packs (e.g., DIY divorce kits), citizens may make more informed choices with regard to these matters. This allows them to be less dependent on the legal profession, take more control over their own lives, and thereby promotes their autonomy. This leads to a distinction between defending liberty (negative freedom) and promoting liberty (positive freedom).

Regan follows Berlin[23] in arguing that the classical liberal preoccupation with ensuring 'freedom from' interference by the state and other citizens is inadequate, and that freedom should include elements of 'freedom to', that is, freedom to do more and to be more human. Legal aid schemes can thus be said

---

[22] See Walker, C., 'Introduction', in Walker, C. and Starmer, K. (eds), *Justice in Error*, London: Blackstone Press, 1993, p. 3.

[23] Berlin, I., *Four Essays on Liberty*, Oxford: OUP, 1979.

to promote citizenship most strongly and comprehensively when they provide a range of legal resources that emphasise both positive and negative freedom. Regan next analyses the development of the Australian legal aid scheme and finds that, whereas legal aid private lawyers tended to emphasise representation in order to promote negative freedom but neglected the promotion of positive freedom, the reverse was true of the salaried state employee legal aid sector. Regan concludes that a mixed model of legal aid provision, involving both the government and the legal profession, will promote citizenship most effectively.

A number of interesting points arise from Regan's discussion. First, there is evidence that the legal aid scheme in England and Wales is beginning explicitly to prioritise representation for criminal matters. For example, the 1995 Green Paper on legal aid states that the civil legal aid scheme requires cash-limiting in order to control costs and encourage the setting of priorities.[24] When it comes to criminal legal aid, however, there is some baulking at the idea of a fixed budget as defendants 'have no choice but to defend themselves against the power of the state ranged against them in the form of the prosecuting authorities'.[25] Secondly, Regan's conclusion that a private practitioner model for delivering legal aid will lead to an emphasis on representation echoes the experience of England and Wales as documented by Tamara Goriely in her contribution to this book. Thirdly, difficult questions arise as to the balance to be struck between defending negative freedom and the promotion of positive freedom. If criminal legal aid is not to be given priority over civil legal aid, does this mean that more defendants must appear unrepresented in the criminal courts in order that civil legal aid's share of the available budgetary cake can be increased? This is not an attractive proposition for those committed to the principles of adversarial justice.

Perhaps the problem here lies in tying legal aid to citizenship in the first place. If the arguments developed by Andrew Ashworth in this book are accepted, then criminal legal aid should be regarded as a human right for all people, including those whose legal status within a state is as an alien rather than as a citizen. This does not mean that civil legal aid must of necessity take lower priority. As a resource which promotes positive freedom, it may be possible to defend it by reference to human rights, especially as regards any educative goal it advances.[26] If the language of citizenship is overlaid with the language of human rights, then convincing arguments can be developed for expanding the overall legal aid budget. By reformulating the debate in this way,

---

[24] Green Paper, *op. cit.*, pp. 28–9.
[25] *Ibid.*, p. 30, para. 4.40. The right to free representation enshrined in Article 6 of the European Convention on Human Rights is also cited to justify the different treatment of criminal legal aid in this regard: *ibid.*, para. 4.41.
[26] See Feldman, *op. cit.*, pp. 887–9.

it may be possible to ensure that both civil and criminal legal aid take priority over other forms of state expenditure which do not advance citizenship or human rights so effectively. Alternatively, the arguments for legal aid may, thus strengthened, override arguments for not increasing taxation further. As we have already noted, restrictions on legal aid expenditure are not a matter of financial necessity but of political preference.

III   THE ROLE OF LEGAL AID IN SOCIETY

We have considered above some of the key arguments surrounding criminal legal aid. The objections to the provision of legal aid should not be dismissed out of hand for they retain material and ideological significance, certainly for those on the right of the political spectrum. Neither can it be said that they are lacking in all force. The balance of the argument seems to us, however, to lie in favour of legal aid as an important way of securing access to justice and defending liberty. This position does not mean that we are blind to the failings of the legal aid scheme, or to its wider sociological significance. The worth, functions and limits of the legal aid scheme are intimately connected to the structures and values of the society within which it operates.

Legal aid may be described as a necessary but insufficient condition of criminal justice. Two ways in which it is insufficient may here be mentioned. The first concerns the way in which some groups are at more risk than others of being the subject of formal police action. There would be little disagreement with the simple proposition that justice requires that equals be treated equally. The problematic aspect of this formulation is to determine which characteristics are to be regarded as relevant for the purposes of comparison.[27] In the case of crime we might want to develop a principle that those who intentionally cause a certain level of harm should be at an equal risk of detection by the police, prosecution by the Crown Prosecution Service, and conviction by the courts. It would offend our sense of justice if one person was at less risk in any of these ways because he or she was well-connected, or white, or for some other irrelevant reason. Yet study after study has demonstrated that the police enforce the criminal law more rigorously against some groups than others, resulting in a pattern of unjustified discrimination — particularly against young black males.[28] Legal aid is essentially individualistic, attaching itself to persons against whom formal action has already been taken by the police. It can therefore do nothing to prevent or remedy this initial biased selection.

---

[27] Ginsberg, M., *On Justice in Society*, Harmondsworth: Pelican, 1965, pp. 72–3.
[28] The research is summarised and discussed in Sanders and Young, *op. cit.*, pp. 96–8.

The second way in which legal aid is insufficient to achieve criminal justice concerns the nature of the services it purchases. We suggested above that access to justice implied access to legal aid lawyers. But as McConville et al. warn, 'it can no longer be taken for granted ... that legal representation is an end in itself and to be valued — and paid for — on that basis alone'.[29] There are two related problems here. One is the empirical fact of low quality services provided by lawyers funded through legal aid,[30] and the other that the criminal process itself contains a variety of devices which have the effect of undermining adversarialism, such as sentence discounts for those who plead guilty.[31] When taken in combination, the effect is that lawyers rarely prepare thoroughly in anticipation of contesting their clients' cases in court. More usually, they transmit to those clients the system's structural imperatives 'whether for cooperation with the police or the administrative convenience of a guilty plea'.[32]

Seen in this light, a worrying aspect of the Green Paper's proposals is that they are predicated on dubious assumptions that existing patterns of criminal legal aid coverage and case work provide the foundations on which, to use the fashionable jargon, a new quality assured cost-controlled system can be erected. As McConville et al. warn, quality measures and cost structures based on existing patterns and standards of legally-aided work risk further institutionalising the poor quality of much criminal defence work. The starting point for reform must therefore lie 'in a wider movement toward re-defining the underlying purpose and values of criminal defence work as a whole'.[33]

The problem here is that the Government's broader programme of criminal justice reform represents an attempt to redefine the underlying purpose of defence work in a quite different direction from that proposed by liberal academics. For example, at the time of writing the Government is pressing ahead with its proposals to require the pre-trial disclosure of the defence case so as to improve the 'efficiency' of the criminal process.[34] Indeed, Leng argues that the accelerating shift away from adversarial principles embodied in such initiatives is intimately connected with the growth of legal aid. As he puts it:

---

[29] McConville et al., *op. cit.*, p. 295.
[30] See, in particular, *ibid.* and Sanders, A., Bridges, L., Mulvaney, A. and Crozier, G., *Advice and Assistance at Police Stations and the 24 Hour Duty Solicitor Scheme*, London: Lord Chancellor's Department, 1989. See also the analysis of legal aid practices by King, M., *The Framework of Criminal Justice*, London: Croom Helm, 1981, pp. 68–75.
[31] See Sanders and Young, *op. cit.*, pp. 318–33.
[32] See McConville et al., *op. cit.*, p. 281.
[33] *Ibid.*, p. 295.
[34] See Leng, R., 'Losing Sight of the Defendant: The Government's Proposals on Pre-Trial Disclosure', *Criminal Law Review*, 1995, p. 704.

11

we are losing sight of the defendant in a process in which the most visible actors are opposing groups of state-funded lawyers. If the process is conceived as a contest between such groups it becomes natural to think in terms of reciprocal duties and shared responsibility for efficiency and results.[35]

This insight leads us to another of the functions of legal aid — the funding in post-Second World War society of a major expansion of the Bar. Abel notes that 'it hardly overstates the case to say that legal aid paid for the doubling of the Bar since the late 1960s'.[36] With regard to solicitors, Karen Kerner, in her chapter, demonstrates that a large number of firms specialising in criminal defence are now heavily dependent on legal aid funding. Any cuts to the scope of the legal aid scheme or to remuneration levels will have serious economic consequences for criminal lawyers, both individually and as a profession. This has created a powerful constituency with a stake in the future of the legal aid scheme. The interests of that constituency are bound to differ from those who are the recipients of its services.[37]

Lawyers are naturally most uneasy about the implications of the Government's programme of legal aid reform for their own profitability and market share; whereas clients, were they sufficiently organised to express a view, would be more concerned with the issue of quality. The legal profession has always been adept, however, at invoking the interests of clients in advancing its own case. Thus, an argument that the profession has deployed repeatedly is that the current low levels of remuneration have forced lawyers into providing services of a lower quality than they would wish.[38] There is clearly something in this claim as private practitioners must either make a profit or go out of business. If the only way of making a profit under legal aid is to offer hurried, standardised services, then access to justice must suffer. Research has shown, however, that some legal aid firms provide a much higher standard than others under the existing fee structure, largely because they have retained a commitment to the client and to adversarial ideals.[39] Higher rates of pay would therefore enable, but not necessarily guarantee, higher quality services. More important is that legal aid lawyers internalise and act in accordance with the values of adversarial justice.

---

[35] *Ibid.*, at p. 711.
[36] See Abel, R., *The Legal Profession in England and Wales*, Oxford: Basil Blackwell, 1988, at p. 116.
[37] See Holland, A., 'Access to justice', *New Law Journal*, 1995, vol. 145, p. 1256.
[38] See, for example, Law Society, *Memorandum on the Future of Criminal Legal Aid: Evidence to Royal Commission on Criminal Justice*, London: Law Society, 1992, p. 6.
[39] See McConville et al., *op. cit.*, p. 271.

We have noted that criminal justice aspires to political and moral legitimacy. Another of the broader functions of legal aid is the legitimation of the processes leading to state punishment. Mel Cousins argues in his chapter that this legitimation function has been the key factor in shaping the Irish legal aid scheme. His starting position is that, while the nominal role of the legal system is to facilitate access to the law, in practice it operates so as to control the operation of the law for the immediate financial benefit of the legal profession and, more broadly, for the benefit of dominant classes and groups. Thus the legal system serves to inhibit rather than facilitate access to the law for those who are not part of these dominant groupings. In his view, the law in a patriarchal and capitalist society will always reflect inequalities in power and wealth. The operation of the legal system increases these imbalances. Criminal legal aid, therefore, plays an important part in upholding the skewed social order by legitimating criminal justice.

The above thesis is echoed in the chapter by Lee Bridges in the context of the English legal aid scheme. Bridges notes that the Government's decision to expand the scope of legal aid by setting up a national duty solicitor scheme for police station work was intended to provide an appearance of fairness and 'balance' in the wake of the increase in police powers achieved through the Police and Criminal Evidence Act 1984. Consistent with the thesis that legal aid exists to legitimise the operation of criminal justice is the fact that legal aid is the norm in the Crown Court[40] whereas fewer than 20 per cent of criminal cases in the magistrates' courts are legally aided.[41] Crown Court trial is the public face of justice in England and Wales. Its elaborate lawyer-dominated rituals have been seen by some as distracting attention from the lack of due process in the magistrates' courts.[42] The almost automatic grant of legal aid at the higher tier of criminal justice assists in lending an air of fairness to a system in which most defendants dealt with at the less publicised lower tier lack representation.[43] Similarly, while legal aid is always granted for those whose cases are heard in open court in the Court of Appeal, it is not so readily available for the more private procedures which defendants must follow if they wish to be granted leave to appeal.[44]

Cousins acknowledges that the legal profession has also played a part in shaping the Irish legal aid scheme, in particular by resisting any departure from the model whereunder private practitioners provide representation in court.

---

[40] Lord Chancellor's Department, *Judicial Statistics 1994*, Cm 2891, London: HMSO, 1995, p. 100.
[41] See the Green Paper, *op. cit.*, p. 103. It should be borne in mind that around one half of criminal cases in the magistrates' courts are for motoring offences.
[42] For discussion, see Sanders and Young, *op. cit.*, p. 354.
[43] See McBarnet, D., 'Two Tiers of Justice', in Lacey (ed.), *op. cit.*
[44] See Sanders and Young, *op. cit.*, p. 434.

Proposals for a pre-court legal advice scheme and for a duty solicitor scheme have fallen on stony ground. This reinforces one of the messages of the chapters by Tamara Goriely and Francis Regan, that where legal aid is delivered through private practitioners, an emphasis on representation in court is likely to result.

The chapters by Ashworth, Regan and Cousins examine the issue of access to justice at a fundamental level. The next three chapters, by Wall, Young, and Wood respectively, consider the issue of access from a more practical standpoint. Criminal legal aid for proceedings in the magistrates' court may lawfully be granted only when it is 'in the interests of justice' that a defendant be represented. The day-to-day administration of criminal legal aid therefore has a direct bearing on access to justice.

IV THE ADMINISTRATION OF CRIMINAL LEGAL AID

Over the last decade a number of studies have been conducted on different aspects of the legal aid scheme. The green form scheme was the subject of large-scale research in the late 1980s by Baldwin and Hill,[45] and the police station duty solicitor scheme has been evaluated by a number of research teams.[46] McConville et al.'s extensive study of advice and representation from the police station through to the Crown Court threw new light on work performed under legal aid by criminal lawyers.[47] That study did not, however, pay much attention to the administration of the criminal legal aid scheme for proceedings in the magistrates' courts. Two empirical projects on this neglected aspect of the legal aid scheme form the basis of the next three chapters in this book. The first, funded by the ESRC,[48] was carried out by Wall and Wood, and the second, funded by the Legal Aid Board, by Young, Moloney and Sanders. Both pieces of research focused on the application practices of solicitors, and the decision-making behaviour of court clerks and the area committees of the Legal Aid Board.

David Wall presents an analysis of applications for criminal legal aid. Although legal aid applications are made formally by defendants, the reality is that solicitors and their staff complete the forms. The applications are highly result-orientated documents, with solicitors anxious to convince the magistrates' courts that their client's case or position is sufficiently meritorious to justify a grant of a legal aid certificate. That this is so is hardly surprising: a

---

[45] Baldwin, J. and Hill, S., *The Operation of the Green Form Scheme in England and Wales*, London: Lord Chancellor's Department, 1988.
[46] See, in particular, Sanders et al., *op. cit.*, and McConville, M. and Hodgson, J., *Custodial Legal Advice and the Right to Silence*, Royal Commission on Criminal Justice, Research Study No. 16, London: HMSO, 1993.
[47] McConville et al., *op. cit.*
[48] Awards Nos. R000232673 and R000234528.

successful application represents not just the possibility of access to justice for the client, but access to legal aid funds for the lawyer. If the magistrates' courts are the gatekeepers to legal aid, then solicitors are the keyholders and the legal aid application the key. There is apparently, however, little call for skill in the use of this key.

Wall's chapter shows that solicitors and their staff rarely apply legal expertise and judgement in assessing whether a case is likely to pass the interests of justice test. Cases regarded as manifestly 'ungrantable' are often weeded out, but, beyond that, an application will be routinely completed and submitted in virtually every case. There is little incentive to do otherwise given that the vast majority of applications are granted. The application process is a hit-and-miss affair, with substantially more hits than misses. The great majority of clients will therefore not be prejudiced by the sloppy way in which applications are completed on their behalf. Some, however, will not obtain legal aid for no better reason than that their legal representatives exercised minimal time and care in constructing their application for legal aid.

Richard Young examines how court clerks exercise discretion in determining legal aid applications. While most magistrates' courts maintain grant rates of around 90 per cent, significant disparities in grant rates between courts persist. This raises the issue of differential access to justice. Drawing on the theoretical insights of previous studies of administrative discretion, Young argues that the sheer number of legal aid applications requiring determination drives hard-pressed court clerks into simplifying their decision-making task. Rather than applying the complex interests of justice test prescribed by law, they grant on the basis of tariff-based rules of thumb. Any defendant in a serious position before the court, where 'seriousness' is constructed primarily by reference to the offence charged, will almost certainly be granted legal aid. The disparity in the rules of thumb operated by magistrates' courts is largely attributable to differing views amongst court clerks as to the value of legal aid in saving court time and maintaining the legitimacy of proceedings.

Young concludes that the rationing of legal aid in the magistrates' courts should not be governed by the idiosyncrasies of individual court clerks operating within particularistic court cultures. Instead, Parliament should substitute for the discretionary 'interests of justice' test detailed prescriptions for the grant of legal aid. The proposal in the Green Paper to replace the Widgery criteria with a simpler interests of justice test is accordingly given a qualified welcome.

The Legal Aid Board has played an increasingly important part in the administration and development of the legal aid scheme since its creation by the Legal Aid Act 1988. It has, for example, taken the initiative in commissioning research into various aspects of the legal aid scheme such as that reported in the chapters by Young and by Alistair Gray and his colleagues. There has, however, been little independent study of its own performance. In his chapter, Adrian Wood employs Sainsbury's model of administrative justice[49] to evaluate the Legal Aid Board's procedures for handling reviews of legal aid applications refused in the magistrates' courts. These reviews are determined by caseworkers and area committees (made up of practising lawyers) operating within the area offices of the Board.

For administrative justice to be achieved, argues Wood, a decision-making system must be operated in such a way as to make its decisions acceptable, particularly in terms of accuracy and fairness. He finds the area committee review procedure to be defective on both counts. In his view, a main cause of the poor quality of decision-making is that legislation and administrative guidance have failed to spell out the proper approach to be taken in determining a review. Some area committees and caseworkers see their function as akin to judicial review, whereas others treat the review as if it were a *de novo* appeal. While acknowledging that steps have recently been taken to improve matters (such as by requiring decision-makers in courts and area offices to give reasons for their decisions), he nonetheless contends that the Board continues to prioritise internal procedural concerns — such as the efficiency and speed of case-handling — over substantive decision-related issues. From this he concludes that the area committee structure is an example of the compromising of the criminal justice process by a managerial ethos.

The new emphasis on managerialism within the criminal process[50] is a theme that is explored by a number of the contributors to this book, in particular Lee Bridges and Hilary Sommerlad. One of its key aspects is the control of costs — a major preoccupation in relation to legal aid. The next three chapters in the book explore this important issue.

V   CONTROLLING THE COSTS OF LEGAL AID

The state can benefit in two key ways through expenditure on legal aid. It enables criminal cases to be processed through the courts more efficiently and it legitimises the operation of criminal justice. While these instrumental gains are attractive to government, they are difficult to measure accurately. Contrast this with the immediate financial costs of the legal aid scheme which are

---

[49] Sainsbury, R., 'Administrative Justice: Discretion and procedure in Social Security Decision-Making', in Hawkins, K. (ed.), *The Uses of Discretion*, Oxford: Clarendon Press, 1992.
[50] See the discussion by Newburn, T., *Crime and Criminal Justice Policy*, London: Longman, 1994, pp. 173–5.

relatively easy to quantify. Over the decade to 1993–94, legal aid expenditure on criminal matters rose by 300 per cent to £519 million.[51]

The mounting costs of legal aid have deeply troubled the Government for some years now, and the 1995 Green Paper asserted baldly that the 'cost of legal aid is rising at a rate which the country cannot afford'.[52] To enter into an analysis of the Green Paper proposals would be to anticipate the discussion contained in some of the chapters which follow. But we should note here that the practical realisation of the Green Paper's holy trinity of quality, economy and cost control carries significant implications for access to justice. If quality plays second-fiddle to cost control and economy, then the gap between access to legal aid lawyers and access to criminal justice is likely to widen.

The Green Paper proposals follow a piecemeal collection of changes to the legal aid scheme, including the introduction of standard fees for Crown Court work in 1986, and for magistrates' court work in 1993, which failed to meet the Government's expectations as regards cost control. The contribution to this book by Alastair Gray, Paul Fenn and Neil Rickman helps us to understand why such fragmentary reforms often fail to achieve the desired results. They present an economic analysis of the likely impact of standard fees on criminal defence work. Under this system, payments received by lawyers are unrelated to the amount of work they put into a case unless one of two thresholds is reached: the first triggers a higher standard fee, the second a reversion to the pre-existing system of payment whereby each item of work performed attracts remuneration ('fee-for-service').

Using economic theory as their starting point, Gray et al. consider how lawyers might react to the financial incentives inherent in the currently existing standard fee structures. They conclude that the aggregate costs of a standard fee system might increase and, moreover, that some clients are likely to receive fewer services than they did before, while others may find their cases prolonged deliberately by their lawyers so that a given fee threshold may be exceeded.

Gray, Rickman and Fenn predict other unwanted effects of the standard fees regime. One effect is that lawyers will redefine and split cases in order to be able to obtain several standard fees in relation to what would previously have been regarded as one case. Another is the shifting of initial advice work from the criminal legal aid scheme into the green form scheme so as to minimise the effort expended under the standard fee regime while maximising the amount of public funds that can be claimed overall. Perhaps of greater concern to the legal profession is that the risk involved in a standard fees regime of losing out

---

[51] Lord Chancellor's Department, *Legal Aid – Targeting Need: The future of publicly funded help in solving legal problems and disputes in England and Wales*, Cm 2854, London: HMSO, 1995, p. 115.
[52] *Ibid.*, p. viii.

financially increases the fewer cases that a firm handles, implying that small, low-volume firms are likely to be driven out of the criminal legal aid market.

In view of the array of problems associated with the standard fees regime identified by Gray et al., it is not surprising that the Government has concluded that standard fees 'have only limited value in controlling growth in legal aid expenditure'.[53] The overall cash limit for criminal legal aid proposed in the 1995 Green Paper is in large part a response to the difficulties of achieving financial control through piecemeal reform to the current patchwork of overlapping schemes.

Many of the proposals in the Green Paper stem from the assumption that under the traditional legal aid arrangements lawyers are encouraged to define problems as needing expensive legal remedies: 'there is an incentive within the system of fees to pursue court-based solutions to problems.'[54] In seeking to explain spiralling legal aid costs in this way, the Green Paper draws heavily on the supplier-induced demand thesis developed in a 1994 Social Market Foundation memorandum.[55] The essence of the thesis is that lawyers (the suppliers) can perform as many services of whatever type they like since clients neither know what services they need nor care how much those services cost, given that a third party is picking up the bill. Lawyers, on the other hand, have every incentive to perform as many services as possible (subject to the points made about standard fees above). The increased 'demand' for legal aid is therefore a social construct, induced or shaped by the suppliers of legal services. Elaine Samuel contests the theoretical assumptions of this thesis in her chapter and subjects it to empirical testing. She points out that it implies an asocial and overly-simplistic model of human behaviour, in which actions are driven only by self-interest, and pays no regard to the social and institutional context shaping and constraining case-related decisions. Drawing on research she conducted for the Scottish Office, she describes ways in which the system itself is responsible for driving up costs.

Samuel concludes that, while the appetite of lawyers for legal aid funding is a factor to be taken into account in attempts to control costs, that factor is shaped by the institutional setting in which lawyers work and by the rules to which their work is subject. A way of controlling costs other than by such drastic steps as capping the budget or reducing the scope of the scheme (i.e., removing the food), would be to manipulate the appetite by changing the setting or the rules. The lessons of this research have been acknowledged and acted upon by Scottish policy-makers. Thus, for example, in order to address the

---

[53] *Ibid.*, p. 18, para. 3.28.
[54] *Ibid.*, para. 3.29.
[55] Bevan, G., Holland, T. and Partington, M., *Organising Cost Effective Access to Justice*, Memorandum No. 7, Social Market Foundation, July 1994.

problem of defendants contesting cases merely in order to secure a grant of legal aid, access to legal representation for those wishing to plead guilty is to be broadened. This is a good illustration of how expenditure on legal aid can, by facilitating the earlier disposal of cases, save the state money in the long run.

The 'supplier-induced demand' thesis, as Lee Bridge's chapter illustrates, is as simplistic and inadequate in England as Elaine Samuel shows it to be in Scotland. The state induced the rising costs of legally-aided advice to suspects detained in police custody by setting up a national duty solicitor scheme for England and Wales, and it is the state through its arrest, cautioning and prosecution policies that determines how many people will require advice and assistance. Furthermore, the state has left decisions on granting legal aid for representation to be made by the courts themselves, and it is magistrates and their clerks who have fuelled the growth in legal aid as much as defence lawyers.

Karen Kerner's chapter, based on a survey of Scottish legal aid lawyers, shows that many of the features of the legal aid scheme of England and Wales are replicated north of the border. Most legal aid work is concentrated in the hands of a relatively small number of high volume, specialist firms. These firms are characterised by their dependency on legal aid funding and by widespread delegation of much of the work of preparing a case for court to less experienced members of the firm or outside agents.

Whereas the supplier-induced demand thesis implies avid self-interest amongst solicitors, Kerner's interviews with defence agents revealed a commitment to cost control and the quality of service provided under legal aid. There was an awareness amongst those she spoke with that some Scottish lawyers were being paid too much given the standard of service they provided, while others were paid too little. There was also a view that the legal aid scheme was open to fraud and abuse and that controls needed to be tightened.

Kerner concludes that defence lawyers share with policy-makers a desire to facilitate the timeous, efficient and cost-effective delivery of justice in Scotland. There appears to be disagreement on the means to achieve these ends, however. That there is a degree of concordance regarding aims is significant and suggests that there may be scope for policy-makers and lawyers to devise an agreed programme of reform for legal aid. On the other hand, the miserable level of debate between the Law Society and the Lord Chancellor in this country from the mid-1980s onwards does not inspire confidence in this regard.[56]

---

[56] See the account by Rozenberg, J., *The Search for Justice*, London: Hodder & Stoughton, 1994, pp. 251–9, 262–9.

VI THE IMPACT OF LEGAL AID REFORMS: STRUCTURAL CONSTRAINTS ON ACCESS TO JUSTICE

The final section of this chapter explores some of the less obvious implications of reforms to the legal aid scheme and the wider criminal justice system. The underlying theme is that the material and ideological structures within which allegations of crime are handled will constrain the extent to which access to justice may be achieved.

In his chapter, Andrew Sanders examines the research findings on the nature and quality of advice provided under the police station duty solicitor scheme. He documents the problems that have been uncovered: only a minority of suspects request and receive legal advice; a smaller minority actually see a legal adviser in person and receive advice and support when interviewed by the police; up to one half of advisers will be para-legals with little or no training; and the nature of that advice and support departs markedly from the adversarial ideal of defending suspects' rights, advising silence wherever that would help the suspect, and intervening when questioning is improper.

Sanders acknowledges the force of well-rehearsed explanatory factors for such findings, such as the negligence of the profession, the ideological commitment to crime control values amongst most criminal firms, and poor legal aid rates which reward only routinised responses. But he goes on to identify a more fundamental cause at work. This is that the police have the structural power to dictate when and how interviews and detention take place.

This power means, for example, that suspects can be detained in conditions where they are unwilling to wait for a duty solicitor to arrive (a stinking cell in the middle of the night) or when qualified legal advisers are unlikely to be available (mid-morning when the magistrates' courts are in full swing). The police, in short, can ensure that the process of detention is so unpleasant that 'standing on one's rights' only produces more suffering. They can also make life difficult for legal advisers they regard as 'unhelpful' (i.e. adversarial), for example, by withholding information from them about the evidence or by rescheduling interviews at the last minute. And so if solicitors wish to do their best for their clients, they have to compromise by becoming acceptable to the police.

Sander's analysis suggests that the system is loaded in favour of the police to such an extent that adversarial justice at the all-important pre-trial stage of the criminal process is bound to remain illusory. While he does not offer a solution, Sanders hints at one. A major flaw he identifies is that too much choice is left to suspects. They are asked by the police if they want a solicitor, and asked by solicitors over the telephone if they want them to come out to the station to give advice. These are not choices most suspects can sensibly make, since they lack knowledge of their rights and of how a lawyer might help them. Sanders concludes from this that, if a proper legal service is to be provided in police stations, the law would need to be changed so as to require suspects to receive advice and support. He does not regard this as a realistic option, contending that it runs counter to liberal legal ideology.

Requiring someone to receive legal advice certainly looks like an infringement of personal autonomy. As Feldman notes, however, 'one can ... justify imposing protection and regulation in situations which are inherently likely to overwhelm people's normal capacity for self-determination and free choice. Being detained in a police station is such a situation.'[57] Since the police are now virtually compelled by PACE to conduct interviews with suspects in no other place than on police territory,[58] it may be in the interests of adversarial justice to compel suspects to receive support and advice before and during those interviews.

There are many other structural aspects of access to criminal justice which we have not yet addressed. For example, questions can be raised as to whether the social and racial composition of the legal profession itself constitutes a barrier to criminal justice. Young, black, jobless people may feel that access to justice is denied to them if there are no black lawyers to whom they can turn when arrested or prosecuted.[59] That perception may or may not be correct, but the cynicism it can breed may in itself make some accused persons less likely to seek representation or contest the charges against them. Arguably, then, it is important that the legal profession attracts entrants from all groups in society.

As Abel notes, the admission policies of law schools are largely responsible for determining the composition of the legal profession.[60] These policies currently place great emphasis on acquired academic qualifications, which puts those from less privileged backgrounds at a disadvantage.[61] This problem is compounded by the differential treatment of those seeking entry into the legal profession by firms of solicitors: a study by Halpern found that black students seeking training contracts were less likely than white students to be successful, even after all other factors (such as degree result and previous legal experience) had been taken into account.[62]

---

[57] Feldman, *op. cit.*, p. 232.
[58] Paradoxically, this restriction was designed, in part, to facilitate the protection of suspects from the police: Sanders, A. and Young, R., 'The Legal Wilderness of Police Interrogation', in *The Tom Sargant Memorial Lecture*, London: JUSTICE, 1994, at pp. 24–5.
[59] The evidence on this point is admittedly anecdotal: see Tzannes, M., 'Strategies for the Selection of Students to Law Courses in the 21st Century: Issues and Options for Admissions Policy Makers', *The Law Teacher*, 1995, vol. 29, no. 1, p. 43 at p. 49.
[60] Abel, *op. cit.*, p. 272.
[61] See Tzannes, *op. cit.*
[62] Halpern, D., *Entry into the Legal Professions*, London: Law Society, 1994, p. 78.

Despite the barriers confronting black people who wish to enter the legal profession, some 'black firms' have established themselves in inner-city areas and built links with their local community. In McConville et al.'s typology, these firms are often 'political', in that they 'have a strong sense of social commitment, are on the side of the individual in disputes with the state and have an empathy with the poor and disadvantaged'.[63] Such a client-centred firm provides the starting point for Lee Bridge's analysis of the Green Paper in his contribution to this book. He argues that the proposal for firms to tender for the right to handle a pre-set number of criminal cases over a given period (block contracts) will lead to the administration of criminal legal aid becoming a matter of political controversy.

The client-centred firm tends to have higher than average costs per case when compared with other types of firm. Whereas the former fights cases and often advises its clients to elect jury trial, the latter prefer to manage their clients through the process, allowing and expecting their cases to peter out through a guilty plea in the magistrates' courts. With its higher cost per case, the client-centred firm is more likely to be unsuccessful in bidding for block contracts, leaving such firms barred from handling legal aid cases in the name of efficiency and cost-effectiveness. This, argues Bridges, will contribute to the increasing racial polarisation in the criminal justice system.

Bridges concludes by arguing in favour of an alternative programme of reform which might retain key elements of the Green Paper while dispensing with others. Thus, he contends that there may be advantages in introducing block contracts, but only if awarded on a non-competitive and non-exclusive basis. Looking beyond the cost control-inspired horizons of the Green Paper, Bridges sees the most pressing need as to address the issue of quality of service through programmes of specialist training and accreditation, such as that now in operation for police station advisers. It is worth adding that these would stand a better chance of success if law schools placed less emphasis on the technicalities of criminal law, procedure and evidence, in favour of inculcating in those intending to enter the legal profession a proper understanding of the basic principles of adversarial justice[64] and the ethical dilemmas of professional practice.[65]

Hilary Sommerlad's chapter focuses on how legal aid reforms are restructuring the ideology and practice of criminal defence work. She begins by outlining the classical view that solicitors held both of themselves and of their function. In this vision, solicitors stood outside the class struggle and acted as

---

[63] McConville et al., *op. cit.*, p. 20.
[64] See *ibid.*, *op. cit.*, p. 296.
[65] Using such techniques as that described by Harris, P., 'The Politics of Law Practice', in Grigg-Spall, I. and Ireland, P. (eds), *The Critical Lawyers' Handbook*, London: Pluto Press, 1992.

impartial mediators between clients and the universal standards embodied in the legal system. Their professional expertise in law was seen as justifying an independent, autonomous status, and self-regulation was presented as inevitable since no other body was qualified to judge whether lawyers were providing high quality legal services. Their mission was to act in the public service by helping clients to achieve access to justice. While these ideals were never fully realised in day-to-day practice, their effectiveness in legitimising the privileges of the profession required them to have some substance.

The rapid growth of legal aid after the Second World War is identified by Sommerlad as one of the main factors behind the crumbling of classical professionalism. State funding led to an ever-increasing level of managerial control over lawyers and their work and represented a challenge to the direct relationship with the client. Moreover, criminal legal aid was stigmatised as dirty, low status work. For these and other reasons, a wide gap opened up in the legal aid sector between the ideal of professional service and its realisation in practice. This in turn produced a questioning of the basic tenets of the classical professional paradigm and, as a corollary, demands to control and regulate the legal aid practitioner's work.

The programme of legal aid reforms which began in the late 1980s and was significantly advanced by the 1995 Green Paper is then analysed in this light. Sommerlad argues the classical paradigm has been replaced by one imbued with the ethic of scientific managerialism. Franchising, block contracts, transaction criteria and standard fees are seen as ways of the state controlling and shaping in detail the work that lawyers do. The loss of professional autonomy implicit in the legal aid reforms will, she argues, further entrench deskilling, discontinuous service and the 'sausage machine' approach whereby the client is processed rather than represented. Adversarialism, involving the testing of the prosecution case and the construction of a defence to throw reasonable doubt upon that case, will remain something to which only the wealthy have full access.[66]

An extreme illustration of this last point was the trial of Mr O.J. Simpson in the United States. The protracted nature of the court proceedings, encompassing 120 witnesses, 45,000 pages of transcripts and 1,110 exhibits,[67] demonstrated that there remains an enormous adversarial potential within the Anglo-American criminal process to be tapped by those with the means to pay

---

[66] Ironically, the 'apparently wealthy' may also derive much more benefit from the legal aid scheme than the manifestly poor for whom it was intended. See Dyer, C., 'How rich can get help denied to paraplegic on benefits', *Guardian*, 20 May 1995. For a Government response to this problem see Lord Chancellor's Department, *Legal Aid for the Apparently Wealthy: A Consultation Paper*, London: December 1994.

[67] See *The Times*, 4 October 1995.

privately for a defence. For those without means, the realistic option available is usually a guilty plea.[68] What Sommerlad's analysis reveals is that the legal aid reforms are likely to widen the gap between the appearance and substance of access to justice and the rule of law.

Adam Crawford's concluding chapter broadens the access to justice debate by looking at alternatives to prosecution, such as cautioning (whether or not linked to some further diversionary scheme), the Scottish prosecutor fine, and mediation and reparation schemes. The latter, in particular, espouse a different set of values to the formal legal process, including reconciliation, voluntariness, agency and free expression of feelings and claims. Crawford's main concern is that these values may become distorted in practice by the state's overriding aim of managing large criminal case-loads more efficiently. Priority is too often given to administrative requirements in which moral and ethical arguments are subordinated to the demands of 'smooth management'. The danger is that even the most normatively driven experiments in diversion may come to constitute exits from, rather than access to, justice.

Alternatives to prosecution are attractive to policy-makers since they do not necessitate the high level of expenditure associated with courtroom procedures, including the costs of legal aid. But is it defensible to exclude defence lawyers from the operation of such alternatives? Crawford assesses this by testing whether the arguments for legal aid as presented by Andrew Ashworth in this book have any application to diversionary schemes. The argument for legal aid based on the need to equalise resources between state and defendant is found by Crawford to have the most purchase. At present, the decision as to whether to accept guilt and proceed to a diversionary alternative is often devolved to the suspect in isolation, without recourse to legal assistance. An informed decision may not be possible in such circumstances. This does not necessarily mean that the defendant requires representation. As Crawford argues, initial legal advice may help to empower the individual in his or her decision-making; whereas legal representation, by contrast, is likely both to distort the values of the diversionary process and to disempower the client.

Crawford notes that any calls for legal aid to be extended even to this limited extent are likely to fall on deaf ears. The restructuring of the criminal process by the proliferation of alternatives to prosecution presents an opportunity to exclude expensive lawyers from the arena. The managerialist ethos which is driving most developments in both the civil and criminal justice systems at present favours cost control, efficiency and convenience over considerations of procedural and substantive justice and fairness. This has extensive implications

---

[68] See further McConville, M. and Mirsky, C., 'The State, the Legal Profession, and the Defence of the Poor', *Journal of Law and Society*, 1988, vol. 15, p. 342.

for the provision and delivery of both civil and criminal legal aid in England and Wales.

VII CONCLUSION

We have seen that legal aid serves a variety of functions within society and that its development, purpose and value can usefully be viewed from a number of different perspectives. We have drawn attention to the potential and limits of legal aid for achieving criminal justice for defendants. From one standpoint the kind of criminal justice to which we can aspire in a society riven by divisions of wealth, gender, class and race must of necessity be deeply flawed.[69] Even so, the potential for criminal justice which subsists within the existing system needs to be exploited to the full. Standing idealistically by while legions of defendants suffer wrongful detention, wrongful treatment and wrongful conviction is not an attractive option. Legal aid can at least be used to ameliorate the injustice of the criminal process itself. It can be used in this way, even if it often is not.

The present legal aid scheme may not in practice contribute much to social justice, and may even play a part in perpetuating social injustice. If legal aid was used self-consciously to advance adversarial justice, however, the ability of the criminal system to perpetuate wider social injustices would be hampered, and there might be other instrumental benefits too. One consequence might be that the state would take more care in its treatment of suspects; another that a growing sense of citizenship might arise as people became more conscious of their rights in relation to the state. It is in this optimistic spirit that we have produced this book.

---

[69] See Cain, M., 'The Symbol Traders', in Cain, M. and Harrington, C.B. (eds), *Lawyers in a Postmodern World*, Buckingham: Open University Press, 1994, pp. 45–6.

2

The Development of Criminal Legal Aid in England and Wales

Tamara Goriely

It is common to assume that defence lawyers are essential to the conduct of a serious criminal trial. In 1979, for example, the Royal Commission on Legal Services declared unequivocally that 'in the adversarial system which prevails in the courts in this country, representation is needed on both sides'.[1] It is worth recalling, however, how recently the presence of defence lawyers has become the norm in English criminal trials: it was not until the 1960s that legal aid was routinely provided to those facing jury trial, while defence lawyers did not become a common feature of magistrates' courts until the 1970s.

The history of criminal justice is usually seen as a progression from the haphazard prosecutions, hangings and transportation of the eighteenth century to the rational professionalised system of the nineteenth century, with armies of police and prison warders ready to apply more certain, bureaucratic justice. In the great professionalisation of criminal justice, however, legal aid is a belated arrival. A paid scheme was first established in 1903, but for most of the century it was used only at the symbolic end of the system — before jury trials and the Court of Appeal. Even before juries, it was used in only a minority of cases. It is only within the last 30 years that legal aid has paid defence lawyers to help in the mass processing of defendants through the courts.

This chapter shows that the development of legal aid has been a gradual evolutionary process, rather than a deliberate government strategy. Legal aid has responded to, and has been shaped by, the changing nature and volume of criminal trials. The result is that the emphasis has been on those aspects of legal

---

[1] Benson, Sir Henry, *Final Report of the Royal Commission on Legal Services in England and Wales*, Cmnd 7648, HMSO, 1979, para. 14.8.

representation which will help the courts in their work: advocacy at trial and representation in preliminary proceedings. Much less emphasis has been placed on police station work and evidence gathering.

I THE MID-EIGHTEENTH CENTURY: JURY TRIAL WITHOUT LAWYERS

During the eighteenth century, trials were essentially amateur affairs, with 'respectable' members of the public heavily involved as jurymen, prosecutors and spectators. Almost all serious offences were tried by juries, either at assizes or at quarter sessions. Assizes in particular were extremely grand occasions, accompanied by processions, addresses and balls. Courts were crowded with spectators, with the wives and daughters of local squires afforded the best views from behind the judge's bench.[2] The frisson of the occasion undoubtedly came from the prevalence of the death penalty, but in practice both jury leniency and post-court lobbying radically reduced the number of hangings. The normal assize would produce only two or three felons to hang as an example to others. Detailed studies of assize courts and the Old Bailey paint a picture of trials mainly for thefts of various kinds, conducted at the rate which one would now associate with summary trials rather than juries.[3] It was common to deal with 13–15 cases per day.[4] In a country without a professional police force, prosecutions were brought by ordinary individuals — usually the victim. A surprising number of prosecutors came from humble backgrounds — farmers, tradesmen or labourers. A third of prosecutors before the Essex quarter sessions could not even sign their names.[5]

The trial was conducted largely without lawyers. Complainants would tell their stories, followed by any witnesses they might bring. Witnesses would be prompted and questioned by the judge, while the defendant might blurt out a denial, often leading to a direct confrontation between the prisoner and

---

[2] For an account of the majesty of assizes and the social meaning of such ritual, see Hay, D., 'Property, Authority and the Criminal Law' in Hay, D., Linebaugh P. and Thompson, E.P., (eds), *Albion's Fatal Tree: Crime and Society in Eighteenth-Century England*, London: Allen Lane, 1975.
[3] A study of Old Bailey trials 1754–56 shows that around 85% of trials were for larceny. Out of 120 convicted, 96 were transported, and 20 were sentenced to death, of whom nine were hanged: Langbein, J. H., 'Shaping the Eighteenth Century Criminal Trial: a view from the Ryder sources', *University of Chicago Law Review*, 1983, vol. 50, p. 1. See also the analysis of quarter sessions and assizes in Surrey by Beattie, J. M., 'Crime and the Courts in Surrey 1736–1753' in Cockburn, J. S. (ed.), *Crime in England 1550–1800*, London: Methuen and Co., 1977 and a study of Essex by King, P., 'Decision-Makers and Decision-Making in the English Criminal Law 1750–1800', *Historical Journal*, 1984, vol. 27, p. 25.
[4] Beattie, *op. cit.*, p. 165. One assizes despatched 35 prisoners in two days.
[5] Based on an analysis of prosecutions from 1748 to 1800: King, *op. cit.*, p. 33.

accuser.[6] Defendants were not allowed to give evidence on oath and usually made statements from the dock. Technically, defendants were not allowed to be represented, but by the 1730s, where barristers could be paid for, they would be allowed to examine and cross-examine witnesses, though not to address the jury. Prosecutors were allowed counsel if they could afford it, but the tradition was that it was not necessary as the trial judge would do the necessary work in examining and cross-examining witnesses. Langbein reports that out of the 171 Old Bailey trials in his study we can be sure that counsel appeared for the prosecution in only six cases and for the defence in eight cases.[7] He suggests that while prosecuting counsel made little obvious difference, the impact of a skilled cross-examination by defence counsel was clear: '... we can point to a couple of cases in [the judges'] notes where the job was done so skilfully that it resulted in acquittals'.[8] Meanwhile, unrepresented defendants had to trust to fate. After long periods in confinement, they found themselves in strange and overwhelming surroundings, where acquittals were much more likely to be the result of the prosecution's failure than anything the accused was able to say or do.[9]

II   1750–1850: INCREASING PROFESSIONALISATION

The amateur trial and harsh penalties of the eighteenth-century process may have been suited to a closely meshed rural society, in which the criminal law was merely an adjunct to the existing patterns of power and deference towards the local ruling elite.[10] They were not suited to deal with crime among a mass urban proletariat. The move from the eighteenth- to the nineteenth-century trial is usually characterised as one of increasing professionalisation: from common informants to professional police; from hangings and transportation to imprisonment; and from haphazard convictions to certain, rational and bureaucratic justice.[11] One particular trend was the slow, steady professional-

---

[6] Beattie, *op. cit.*, p. 166.
[7] Langbein, *op. cit.*, p. 124. A similar picture emerges from Beattie's study of Surrey courts, *op. cit.*
[8] Langbein, *op. cit.*, p. 129.
[9] Beattie, *op. cit.*, p. 166.
[10] Hay, *op. cit.*
[11] For the most eloquent (if somewhat rhetorical) exposition of this thesis, see Foucault, M., *Discipline and Punish: The Birth of the Prison*, London: Allen Lane, 1977. Further discussion is provided by Hay, *op. cit.*, n. 2, and Cornish, W. R. and Clark G. de N., *Law and Society in England 1750–1950*, London: Sweet and Maxwell, 1989, pp. 568–613. See also Davis, J., 'A Poor Man's System of Justice: the London Police Courts in the Second Half of the Nineteenth Century', *Historical Journal*, 1984, vol. 27, p. 309, and Philips, D., 'A New Engine of Power and Authority: the Institutionalization of Law-Enforcement in England 1780-1830', in Gatrell, V. A. C., Lenman, B. and Parker, G. (eds), *Crime and the Law: the Social History of Crime in Western Europe since 1500*, London: Europa Publications, 1980.

isation of criminal prosecutions. In the eighteenth century it had been common to offer rewards to encourage prosecutions, but such 'blood money' payments inevitably led to scandals.[12] The emphasis slowly switched to helping prosecutors by paying their expenses: expenses were first allowed in 1752, but only for poor prosecutors, and only on conviction of a felon. In 1778 the provisions were extended to acquittals; in 1818 all prosecutors were allowed to claim, irrespective of their means; and in 1826, expenses were allowed before committing magistrates and for some misdemeanours.[13] One study found that in Essex in the 1760s around a quarter of prosecutors to the assizes were paid expenses, and that by the 1780s this had increased to nearly half.[14] As available expenses covered lawyers, witness payments and the time involved, they acted as incentives to more organised prosecutors through both voluntary associations and the nascent police forces, and by the end of the century it was much more common for prosecutors to be legally represented.

All this raised the question of whether defendants should also be represented, and whether, in particular, defence counsel should have the right to address the jury on behalf of the accused. Many barristers were keen to see an extended role for defence counsel, and bills to permit counsel to address the jury were introduced into Parliament in 1821, 1824, 1826, and 1834. All met considerable opposition from judges and all were defeated.[15] The law was eventually changed in 1836, when a further bill was supported by a report from the highly rational Benthamite Criminal Law Commissioners. The Commissioners argued that excluding lawyers was unprincipled and led to injustice as innocent defendants were often too ignorant, confused and worried to conduct their own defence: 'The advancement of justice' required that defence counsel should

[12] The most famous was the Macdaniel scandal of 1754, in which a gang was discovered to be deliberately framing victims and prosecuting them to their death for the reward. For an account, see Langbein, *op. cit.*, pp. 105–114.

[13] Prosecution expenses can be seen as the first form of state-funded legal aid, and cost-control proved as politically contentious then as now: see *Report of the Departmental Committee Appointed to Inquire into the Allowances to Prosecutors and Witnesses in Criminal Prosecutions*, Cd 1650, London: HMSO 1903. Originally costs were met from local funds but, as a sop to the agricultural interest during the repeal of the corn laws, Peel offered to reimburse county treasurers from central funds. Central government met half the cost in 1836, and took over the full cost in 1846. At this, the budget increased steeply, and the Treasury decided to take action. In 1853 they appointed gentlemen to go on circuit to the assizes and quarter sessions to examine bills: apparently 'these gentlemen did their duty with energy and caused large disallowances to be made' (para. 16). This led to vociferous complaints from local authorities, and the matter was referred to a number of committees and Royal Commissions. In 1888, central government was only too glad to hand the matter back to the local authorities, in exchange for a fixed grant from central government.

[14] King, *op. cit.*, p. 32.

[15] It was argued that it was sufficient for judges to act as counsel for the accused, and that it would be wrong 'to convert the court into an arena where opposing advocates might meet in professional conflict'. *Hansard* NS, vol. 15, 25 April 1826, quoted in Hostettler, J., *The Politics of Criminal Law Reform in the Nineteenth Century*, Chichester: Barry Rose, 1992, p. 46.

have the right to address the jury.[16] Many judges, however, looked on the intrusion of defence counsel with alarm: they thought that most trials were simple, that judges could help prisoners, and that innocence could best be assessed by the 'simplicity' and 'artlessness' of one 'acquitted by his own conscience'.[17] They feared that trials would be diverted from the dispassionate inquiry into truth by the 'obstreperous contention of counsel' as barristers flattered, threatened or deceived juries through 'vicious eloquence'.[18] Finally the Law Magazine worried that as lawyers assumed a more central place within trials, the position of those who could not afford counsel would worsen.[19] Despite such anxieties, however, the Prisoners' Counsel Act 1836 was passed and, from then on, where prisoners could afford to pay, counsel was allowed to address the jury.

The 1836 Act was accompanied by a rapid expansion of the Bar, as assizes became a regular training ground for young lawyers. One estimate suggests that while in 1809 there had been only 456 barristers, by 1846 there were over 3,000.[20] Philips reports that by the 1840s around 30 to 40 barristers travelled the Oxford circuit, taking prosecuting and defending roles interchangeably. The normal fee was one guinea, or perhaps two for a lucrative prosecution, and most took instructions directly from prosecutor or prisoner. If a solicitor was required as well, that would cost another guinea.[21] By this time, prosecutors were a mixed bunch — sometimes the victim, or his or her friends and relatives; sometimes a policeman, and sometimes the magistrates' clerk.[22] By 1843, just over half of those prosecuting in the assizes and at quarter sessions in the Black Country were represented by counsel. The position of defendants, however, was more difficult, with only a quarter represented.[23] Some, with the help of friends and relatives, might be able to scrape together the required guinea. Others might be funded by newspapers in return for a story, and in murder cases judges would ask barristers to act for no fee. For the great majority of those

---

[16] Report of the Criminal Law Commissioners, P.P. 1936 (343) XXXVI, cited in Hostettler, *op. cit.*, p. 47.
[17] Evidence of Serjeant Hawkins to the Commissioners, cited by Hostettler, *op. cit.*, p. 48.
[18] Letter of Serjeant Spankie to the Commissioners, 28 May 1935, reproduced in Appendix 2 to the report and cited by Hostettler, *op. cit.*, p. 50.
[19] Vol.15 (May 1836) p. 394, cited by Hostettler, *op. cit.*, p. 51.
[20] Hostettler, *op. cit.*, p. 45. He cites the *Law Review*, 1845–46, vol. 3, p. 349. It is an open question whether the rise in the number of barristers was a cause of the 1836 Act (on the basis that lawyers set out to create demand for their services) or an effect. There is probably an element of both — see the discussion on the rise of legal aid firms in the 1970s which follows.
[21] Philips, D., *Crime and Authority in Victorian England*, London: Croom Helm, 1977, p. 104.
[22] Kurland, P. B. and Waters, D. W. M., 'Public Prosecutions in England 1854–79: an Essay in English Legislative History', *Duke Law Journal*, 1959, p. 493.
[23] Philips, *op. cit.*, p. 104.

charged with theft, however, any form of legal defence was beyond their means and they met an increasingly adversarial, lawyer-dominated procedure on their own.[24] As the century progressed, the 'dock brief' came to be seen as a semi-charitable act in which prisoners could ask to be defended by any counsel in the room on payment of £1 3s 6d — one guinea for the barrister and half a crown for the clerk. Until well into the twentieth century, however, this was a far from nominal sum: in 1903 it represented the standard fee paid by Lancaster Borough Council for all its prosecution briefs.[25] Only a minority of prisoners were able to raise such a large amount.[26]

III THE CRIMINAL TRIAL AT THE END OF THE NINETEENTH CENTURY

John Hostettler describes the Prisoners' Counsel Act 1836 as if it were part of the remorseless march of progress: '... the Act was clearly correct in principle and was soon accepted as if it has always existed'.[27] It underpinned adversarial procedure so that 'by 1845 the lawyers had captured the court room, made the trial accusatorial and obliged the accused to recede into the dock'.[28] This overstates its effect. According to Philips, in the 1840s half of all larceny trials were conducted entirely without lawyers.[29] Even by 1903, it would appear that the majority of defendants facing a judge and jury were unrepresented.[30] What is clear, however, is that in the decades following the Prisoners' Counsel Act trial procedure became more adversarial so that, arguably, the position of the unrepresented prisoner became even more difficult.

In his classic *History of the Criminal Law* published in 1883, Sir James F. Stephen provides a portrait of the 'modern criminal trial' based on 'nearly thirty years' experience as a barrister and as a judge'.[31] He describes a trial procedure in which the prosecution is invariably represented by counsel and which relies crucially on formal examination and cross-examination of witnesses by barristers. When both sides are represented, he suggests, 'nothing can be fairer

---

[24] For non-larceny offences, 49% of prisoners were represented, but for larceny offences the figure fell to 16%.

[25] See evidence of Mr T. Cann Hughes, Town Clerk of Lancaster, to the Departmental Committee, *op. cit.*, n. 13, para. 3034.

[26] Abel-Smith, B. and Stevens, R., *Lawyers and the Courts*, London: Heineman, 1967, p. 149.

[27] Hostettler, *op. cit.*, p. 58.

[28] *Ibid.*, p. 43.

[29] Philips, *op. cit.*, p. 105.

[30] In 1903, Mr Slade Butler, a barrister with 25 years' experience, conceded in his evidence before the Departmental Committee, *op. cit.*, n. 13, that the majority of prisoners in London were undefended: 'Yes, but not a large majority, it is a majority' (para. 2278).

[31] Stephen, J. F., *A History of the Criminal Law of England*, vol. 1, London: Macmillan and Co., 1883, p. 428.

or more completely satisfactory than a great criminal trial'.[32] On the other hand, Stephen concedes that many prisoners were not properly advised, with lamentable results:

> It must be remembered that most persons accused of crime are poor, stupid and helpless. They are often defended by solicitors who confine their exertions to getting a copy of the depositions and endorsing it with the name of some counsel to whom they pay a very small fee, so that even when prisoners are defended by counsel the defence is often extremely imperfect, and consists rather of what occurs at the moment to the solicitor and counsel than of what the man himself would say if he knew how to say it. When a prisoner is undefended his position is often pitiable, even if he has a good case. An ignorant uneducated man has the greatest possible difficulty in collecting his ideas, and seeing the bearing of facts alleged. He is utterly unaccustomed to sustained attention or systematic thought, and it often appears to me as if the proceedings on a trial, which to an experienced person appear plain and simple, must pass before the eyes and mind of the prisoner like a dream he cannot grasp.[33]

This is a powerful description of the problem, but Stephen suggests no solutions. In fact, when he summarises the chapter for his shorter student handbook in 1890, he leaves out all mention of unrepresented defendants. Instead, one aside suggests to the casual reader that undefended prisoners no longer existed.[34] Stephen does not blame either the bar or criminal procedure for the difficulties prisoners face. Rather, any blame is laid at the door either of solicitors or of men 'incapable of systematic thought' who cannot understand how plain and simple trial procedure really is. For many mid-Victorian commentators, the 'problem' of unrepresented defendants was one which simply had to be tolerated within what was normally the fairest procedure in the world. Although there were spasmodic calls for public defenders, these made little headway.[35] The only concession to state funding for the defence was the Criminal Law Amendment Act 1867, under which the expenses of defence

---

[32] *Ibid.*, p. 444.

[33] *Ibid.*, p. 442.

[34] He states that 'so long as prisoners were really undefended by counsel in serious cases, their cross-examination of the witnesses against them was trifling and of little or no importance', Stephen, J. F., *A General View of the Criminal Law of England*, London: Macmillan and Co., 1890, p. 169.

[35] A pamphlet by Frederic Clavert on the Prisoners' Counsel Bill in 1936 argued for government agents employed at public expense. See review in the *Law Magazine*, May 1936, vol. 15, p. 394, cited by Hostettler, *op. cit.*, p. 51. In 1919, Horatio Bottomley MP unsuccessfully introduced a bill to set up a Public Defender's Department: see Abel-Smith and Stevens, *op. cit.*, n. 26, p. 152.

witnesses could be met out of public funds in the same way as those of prosecution witnesses. The recital to the Act takes a somewhat grudging tone:

> Complaint is frequently made by persons charged with indictable offences, upon their trial, that they are unable by reason of poverty to call witnesses on their behalf, and that injustice is thereby occasioned to them; and it is expedient to remove as far as practicable all just ground for such complaint.[36]

Nevertheless, the Act established an important principle, which in 1903 made Parliament much more prepared to accept the idea of paid legal aid in the criminal than in the civil field.

The final cornerstone of the adversarial trial was laid by the Criminal Evidence Act 1898, by which defendants were allowed to give evidence on oath. Almost 70 years earlier, Bentham had inveighed against the irrationality of preventing those who best knew the facts of the case from giving evidence.[37] The Act may therefore be seen as a long delayed Benthamite reform made in the name of progress and rationality. It was also a reaction against the way in which, with the increasing professionalisation of criminal defence, the voice of the defendant was no longer being heard. The promoters were keen to put prisoners 'on the spot' by encouraging them into the witness-box where they might be cross-examined.[38] The effect was to increase substantially the role of prosecuting counsel as, for the first time, they could use their forensic cross-examination skills on the defendant. In 1903 a committee remarked that cross-examining defendants was 'one of the most delicate and difficult duties a barrister is called on to perform'.[39] It also exposed even more starkly the imbalance between prosecution counsel and the unrepresented defendant.

By the end of the century the purpose of jury trials had changed. They were no longer the central way of disposing of criminals, and were increasingly assuming symbolic importance in a criminal system which relied mainly on summary trials. This can been seen in the figures. In the first half of the nineteenth century the number of jury trials had increased substantially as the law turned from an amateur and haphazard system for subjecting people to exemplary punishments to a mass system of bureaucratic justice. In 1805 there had been a mere 4,605 committals for trials, which by 1848 reached a peak of 30,349. In the second half of the century, however, the number of committals fell steeply, so that by 1891 they had reached a low of 11,695, despite a 62 per

---

[36] 30 and 31 Vict., c.35, s. 3.
[37] See Twining, W., *Theories of Evidence: Bentham and Wigmore*, London: Weidenfeld and Nicolson, 1985, ch. 2.
[38] See Cornish and Clark, *op. cit.*, n. 11, p. 619.
[39] Departmental Committee, *op. cit.*, n. 13, para. 78.

cent increase in population.[40] This was partly the result of what was perceived as the 'English miracle', by which the rate of recorded crime per head of population fell from the 1860s to 1900.[41] More significantly, it reflected a shift from jury to summary trial, as the powers of magistrates were gradually extended. By 1879, magistrates could try children for a wide range of offences and could try adults for thefts up to £2.[42] The percentage of indictable offences tried by jury fell from over 30 per cent in 1876 to under 20 per cent in 1900.[43]

As a symbol of the perfection of English justice, however, jury trials were tarnished by the obvious imbalance between prosecution and defence. Prosecutions were now much more professional. Stephen, while lauding the theory of private prosecution, admitted that in fact prosecutions were usually instituted by the police.[44] Moreover, the police were increasingly using specialist solicitor departments, who could bring a much greater level of expertise to the process, while prosecution barristers could use their skills to cross-examine defendants to great effect. Meanwhile, the majority of defendants appeared to be in the 'pitiable position' of being undefended in which the splendour of the adversarial process passed before them 'like a dream they could not grasp'. By the end of the nineteenth century, some members of the Bar were becoming uncomfortably aware that unrepresented defendants damaged the image of English justice.[45]

IV THE POOR PRISONERS' DEFENCE ACT 1903

A paid legal aid scheme was first introduced in 1903. Far from representing a new consensus in support of unrepresented defendants, however, the 1903 Act was passed almost by accident. It represented a compromise that no one really supported, and it was to help very few defendants.

---

[40] Gatrell, V. A. C. and Hadden, T. B., 'Criminal Statistics and their Interpretation' in Wrigley, E. A. (ed.), *Nineteenth Century Society: Essays in the Use of Quantitative Methods for the Study of Social Data*, Cambridge: Cambridge University Press, 1972. The population of England and Wales rose from 17.9 million in 1851 to 29 million in 1891.

[41] For further discussion of this phenomenon, see Radzinowicz, L. and Hood, R., *The Emergence of Penal Policy in Victorian and Edwardian England*, Oxford: Clarendon Press, 1990, ch. 5.

[42] Radzinowicz, L. and Hood, R., *op. cit.*, pp. 113–24 and 619–24.

[43] Jackson, R. M., 'The Incidence of Jury Trial during the Past Century', *Modern Law Review*, 1937, vol. 1, p. 132.

[44] *Op. cit.*, n. 34, p. 156.

[45] The campaign was led by Mr W. R. Bousfield, KC, MP. When he introduced a bill into the House of Commons he was supported by six other KCs and two solicitors: see Abel-Smith and Stevens, *op. cit.*, n. 26, p. 150.

So how did it come about? In the wake of the Criminal Evidence Act 1898, increasing concern was expressed about the plight of unrepresented litigants,[46] especially as it became clear that England fell far behind Scotland in making voluntary provision for poor defendants. In Scotland, each year volunteer advocates and solicitors were appointed to act as Counsel or Agents for the Poor. While the English survived on an *ad hoc* system, in which in serious cases the judge would appoint a barrister to act for free as the trial started, in Scotland agents would take instructions from defendants in prison, and would brief the Counsel for the Poor before the trial started. Although the Bar Council itself stopped short of recommending either a paid or a voluntary scheme, in 1903 a group of leading lawyers promoted a bill before Parliament to establish a voluntary scheme along Scottish lines to assist poor prisoners.

Within the Home Office, officials regarded the bill with mixed feelings. Clearly it would be difficult to oppose 'in principle', but they doubted it would work. The Law Society had shown little interest in the scheme, there would be insufficient solicitors to carry out the work, and when provision failed, there was a danger that defendants would expect the Home Office to remedy the deficiency.[47] Officials already received many petitions in which convicted felons blamed their lawyers for their convictions: with more gratuitous representation from young and inadequately prepared barristers, they feared that the number of such complaints would increase. Lastly, they worried that more representation would encourage defendants to contest trials: barristers would be given long lists of mostly irrelevant witnesses, and trials would become longer and more expensive. When the bill was referred to a Select Committee, H. B. Simpson, Principal Clerk to the Criminal Division, was sure that it would be persuaded to drop the idea. In July 1903 he noted that 'there is no chance of the bill passing in its present form. I should think these papers may be laid by'.[48]

In fact, the Select Committee, instead of deciding to drop the scheme, became persuaded that lawyers should be paid. It argued that 'the basis of an effective defence generally involves preliminary communication with the accused, obtaining evidence for the defence and inquiry into the case for the prosecution'.[49] If a voluntary scheme could not deliver this, the cost should be borne by the ratepayer. After all, prosecutors were already paid their expenses from local funds and it would be relatively simple to meet defence expenses in

---

[46] Abel-Smith and Stevens cite a paper by W. S. Coldstream given to the International Bar Association in Glasgow in 1901 calling for a state-funded scheme, which was apparently well received, *op. cit.*, n. 26, p. 150.

[47] See the memoranda of H. B. Simpson, 19 March 1903, and undated: PRO File HO45 10282.

[48] Note dated 1 July 1903, PRO file HO45 10282.

[49] *Report and Special Report of the Select Committee on Poor Prisoners' Defence Bill*, HC 254, London: HMSO, 1903, para. 7.

the same way. On the other hand, the committee was alive to the many arguments against extending representation. It was pointed out that 40 per cent of defendants pleaded guilty, and they did not wish to tempt them by 'the offer of solicitor and counsel to try for the chance of an acquittal'.[50] If lawyers were to be paid, the amount of legal aid provided would need to be strictly limited. When the bill returned to the House of Commons, it had been re-written to allow solicitors and barristers to be paid from local funds, but only in very limited circumstances. Magistrates should have discretion to grant legal aid only when the prisoner raised a defence at the committal. Before the Home Office woke up to what had happened, the bill had passed, and the Poor Prisoners' Defence Act 1903 was on the statute book.

It was only after the Act had been passed that the complaints flooded in. The bill's original supporters objected that the poor would be helped only if they disclosed their defences at committal, while the rich enjoyed a right of silence. Many of those who were most vulnerable — children, foreigners, the deaf and dumb and the mentally ill — would not be able to make themselves understood at committal and would therefore go without help. [51] The Bar complained that the Act paid counsel only when they were instructed by solicitors: where barristers stepped in at the last moment they could not be paid. The Clerk to the Old Bailey thought that the Act would merely encourage disreputable solicitors:

> I think that it is pretty certain that no solicitor of standing and experience will be willing to undertake the defence of poor prisoners, but that it will be left to the lowest class whose presence at this court has hitherto been discouraged as much as possible.[52]

Meanwhile judges denied that it was needed at all, as the interests of defendants 'are safe in the hands of the presiding judge, whose duty it is, according to long-standing tradition, to see that every point which can be made in favour of the accused is properly considered'.[53]

When it was suggested that at committals magistrates should tell defendants about the possibility of legal aid, there were widespread protests. Even the bill's supporters explained that 'it is not desirable that this Act should be put into operation too quickly and it should . . . be left to the discretion of the magistrates

---

[50] *Ibid.*, para. 3.
[51] See Sir Harry Poland's comments on the draft rules, 6 January 1904, and a letter from B. Fossett Lock to the Home Office dated 24 January 1904: PRO file HO45 10282.
[52] Evidence of Mr H. K. Avory, reproduced in 'Comments on Draft Rules', 6 January 1904, PRO file HO45 10282.
[53] Jelf J's address to the Grand Jury at Carlisle, 21 January 1904, as reported in *Justice of the Peace*, 5 March 1904.

to say nothing whatever about the Act'.[54] According to the Society of Clerks of the Peace, telling a prisoner about legal aid would 'simply act as an incentive to him to trust to a possible, however desperate, chance of getting off, if he felt he could avail himself of this chance at the public expense'.[55] In the end it was agreed that magistrates would not need to tell anyone about the scheme.

In January 1904, Mr Justice Jelf explained to the Grand Jury at Carlisle that the 1903 Act was 'an exceptional remedy intended to meet an exceptional difficulty'.[56] Normally judges would look after the interests of the accused, or if they could not, would ask a member of the Bar to act for free. It was only in a very few cases that legal aid would be needed: where the defendant raised an alibi defence at committal, for example, or in a case of fraudulent bankruptcy where the investigation of books and documents was essential.

V CRIMINAL LEGAL AID IN THE 1920s

The Home Office kept no figures about how often legal aid was granted,[57] but judging from the regular protests in the House of Commons the number of times it was granted was extremely low.[58] Not only were defendants unaware of the provisions, but so were some magistrates,[59] and many of those who did know about them were anxious to prevent any further burden on their local ratepayers. By 1925, the original remuneration rates, set at £2 2s for solicitors and £1 3s 6d for counsel in 1903, had not been uprated. Most lawyers came to regard acting under the scheme as equivalent to charity, and solicitors showed some reluctance to include their names on the court lists.

During the 1920s there was mounting pressure to improve legal aid and advice for both criminal and civil matters. The most active and effective lobby was undoubtedly the women's movement. The Suffragist movement had gained a partial victory in 1918 when women over 30 were given the vote, and during the 1920s many leading campaigners turned their attention to issues of

---

[54] Comments of Mr W. R. Bousfield MP, reproduced in 'Comments on Draft Rules', *op. cit.*, n. 52.
[55] R. Nicholson, 'Observations of the Society of Clerks of the Peace of the Counties', reproduced in 'Comments on Draft Rules', *op. cit.*, n. 52.
[56] Reported in *Justice of the Peace*, 5 March 1904.
[57] For the Home Office views on the operation of the Act, see Memorandum, 'The Provision of Legal Aid for the Poor', 28 February 1925, PRO File HO45 11857. Figures were kept from 1931 onwards.
[58] See Hansard (H of C), vol. 117, 4 July 1919, col. 1359 and vol. 189, 10 December 1925, col. 723. In 1929, His Honour Judge Sturges is reported as saying that after 16 years as a Vice-Chairman of Quarter Sessions he could not recall a single instance in which legal assistance was granted under the 1903 Act: *The Times*, 23 February 1929.
[59] See the evidence submitted by the Howard League for Penal Reform to the Rushcliffe Committee in 1944: PRO file 3900. One member declared that when he had been appointed as a magistrate in 1935 he found that not one of his fellow justices 'knew anything about legal aid for the poor'.

wider social concern. Many leading Labour women were magistrates, and knew from experience the problems that defendants, separated wives and unmarried mothers faced in court; and a small group of leading figures worked within their respective organisations to organise a more general protest.[60] By December 1924 their campaign was well underway, as 17 leading churchmen, led by the Bishop of London, wrote to *The Times* to demand an enquiry into legal aid. A petition to that effect was signed by 100 MPs. Meanwhile, a committee of the Labour Party was advocating improvements. [61] Sir Claud Schuster, Secretary to the Lord Chancellor, was appalled. 'Personally, I look upon the whole thing with horror,' he wrote. He saw no prospect of further state funding so any improvement would have to rely on the good will of the solicitors' profession — and that was 'insufficient to carry on the work which we actually have in hand'.[62]

The pressure, however, required a response, and in 1925 the Lord Chancellor's Department was forced to appoint a committee to investigate. All Schuster could do was to select members unlikely to recommend any radical ideas.[63] Considerable evidence was presented that the Poor Prisoners' Defence Act 1903 was not working: defendants who failed to disclose their defence on committal were excluded; many judges refused to allow the services of a solicitor, granting legal aid for counsel only; and legal aid was often provided so late that defences could not be investigated. Both solicitors and barristers complained of the low fee rates, and no help at all was available in magistrates' courts. Despite the strength of the protest, the committee took a highly complacent view: 'in criminal cases the present system works satisfactorily,'

---

[60] In 1924, the National Conference of Labour Women discussed a report on the need for greater legal aid. The main campaigners were Gertrude Tuckwell, Dr Marion Phillips, Eleanor Rathbone and Elizabeth Fry at the Howard League for Penal Reform. Gertrude Tuckwell appears to have played the lead role, becoming chair of a committee of the Magistrates' Association to consider legal assistance to poor people in police courts. She bombarded the Lord Chancellor's Office with good ideas for harnessing more voluntary work from the profession: see PRO file LCO2 979.

[61] See *Daily Herald*, 31 January 1924, which reported the work of Mr Halford Knight, a Labour barrister. See also *Daily Chronicle*, 17 January 1925.

[62] PRO file LCO2 979.

[63] It was to be chaired by a judge, Mr Justice Finlay, and was to consist of two barristers, two solicitors (one a Conservative MP), three other MPs, one woman, representatives of the Treasury and Home Office and himself. The selection was immediately criticised for not including any county court judges or magistrates. Neither did it include anyone from a church or social work background. It did not include Marion Phillips, Secretary to the Standing Joint Committee of Industrial Women's Organisations, whose name was being constantly urged upon the Department by Gertrude Tuckwell: PRO File LCO2 979 (and see n. 60).

it declared, and 'no alterations are urgently or imperatively required'.[64] In most cases 'the prisoners are manifestly so guilty as to leave no room for doubt'.[65]

Nevertheless, the protests were too strong to ignore, and the committee did recommend some improvements. The committee thought that defendants should not be precluded because they failed to disclose their defence. Instead, magistrates should have discretion to grant legal aid for jury trial when it was in the interests of justice to do so. In grave charges, such as murder, it was recommended that help should be available at committal. Lastly, in a few, limited summary trials, magistrates should be able to grant legal aid if it was 'necessary in the interests of justice, by reason of the exceptional circumstances in the case'.[66] The committee wholly rejected proposals for lay advocates, in which help would be provided by friends of defendants or by probation officers: any such system would be 'most dangerous' and could 'lead to grave abuses'.[67] Also rejected were schemes for public defenders, which were considered 'exceedingly expensive and difficult to work'.[68]

VI THE POOR PRISONERS' DEFENCE ACT 1930

The committee's recommendations were generally well received, but there was little urgency about them. Left to its own devices the Home Office would have done nothing, noting privately that 'the public should not spend money in helping a guilty man to establish a false defence'.[69] The Howard League for Penal Reform, however, was active in organising conferences and in lobbying MPs. In 1928, J. J. Withers MP introduced a private member's bill sponsored by the League to improve criminal legal aid. When the following year he reintroduced it and gained considerable support, the Home Office reluctantly agreed to back it, provided the Home Office could rewrite its provisions. In particular it wished to omit any requirement that the Act should be publicised. Civil servants commented, for example, that a provision for summonses to carry information about legal aid 'can only be considered as absurd'.[70] Thus with much official hesitation and reluctance, the Poor Prisoners' Defence Act

---

[64] Finlay, Mr Justice, *First Report of the Committee on Legal Aid for the Poor*, Cmd 2638, London: HMSO, 1926, para. 22. When the Committee turned to civil legal aid the following year, it was even more contemptuous of reform and became famous for rejecting any analogy between medical and legal aid: 'It is manifestly in the interests of the state that its citizens should be healthy, not that they should be litigious': Finlay, Mr Justice, *Final Report of the Committee on Legal Aid for the Poor*, Cmd 3016, London: HMSO, 1928, para. 17.

[65] *First Report*, para. 9.

[66] *Ibid.*, para. 15.

[67] *Ibid.*, para. 16.

[68] *Ibid.*, para. 21.

[69] PRO file HO45 13774.

[70] Memorandum on Poor Prisoners' Defence Bill, 20 November 1928, PRO file HO45 13774.

1930 became law and was to lay the foundations of the criminal legal aid scheme as we know it today.

The 1930 Act introduced three main changes. First, in jury trials, it removed the requirement that prisoners should disclose their defence at committal. Instead, legal aid was automatic in murder trials. In other cases, magistrates were given wide discretion to grant legal aid where the defendants' means were insufficient and it appeared to them 'to be desirable in the interests of justice'.[71] Secondly, the Act provided some limited help in summary trials, where 'by reason of the gravity of the charge or of exceptional circumstances it is desirable in the interests of justice'.[72] Lastly, it allowed the possibility of legal aid before committals: again this was only for grave charges or in exceptional circumstances.[73]

Following the 1930 Act, the Home Office started to keep figures on the number of certificates granted. In 1931, 1,321 certificates were granted for representation at assizes and quarter sessions, representing 15 per cent of all those standing trial. By 1938, the figure had risen gradually to around 2,000 or 20 per cent of those standing trial. Within summary courts, however, magistrates rarely saw any need for representation and only tiny numbers of certificates were granted: in 1938 there were a mere 327 certificates for help with summary trials.[74]

Although the limitation to exceptional requirements in magistrates' courts was eventually repealed in 1963, the 1930 Act's provisions formed the basis of legal aid for the next 50 years. Several characteristics of the Act are important to understanding criminal legal aid today. First, criminal legal aid developed quite separately from civil legal aid, where a paid scheme was not introduced at all until 1950. This division was reflected within government, where the Home Office had responsibility for overseeing the criminal scheme while civil legal aid was a matter for the Lord Chancellor's Department, a division of responsibility which persisted until 1980. Secondly, the emphasis was on court proceedings, with no provision for advice about criminal matters until 1959. Thirdly, the key decision-makers under the scheme were magistrates and their clerks, who were granted great discretion to provide legal aid as and when they saw fit. Lastly, there was little planning or coordination of the scheme. The Government did not monitor whether the Act was working, whether there were sufficient solicitors, or whether they did a good job. Instead, legal aid was perceived as a relatively minor way of paying existing lawyers in a few cases.

---

[71] Poor Prisoners' Defence Act 1930, s. 1(3)(b).

[72] *Ibid.*, s. 2.

[73] *Ibid.*

[74] Home Office, *Criminal Statistics – England and Wales 1938*, Cmd 6167, London: HMSO, 1940.

VII THE SECOND WORLD WAR, RECONSTRUCTION AND THE RUSHCLIFFE COMMITTEE

Before 1939, official attitudes to legal aid were at best grudging and sometimes overtly hostile. Although the principle of state payments had been accepted in the criminal sphere, in civil work it was an article of faith with both the Law Society and the Lord Chancellor's Department that help should be provided only on a voluntary basis to the very poor. The experience of war was to bring about fundamental change.

By 1942 the voluntary High Court Poor Persons Procedure had collapsed as the number of divorces rose and the number of lawyers available to do the work fell. By 1944 it was clear that a voluntary civil scheme could not be resurrected after the war. Private charity was no longer acceptable, and there was widespread agreement that in the post-war reconstruction the state should assume responsibility for social ills. In May 1944, Lord Simon, the Liberal Lord Chancellor in the coalition government, wrote to Herbert Morrison, the Labour Home Secretary, informing him that he was setting up a committee under the chairmanship of Lord Rushcliffe to consider the reform of legal aid within the civil courts. In direct contradiction of the views of the Finlay Committee[75] he commented that 'if we make efforts to get a better medical service for people who are ill, had we better not see whether there is anything to be done about better legal advice and assistance for those who have the misfortune to be involved in a legal dispute'.[76] Simon's initial idea was that the committee's remit should be confined to civil work, but Morrison, anxious not be outdone by a Liberal colleague, demanded that criminal legal aid should be included. He argued that legal aid was not always granted where it ought to be and that there was a lack of legal advice before court appearances.

The Rushcliffe Committee was appointed in June 1944, at the time of the 'D day' landings, and reported in May 1945,[77] the month when victory was declared in Europe. It shows all the optimism of those final months of the war, when it was becoming clear that Britain would emerge victorious and could turn its mind to 'winning the peace'. On the civil side, the Committee recommended a comprehensive scheme in which the state would pay private lawyers to represent poor and middle-income litigants before a wide range of courts and tribunals. It also wanted a salaried advice scheme to provide initial help with both civil and criminal matters. In the area of criminal legal aid, however, its proposals were less radical. It approved of the 1930 Act in

---

[75] See n. 64, above.
[76] Letter dated 5 May 1944, PRO file HO45 25130.
[77] Rushcliffe, Lord, *Report of the Committee on Legal Aid and Legal Advice in England and Wales*, Cmd 6641, London: HMSO, 1945.

principle and wanted to see greater use made of it. The Committee rejected Law Society proposals that they should grant certificates and run criminal legal aid in the same way as the civil scheme.[78] It also rejected suggestions for public defenders. Instead the Committee looked for incremental changes.

Almost all of those giving evidence about criminal legal aid criticised the lack of publicity. As the Magistrates' Association observed, it was usually only 'old lags' who knew the system well who ever asked for it.[79] The Howard League for Penal Reform also complained that magistrates lacked knowledge about the Act or sympathy with defendants and that there was no generally accepted standard of need.[80] There was evidence that some magistrates still required prisoners to disclose their defence at committal. Furthermore, the low payments meant that the scheme failed to attract the interest and cooperation of the legal profession. When legal aid was granted it was often provided too late for the case to be prepared adequately.

The Rushcliffe Committee agreed with these criticisms, and made five recommendations for change.[81] First, the limitations to grave charges and exceptional circumstances should be repealed. Legal aid should be granted in all criminal courts where it was desirable in the interests of justice, and any doubt should be resolved in favour of the applicant. Secondly, publicity should be improved. Revisiting an issue which had caused such problems 40 years before, the Committee thought that magistrates should always tell defendants about legal aid at committal and confirm this by handing out information slips. Similarly, people should be given slips about legal aid when charged by the police or when sent a summons for offences carrying terms of imprisonment. Thirdly, solicitors should be given at least four days to prepare cases. In order to grant legal aid earlier, defendants should be able to apply by letter to the clerk before the hearing. Fourthly, the Committee recommended that lawyers should no longer be paid fixed fees. Although fees had been raised after the Finlay Committee's report, they had again slipped to levels at which lawyers viewed the work as almost charitable.[82] Instead, they should be fairly remunerated with bills taxed by the clerk of the justices, and allowances made for expenses such as travel and witnesses. The final recommendation was slipped into the report with no explanation: that the costs of legal aid should be borne by taxpayers rather than ratepayers. In doing this the Committee

---

[78] For criticism of the Committee's failure to accept the Law Society's case, see Lund, T. G., 'Legal Aid and Advice Scheme', *Solicitors' Journal*, 1948, vol. 92, pp. 716 and 728.

[79] Written evidence to the Rushcliffe Committee, PRO file LCO2 3899.

[80] Evidence to the Rushcliffe Committee, *op. cit.*, n. 59.

[81] Rushcliffe Committee, *op. cit.*, para. 140.

[82] Solicitors were allowed £3 3s plus an additional £1 11s 6d for every additional day of substantive hearing, but no extra fees were allowed for simple adjournments or remands on bail. Counsel were allowed £3 5s 6d plus a £2 4s 6d refresher fee.

followed a proposal put forward by the Howard League for Penal Reform designed to encourage magistrates to be more generous with public money. When this recommendation was eventually implemented in 1960 it was to have a major effect on the grant of legal aid. Magistrates felt some compunction to be careful with local ratepayers' money, but they were to have few such worries about the remote national exchequer.

VIII INITIAL ENTHUSIASM MEETS ECONOMIC REALITY: RUSHCLIFFE'S SLOW IMPLEMENTATION

In the July 1945 election, Labour was returned with a strong mandate to build the welfare state. In the first bout of enthusiasm, the Home Office issued a circular to magistrates urging them to grant legal aid more readily and at an earlier stage, and to resolve any doubts in the applicant's favour.[83] In April 1948, the Home Office — in a reversal of earlier policy — produced information slips for courts and police to hand to defendants. This had a marked effect on the number of certificates granted for the assizes and quarter session: by 1950, 43 per cent of defendants before these courts were granted legal aid. There was no acceptance, however, that lawyers were needed in summary courts, where the number of certificates was only 0.3 per cent of all those dealt with. Even with jury trials the effect of publicity proved short-lived, and during the 1950s the number of certificates fell, reaching a low of 27 per cent in 1958.

The Labour Government proved less successful with legislative changes. Legal aid was hardly a priority amid all the other welfare reforms, and a bill could not be fitted into the crowded parliamentary timetable until Autumn 1948. In 1949, the Legal Aid and Advice Act was passed, giving effect to the Rushcliffe recommendations, but the Government was unable to implement it. Throughout 1949 the Chancellor of the Exchequer, Sir Stafford Cripps, tightened controls on expenditure, and when, in September, he was forced to devalue sterling it was clear that the welfare paradise would have to be postponed. The only part of the Rushcliffe proposals which the Labour Government was able to introduce was a High Court scheme to deal with the divorce crisis. Any improvements to criminal legal aid were left to subsequent Conservative governments.

Although the Conservatives of the 1950s were sympathetic to the welfare state in general, and to the Rushcliffe proposals in particular, it took a long time for money to be found for extensions. The salaried advice service never happened. When the first legal advice scheme was eventually set up in 1959 it paid private solicitors on a case-by-case basis.

---

[83] Issued 18 December 1945, reference HO328/45.

The most significant changes occurred in March 1960, when the Government accepted that lawyers should be paid hourly rates for their work and costs were transferred from ratepayers to taxpayers. From 1960 onwards, local funds for legal aid were abolished. Instead, magistrates' courts' bills were met by the Legal Aid Fund, while in the higher courts bills were paid by the clerk to the court and reimbursed by the Home Office. Finally, in April 1963, the limitation of help before magistrates' courts to 'grave charges' or 'exceptional circumstances' was repealed. Legal aid was available whenever 'the interests of justice' demanded.

IX THE WIDGERY COMMITTEE

The effect of these changes on representation at assizes and quarter sessions was immediate and dramatic. As a proportion of defendants dealt with in these courts, the number of certificates granted rose to 39 per cent in 1962, 55 per cent in 1963, 72 per cent in 1964, and 79 per cent in 1966. By 1964, when the Widgery Committee was set up to carry out a further investigation of legal aid, it was rare for anyone to appear before a jury unrepresented. The Committee's small-scale survey found that among those pleading not guilty, 96 per cent were represented and among those pleading guilty, 81 per cent were represented. The great majority were represented by legal aid — less than 20 per cent paid privately, and only 1 per cent received dock briefs.[84] The Widgery Committee confirmed that anyone facing a trial on indictment whose means were insufficient should be granted legal aid as a matter of course. It thought that legal aid was equally important for those pleading guilty in the higher courts, and therefore recommended that magistrates should grant legal aid irrespective of the applicant's intended plea.

Although every previous committee which had enquired into criminal legal aid had paid lip-service to the importance of good preparation, it is clear from the Widgery Report that the emphasis in practice was on court advocacy. The Committee found that over 1,000 defendants facing jury trial were still granted last minute legal aid for counsel only, often as an economy measure rather than because they had slipped through the net.[85] The concentration on advocacy was particularly clear when it came to appeals. Lawyers engaged for the trial were under no duty to advise on the possibility of an appeal and few did so, even

---

[84] Of those pleading not guilty, 78% were legally aided, 18% paid privately and 4% were unrepresented. Of those pleading guilty, 71% were legally aided, 8% paid privately, 1% received dock briefs and 19% were unrepresented: Widgery, *Report of the Departmental Committee on Legal Aid in Criminal Proceedings*, Cmnd 2934, London: HMSO, 1966, para. 45.
[85] *Ibid.*, para. 39.

though the work involved could be charged for.[86] Although the Court of Appeal had wide powers to grant legal aid, they almost never provided aid for an application for leave to appeal. If leave was granted, legal aid was granted for virtually all appeals, but was usually limited to counsel. Solicitors were rarely paid to find new evidence.[87]

Lawyers had become a routine part of jury trials and full Court of Appeal hearings, but the position before the magistrates' courts was very different. The number of magistrates' court certificates was increasing, but as a proportion of all those dealt with summarily, the numbers were still tiny. The growth was from 0.3 per cent in 1955 to 1.2 per cent in 1964.[88] In 1967, a study of five magistrates' courts found that of those pleading not guilty in non-motoring cases, 70 per cent were unrepresented.[89] The Committee denied that legal aid was necessary for all summary trials, but it did want to see greater and more consistent use of legal aid. It established a set of tests to guide magistrates, known as the 'Widgery Criteria', which are now incorporated in the Legal Aid Act 1988[90] and form the statutory basis of summary legal aid. Briefly the criteria state that legal aid is in the interests of justice if the accused is in danger of losing his liberty, livelihood or reputation, if the case involves questions of law, if the accused is unable to understand the proceedings, or if the case involves tracing witnesses or expert cross-examination.[91]

X 1967–82: FIFTEEN YEARS OF EXPANSION WITHIN MAGISTRATES' COURTS

In the 15 years following the Widgery Report, there was an explosion of magistrates' court legal aid. The net cost rose from a mere £549,215 in 1966–67 to almost £54 million in 1982–83, a five-fold increase in real terms. Representation grew from a rarity to the normal way in which serious summary trials were dealt with. By 1983, 71 per cent of those pleading guilty and not guilty for either way offences received legal aid certificates, as did 55 per cent of those facing committal proceedings.[92]

How and why did this change occur? During this period there was an active lobby of radical lawyers calling for improvements. In 1968 the Society of

---

[86] *Ibid.*, paras 240–41.
[87] *Ibid.*, para. 244.
[88] *Ibid.*, para. 32.
[89] Zander, M. and Glasser, C., 'A Study in Representation', *New Law Journal*, 1967, vol. 117, p. 815. See also Zander, M., 'Unrepresented Defendants in the Criminal Courts', *Criminal Law Review*, 1969, p. 632.
[90] Section 22.
[91] See Widgery Committee, *op. cit.*, para. 180.
[92] Home Office, *Criminal Statistics England and Wales*, Cmnd 9349, London: HMSO, 1984, p. 188.

Labour Lawyers argued strongly that defendants should be represented before receiving lengthy prison sentences.[93] In 1971, JUSTICE published an influential report, which concluded that there was 'an overwhelming and incontrovertible body of evidence that the legal aid system is not working in the magistrates' courts in the way the Widgery Committee intended it should'. It proposed that there should be duty solicitor schemes within courts to encourage greater representation, a idea which had been specifically rejected by the Widgery Committee in 1966.[94] This was followed, in 1972, by the formation of the Legal Action Group (LAG) to campaign for improved access to justice. The movement drew support from empirical studies which showed that unrepresented defendants were less likely to be given bail,[95] less likely to be acquitted[96] and often bewildered by the whole atmosphere of courts.[97] It is unlikely, however, that such a massive change in the grant of legal aid was brought about by the efforts of a few left-wing lawyers. The answer must lie within the attitudes of the key decision-makers of the legal aid system — magistrates and their clerks.

The Widgery criteria allowed courts great discretion in how they used legal aid. From 1979 onwards, LAG published annual 'league tables' highlighting differences between courts.[98] In 1980, for example, outer London courts varied between Uxbridge, which refused 36 per cent of applications, and Watford which refused only 6 per cent. LAG showed how the personal views of one clerk could lead to a significant reduction in the grant of legal aid certificates.[99] Although there were a few exceptions, however, most clerks and magistrates came to value legal aid, and to provide it much more readily. It was a time of significant growth in the jurisdiction of magistrates and in their case-loads: between 1970 and 1980, the number of defendants facing indictable offences increased from 351,000 to 507,000, while the total number of non-motoring

[93] Society of Labour Lawyers, *Justice for All*, London: Fabian Research Pamphlet no. 273, 1968.
[94] JUSTICE, *The Unrepresented Defendant in the Magistrates' Courts*, London: Stevens and Sons, 1971.
[95] King, M., *Bail or Custody*, London: Cobden Trust 1971. See also Zander, M., 'A Study of Bail/Custody Decisions in London Magistrates' Courts', *Criminal Law Review*, 1971, p. 191, and, by the same author, 'Operation of the Bail Act in London Magistrates' Courts', *New Law Journal*, 1979, vol. 129, p. 108.
[96] Zander, M., 'Unrepresented Defendants in Magistrates' Courts', *New Law Journal*, 1972, vol. 122, p. 1041. This found that the great majority of those on theft and drug charges were not represented. Out of 11 defendants pleading not guilty, 30% were acquitted, compared with 64% of those who were represented. See also Borrie, G. J. and Varcoe, J. R., *Legal Aid in Criminal Proceedings: A Regional Survey*, Birmingham: Institute of Judicial Administration, 1970.
[97] See Dell, S., *Silent in Court*, London: Bell, 1971.
[98] *LAG Bulletin*, January 1979, April 1980, May 1980 and February 1982.
[99] Hansen, O., 'What a Difference a Clerk Makes', *LAG Bulletin*, March 1982, p. 11.

defendants increased from 771,000 to over a million.[100] At the same time, there were attempts to routinise the work. The Criminal Justice Act 1967, for example, introduced 'paper committals' in which committals could be reduced to an administrative formality, provided the defendant was represented. As courts had no responsibility for the legal aid budget, there were few restraints on granting it. Most magistrates came to see the involvement of solicitors as a way of smoothing the administration of their court, and preventing the hiccups caused by difficult unrepresented defendants.

For jury trials, legal representation for the defence followed that for the prosecution. This, however, was not true for magistrates' courts. During the late 1960s the majority of magistrates' courts' prosecutions were still conducted by the police.[101] The motivation for granting legal aid was not so much to provide equality with the state as to process defendants through the courts. As McConville et al. comment:

> more and more of the routine decision-making about the processing of cases through the courts, from initial questions about terms and conditions of bail and choice of trial venue through to pleas and 'paper committals', could be effectively transferred out of the courtroom to be determined through a process of inter-professional negotiation.[102]

In her study of a metropolitan magistrates' court in the early 1970s, Carlen found that few defendants spontaneously asked for legal aid. Instead magistrates often directed them to apply for it. Carlen commented that legally aided defendants 'are subjected to an outside-court training on what they *have* to say inside, such training often being given in the last ten minutes before the case is heard and often by a young solicitor whom they have never seen before'.[103] The Home Office had been wrong in 1903: lawyers, far from wasting valuable court time by putting forward troublesome defences, instructed defendants to conform. Indeed, since the introduction of legal aid, the proportion of all

---

[100] See the Appendix to McConville, M., Hodgson, J., Bridges, L. and Pavlovic, A., *Standing Accused: The Organisation and Practices of Criminal Defence Lawyers in Britain*, Oxford: Clarendon Press, 1994.
[101] Zander and Glasser's study of non-motoring cases in five London magistrates' courts (*op. cit.*) found that in 76% of not guilty pleas, the prosecution was conducted by a police officer.
[102] *Op. cit.*, pp. 6–7.
[103] Carlen, P., *Magistrates' Justice*, London: Martin Robertson, 1976, p. 91. A 1983 survey confirmed that courts had a strong influence on whether defendants applied for legal aid, with striking differences in the rate of applications between courts: Lord Chancellor's Department, *Report of a Survey of the Grant of Legal Aid in Magistrates' Courts*, 1983.

completed trials before jury courts in which the defendant pleads guilty has risen from 40 to over 60 per cent.[104]

XI THE CRIMINAL LEGAL AID FIRM

When in 1904 the Clerk to the Old Bailey prophesied that criminal legal aid would be left to the 'lowest class' of solicitor, he started a theme which has echoed through the century. In 1975, White spoke of the 'element of distaste, sometimes even of disdain which is to be found amongst some solicitors of standing for those solicitors who do legal aid work'.[105] A pioneering survey of solicitors in Birmingham in the late 1960s found that out of 161 firms in the city, ten did half of all legal aid work, and 40 did three-quarters of the work. In order to make a profit from criminal legal aid, it was necessary to be 'geared up' to it: cases had to be handled in bulk, according to standardised routines, with maximum delegation to support staff. Many commercial solicitors dismissed such firms as 'sausage machines', and it was true that potentially diverse clients' problems had to be forced through the narrow range of services provided.[106] The emphasis on turnover required criminal legal aid firms to attract business, which could cause difficulties at a time when advertising and touting were regarded as unprofessional. Firms had offices right next to the court to catch passing trade and developed 'quasi-corrupt relations with local police and court officials'.[107]

The expansion of criminal legal aid would not have been possible without an increase in the number of providers, and the growth in criminal legal aid is clearly related to the rapid increase in the size of the profession.[108] The voluntary magistrates' court duty solicitor schemes which developed in the wake of the JUSTICE report provided the ideal opportunity for new firms to break into the market — so it is hardly surprising that such schemes became

---

[104] Stephen tells us that between 1885 and 1889, of the 1,178 trials he completed, only 17% of defendants pleaded guilty (*op. cit.*, 1890, p. 174). The 1903 Select Committee heard that in 1902, guilty pleas accounted for 39% of completed trials before the Old Bailey, and 46% of those at London quarter sessions (*op. cit.*, paras 119, 126 and 128). In 1974, guilty pleas accounted for 57% of completed trials, a proportion which rose to 71% in 1990, and in 1993 stood at 64% (see Lord Chancellor's Department, *Judicial Statistics*, London: HMSO).
[105] White, R., 'The Distasteful Character of Litigation for Poor Persons', *Juridical Review*, 1975, vol. 3, p. 233.
[106] Bridges, L., Sufrin, B., Whetton, J. and White, R., *Legal Services in Birmingham*, Birmingham: Birmingham University, 1975.
[107] McConville et al., *op. cit.*, p. 3.
[108] See Bridges, L., 'The Professionalisation of Criminal Justice', *Legal Action*, August 1992, pp. 7–9. The numbers increased from just over 20,000 practising solicitors in 1964 to almost 45,000 in 1984: Jenkins, J., *Annual Statistical Report 1994*, London: Law Society, 1994.

popular.[109] As Bridges points out, however, duty schemes did not create the demand for legal aid: grant rates rose equally fast in courts without schemes.[110] Although it is becoming increasingly popular to accuse solicitors of having 'created' a demand for legal aid,[111] this is overly simplistic.[112] New markets require both supply and demand factors to come into existence, and without the active participation of magistrates' court clerks the increase would never have come about.[113]

What is more of an open question is whether the new firms of criminal practitioners followed the pattern set by the 'sausage machines' of the 1960s, or whether they set new patterns of practice. The new young recruits leaving university from 1968 onwards were often more idealistic than their predecessors, and, during the 1970s, working for the poor became less stigmatised, and in some quarters even acquired a social cachet. A mythology is developing among the more nostalgic of the profession that during this time legal aid provided a high quality, individualised service equivalent to that given to the rich.[114] The evidence suggests, however, that while in 1979–80, there were many more firms carrying out criminal legal aid, the work was concentrated in much the same sort of proportions as it had been in 1969: one third of magistrates' court work was done by fewer than 300 offices and 60 per cent was concentrated in fewer than 1,000 offices.[115] The highly routinised firms described so graphically by McConville et al. appear to be working within a long tradition of solicitors' 'police-court' work.[116]

---

[109] See Mungham, G. and Thomas, P., 'Solicitors and Clients: Altruism or Self-Interest?', in Dingwall, R. and Lewis, P. (eds), *The Sociology of the Professions*, London: Macmillan, 1983. In June 1975 there were 30 such schemes, and they received the blessing of the Law Society: see 'Guide to Duty Solicitor Schemes', *Law Society's Gazette*, 2 June 1975, vol. 72, no.20, p. 577.

[110] *Op. cit.*, p. 8. See also McConville et al., *op. cit.*, p. 5.

[111] For an academic exposition of the demand creation thesis, see Abel, R., 'Law without Politics: Legal Aid under Advanced Capitalism', *UCLA Law Review*, 1985, p. 474, and, by the same author, 'Between Market and State: the Legal Profession in Turmoil', *Modern Law Review*, 1989, vol. 52, p. 285. For the policy ramifications, see Bevan, G., Holland, T. and Partington, M., *Organising Cost-Effective Access to Justice*, London: Social Market Foundation, 1994. In 1995, the Lord Chancellor declared that he found such an analysis 'compelling': Speech to the Social Market Foundation, 11 January 1995.

[112] See Samuel, E., 'Criminal Legal Aid Expenditure: Supplier or System Driven? The Case of Scotland', at chapter 10 of this volume.

[113] For further discussion of legal aid decision making by court clerks see Young, R., 'Will Widgery Do?: Court Clerks, Discretion, and the Determination of Legal Aid Applications', at chapter 7 of this volume.

[114] Thus Tony Holland comments that 'there was a time in the 1960s and 1970s when we could put our hands on our hearts and say that the poor received as good a quality service as the rich': 'An Open Letter to the Lord Chancellor', *Law Society's Gazette*, 12 December 1990, vol. 87, no.45, p. 2. See also Pannone, R., 'Enough is Enough', *Law Society's Gazette*, 23 March 1994, vol. 91, no. 12, p. 2.

[115] Bridges, *op. cit.*, n. 108, p. 8.

[116] McConville et al., *op. cit.*

XII   THE CONTENT OF CRIMINAL LEGAL AID WORK

What were lawyers paid to do under legal aid? From 1959, legal aid was available for advice on any issue, including criminal, and this 'green form' scheme, as it became known, was widened in 1972, so that more people were eligible and solicitors were better paid. However, pay rates were still set lower than for other forms of work and authority was required for advice over the initial limit (set at around two hours' worth of time). Few applications were made to exceed the limit, and one of the most common uses of the scheme was to apply for full legal aid.[117]

Despite official pronouncements about the importance of preparation and evidence gathering, solicitors perceived this as unprofitable, with high up-front costs, low pay rates and a high risk that costs would be disallowed. One example is given by a research study conducted in 1992. The Widgery criteria state that the case for granting legal aid is stronger where witnesses need to be traced. As one lawyer pointed out, however, solicitors are office-based, and can rarely spend time knocking on doors without incurring substantial up-front costs, which might easily be disallowed: 'we don't have the funds, we don't have the staff to go out and trace people on legal aid'.[118] Thus it was not uncommon for solicitors to argue that legal aid should be granted on the basis that witnesses did need to be traced, but to fail to carry out the necessary work for fear of not being paid for it.[119] In order to understand what solicitors do for their clients it is necessary to consider how their bills are assessed.[120]

Fee rates reinforced the message that the proper place for a solicitor to be was in court. Until 1960, lawyers were given fixed fees with no additional payments for simple remands; but with the change to hourly fees, all court appearances — including remands and bail applications — were not only paid, but paid at the more generous rate appropriate for court advocacy, with relatively little danger of being disallowed.

---

[117] Baldwin, J. and Hill, S., *The Operation of the Green Form Scheme in England and Wales*, London: Lord Chancellor's Department, 1988.

[118] Young, R., Moloney, T. and Sanders, A., *In the Interests of Justice? The Determination of Criminal Legal Aid Applications by Magistrates' Courts in England and Wales, Report to the Legal Aid Board*, Birmingham: Institute of Judicial Administration, 1992, p. 75.

[119] Under a standard fees regime, the tendency towards minimal research and preparation of the defence case is likely to be even more pronounced: see Gray, A., Fenn, P. and Rickman, N., 'Controlling Lawyers' Costs Through Standard Fees: An Economic Analysis', at chapter 9 of this volume.

[120] See also Samuel, *op. cit.*

XIII THE GOVERNMENT'S REACTION

By the mid-1990s, government policy towards legal aid appeared to be driven solely by the exigency of cost control. It is worth recalling, however, how recent this trend is. Despite the explosion in magistrates' costs between the mid-1960s and mid-1980s, successive governments showed remarkable tolerance. In the context of Home Office expenditure generally, legal aid expenditure was small change, and Home Office cost-control amounted to little more than the occasional reminder to courts to remember the 'present restrictions on public spending'.[121] When the Lord Chancellor's Department took over in 1980 the sums involved featured more prominently on their budget, and in 1981, the department issued a sterner warning that 'every effort must be made to avoid waste'.[122] It was objected, however, that such guidance broke with the wording of the Legal Aid Act which required doubt to be resolved in favour of the applicant, and a 1984 circular was more neutral in tone.[123]

A major way in which the Government sought to mitigate criminal legal aid costs was to seek contributions from clients. As a strategy, however, it has proved a repeated failure. In 1967, the Government accepted the Widgery Committee's recommendation that the courts should have discretion to order defendants to make legal aid contributions at the end of cases.[124] Realistically, however, there is little prospect of recouping money from those sentenced to prison, and the contributions fell disproportionately on those acquitted of offences. When in 1972 a man acquitted of stealing a 7p magazine was ordered to pay a £100 contribution (and threatened with jail if he did not pay), it was asked whether the bad press engendered by such decisions was worth the money raised.[125] The Legal Aid Act 1982 purported to take a firmer line, by requiring contributions on a more systematic basis in advance. In 1986, however, the Legal Aid Scrutiny found that fewer than 3 per cent of orders were contributory. Contributions raised only £1.8 million and cost £800,000 to assess and collect.[126] The contributions raised were very unlikely to have offset those provisions of the 1982 Act designed to improve legal aid — by placing

---

[121] Home Office Circular 97/1978, issued 25 July 1978.

[122] LCD 81(3), reprinted in *Law Society's Gazette*, 13 May 1981, p. 513.

[123] *New Law Journal*, 1984, vol. 134, p. 1035. See also Zander, M., *Cases and Materials on the English Legal System*, 5th ed., London: Weidenfeld and Nicolson, 1988, p. 482.

[124] For a full analysis of how such contributions worked, see Levenson, H., *The Price of Justice*, London: Cobden Trust, 1981.

[125] *Ibid.*, p. 50. In 1973–74, contributions amounted to £221,000 towards a magistrates' criminal legal aid budget of £6m (*24th Legal Aid Annual Reports [1973–74]*, HC 20, London: HMSO 1974, p. 31).

[126] Lord Chancellor's Department, *Legal Aid Efficiency Scrutiny*, London: LCD, 1986.

duty solicitor schemes on a statutory footing and allowing applicants refused legal aid to appeal to a committee of lawyers.[127]

XIV   1984 ONWARDS

Since 1983, the rate of increase in criminal legal aid has slowed, but the overall trend continues upwards. The number of bills for magistrates' courts' work rose from 334,000 in 1984–85 to a peak of 477,000 in 1991–92.[128] A much greater proportion of juveniles are now represented (74 per cent in 1989, compared with 38 per cent in 1984) and many more orders are now granted for summary offences.[129] The overall budget for criminal cases in the magistrates' court has increased even more steeply, from £61 million in 1983–84 to a peak of £209 million in 1990–91, an increase from £90 million to £209 million in constant prices.[130]

The professionalisation of criminal justice continues apace. In 1984, the Police and Criminal Evidence Act provided a statutory right to legal advice within the police station, backed by a 24-hour scheme to provide a duty solicitor free of charge to all suspects in custody who asked for help. In 1981, the Royal Commission on Criminal Procedure had estimated that this would cost a mere £6 million (equivalent to £12 million in 1994 prices), but by 1994 costs exceeded £66 million. At the same time, the Crown Prosecution Service took over the representation of the prosecution, a task which for most summary offences (and many indictable offences tried summarily) had previously been handled by the police.

Meanwhile, the political climate has changed: government is increasingly concerned to limit costs and monitor the service provided. There is a new emphasis on planning and control of a system which for so long has developed in an *ad hoc* and, at times, almost accidental fashion. This book represents an attempt to analyse the existing legal aid scheme and the transformation the Government has planned for it. The history of legal aid should alert us to the complex motivations or causes likely to underlie any development in this area of social welfare provision. It is clear, however, that the interests of defendants have rarely been uppermost in the minds of those who, at a macro and micro level, have been responsible for taking decisions on legal aid.

---

[127] See Bridges, *op. cit.*, n. 108, p. 8.
[128] *35th Legal Aid Annual Reports [1984–85]*, HC 156, London: HMSO, 1986, and *Legal Aid Board Annual Report 1991–92*, HC 50, London: HMSO, 1992.
[129] 72,000 in 1993 (Lord Chancellor's Department, *Judicial Statistics 1993*, Cm 2623, London: HMSO, 1994) compared with 37,000 in 1983 (Home Office, *Criminal Statistics England and Wales 1983*, Cmnd. 9349, London: HMSO, 1984).
[130] Calculated from *Legal Aid Annual Reports*.

XV CONCLUSION

For the most part, criminal legal aid, like Topsy, just growed. Its history shows few articulations of grand principle: little has been planned. So why has such a scheme developed? Later in this volume, Andrew Ashworth states the classic argument in favour of criminal legal aid: that an adversarial trial requires equality of arms between the prosecution and the defence. This has been recognised, albeit tacitly and belatedly. By the end of the nineteenth century the growing sophistication of criminal prosecutions highlighted the glaring inequality between prosecutor and defence before jury trials and led to the 1903 Act. While the 1903 Act established an important principle, however, it did little to help the great mass of criminal defendants. Indeed, many lawyers who conceded that equality of arms was necessary in principle, vehemently denied that it was necessary in the bulk of cases.[131] According to the Finlay Committee, most defendants were so obviously guilty that legal aid could not be justified.

The development of mass legal aid for the majority of defendants is thus a recent phenomenon. Its development, from the early 1960s onwards, was not the result of political debate or new legislation but was triggered by financial considerations. The increase in pay-rates provided lawyers with an incentive to develop the work, while the transfer from ratepayers to taxpayers meant that those granting legal aid were freed from financial accountability for their actions. For jury trials, the principle that defendants should be represented was accepted immediately, and within five years almost all those pleading not guilty and most of those pleading guilty were receiving help. The idea that legal aid was necessary in the magistrates' court took longer to become established and met with resistance from a few clerks and courts. Within 15 years, however, it had become accepted. Instead of courts perceiving it as a threat, they came to see legal aid as a way of smoothing the administration of the courts, allowing more decisions to be made out-of-court and training defendants in what was expected from them. In 1983, the introduction of an appeal against the refusal of legal aid to a committee of lawyers allowed the few remaining recalcitrant courts to be brought into line.

For many years, government regarded the increasing cost of criminal legal aid with equanimity. It was seen as such a small part of the overall law and order budget as to require little attention. That has now changed — government worries incessantly about the cost and talks about efficiency saving and

---

[131] When giving evidence before the 1903 Select Committee, Sir Harry Poland KC argued that although it was of 'vital importance' for an innocent prisoner to have an experienced solicitor and counsel, this was not necessarily the case where one was dealing with 'the mass of prisoners who are sent for trial' (*op. cit.*, n. 49, para. 143). The implication is that the mass of defendants are clearly guilty.

improving the quality of service. But this means little without a discussion of basic principle: one cannot measure quality without considering what legal aid is meant to do. The time for such a discussion has arrived.

3

Legal Aid, Human Rights and Criminal Justice

Andrew Ashworth

By what criteria can we judge the provision of legal aid in criminal cases? Many of the chapters of this book point out deficiencies in the legal aid schemes of a number of jurisdictions, but the aim of this chapter is to explore the answer to this question at a more general and more fundamental level. The provision of legal aid to defendants can be regarded as an essential element in criminal justice. This proposition is developed in two main ways in this chapter — by outlining the relevant Articles of, and case law under, the European Convention on Human Rights; and by exploring the arguments for going beyond the European Convention. First, however, there is brief consideration of deeper philosophical justifications for the provision of criminal legal aid.

I WHY LEGAL AID?

We may start from the proposition that the right of an innocent person not to be convicted is fundamental. It is a serious moral harm, and the acme of injustice, to be convicted of an offence one did not commit.[1] The whole concept of individual rights is based, to a greater or lesser degree, on respect for the autonomy of each individual as a thinking and choosing being.[2] It is bad enough to be convicted of an offence which does not require a significant fault element,

---

[1] Dworkin, R. M., 'Principle, Policy, Procedure', in Tapper, C. (ed.), *Crime, Proof and Punishment*, London: Butterworths, 1981.

[2] This is recognised even in accounts of criminal justice that are not exclusively rights-based: see Lacey, N., *State Punishment: Political Principles and Community Values*, London: Routledge, 1988, pp. 160–68.

such as a 'strict liability' crime.[3] It is fundamentally wrong to be convicted of an offence when one did not do the acts alleged or did not satisfy the fault elements required. This is not only wrong because it impairs the ability of individual citizens to organise and predict their lives, to the extent of avoiding conflict with the criminal law. It is also unjust because it involves a public misapplication of blame and censure, and because it may unfairly bring upon the citizen the deprivations entailed by a court sentence — at worst, deprivation of liberty. While it is true that the principle that innocent persons should not be convicted cannot be treated as an absolute, since that would consume disproportionate public resources, it should always be regarded as fundamental and should be assigned a high value whenever procedures in criminal justice are being assessed.[4]

Without going further into the causes and consequences of miscarriages of justice,[5] we may quickly sketch the relevance of legal aid and assistance to the fundamental right not to be wrongly convicted. Four important strands come to the fore and will be examined in turn.

First, courts and lawyers operate with a fair degree of complexity, technicality and jargon. Even in the magistrates' courts it is not always clear to the uninitiated what is going on, and what is the significance of certain statements, questions and procedures. The professionalisation of criminal justice has increased considerably, particularly in magistrates' courts since the creation of the Crown Prosecution Service. At the most basic level, words may be spoken too quickly, regular participants may assume that everyone understands certain things, and there may be neither the time nor the inclination to stop and explain.[6] Without denigrating the efforts of some magistrates' clerks to assist the unrepresented defendant, it remains true that even a fairly intelligent and self-confident citizen might fail to grasp the significance of some important steps in court procedure. This applies *a fortiori* to citizens who do not possess great intelligence or self-confidence, and *a fortiori* to trials at the Crown Court.[7]

Secondly, the police and Crown Prosecution Service can call upon immense public resources, both human and financial, in the prosecution of crime and criminals. No doubt the police and prosecutors complain that they have insufficient resources, but that should not be allowed to mask the enormous

---

[3] For discussion, see Ashworth, A., *Principles of Criminal Law*, 2nd ed., Oxford: Oxford University Press, 1995, ch. 5.3.

[4] See the discussion in Ashworth, A., *The Criminal Process: an Evaluative Study*, Oxford: Oxford University Press, 1994, pp. 29–31.

[5] On which see Greer, S., 'Miscarriages of Justice Reconsidered', *Modern Law Review*, 1994, vol. 57, p. 58.

[6] See Carlen, P., *Magistrates' Justice*, London: Martin Robertson, 1976.

[7] Rock, P., *The Social World of an English Crown Court*, Oxford: Clarendon Press, 1993.

sums of public money invested in these services. It is not being claimed here that this investment is unnecessary, or that in an ideal world precisely the same amounts of public money should be devoted to matters of prosecution and to matters of defence. Without running either of those arguments, one can nonetheless contend that the immense resources of law enforcement agencies should not be allowed to result in prejudice to defendants' rights in the criminal justice system.

Thirdly, the consequences of conviction for an individual citizen may be devastating. We have already noted that conviction involves public censure. Further, the sentence of the court may deprive the individual of money, restrict the individual's liberty, or even result in incarceration. This increases the moral and social significance of the first two points — the difficulty in comprehending many court proceedings, and the disparity in resources between prosecution and defence — and builds a compelling case for proper legal representation for accused persons.

Fourthly, it is contrary to the principle of equality before the law that the ability to defend oneself adequately against a criminal charge should depend on one's financial resources. Thus, to allow legal representation without providing state funding for the indigent would be to respect the right of the innocent not to be convicted only in so far as they have money, and would fail to ensure equal access to justice. Innocent people without money would be liable to wrongful conviction in circumstances when the wealthy would not. The blatant injustice of such a distinction seals the argument for the state provision of legal aid and assistance in criminal cases.

These four themes will re-emerge at various stages in the chapter. They have been set out in elementary and theoretical form here in order to prepare the ground for an examination of relevant provisions of the European Convention, which now follows.

II THE EUROPEAN CONVENTION ON HUMAN RIGHTS

Before explaining the provisions of the European Convention relevant to our topic, a few words about the history and application of the Convention are in order. The European Convention on Human Rights and Fundamental Freedoms was signed in 1950 and came into force in 1953. Some European countries allow the direct application of the Convention in domestic law, which means that an ordinary court can draw upon the Convention to hold that a particular procedure authorised by domestic law is invalid because contrary to the Convention. The United Kingdom is one of the countries that has ratified the Convention but does not allow direct application. This means that the Convention cannot be regarded as binding or direct authority in any British court, and that it can be invoked only by an application to Strasbourg. The first step is to apply to the European Commission on Human Rights, which will rule on the admissibility of the petition. If it is admissible, the Commission will give a preliminary opinion on it and then pass the case to the European Court of Human Rights. The Court is in no way bound by the Commission's opinion: it will reach its own conclusion on whether there has been a breach of the Convention. If the Court rules against a member state, its government may be ordered to pay compensation to the applicant. Judgments of the Court do not have direct effect in the United Kingdom: the Government is supposed to take steps to ensure that the domestic law is altered so as to conform with the ruling. The whole process may take several years.[8]

Perhaps the most relevant of the provisions of the European Convention are the following: Article 3 prohibits 'torture or inhuman or degrading treatment or punishment'; Article 5 provides that 'everyone has the right to liberty and security of person', and sets out a number of cases in which deprivation of liberty may be lawful (e.g., arrest, remand pending trial, sentence after conviction); Article 5.3 affirms the right to be brought promptly before a court; Article 6.1 declares the right to a fair trial; Article 6.2 declares the presumption of innocence in criminal proceedings; Article 6.3 enumerates five particular rights of defendants in criminal cases, to which we will refer more fully below; Article 7 states that criminal laws should not be retroactive; Article 8 proclaims a right to privacy, and the freedoms of thought, expression and peaceful assembly are provided for in Articles 9, 10 and 11 respectively; Article 14 sets out the right to equality of treatment and non-discrimination.

Our main concern here lies with Article 6, from which the following extracts are the most relevant:

Article 6

1. In the determination of his civil rights and obligations or of any criminal charge against him, everyone is entitled to a fair and public hearing within a reasonable time by an independent and impartial tribunal established by law. . . .

3. Everyone charged with a criminal offence has the following minimum rights:

    (a) to be informed promptly, in a language which he understands and in detail, of the nature and cause of the accusation against him;

    (b) to have adequate time and facilities for the preparation of his defence;

---

[8] For a relatively brief introduction to the subject, see Gearty, C., 'The European Court of Human Rights and the Protection of Civil Liberties: an Overview', *Cambridge Law Journal*, 1993, vol. 52, p. 89.

(c)   to defend himself in person or through legal assistance of his own choosing or, if he has not sufficient means to pay for legal assistance, to be given it free when the interests of justice so require;

(d)   to examine or have examined witnesses against him and to obtain the attendance and examination of witnesses on his behalf under the same conditions as witnesses against him;

(e)   to have the free assistance of an interpreter if he cannot understand or speak the language used in court.

It will be observed that the right to a fair trial declared in Article 6.1 applies equally to civil and criminal proceedings, but that Article 6.3 is focused on criminal cases. The relationship of Articles 6.1 and 6.3 in criminal cases is not entirely clear. On a straightforward reading it may appear that the specific rights granted in Article 6.3 are but examples of the right to a fair trial, and that an applicant might try to rely on Article 6.1 to extend some of the Article 6.3 rights where they are expressed in limited or circumscribed form. The Court[9] has certainly not regarded the application of Article 6.3 as excluding the application of Article 6.1,[10] and it therefore remains possible for an applicant to argue a case for legal aid by reference to the general notion of a fair trial in Article 6.1.[11]

Two more points should be made before we look closely at Article 6.3(c). The first is that the Court has developed, through its interpretation of Article 6.1, the principle of 'equality of arms'. This principle, unconstrained by any particular words in the Convention itself, has already enabled the Court to insist on equal access to documentation for both parties and to equal access to expert evidence.[12] In view of its resonance with the second argument for legal aid presented in the first part of this chapter, the potential power of this principle must be borne in mind. The other point is that Article 6.3(c) must clearly have a close relationship to Article 6.3(b), which refers to adequate time and facilities for preparing a defence. The Commission has held that the reference to adequate time applies equally to counsel, and that where there is legal aid the nominated lawyer must be allowed sufficient time to prepare the case.[13] In

---

[9] 'The Court' refers to the European Court of Human Rights.

[10] E.g., the case on hearsay evidence, *Unterpertinger* v *Austria*, A. 110 (1986), pp. 14–15.

[11] For general discussion of the European Convention and its case law, see van Dijk, P. and van Hoof, G. J. H., *Theory and Practice of the European Convention on Human Rights*, 2nd ed., Dordrecht: Kluwer, 1990; Robertson, A. H. and Merrills, J., *Human Rights in Europe*, 2nd ed., Manchester: Manchester University Press, 1993; Beddard, R., *Human Rights in Europe*, 3rd ed., Cambridge: Cambridge University Press, 1993.

[12] E.g., *Bonisch* v *Austria*, A. 92 (1985).

[13] *Ofner* v *Austria*, Yearbook III (1960), *X and Y* v *Austria* (1979), D & R 15, p. 160.

the well-known case of *Campbell and Fell* v *United Kingdom*[14] it was held that the proper preparation of a defence requires private and confidential discussions between the accused and the lawyers.[15]

We now turn to Article 6.3(c). First of all, it provides that any person charged with a criminal offence should have the right 'to defend himself in person or through legal assistance of his own choosing'. The Court has held that this wording does not give defendants the right to conduct their own defence: it seems that the procedural rules of a state may provide that in certain circumstances it is sufficient for a defendant to be represented by counsel rather than being present himself.[16] More recently, in *Lala* v *Netherlands*[17] the Court held that Article 6.3(c) had been breached in a case where, the defendant having declined to attend his appeal in order to avoid arrest on another matter, the local appeal court refused to allow his counsel (who was present) to address it. The Court observed that there should be no 'unduly formalistic rules' standing in the way of the basic right of representation in a criminal court.

The second phrase in Article 6.3(c) is 'or, if he has not sufficient means to pay for legal assistance, to be given it free when the interests of justice so require'. This does not imply that an accused person has a right to choose the lawyer if state legal aid is given. A defendant may have 'legal assistance of his own choosing' if he is paying for it. Otherwise, it is sufficient if a lawyer is nominated according to local procedures. The Court went so far in *Croissant* v *Germany*[18] as to argue that the accused's wishes should be considered, though accepting that they may be overridden when there are relevant and sufficient grounds for holding this necessary in the interests of justice. There is some authority for the view that, if the relationship between the assigned lawyer and the accused is unsatisfactory, compliance with the Article requires the nomination of a fresh lawyer.[19] Certainly it is well-established that it is not sufficient simply to nominate a lawyer and then do nothing further: in *Artico* v

---

[14] A. 80 (1984).

[15] van Dijk and van Hoof, *op. cit.*, who argue (at p. 348) that Article 6.3(b) may be more powerful in this regard than Article 8 on privacy, the terms of which are somewhat qualified. Those authors criticise the Commission's failure in certain instances to insist on the terms of Article 6.3(b) in criminal cases.

[16] *X* v *Austria*, Coll. 23 (1967).

[17] A. 297 (1994), 18 EHRR 586.

[18] (1992) 16 EHRR 135.

[19] *Pakelli* v *Germany* A. 64 (1983), a decision that involves a close examination of the wording of Article 6.3(c). It may be noted that there is a considerable North American jurisprudence on a defendant's right to the 'effective assistance' of counsel. The test adopted in the United States is whether counsel's performance in the case fell below an objective standard of reasonableness, reference usually being made to the Bar standards: see, e.g., *Strickland* v *Washington* (1984) 466 US 668, and in Ontario (Canada) the cases of *Silvini* (1991) 68 CCC (3d) 251 and *Collier* (1992) 77 CCC (3d) 570. Compare the more restrictive English decision in *Ensor* [1989] 1 WLR 497.

Italy[20] the accused had been sentenced to custody for various fraud offences in his absence and without his knowledge. Wishing to appeal, he applied for legal aid and was assigned counsel. The lawyer declined to act, pleading ill-health and the onerousness of the brief. The accused's many efforts to have a new lawyer appointed were unsuccessful and, by the time he succeeded several months later, his appeal had been disallowed. The Court gave short shrift to the Italian Government's argument that it had complied with Article 6.3(c) by appointing the first lawyer. The Court held that 'the Convention is intended to guarantee not rights that are theoretical or illusory but rights that are practical and effective'.[21]

In reading the second part of Article 6.3(c), one's eyes are drawn to two rather open-textured phrases, 'not sufficient means to pay for legal assistance' and 'free when the interests of justice so require'. There has been remarkably little discussion of the former phrase in the Commission or the Court: in many cases the point has been conceded, and so there has been no reason to consider the appropriate financial limits. The latter phrase, however, has been interpreted in several cases. The Court has been reluctant to lay down any firm criteria, but it emerges clearly that the complexity of the case and the potential consequences for the accused are the foremost considerations. Thus in the *Artico* case, already mentioned, the Italian Government also raised the argument that the case was relatively straightforward: once again, the Court dismissed this readily, since one of the nominated lawyer's reasons for declining to act was the onerous nature of the brief. The leading decision is probably *Quaranta* v *Switzerland*,[22] where the accused had received a custodial sentence (including the activation of a suspended sentence) on a drugs charge without having counsel assigned to him. One interesting feature of the procedure in this case was that the prosecution was not represented in court either, since the court had merely reached its decision on the basis of the dossier, and so this is one case which did not depend even indirectly on 'equality of arms'. The Court made the point that Article 6.3(c) does not create an absolute right to legal aid, in view of the two open-textured phrases it contains. However, 'the interests of justice' depended on the complexity of the case, the seriousness of the charge, and the severity of the possible sentence. In view of the likely (and actual) prison sentence, the Court held, 'free legal assistance should have been afforded by reason of the mere fact that so much was at stake'.[23] The Court has not restricted the 'interests of justice' to cases

---

[20] A. 37 (1980).
[21] *Ibid.*, at p. 16.
[22] A. 205 (1991).
[23] *Ibid.*, at p. 17.

where imprisonment is a possibility: in *Pham Hoang* v *France*[24] the Court upheld the accused's right to free legal aid, denied to him by an appeal court despite the fact that 'the proceedings were clearly fraught with consequences for the appellant', who had been convicted of drug importation and had been ordered to pay a large fine.

III   THE EUROPEAN CONVENTION AND THE ENGLISH SYSTEM

These are the main points of the Court's jurisprudence on the right to legal aid and assistance. What implications do they have for the English system of criminal legal aid? One point is whether the income limit for legal aid is now so low that a test case under the European Convention might be worthwhile. It could be argued that, by lowering the financial threshold as the Government has done in the last few years,[25] free legal assistance may now be refused to defendants who, objectively speaking, have 'insufficient means to pay' according to Article 6.3(c). It is doubtful whether the Court would uphold such a challenge, however. It has thus far avoided setting any limits, and its tendency on matters of this kind is to allow member states a considerable margin of latitude.

Is legal aid ever refused in England when, according to the European Convention, 'the interests of justice' would require it to be granted? Section 21(2) of the Legal Aid Act 1988 uses the same phrase as the European Convention, 'the interests of justice': that might in practice make the European Commission and Court reluctant to intervene, especially since more detailed guidelines have also been issued. Reporting on the Birmingham study of decision-making on legal aid, Richard Young concluded that magistrates' clerks vary considerably in their practices and that, overall, they tend to be too generous in some respects and too severe in others.[26] The clerk's view of the seriousness of the offence tended to be the most powerful pointer to the decision:[27] in so far as some clerks would grant legal aid on this ground only if custody was a real possibility, this sounds to be an over-restrictive interpretation and compares unfavourably with the European Court's decision in *Pham Hoang* v *France*,[28] where liability to a large fine was sufficient to trigger Article 6.3(c). Many clerks were also reluctant to grant legal aid on the basis of

---

[24] A. 243 (1993) 16 EHRR 53.

[25] See Sanders, A. and Young, R., *Criminal Justice*, London: Butterworths, 1994, p. 256.

[26] Young, R., 'The Merits of Legal Aid in the Magistrates' Courts', *Criminal Law Review*, 1993, p. 336.

[27] See further Young, R., 'Will Widgery Do?: Court Clerks, Discretion, and the Determination of Legal Aid Applications', at chapter 7 of this volume.

[28] See n. 24 above.

potentially serious damage to the defendant's reputation,[29] an issue not directly considered by the European Court (although in *Pham Hoang* the Court referred to the case as 'fraught with consequences for the appellant'). The European Court has recognised the complexity of the case as a significant factor, but this is clearly a matter of degree. Young reports that magistrates' clerks seem reluctant to find complexity in most magistrates' court cases,[30] and it is not clear that the European Convention would be interpreted so as to admit that many magistrates' court cases are sufficiently 'complex', particularly those that have not also qualified for legal aid under the seriousness criterion.

The various efforts of the Government to cut back on legal aid expenditure in recent years may mean that significantly fewer defendants are now receiving legal aid, leaving open the possibility of challenge in Strasbourg. The difficulty is that the European Court has tended to find contraventions of Article 6.3(c) only in fairly extreme cases, and the procedure may not be apt to combat gradual reductions in the extent of provision. On the other hand, it would be hoped that the European Court would not accept the bland assertion that legal aid costs must be curtailed in times of restraint on public expenditure: as has often been pointed out,[31] legal aid funding is only a small fraction of the amount spent on policing and prosecutions, and it can be argued strongly that the right of the innocent not to be convicted deserves greater protection.

The new scheme for legal aid proposed by the Government in its Green Paper[32] may also create problems of conformity with the European Convention. The approach of allocating block contracts to certain firms suggests that it may be solicitors' firms that decide who will and who will not receive legal aid, and it is unclear to what extent the criteria will reflect the principles of the European Convention and the Court's case law. Also, if the Government decides to impose 'cash limits' on criminal legal aid, there is the possibility that a defendant might be refused legal assistance because the budget had already been spent. It is unlikely that the Court would find this to be 'in the interests of justice'.

In some spheres English law appears to fulfil the Convention straightforwardly. Thus s. 21 of the Powers of Criminal Court Act 1973 provides that a court may not pass a sentence of imprisonment on a person who was not legally represented at some time after being found guilty and before being sentenced, unless that person either failed to apply for legal aid or was refused legal aid

---

[29] Young (1993), *op. cit.*, at p. 340.
[30] *Ibid.*, pp. 341–2; the problem was exacerbated by the tendency of many solicitors to fill in the forms in a rather unconvincing and over-optimistic manner.
[31] E.g., Sanders and Young, *op. cit.*, p. 266.
[32] Lord Chancellor's Department, *Legal Aid – Targeting Need: The future of publicly funded help in solving legal problems and disputes in England and Wales*, Cm 2854, London: HMSO, 1995.

on the ground that his means were sufficient. In *Wilson*[33] the defendant had dismissed two sets of legal advisers and then addressed the Crown Court at length in person, ultimately asking the judge to assign her another firm of solicitors. The judge declined any further adjournment and sentenced her to seven years' imprisonment for arson. The Court of Appeal quashed the sentence because it was unlawful to impose imprisonment without representation. The Court then appointed counsel, but the appellant did not wish to be represented by this counsel. The Court appointed an *amicus curiae*, heard argument, and re-imposed seven years' imprisonment. It therefore appears that, although legal aid need not be granted in cases where custody is or may be a real possibility, it must be granted before a custodial sentence is actually imposed.

A considerable improvement in legal aid provision has been effected in recent years through the spread of court-based duty solicitor schemes.[34] Access to justice has been broadened by the availability of lawyers at courts. However, it must be said that the criteria governing the use of duty solicitors tend to focus on the more serious type of case, once again leaving many defendants in the magistrates' courts without legal assistance.

IV CRIMINAL JUSTICE BEYOND THE EUROPEAN CONVENTION

The contours of the discussion in parts II and III of this chapter were dictated by the European Convention on Human Rights and relevant rulings of the Commission and the Court. Important (and, in the United Kingdom, neglected) as the European Convention is, its parameters, set in 1950, should not be allowed to constrain examination of the issues. We must now return to the arguments of principle in favour of legal aid, and re-assess its proper scope in criminal justice. In part I it was argued that criminal legal aid should be available because (i) criminal proceedings are complex and largely professionalised, (ii) the police and prosecution have massive resources at their disposal, (iii) the consequences of criminal conviction for individual citizens can be devastating, and (iv) it would be contrary to the principle of equal access to justice if some citizens were at greater risk of wrongful conviction simply through lack of money.

Should there be an absolute right to legal aid in criminal proceedings for those with insufficient money to pay for legal representation? It seems that the most important international and constitutional declarations stop short of this.

[33] [1995] Crim LR 510; see generally *Blackstone's Criminal Practice 1996*, D16.30.
[34] For discussion, see Sanders and Young, *op. cit.*, pp. 254–56.

Thus the International Covenant on Civil and Political Rights, Article 14(3)(d), uses the phrase 'when the interests of justice so require', as the European Convention does, and more recent declarations such as the Canadian Charter of Rights go no further. It is not difficult to mount an argument against this position: given the increasing professionalisation of the administration of criminal justice, and the spread of public prosecutor systems, it is arguable that principles such as equality of arms and equal access to justice militate in favour of state-funded legal assistance for those unable to pay for their own representation. It could be argued that no criminal proceedings are so trivial that they matter little to defendants; or, alternatively, it could be argued that the state should be obliged to provide legal aid for the indigent in all proceedings serious enough to involve the criminal law, which might in turn persuade states to ensure that their criminal process was reserved for non-minor wrongs. Most governments would be reluctant to accept such a general proposition for fear of the consequences for public expenditure. However, this is a question of financial and political preference, and should not be allowed to masquerade as financial necessity. Most governments manage to lavish much greater expenditure on the police and public prosecutors than on provisions for legal aid and assistance for defendants. If the principle of equal access were taken seriously, the gulf would not be so wide, and public defender services would be no less prominent than public prosecution departments.

Could the common law be tapped as a source of fuller defence rights? In the Australian High Court an attempt was made in *Dietrich* v *The Queen*[35] to argue that the right to legal assistance could be derived from the common law duty of the court to ensure a fair trial. Dietrich had been charged on three counts of importation and possession of heroin. He pleaded not guilty, but his attempts to obtain legal aid (and his appeals against refusal) were all rejected on the ground that his defence had no reasonable prospect of success. He was convicted after a lengthy trial, at which he was unrepresented throughout. The case went up to the High Court of Australia which, by a majority of five judges to two, set the conviction aside and ordered a new trial. The essence of the majority's reasoning is that defendants have a right to a fair trial, and courts have the discretion to stay proceedings to prevent any abuse of process. Although the High Court rejected the proposition that this requires the provision of legal aid for the indigent in every case on indictment which might result in imprisonment, and the majority insisted that the matter remains one of judicial discretion, it was held that the discretion should be favourably

---

[35] (1992) 177 CLR 292; for analysis, see Zdenkowski, G., 'Defending the Indigent Accused in Serious Cases: a Legal Right to Counsel?', *Criminal Law Journal*, 1994, vol. 18, p. 135; Fairall, P., 'The Right not to be Tried Unfairly without Counsel: *Dietrich* v *The Queen*', *University of Western Australia Law Review*, 1992, vol. 22, p. 396.

exercised when a person faces a serious charge, in the absence of exceptional circumstances. The decision therefore stops short of recognising an absolute right even in serious cases, but the judgments contain several affirmations of a defendant's right to a fair trial, of the connection between the absence of legal representation and the fairness of the trial, and of the possibility of miscarriages of justice through denial of legal assistance.

The next step in the argument should be to challenge the trial-centred nature of the European Convention and of many other declarations of the right to legal assistance. It is now a commonplace, among those who study and think about the criminal justice system, that trials are of significance in relatively few cases. Certainly in most common law systems the vast majority of cases proceed on a plea of guilty. In many of these cases the defendant freely admits the offence from an early stage,[36] but there is a significant number of cases which do not fall into this category. Some of these involve vulnerable suspects, and even for those who would not be described as vulnerable the psychological pressures of being questioned in a police station may prove to be overbearing or distorting. Confessions are still central to many prosecution cases, and have featured in several of the notorious cases of miscarriage of justice. English law has now gone further than the European Convention and than the laws of many other European countries in recognising the importance of securing legal assistance in the earlier stages of the criminal process.[37] Section 58 of the Police and Criminal Evidence Act 1984 provides a right of access to legal advice in the police station, subject only to a fairly narrow exception.[38] However, if rights of this kind are to be 'practical and effective', not 'theoretical and illusory',[39] it is necessary to ensure that suspects are informed fully of their right and are given a proper opportunity to exercise it. Research has demonstrated that this is not always the case.[40]

In interpreting s. 78 of the Police and Criminal Evidence Act 1984, the English courts have recognised the argument that pre-trial events may be important to the fairness of the trial. Section 78(1) allows a court to exclude evidence if, 'having regard to all the circumstances, including the

[36] See, e.g., Bottoms, A. E., and McClean, J. D., *Defendants in the Criminal Process*, London: Routledge & Kegan Paul, 1976, p. 115.
[37] Note, however, the decision of the Conseil Constitutionnel in France on 11 August 1993, holding that there is a fundamental right to consult a lawyer during the period of *garde à vue* in France. Although this is a right to consult, and does not contemplate the presence of a lawyer during interrogation, it is a significant step in French domestic law.
[38] For discussion, see Sanders and Young, *op. cit.*, pp. 124–46. For two contrasting decisions on the exception, see *Samuel* (1988) 87 Cr App R 232 and *Alladice* (1988) 87 Cr App R 380.
[39] To adopt the words of the European Court of Human Rights in the *Artico* case, above, n. 20, albeit in the context of legal assistance at trial.
[40] See Sanders, A., 'Access to Justice in the Police Station: An Elusive Dream?', at chapter 12 of this volume.

circumstances in which the evidence was obtained, the admission of the evidence would have such an adverse effect on the fairness of the proceedings that the court ought not to admit it'. The Court of Appeal has been quite prepared to find that departures from proper pre-trial procedures may have an 'adverse effect on the fairness of the proceedings', excluding evidence obtained after a wrongful refusal to allow access to legal advice,[41] a failure to notify a suspect properly of the right to legal advice,[42] an attempt to avoid the 1984 Act by surreptitious questioning of a suspect,[43] and so on. It is not necessary to make a full survey of the decisions here, or to deal with the cases in which evidence has not been excluded. The indisputable point is that the courts have recognised that the fairness of court proceedings can be affected adversely by failures to accord suspects and defendants their rights in the pre-trial stages. The failure to allow access to legal advice is a clear example of this.

This argument appears not to have been pressed under the European Convention. However, there is nothing in the wording of Article 6 to stand in its way. The terms of Article 6.3(c) refer to the right of a person charged with a criminal offence 'to defend himself', and this is not expressly limited to proceedings in court. Article 6.1 refers more broadly to the right to a fair hearing, rather than a fair trial. Moreover, the Court has developed the principle of equality of arms, and it would not be difficult to apply the argument of the foregoing paragraph to this. The only relevant passage in the leading texts is the following, in the context of Article 6.3(c):

> If the accused is not assisted by a lawyer during the pre-trial phrase, the question arises as to the propriety of the evidence collected there in view of the requirements of a fair trial. In that context it is considered to be highly relevant that the evidence is evaluated by the court during the trial in the presence of the accused and his counsel, who then have the opportunity to contradict the evidence, and that any confession is proved by the prosecution to have been made voluntarily.[44]

Although the first part of this passage recognises the connection between the fairness of the trial and the fairness of evidence-gathering, the passage as a whole assumes that there is no right to legal advice and assistance at all pre-trial stages, and that somehow this deficiency can be remedied in the courtroom.

---

[41] *Samuel* (1988) 87 Cr App R 232.

[42] E.g., *Absolam* (1989) 88 Cr App R 332; *Beycan* [1990] Crim LR 185.

[43] *Bryce* (1992) 95 Cr App R 320.

[44] van Dijk and van Hoof, *op. cit.*, p. 352; the only authority they cite is an unpublished opinion of the Commission in the case of *X* v *United Kingdom*. That case went on to the Court, but the Court made no pronouncement on this point.

This is unconvincing, and it illustrates the limited protection afforded by the European Convention in its present form. For the Court to insist on access to free legal advice during pre-trial questioning in all member states would probably be too much, politically, for most European governments to contemplate, and the Court might therefore shrink from this.

V CONCLUSIONS

The purpose of this chapter has been to examine the arguments for a right to legal aid and assistance in criminal cases, and to consider the relevance of the European Convention on Human Rights. While there is a vigorous European jurisprudence on some aspects of the right, which might have some application to English cases if the lower threshold for criminal legal aid were to be challenged, the main shortcoming of the European Convention and its interpretation is that they appear to be trial-centred, and that they fail to insist on proper standards of fairness and equal access to justice at the pre-trial stages. The Court's principle of equality of arms could be developed in a way that met these concerns, but the result would be to require such fundamental change in so many countries' systems of criminal justice that the Court may well be reluctant for pragmatic reasons to take this step.

This is not to suggest that the Convention is not relevant to legal aid in England and Wales, for one of the paradoxes is that the English system seems to provide greater access to legal assistance in the police station than it does at trials, certainly in magistrates' courts.[45] Since the European Convention is stronger on assistance at trial, resort may be had to it on those issues. In relation to the pre-trial stages, it may be that the English courts provide a more fruitful forum, in view of their interpretation of s. 78 of the Police and Criminal Evidence Act, together with the doctrine of abuse of process.[46] Some assistance might be derived from the decision of the High Court of Australia in the *Dietrich* case. Whether even these doctrines could cope with the true breadth of the problem is a difficult question. For example, many people are now cautioned for criminal offences instead of being prosecuted[47]: although this may be welcomed in general as an enlightened approach, some people may accept a caution when they are not in fact guilty of the alleged offence, and the caution is then recorded and may be cited against them subsequently. This suggests that there should be the possibility of access to legal advice before

---

[45] See Young (1993), *op. cit.*, on the vagaries of court clerks' decisions.
[46] On which see Choo, A., *Abuse of Process and Judicial Stays of Criminal Proceedings*, Oxford: Oxford University Press, 1993, ch. 4.
[47] See further Ashworth (1995), *op. cit.*, pp. 137–58.

accepting a caution.[48] A second example concerns expert evidence: research for the Royal Commission on Criminal Justice demonstrated quite clearly that it is much more difficult for the defence to obtain expert evidence than for the prosecution,[49] which has clear implications for 'equality of arms' and for making legal assistance 'practical and effective' rather than 'theoretical or illusory'. Perhaps this second example does reveal an area in which the European Convention could be used.

This chapter began with the proposition that the provision of legal aid to defendants is an essential element in criminal justice. While it has been argued here that the right to legal assistance ought to be developed in various ways in practice, it should not be inferred that improvements in legal aid will, of themselves, bring about improvements in criminal justice. Several other conditions — the availability of lawyers of a high standard, their willingness to defend stoutly rather than to fall in too readily with the prosecution — need to be fulfilled in relation to legal services, and there are many other aspects of fairness in the criminal process as a whole which need addressing. Nonetheless, effective legal assistance is an essential minimum. The argument here has been that, important as the European Convention on Human Rights is, neither the Convention nor domestic law (existing, or as proposed in the Green Paper) takes sufficient account of the principles of equal access to justice and equality of arms. So long as this remains true, assertions that 'too much money' is being spent on criminal legal aid should be challenged vigorously.

[48] See further Crawford, A., 'Alternatives to Prosecution: Access to, or Exits from, Justice?', at chapter 15 of this volume.
[49] Roberts, P. and Willmore, C., *The Role of Forensic Science Evidence in Criminal Proceedings*, Royal Commission on Criminal Justice Research Study No. 11, London: HMSO, 1993.

4

Criminal Legal Aid: Does Defending Liberty Undermine Citizenship?

Francis Regan*

I INTRODUCTION

After 45 years of large scale public funding, legal aid seems to be in decline in most of the rich societies as part of the dismantling of the welfare state.[1] So it is reasonable to ask after 45 years: What has legal aid achieved? One of the remarkable success stories is the way that legal aid has significantly reduced the number of poor people who go to court without a lawyer to defend them. Legal aid in many countries has given a heavy emphasis to providing representation in criminal matters in particular. In this way it has played an important role in protecting individual liberty. But governments are currently elevating legal aid in criminal matters to be the main legal aid priority. In many countries criminal legal aid as a proportion of all cases is increasing, as is the proportion of legal aid budgets devoted to protecting liberty. There are two reasons for the change in priorities to favour criminal legal aid: first, legal aid budgets generally are being capped or cut and new restrictions on types of cases and eligibility are commonly used to achieve this; secondly, and as a result of declining resources, governments and legal aid administrators are making

* The arguments in this chapter have benefitted from ongoing discussions with many scholars. In particular the author wishes to record his thanks to Annaliese Groothedde, Jenny Burley, Peter Travers and Liz Mumford in Adelaide. Alan Paterson's initiative to establish the 'Legal Aid Legal Services Research Group' of the ISA has also been very helpful for establishing links with other scholars. In particular the author has benefitted from discussions with Tamara Goriely over the last two years. Research assistance for this chapter was undertaken by Suzanne Legena and Liz Mumford.
[1] For a recent comparative overview of the decline of public legal aid, see Regan, F. and Fleming, D., 'International Perspectives on Legal Aid', *Alternative Law Journal*, 1994, vol. 19, p. 183.

decisions to give priority to protecting liberty by way of criminal legal aid. In the process other priorities are being scaled back or jettisoned altogether. The prospect of future legal aid schemes embracing criminal work only, and then not very much of it, is now a frightening but distinct possibility.

While no one would deny the importance of legal aid's role in criminal work, a world where that was the only work undertaken would not be an attractive one. How would poor people's civil and matrimonial work get done? In addition there is a strategic concern here: it is possible that if attempts are not made to stop the cuts and the increasing emphasis on criminal work, there may be no legal aid at all in the future.

There is, then, a need to develop arguments to defend legal aid's historic role of assisting poor people with legal services. But it is also clear that the traditional arguments that stressed how legal aid assists the poor to receive equal treatment in court no longer hold much weight in political debate in most societies. So other arguments, particularly if they are based on achievements, may be helpful. But what is the best way to evaluate legal aid's achievements?

The available literature offers little help as it is dominated by discussion of the service delivery models used in different schemes.[2] The service delivery models do need to be discussed in terms of cost and efficiency, but other issues are also important. For example, individual legal aid schemes could be analysed in terms of issues such as: the range of services provided; the type of legal matters and legal institutions for which legal aid was available; the success or otherwise of providing services to those who needed them; and whether legal aid eligibility has kept pace with changes in the legal system and society. Research into any, or all, of these issues could provide valuable insights into what legal aid has achieved. Each would also be an advance on the studies that discussed only service delivery models. Further valuable insights would be gained by study of these issues on a cross-national basis. And, as suggested, it may be that these sort of studies will also provide important new arguments that could be used to defend legal aid.

In this chapter it is not intended to argue for the worth of one particular type of these studies. But it is argued that there is a role for studies that allow different perspectives on what legal aid has achieved. To develop new perspectives, two basic conditions of social science research should be met: first, a careful description of the scheme(s) under study; and, secondly, a means for interpreting the data that are collected. Recent cross-national comparisons demonstrate the need to meet these conditions. That is, they have described the

---

[2] For a critique of the way that this framework dominates the literature see Regan, F., 'Is It Time To Rethink Legal Aid? Beyond Lawyers and Money', Paper to the SLSA Conference, Exeter, England, March 1993.

schemes but have not interpreted differences between them.[3] Blankenburg,[4] for example, analysed the spending and services of three European schemes, noted that there were major differences, but did not interpret them. Cousins'[5] discussion of four European schemes demonstrated that priorities vary markedly if measured in terms of the range and scope of services provided, the expenditure, and eligibility tests. He also made no attempt to interpret the differences, but he concluded his paper with the observation that debate about legal aid has not been driven by a 'desire to find out what legal aid is doing and why'.[6] In an earlier work the author compared schemes in Sweden and Australia using a framework adapted from recent comparative welfare state analysis.[7] It was hypothesised that legal aid in the former would be more generous given that Sweden has a highly developed welfare state. The conclusion was that both countries provided similar levels of legal representation, but that Australia's range of services was more extensive; Australia was 'doing more with less' by providing more legal advice, duty lawyer services and legal education but spending less per capita. However, no attempt was made to interpret the differences between the schemes.[8]

It is proposed to use an approach here that develops new insights into the achievements of legal aid. The approach builds on the recent comparative research but goes beyond it in two ways: first, by describing the full range of services provided by a legal aid scheme and not just highlighting one type of service such as representation; secondly, by offering a fresh device for

---

[3] Such comparisons are also fraught with difficulties due to factors such as the variety of activities undertaken by different schemes and the differences between legal systems.

[4] Blankenburg, E., 'Comparing Legal Aid Schemes in Europe', *Civil Justice Quarterly*, 1992, vol. 11, p. 106.

[5] Cousins, M., 'Civil Legal Aid in France, Ireland, The Netherlands and the United Kingdom', *Civil Justice Quarterly*, 1993, vol. 12, p. 154.

[6] Cousins, *op. cit.*, p. 166. In a later work Cousins addresses the question of why legal aid emerged in different societies. He discusses a range of explanations and concludes that the economic needs of the legal profession were a key and common factor. See Cousins, M., 'The Politics of Legal Aid: A Solution in Search of a Problem', *Civil Justice Quarterly,* 1994, vol. 13, p. 111. Further systematic historical, national and comparative studies are needed in order to explain the development of legal aid. Compare the innocent evolutionary approach proposed in Cappelletti, M., Gordley, J. and Johnson, E., *Toward Equal Justice*, Dobbs Ferry, New York: Oceana, 1975.

[7] The classification was adapted from that developed in Esping-Andersen, G., *The Three Worlds of Welfare Capitalism*, Cambridge: Polity, 1990. See Regan, F., *Are There 'Mean' and 'Generous' Legal Aid Schemes?*, Paper to the 'Legal Aid in the Post Welfare State Society Conference', Den Haag, The Netherlands, April 1994.

[8] These results are in stark contrast to the uniformity that is implied in the literature where modern legal aid schemes are classified as examples of either the 'judicare', 'salaried' or so-called 'mixed' model. See Cappelletti et al., *op. cit.* According to this classification the major difference between schemes relates to whether the private legal profession or salaried legal officers undertake the legal work and where payment derives from. But, as we have seen, when more sophisticated approaches are used the differences between schemes are marked. The critique is developed in Regan, *op. cit.* (1993).

72

interpreting the services provided. As a result the chapter suggests major new insights into legal aid's achievements. The approach asks whether legal aid provides a range of legal resources that promote citizenship for citizens generally, and especially for the poor. That is, whether the legal resources which are necessary for citizens to mobilise the law have been provided by legal aid. The 'citizenship approach' is applied to the case of legal aid in one society in this chapter, but it could be applied to either national or cross-national studies.

The theoretical bases of the approach are outlined in the next part of the chapter and then applied to legal aid in Australia. How and why Australian legal aid developed is summarised, and then the range of services provided is described and interpreted. In the final part of the chapter we reflect on issues raised in the text. In particular it is argued that, paradoxically, the trend in modern schemes to give priority to legal representation in criminal matters can be interpreted as a threat to citizenship. The citizenship approach can therefore be part of developing important new arguments to use to defend legal aid.

II LEGAL AID AND CITIZENSHIP

The relationship between legal aid and citizenship has not been well developed in the literature.[9] Marshall's classic essay 'Citizenship and Social Class' drew attention to what he referred to as the 'civil rights' of citizenship, by which he meant the right to justice, or equal treatment before the law. For Marshall, legal aid was essential for making the civil right of equality before the law a right in practice. It was understood by him as the provision of state-funded legal representation services for citizens who might not be able to afford the cost of lawyers' services. Legal aid gave priority to providing legal representation for citizens charged with criminal matters, for those involved in matrimonial disputes, or those involved in litigation.[10] But there have been few other

---

[9] There has been a resurgence of interest in citizenship in recent years in academic literature. See Turner, B., 'Outline of a Theory of Citizenship', *Sociology*, 1990, vol. 24, p. 189; Turner, B. (ed.), *Citizenship and Social Theory*, London: Sage, 1993; King, D. and Waldron, J., 'Citizenship, Social Citizenship and the Defence of Welfare Provision', *British Journal of Political Science*, 1988, vol. 18, p. 415; Meehan, E., *Citizenship and the European Community*, London: Sage, 1993; Oldfield, A., 'Citizenship: An Unnatural Practice', *Political Quarterly*, 1990, vol. 61, p. 177. There is a survey of recent literature in Kymlicka, W. and Norman, W., 'Return of the Citizen: A Survey of Recent Work on Citizenship Theory', *Ethics*, 1994, vol. 104, p. 352. Much of the recent scholarship can trace its origins to the work of Marshall, T. H., *Citizenship and Social Class and Other Essays*, London: Heineman, 1950.

[10] The discussion of legal aid referred to the 1949 Legal Advice and Assistance Bill. See Marshall, *op. cit.*

attempts in the literature to explore and develop the relationship between legal aid and citizenship.[11]

Legal aid schemes have traditionally given priority to legal representation for the poor, and particularly in criminal and matrimonial matters. But is the role of legal aid in promoting equality before the law achieved only by providing legal representation for the poor, and only in these areas of law? It would be a very limited view of citizens' equality before the law if this were so. But much of the literature has focused on that service, namely representation, rather than on the inability of citizens to pay for that service. The issue for Marshall was that the state effectively ensured that those citizens who could not purchase the service of representation were assisted. That is, the state overrode the market mechanism whereby citizens had access only to services that they could afford to purchase on the market. The state stepped in to provide a service, or to pay for it, because it was deemed to be an important good required by citizens in order to be treated equally before the law. The point to note, therefore, is not just that the state funded representation, but also that it provided a service which would not be available to certain citizens unless the state intervened. It is important to understand this point if we are to recognise what was the effect of legal aid schemes when they were established: it was not just the provision of a service, or payment of legal bills; the market was being overridden.

Recognising this point requires that we look carefully at the ways in which the state ensures that some goods are provided by legal aid which would normally be provided only on the market, or otherwise not at all. One other implication is that legal aid could therefore be expected to play a role in providing services to citizens who may not even be poor, as well as to the poor. It is conceivable that some things relating to equality before the law for all citizens will not be provided at all unless by legal aid. The importance of this point becomes clearer below.

Legal representation in criminal matters is important as it ensures that the liberty of the citizen is not jeopardised by the state due to the citizen's inability to pay for legal services.[12] It may also protect citizens from bankruptcy or

---

[11] There are exceptions of course. For example, the development of the European Union has resulted in attention being given to issues of equality before the law and legal aid has sometimes been mentioned. See Meehan, *op. cit.* Some recent historical research has also emphasised the link between legal aid and citizenship in the context of the rise and fall of the British welfare state. See Goriely, T., 'Rushcliffe Fifty Years On: The Changing Role of Civil Legal Aid Within the Welfare State', *Journal of Law and Society*, 1994, vol. 21, p. 545.

[12] For a recent discussion of the contemporary importance (and the varying interpretations of the importance) of the role of the 'loss of liberty' principle in granting criminal legal aid in the UK, see Young, R., 'The Merits of Legal Aid in the Magistrates' Courts', *Criminal Law Review*, 1993, p. 336.

poverty caused by the cost of matrimonial or civil proceedings. But is legal representation to protect liberty the only element, or even the most important part, of the relationship between legal aid and citizenship? One way to answer that question is to consider it from the citizen's point of view. Do these matters exhaust the legal matters that the poor, or any other citizens, will experience in life? And does legal representation exhaust the range of ways in which the poor, or citizens generally, will want to use the law and legal system? If legal aid promotes equal citizenship then we would expect that it should and could promote equality before the law in other ways. Ideally, if it does promote citizens' equality before the law, it should play a role of promoting equality of citizens in all areas of law. And it should promote equality in the use of law in all ways by citizens. Or to put it another way, legal representation in criminal and matrimonial matters does not exhaust the areas of law that affect citizens' equality before the law and at a basic empirical level legal representation does not exhaust the number of ways that citizens can use law.

But what else could legal aid schemes provide apart from legal representation? What other services could be offered that would not otherwise be provided unless by the market on the basis of the citizen's capacity to pay? This question is considered here from the perspective of both demand and supply, that is, first, the legal problems experienced by citizens, and secondly, the services that legal aid sometimes provides. The citizens of most societies report that they experience civil and matrimonial problems in particular, where there is little likelihood of legal proceedings eventuating.[13] They also experience civil and matrimonial problems where they choose, for a variety of reasons, not to pursue actions through the formal legal system. As a result modern legal aid schemes often provide services that assist citizens to recognise when they have experienced an event where the law is involved, to understand how the law can be used, and to decide what choices are available — whether to use the mechanisms of the legal system or not. The services that are often provided for these problems include legal advice, legal education and training. They are particularly important in as much as they do not concentrate on the use of lawyers' services to initiate court proceedings. This is not to say that representation is unimportant, but rather that citizens, including the poor,

---

[13] The literature in this area is vast. For the USA data see Curran, B., *The Legal Needs of the Public*, Chicago: American Bar Foundation, 1977; and the extensive discussion of the studies of citizens' experience of 'legal' problems and what they do about them in Zemans, F. K., 'Framework for Analysis of Legal Mobilization: A Decision-Making Model', *American Bar Foundation Research Journal*, 1982, p. 911. For the UK see the survey data discussed in The Royal Commission on Legal Services, *Final Report: Volume Two – Surveys and Studies*, London: HMSO, 1979. Also see Kempson, E., *Legal Advice and Assistance*, London: Policy Studies Institute, 1989. For Australian data see Australian Bureau of Statistics, 'Usage of Legal Services, New South Wales, October 1990', Canberra: ABS, 1991.

experience events in life which do not require legal representation and that some schemes have developed services to respond which exist alongside the provision of legal representation.

What legal problems do citizens seek legal advice and minor assistance for? Examples include: the need for advice about divorce provisions; negotiation with insurance companies after vehicle collisions; preparation for hearings in a small claims court; tenancy disputes; and advice about contracts with car sales companies.[14] Citizens in many countries experience these matters and attend legal aid (and other) institutions to seek help. Advice and assistance allows citizens to be 'legally competent'. They may, as a result, be in a better position to comprehend and deal with the matter themselves, and to deal with similar situations should they occur in the future. They may also feel less alienated from the legal system and be more prepared to use the law in the future. And they may be able to assist other citizens to identify the options available if similar situations occur, even if the only viable option is to go and see a lawyer.

Legal education and training services are also provided by legal aid in many countries. Legal education includes: citizen education about common legal problems; written materials informing citizens how to undertake their own legal actions in small claims and other tribunals; and guides or manuals for citizens to draw up documents such as simple wills or power of attorney documents. Legal training includes: classes for citizens in particular aspects of the law; 'Do-your-own-divorce' classes; information about child support; and training workshops for citizens, welfare workers, or public servants to enable them to recognise and deal with common legal problems. Legal education and training promote the possibility of citizens taking control over more areas of their life. They enable citizens to understand more about legal matters, allow them to make informed choices, and ensure that they do not have to rely totally on the services of the legal profession.

III   LEGAL MOBILISATION

The importance of these non-representation services can be more clearly understood if we consider the relationship between citizens and the law, and in particular the way that citizens 'mobilise' the law. The initial focus of the legal mobilisation literature was on the state mobilising the law against citizens — Black defined legal mobilisation as 'the process by which a legal system acquires its cases'.[15] But that definition is problematic — it reduces the role of law to one of social control, where citizens are objects that are 'done to' by the

---

[14] See the survey data referred to in n. 13 above.
[15] Black, D., 'The Mobilization of Law', *Journal of Legal Studies*, 1973, vol. 2, p. 125.

state. It also means that the only relevant 'cases' are those dealt with by the formal mechanisms of the legal system.[16] Lempert, by contrast, saw legal mobilisation as 'the process by which legal norms are invoked to regulate behaviour'.[17] The emphasis here was upon the way that citizens transferred problems and disputes from the private to the public arena to be processed by the formal legal system.[18] But disputes are disregarded by this model if they do not come to the attention of lawyers.

Zemans,[19] by contrast, proposed a citizen's view of legal mobilisation, arguing that citizens make a series of rational decisions when they experience legal problems. These include doing nothing, talking with family and friends, and self-help, all of which would normally take place prior to a citizen contacting a lawyer. Drawing on the theory of political mobilisation, she argued, in effect, that citizens are the subject not the object of legal mobilisation. So if citizens did not contact a lawyer when they experienced a legal problem it did not mean that they did not mobilise the law. They may have decided to do nothing after considering the consequences of legal action; they may have negotiated a settlement based on legal rules, or proposed further action if settlements were not reached. But all these choices would have involved some degree of mobilising law, or using the norms of the law. For Zemans poverty was, therefore, not the central variable which determined citizens' use of the law and lawyers. She argued that knowledge of the law and capacity to pay for the cost of a lawyer were only two factors, among many, to take into account when explaining citizens' rational choices to mobilise the law

---

[16] There was initial enthusiasm for Black's conceptualisation in the literature, but then interest waned. Recent scholarship has focused on the role of the courts in legal mobilisation for social reform. For the USA see Kessler, M., 'Legal Mobilisation for Social Reform: Power and the Politics of Agenda Setting', *Law and Society Review*, 1990, vol. 24, p. 121; Burstein, P. and Monaghan, K., 'Equal Employment Opportunity and the Mobilization of Law', *Law and Society Review*, 1986, vol. 20, p. 355; Silberman, M., *The Civil Justice Process: A Sequential Model of the Mobilization of Law*, Orlando: Academic Press, 1985. For Spain see Giles, M. and Lancaster, T., 'Political Transition, Social Development and Legal Mobilization in Spain', *American Political Science Review*, 1989, vol. 83, p. 817. A recent article that stresses the importance of the concept and which attempts to develop it is McCann, M., 'Legal Reform and Social Reform Movements: Notes on Theory and Its Application', *Studies in Law, Politics and Society*, 1991, vol. 11, p. 225.
[17] Lempert, R., 'Mobilizing Private Law: An Introductory Essay', *Law and Society*, 1976, vol. 11, p. 173.
[18] Lempert, *op. cit.*, p. 174.
[19] The legal mobilisation model is explained in detail in Zemans, *op. cit.*, n. 13. The model is applied to the relationship between law and the political system in Zemans, F. K., 'Legal Mobilization: The Neglected Role of Law in the Political System', *American Political Science Review*, 1983, vol. 77, p. 690.

or not.[20] Legal mobilisation was therefore an 'interactive process' between the citizens and the law, where citizens can activate law in a variety of ways, with or without a lawyer, and where the state and other citizens can also bring the law to bear on the lives of citizens. But legal mobilisation was therefore not unidirectional — from the state to the citizens.[21] Individual citizens can and do activate legal norms and rules inside or outside the formal legal system, and with or without the help of a lawyer. Lastly, and again drawing upon theory of political mobilisation, Zemans argued that citizens can also mobilise to change law; that they can activate processes of law reform by drawing upon the legal problems they experience collectively.

Zemans' model is significant in the emphasis it gives to the citizen's view and experience of law. The emphasis on citizens' interaction with the law both within, and outside, the formal legal system, suggests a significant extension of the idea of citizens' equality before the law. The model suggests that citizens are often capable of using the law to solve their legal problems with or without a lawyer. Equality before the law therefore does not mean only the provision of legal representation in criminal and matrimonial matters. But the implication is certainly not that citizens are best left to their own devices to mobilise law. According to Zemans, they require a range of resources (including lawyers' services) that allow and encourage them to mobilise law. The model therefore implies a role for institutions (such as legal aid schemes) to provide legal resources, for the poor especially and citizens generally, as the capacity to mobilise law will at least partly depend on the ability to locate and utilise relevant legal resources. Or, to put it another way, the study of citizen mobilisation of law must take account of both the demand for, and supply of, legal resources. And the range of legal resources required to promote citizens' equality before the law is therefore likely to be substantial. It is therefore important to identify what legal resources are provided and by which institutions.[22]

---

[20] She was in part concerned to argue that the poor made similar choices to the non-poor in mobilising the law. To attribute fewer choices to the poor was not only empirically incorrect, but also meant that the poor were being destined to a far greater reliance upon lawyers than other citizens: Zemans, *op. cit.*, 1982, p. 991.

[21] In the later paper Zemans makes explicit connections between legal and political mobilisation and refers to the former as a form of political participation that has been neglected in research: Zemans, *op. cit.*, 1983, p. 701.

[22] The emphasis upon individuals interacting with the law implies that collective citizen mobilisation is unimportant. Zemans, *ibid.*, acknowledges the lack of discussion of the role of collective organisations and collective action, but argues that her emphasis on the individual citizen was fundamental to a discussion of the collective element, and 'because that is where the argument needs to be made most strongly'.

IV INTERPRETING LEGAL RESOURCES

It has been argued that citizens require a range of legal resources to mobilise, and to be treated equally before, the law. But what else is required apart from lawyers' services? Dias and Paul define legal resources as 'the capacity to use law' and propose that:

> By *legal resources* we mean that functional knowledge and skills which enable people, working collectively and with other groups, to understand law and use it effectively.... Thus legal resources are simply *part* of an aggregate of knowledge and skills which create or enhance incentives and capacities to promote or defend shared interests.[23]

If the citizens' relationship with the law is to be interactive they require resources that respond to the legal problems — both individual and collective — that they experience.[24] The resources will include the following: legal services (advice and representation) provided by private lawyers or public legal aid schemes; public legal education to the community; legal education for the legal professions; and community-based and other mechanisms for articulating the need for law reform in response to the legal problems of the people.[25] All these resources are necessary for citizens to mobilise the law effectively. All should be available if citizens are to interact with, and be equal before, the law. Legal aid schemes can be, and are, involved in providing some of these resources. But clearly legal aid cannot provide them all — they are the resources that are required in society generally. (For example, it is hard to imagine legal aid providing dispute resolution mechanisms or processing complaints against public agencies.) But if legal aid promotes citizen equality before the law by providing legal resources then there is a role to provide legal representation, legal advice and assistance, legal education and training, and also to take a role in law reform processes. And in particular the range of legal resources must be broader than legal representation in criminal and matrimonial matters. This is but one, albeit very important, legal resource to provide. But it is not and should not be the only resource provided. The resources should respond to what citizens need and not give exclusive priority to what lawyers do in court for them.

---

[23] Dias, C. and Paul, J., *Lawyers in the Third World*, Uppsala: Scandinavian Institute of African Studies, 1981, p. 20. The term 'legal resources' has been commonly used in the literature to refer to the resources provided by lawyers. That is, the services provided by lawyers in legal practice, especially legal representation and legal advice. The term is used in a very different way here.

[24] Dias and Paul's approach is applied to a developing society in Regan, F., 'Legal Resources Development in Uganda', *International Journal of the Sociology of Law*, 1994, vol. 22, p. 203.

[25] The list of resources is adapted from Dias, C. and Paul, J., 'Developing Legal Resources for Participatory Organisations of the Rural Poor', *Third World Legal Studies*, 1985.

Lastly, while it has been argued that a range of resources should be provided by legal aid, we need to consider whether different resources promote citizenship in different ways. How do we decide this and interpret differences? For example, how do we interpret the difference between representation in criminal matters and legal education materials? Berlin's discussion of liberty offers a way of understanding and interpreting the importance of different legal resources. For Berlin, liberty included a concern for loss of liberty, but he refused to limit freedom to this.[26] He argued that the classical liberal preoccupation with ensuring 'freedom from' interference by the state and other citizens was inadequate, and that freedom should include elements of 'freedom to', that is, freedom to do more, and to be more human. One implication of positive freedom is that certain things need to be provided, by the state in particular, which, while they may interfere with negative liberty, are necessary in order to promote positive freedom, to be more human. In compulsory schooling, for example, the state interferes with freedom but on the basis that education is a way of enabling citizens to be more human. Education improves choices at various points in life. For example, it may improve the capacity to understand legal issues and to read legal education materials, contracts and other documents.[27]

The range of legal resources provided by legal aid schemes can be interpreted in this light.[28] Legal advice can be provided after arrest, and representation in court may be made available if citizens are charged with criminal offences by the state. The accused may not necessarily stay out of jail, but the representation ensures that they do not appear in court alone and at the mercy of the state. In this way their freedom from interference, negative freedom, is promoted. Legal representation in many matrimonial matters can also be seen in terms of ensuring freedom from interference; for example, divorce may allow escape from violent partners, or from the suffering and restrictions of unhappy marriages. Other resources can be similarly interpreted. Legal advice and legal education and training can be seen to promote positive freedom. They allow citizens to be more and do more, by taking control of the legal problems that they experience and by making informed choices about

---

[26] Berlin, I., *Four Essays on Liberty*, Oxford: OUP, 1979. Berlin's conceptualisation is experiencing a new prominence in the literature. For mental health policy see Cavadino, M., *Mental Health Law in Context*, Aldershot: Dartmouth, 1989; for a study of the standard of living in Australia see Travers, P. and Richardson, S., *Living Decently*, Melbourne: OUP, 1994.

[27] For a perspective on the importance of education for 'human development' see the UNDP's Human Development Report (HDR). The HDR ranks countries by combining three measures of human development: life expectancy, purchasing power, and adult literacy rates. The resulting measure emphasises what people can be rather than emphasising only freedom from interference. See United Nations Development Program, *Human Development Report*, New York: OUP, 1990.

[28] Not all services in all types of law are discussed in detail in the present chapter. The aim is to test an alternative approach, not to claim that all conceptual or measurement problems are resolved.

what action to take. Regardless of whether their problems enter the formal legal system, these services can promote citizens' capacity to mobilise the law on their own behalf either within or outside of the legal system.

Berlin's distinction between forms of freedom can also be used to interpret legal aid schemes overall. Some schemes will emphasise both positive and negative freedom by providing a wide range of legal resources. In practice we would expect that most schemes would not give an exclusive priority to services that promote just one form of freedom but would attempt to promote both. And to some extent, as we have seen, different services incorporate elements of both positive and negative freedom.[29] We would also expect that the priorities (in terms of positive and negative freedom) may alter over time due to the changing needs of the society and other factors. Indeed, one way to view the development of legal aid schemes is to see them as involved in an ongoing process of trying to accommodate pressures to promote both forms of freedom in the services provided. At different stages in history the priority is inevitably placed on one more heavily than on the other. As we see below, the history of legal aid in Australia can certainly be viewed in this light.

In summary, a citizenship-oriented device is suggested to describe and interpret the resources provided by the services of legal aid schemes. Legal aid schemes can be said to promote citizenship most strongly and comprehensively when they provide a range of legal resources that give priority to both positive and negative freedom. Citizens can then mobilise the law in a variety of ways which enhance their equality before the law. Citizenship will be promoted only weakly if representation in criminal matters is the main priority. But it will also be promoted weakly if legal education and training are the main priorities.[30] The challenge is therefore to devise schemes that provide a range of resources which allow citizens, especially the poor, to be treated equally in all areas of law and in all ways that they use the law. The citizenship approach therefore calls for careful description of the full range of legal resources provided by legal aid schemes. The resources should be interpreted in terms of promoting citizens' equality before the law, making use of the distinction between those resources that promote positive and those that promote negative freedom. In

---

[29] If the distinction is pushed too far it also tends to break down. For example, freedom from interference does allow citizens to do other things, i.e., to do more and be more. The point here is to use Berlin's distinction to shed light on the importance of what have often been seen to be peripheral activities of legal aid.

[30] In practice most societies do not provide only one of the two groups of legal resources. But representation is almost the exclusive priority of Sweden's legal aid, and legal education and training is almost the exclusive priority in Uganda. For Sweden see Regan, 'Are there 'mean' and 'generous' legal aid schemes?' op. cit. (1994); for Uganda see Regan, 'Legal Resources Development in Uganda', op. cit. (1994).

the next part of the chapter the legal aid scheme in one country is described and interpreted as a case study of the role of legal aid in promoting citizenship.

V NATIONAL LEGAL AID IN AUSTRALIA

(i) Early developments

Australia's first national, comprehensive legal aid scheme, the Australian Legal Aid Office (ALAO), was established in 1973. The ALAO built upon a complex historical legacy of legal aid schemes that reflected the federal nature of government, the multi-jurisdictional legal system, a high but unsustained level of government involvement in legal aid and a historically low level of involvement in establishing legal aid schemes by the legal profession. The development of these schemes leading up to the ALAO is summarised below.

Public provision of legal aid emerged early in the twentieth century when state governments established Public Solicitors Offices (PSOs).[31] The South Australian PSO (SAPSO), for example, provided what was effectively a state-wide legal aid service.[32] A salaried lawyer was employed to provide free legal advice, minor assistance and legal representation in most areas of law for low income citizens.[33] In the early 1930s, amidst the crisis brought on by the Great Depression, the Government handed the scheme over to the private legal profession in that state,[34] resulting in the first private legal profession scheme

[31] Prior to the development of the organised legal aid schemes, assistance was provided on the basis of the 'in forma pauperis' procedure. Provisions were enshrined in numerous state and Commonwealth statutes.
[32] The South Australian government established the SAPSO in 1926. Other states also enacted legislation to establish similar offices, but the SAPSO was most significant in view of the fact that it was later taken over by the private legal profession as discussed below. The development of the PSOs is discussed in Sackville, R., *Legal Aid in Australia*, Canberra: AGPS, 1975.
[33] The work of the PSO was extensive. The Public Solicitor, Chas A. Sandery, commented on the work during 1931 as follows:

During the year 1931 the Public Solicitor was required to assist 173 persons who had been committed for trial or for sentence in the Supreme Court, and the number of dissolutions of marriage totalled 60.... At the present time there are over two hundred applications for divorce which require attention and will in due time come before the Supreme Court for hearing and determination. In one way and another over four thousand people applied to the Public Solicitor for assistance throughout the year 1931.

SAPSO Annual Report 1931. *Source:* State Records Office of SA, GRG/1, Series 69, Box 3, File 91.
[34] The Law Society of South Australia had argued against setting up the SAPSO in 1925 and refused a government request to assist by doing some of the scheme's work. The Law Society offered only to take over the scheme. See Ross, D., 'A Legal Assistance Scheme', *The Australian Law Journal*, 1948, vol. 22, p. 51.

in Australia. It was also the only major legal profession scheme in the country until the 1950s.

The first national legal aid scheme was also public. The Legal Service Bureaux (LSB) were established by the Commonwealth Attorney General, Dr Evatt, in 1942. The LSB employed salaried lawyers to provide free legal advice and minor assistance in any legal matter to armed service personnel, returned armed service personnel, and their families.[35] Legal representation was not provided[36] and no assistance was available for citizens outside the defence force related group. The LSB survived into the post-war period and Evatt increased the eligible population dramatically when he announced to Parliament in 1949 that the LSB's services were to be extended to all social security recipients.[37] However, the Government lost power before the decision was implemented. The LSB gradually declined in importance under the Conservative Governments from 1949–72. The decline was at least partly in response to claims from the private legal profession and conservative lawyers in Parliament that the LSB was no longer necessary. The Commonwealth, it was argued, did not need to outlay money on legal assistance for that group of citizens. Nevertheless the LSB survived, and in 1973 it became the basis of the ALAO in terms of its services (advice and minor assistance in any matter), employment practices (salaried lawyers) and its structures (the ALAO used the LSB offices in each capital city as the basis of a network of offices).

The private legal profession historically has played a small role in the development of legal aid schemes in Australia.[38] In most states the profession was slow to establish schemes despite discussions with governments, particularly in the post war-period.[39] By the late 1960s profession schemes existed in

---

[35] The LSB assisted more than one million people between November 1942 and September 1949 (Commonwealth Parliamentary Debates, House of Representatives, 30 September 1949, p. 776). The LSB employed 44 lawyers and 63 support staff at its peak in 1946. Other societies also established legal services organisations for service personnel. For the US, see Blake, M., 'Legal Assistance for Servicemen', *American Bar Association Journal*, 1951, vol. 37, p. 9. Abel, R., 'Law without Politics: Legal Aid under Advanced Capitalism', *UCLA Law Review*, 1985, vol. 32, p. 474, noted the fact that the US and Australian national legal aid schemes had their origins in defence force schemes, but he is dismissive of their importance arguing that they were concerned with the morale of the defence forces. Abel is correct in part, but the LSB was established to assist the families as well as the defence personnel. Help was provided in matters where those in the forces would not have known about the problems their partners faced.

[36] The LSB did not provide legal representation but it did provide a referral service to members of the private profession, who traditionally undertook representation at a reduced rate for this client group.

[37] Commonwealth Parliamentary Debates, House of Representatives, 30 September 1949, p. 776.

[38] This is not to deny the role of members of the profession in providing legal aid under '*in forma pauperis*' provisions of various Commonwealth and state government statutes.

[39] The Queensland profession delayed establishing a scheme until 1966 despite discussions with the state government. See Gregory, H., *The Queensland Law Society Inc.*, Brisbane: Queensland Law Society, 1991.

all states,[40] but while they undertook a significant amount of work they had major limitations. In particular: legal advice was not a priority in most schemes; representation was provided as the main priority, but primarily in relation to serious criminal and complex matrimonial matters; representation was not available for magistrates' courts' matters; and there was little help available in non-litigious civil matters. In addition the eligibility criteria and level of assistance varied considerably from one state to another.[41]

(ii)   The ALAO

The first national comprehensive legal aid scheme in Australia, the ALAO, was established by a national Labor Government elected at the end of 1972, after 23 years in opposition. The Attorney-General, Lionel Murphy, was keen to reform many areas of the law; and while legal aid was not mentioned in the campaign speech, Murphy moved quickly to establish a comprehensive, national, publicly-funded and coordinated scheme. Murphy rejected advice from the state Law Societies that legal aid should be organised through the existing profession schemes. Instead he announced — without advising the profession — that the Government was to establish a national public scheme, the ALAO.[42] The ALAO took over the offices and staff of the LSB, inherited

---

[40] The legal profession schemes were established in the states as follows: South Australia 1933; Tasmania 1954; Western Australia 1960; Victoria 1964; Queensland 1966; New South Wales 1971. The profession was aware of the problems with the state profession schemes. The national body of the profession, the Law Council of Australia, proposed a national legal aid scheme to the Menzies (Conservative) Government in 1964 to overcome the differences that existed between the state schemes. The private profession was to deliver services and the Commonwealth was to pay 90% of the cost. The Government refused to establish the scheme. See Gray, G., 'Identifying the Differences: The Development of Legal Aid Policy', in Alexander, M. and Galligan, B., *Comparative Political Studies: Australia and Canada*, Melbourne: Pitman, 1992.

[41] For a detailed description and critical evaluation of the legal aid schemes available in Australia in the early 1970s prior to the ALAO, see Sackville, *op. cit*, n. 32. For other critiques see Spigelman, J., 'Poverty and the Law', *Australian and New Zealand Journal of Criminology*, 1969, vol. 2, p. 87; Cranston, R. and Adams, D., 'Legal Aid in Australia', *The Australian Law Journal*, 1972, vol. 46, p. 508.

[42] Murphy was not opposed to the Law Society schemes as such. For example, early in 1973 he provided $2 million funding 'on a per capita basis' to the states to support existing schemes. The money went primarily to the Law Society schemes. But he was not convinced that the profession had the interests of the citizens at heart and was not sure that the profession would be able to coordinate a comprehensive scheme.

its priorities, but also added further services.[43] In a statement to the Senate of the Australian Parliament on 13 December 1973, Murphy outlined the Government's policy on legal aid, noting that the ALAO would have special responsibility for particular groups and:

> ... will provide legal advice and assistance on all matters of Federal law, including the Matrimonial Causes Act, to everyone in need; and on matters of both Federal and State law, to persons for whom the Australian Government has a special responsibility, for example: pensioners, aborigines, ex-servicemen and newcomers to Australia. The offices will provide a referral service in other cases.[44]

He concluded his statement by noting, in the language of citizenship, that a range of resources need to be provided by legal aid:

> The Government's aim is that eventually no person anywhere in Australia should suffer injustice because of the unavailability of legal advice or inability to afford the cost of representation in court proceedings.[45]

The ALAO continued the LSB's priorities, providing free legal advice and minor assistance, on a non means-tested basis, in all areas of law. But in contrast to the LSB, advice and assistance was available to all citizens: it was not just for the poor, or for the defence related clients of the LSB. Legal representation, by contrast, was targeted at the poor and was subject to tests, including a means test and a 'reasonableness' test. But representation was available for most legal matters. It was provided by ALAO salaried lawyers, or by referral to the private profession who were paid by the ALAO to conduct the litigation. The ALAO lawyers conducted some representation but most was done by private lawyers. The ALAO lawyers undertook the simple, quickly

---

[43] The ALAO commenced operations in September 1973 through the offices of the LSB in the capital cities of the six states and territories. The LSB staff at the time included 13 lawyers, eight lay advocates and ten support staff, all of whom were transferred to the ALAO. By late 1976 the ALAO had a staff of 150 lawyers and 210 administrative staff serving branch offices in each state and territory capital city, and 62 regional offices located in the suburban and provincial centres in Australia. See Harkins, J. P., *Federal Legal Aid in Australia*, Canberra: Attorney-General's Department, 1976.

[44] *Ibid.*, p. 6.

[45] Murphy's contribution to the development of legal aid in Australia was extensive. In addition to the ALAO, a national aboriginal legal aid scheme was established, a community legal centre funding program was initiated, and a special scheme for legal aid in 'environmental and conservation issues' was established.

disposed of, and undefended cases.[46] The ALAO also moved to establish duty lawyer services for the many citizens who were unrepresented in the lower (magistrates') courts.

The ALAO salaried lawyers worked in a network of 'shopfront offices' in urban and rural centres and they worked in liaison with other agencies dealing with the problems faced by citizens, especially those from disadvantaged groups.[47] Attorney-General Lionel Murphy said:

> I see the role of the Australian Legal Aid Office as taking the law to the people who most need it. I want to see small unpretentious 'storefront' offices opened in the suburbs of the cities and in country centres. I want them to be the kind of offices to which the ordinary man or woman faced with a legal problem will go as readily as he or she would go the garage with an ailing motor car. My intention is that the Australian Legal Aid Office would work alongside and in cooperation with bodies of all kinds that are concerned with solving the problems of the citizen and especially, of course, with the private legal practitioner.[48]

The provision of services through legal aid schemes continued to be contested by the private profession after the ALAO was established. Harkins[49] cites three examples of the legal profession mounting legal challenges either to the existence of the ALAO or to its practices. First, the Law Institute of Victoria mounted a High Court challenge to the constitutional validity of the ALAO which was not established by legislation due to the fact that the constitution did

---

[46] According to Harkins there were three reasons why the ALAO lawyers were not expected to undertake all the representation: first, the ALAO was in the process of being established and could not do all the work; secondly, it would have cost too much and there were reservations within the Government about the projected cost of legal aid; thirdly, it was politically more astute to involve the profession in this way rather than to try to exclude it altogether. Interview with Mr J. P. Harkins (first Director of the ALAO), 4 November 1994.

[47] The ALAO was also to fulfil the role of complementing existing legal services work in the society. The Attorney-General's Directive of 6 September 1973 outlined the role:

> The role of the Australian Legal Aid Office will be to provide a service of legal advice and assistance, including assistance in litigation, in co-operation with community organisations, referral services, existing legal aid schemes and the private legal profession. In particular, its decentralised offices will provide administrative support bases for community advice centres and legal or welfare advice groups generally.

Quoted in Harkins, *op. cit.*, p. 7.

[48] *Ibid.*, p. 45.

[49] *Ibid.*, pp. 23–7.

not give the Commonwealth power in that area.[50] The ALAO was also challenged in relation to the right of ALAO lawyers to appear in court in the Full Court of the Supreme Court of the Australian Capital Territory in 1975. Thirdly, the practice of advertising the work of the ALAO came into conflict with a traditional ban by the legal profession upon lawyers advertising. None of the challenges stopped the ALAO from functioning.

For both Murphy and Evatt, legal aid was important because it provided resources in the form of services to improve the capacity of citizens to respond to the legal problems of everyday life. Legal representation, especially in criminal matters, was valuable, but it was not the only priority. Indeed for Evatt, a civil liberty lawyer, legal advice and assistance had been the LSB's priority and no legal representation was provided. Murphy's ALAO continued that priority, but complemented it with representation for criminal and other matters, a duty lawyer service and an emphasis upon educating the community about the law. Or, in terms of freedom, the move from the LSB to the ALAO represented a public program that moved to incorporate a new emphasis on promoting negative freedom by way of legal representation in criminal and other matters, and duty lawyer services in criminal matters. The new emphasis was added to the existing emphasis on positive freedom, although the latter was also strengthened by extending legal advice to the whole population and developing a role in legal education.

(iii) The Legal Aid Commissions

The private profession was instrumental in shaping the next stage of the development of the national legal aid scheme in Australia. A Conservative Government was elected in December 1975 and devolved responsibility for provision of legal aid services and administration to the states in the late 1970s. The ALAO was disbanded and Legal Aid Commissions (LACs) were established in each state under state legislation to administer grants of legal aid, from funds largely supplied by the Commonwealth.[51]

---

[50] The ALAO was established in a similar fashion to the LSB. The Attorney-General did not introduce legislation but set up a unit within the Attorney-General's Department to establish the scheme without delay. According to Harkins, Murphy wanted the scheme 'set up overnight' and did not want to give opportunities to the Conservative opposition to block or delay the setting up of the scheme. Interview with Harkins, 4 November 1994.

[51] For comment on the rise and fall of the ALAO and the rise of the state LACs, see Armstrong, S., 'Labor's Legal Aid Scheme: The Light That Failed', in Scotton, R., and Ferber, H. (eds), *Public Expenditure and Social Policy in Australia Vol. 2*, Melbourne: Longman Cheshire, 1979; Armstrong, S., 'The Objective and the Reality: Legal Aid in Australia 1984', *Labor Forum*, 1985, vol. 6, p. 6; Hawker, G., 'The Rise and Fall of the Australian Legal Aid Office', in Encel, S., Wilenski, P. and Schaffer, B. (eds), *Decisions: Case Studies in Australian Public Policy*, Melbourne: Longman Cheshire, 1981; Gray, *op. cit.*

The organisation of legal aid provision in Australia has not altered substantially since the LACs were set up, but big changes have occurred in relation to the operations, including reductions in means test levels and the matters for which representation is available.[52] For example, legal representation for divorce was abolished in the late 1970s. The most significant alteration of priorities has been the increase in aid for criminal matters as a proportion of all representation, and a corresponding decline in aid for civil matters. Representation in criminal matters has increased from approximately 50 per cent of representation in 1985–86 to 68.5 per cent in 1993–94. The role of legal aid in defending liberty has increased significantly. At the same time Australian legal aid has largely retained its historical commitment to free, non means-tested legal advice and minor assistance.[53] Education, training and law reform have also expanded under the state LACs.[54]

(iv)   Legal aid in the 1990s

In the 1990s, legal aid in Australia consists of three different programs which together provide a wide range of services reflecting, in effect, a range of priorities for assisting citizens.[55] This overview of the development of Australian legal aid concludes with a brief summary of the services provided by the major program, the LACs. A snapshot of the LACs in 1993–94 demonstrates that legal representation is a major priority, but that it is not the only resource provided. In fact the total number of legal advice and duty solicitor services provided was higher than the number of representation

---

[52] Other changes include: funding from the Commonwealth has decreased as a proportion of all funding; and the debate over legal aid policy declined in importance until the late 1980s when cost containment became an issue. Currently legal aid is again part of national policy debate in the context of broad concerns about the accessibility of the justice system, and gender equality before the law. For a summary of developments since 1975 see National Legal Aid Advisory Committee, *Legal Aid For The Australian Community*, Canberra: AGPS, 1990.

[53] Two state LACs (Queensland and Western Australia) now impose a means test and charge a small fee for legal advice and minor assistance.

[54] Indeed the provision of the latter resources has increased rapidly due to the growth in the number of Community Legal Centres (CLCs) which undertake little legal representation but provide advice and other services. A description of the CLCs is available in Office of Legal Aid and Family Services, *Community Legal Centres: A Study of Four Centres in New South Wales and Victoria*, Canberra: OLAFS, 1991.

[55] The LAC is the largest program in terms of funding and services. In addition, approximately 100 CLCs provide advice, small amounts of legal representation and education services. The Aboriginal Legal Services provide legal advice, representation and small amounts of education to the Aboriginal community. For a detailed discussion see Fleming, D., *The Mixed Model of Legal Aid in Australia*, Paper to the 'Legal Aid in the Post Welfare state Society Conference', Den Haag, The Netherlands, April 1994.

services. Table 4.1 highlights the fact that the number of applications for legal representation approved[56] makes up only 24.4 per cent of these services.

Table 4.1: Legal aid services provided by LACs, 1993–94

Type of service	No. provided	%	Per 1,000 Population
Legal advice	184,776	34.6	10.4
Duty solicitor	219,236	41.0	12.4
Legal representation	130,563	24.4	7.4
TOTAL	534,575	100	30.2

Source: Legal Aid & Family Services, *Legal Aid in Australia 1993/4 Statistical Yearbook*, Canberra: LAFS, 1994.

Another perspective is to view the work undertaken in terms of the number of the services provided compared to the size of the whole population. Overall the LACs provided services to 408,926 individuals,[57] or 2.3 per cent of the population. Table 4.1 also expresses the work undertaken in terms of the size of the population, but calculates the number of services provided per 1,000 head of population. The total number of services in 1993–94 was 30.2 per 1,000 members of the population. But of these only 7.4 per 1,000 population were for legal representation — the remaining 22.8 per 1,000 population were for advice or duty solicitor services.

A breakdown of the LACs' services by type of law highlights the dominance of criminal law in legal representation — more than two thirds of representation (68.5 per cent) is provided for criminal matters. In Table 4.2 we also see that

---

[56] The data used in the following tables refer to applications for legal representation approved in 1993–94. These data are used in preference to the number of legal matters, because in criminal cases in particular there is often more than one legal matter involved. The approved applications for legal aid (representation) is a more useful figure as it counts the actual services provided, not the legal issues. However, the approved applications are not necessarily provided in the year they are approved due to the time lags occurring in the legal system.

[57] The number of services provided or approved is used in most of the tables of data here. That figure is used in contrast to the number of individuals who received services. The latter figure distorts the fact that citizens may receive more than one service in a year. The number of services is a more useful figure for this chapter.

Criminal Legal Aid: Does Defending Liberty Undermine Citizenship?

about a quarter (21.4 per cent) of representation is for family law matters and that a very small proportion is for civil matters (10.1 per cent). But the dominance of the criminal law and the defence of liberty is actually understated due to the fact that almost all the duty solicitor work undertaken or funded by LACs is in criminal matters. Of these three services, legal advice is the only one where criminal matters do not dominate.

Table 4.2: Legal representation services approved by LACs, 1993–94

Area of law	Representation services (No.)	%
Family	27,902	21.4
Civil	13,153	10.1
Criminal	89,496	68.5
TOTAL	130,551	100

Source: As for Table 4.1.

We saw in Table 4.1 that the provision of legal advice is a major priority of the LACs — more than one third of all services provided were legal advice. The point to note is that advice and representation are provided for different types of legal matters. As we have seen, most of the representation is for criminal matters, with a small proportion of civil matters, but the proportions are almost reversed when we consider legal advice. Civil and family matters each account for more than a third of all advice, 38.6 per cent and 36.6 per cent respectively (see Table 4.3). Criminal matters account for less than 25 per cent of advice, mainly because these clients apply for representation not advice.

Table 4.3: Legal advice and minor assistance provided by LACs, 1993–94

Area of Law	No. of legal advice services	%
Family	67,581	36.6
Civil	71,355	38.6
Criminal	45,308	24.5
Not stated	532	0.3
TOTAL	184,776	100

Source: As for Table 4.1.

This snapshot of the work of the LACs demonstrates that a range of legal resources is provided, some of which give a priority to promoting negative freedom (e.g., criminal representation) and others which promote positive freedom (e.g., advice for civil matters). Representation and duty solicitor work in criminal matters is the dominant priority, but large amounts of advice in non-criminal matters are also provided.

But are these the LACs' only priorities? In fact the LACs also provide a range of other legal resources that promote the citizen's ability to mobilise the law and therefore to be treated equally before the law. In particular, some of the LACs provide telephone legal advice, legal education and training, and law reform activities. As has been argued above, to ignore these services is to ignore an important range of legal resources and, in effect, gives support to the implied argument that legal aid should promote only negative liberty.

In addition to face-to-face interviews, LACs provide advice over the telephone in simple matters. The aim is to provide a wider range of services to the public, to lessen the need for interviews in simple matters, and to provide a source of advice for citizens who live in rural areas or who cannot easily travel to a legal aid office. While telephone advice has not traditionally been highlighted in government reports and statistical summaries of the LACs, it is an important service.[58] Table 4.4 shows that four LACs gave 209,930 legal advice services over the telephone in 1993–94 compared with 184,776 face-to-face advice interviews nationally. That is, in those four states the number of telephone advice services was greater than the total number of face-to-face advice interviews provided by all the LACs in the country. In total nearly 400,000 advice services were provided to Australians. The breakdown of the problem types shows that most calls (53 per cent) were for civil matters, with family matters accounting for another third (30 per cent). A similar pattern was noted above for legal advice interviews.

Table 4.4: Telephone legal advice provided by four LACs, 1993–94

Legal Aid Commission	Family %	Criminal %	Law Type Civil %	Other %	TOTAL No.
South Aust.	—	—	—	—	56,112
Queensland	30	6	53	11	59,022
West. Aust.	—	—	—	—	29,224
Victoria	—	—	—	—	65,572
TOTAL					209,930

Source: Annual Reports 1993/4, Legal Aid Commissions.
Note: Data are incomplete and need to be treated with caution. The total is not calculated on a national basis.

LACs also undertake a wide range of legal education and training activities (Table 4.5). Large numbers of education pamphlets are distributed on topics such as 'Divorce', 'Dividing Fences', 'Neighbours', 'Going to Court', 'Motor

[58] The Commonwealth government agency responsible for production of reports on legal aid has traditionally not included data in relation to telephone advice provided, or the other services discussed here. According to Legal Aid and Family Services, detailed analysis of telephone advice will be available in the future but no mention has been made of whether other services discussed here will be included.

Vehicle Accidents', and 'You and the Police'. Many state LACs produce 'legal kits' to assist citizens with common legal events and problems such as changing one's name, or negotiating with neighbours over building/ repairing fences, and one publishes a lay person's guide to the law explaining national and state legislation.[59] The LACs are moving to publish their legal education materials in languages other than English because of the high number of citizens who do not speak English as their first language. Table 4.5 demonstrates that publication of pamphlets and other materials about the law is an important way of increasing the citizen's legal resources.

Table 4.5: Legal education activities provided by LACs of South Australia, Western Australia, Queensland and Victoria, 1993–94

| | State Legal Aid Commission | | | |
Activity	SA	WA	Qld	Vic
Pamphlets, kits, booklets	200,000	193,273	N/A	N/A
DIY divorce classes (people attended)	729	459	349	1,098
Education classes and workshops/forums (people attended)	1,000	1,061	1,469	1,198

Source: Annual Reports 1993/4, Legal Aid Commissions.
Note: Data are incomplete and need to be treated with caution. No attempt is made to total the columns as this would be a misleading summary of the activities on a national basis.

The LACs also run 'Do-Your-Own-Divorce Classes' in most states, where citizens are guided in the steps of applying for divorce. These classes are for simple divorces, where there are no complex issues of child custody and

---

[59] The South Australian Legal Services Commission publishes the *Law Handbook*. In other states the *Law Handbook* is published by Community Legal Centres.

property.[60] The LACs also provide a variety of legal education activities, including educating community and other workers about particular areas of the law relevant to their work and training citizens affected by the child support scheme. One state LAC (South Australia) provides a 'paralegal' training course for community workers and runs fee-paying courses for the public on different areas of the law.

Lastly, the LACs undertake one other aspect of the work of building the legal resources of Australian society. They use the collective legal experience of their clients to shape and influence the way that the law develops by undertaking law reform activities. Some law reform projects originate within the LACs; others respond to law reform proposals from governments or law reform commissions. The LAC Annual Reports for 1993–94 identify the wide range of law reform work undertaken. The New South Wales LAC lists 18 law reform projects, including submissions in relation to proposed domestic violence legislative amendments and a review of the anti-discrimination legislation in that state. The Victorian LAC lists 13 law reform projects, and the Queensland LAC lists nine projects.

The development of legal aid in Australia suggests three conclusions. First, the Australian experience is an example of how a legal aid scheme can develop over time which incorporates a balanced and comprehensive range of legal resources. It has been shown that the roles of both the public sector and the private profession have been important, although they have been very different. The SAPSO provided a comprehensive, state-wide service with a range of legal resources for citizens; while the LSB assisted services personnel and their families with the common legal problems experienced by citizens but provided no legal representation. The LSB was also the foundation of the ALAO, which retained the emphasis on providing legal resources to assist with the citizen's everyday legal problems. The private legal profession schemes developed alongside the public schemes and slowly expanded the availability of representation in criminal and matrimonial matters in particular, from the 1960s. In 1973, the national, publicly-funded scheme, the ALAO, ushered in an era when the range of legal resources promoted citizenship comprehensively. Free legal advice, minor assistance and other services, including legal representation, were widely available to all Australians. The ALAO effectively promoted citizens' equality before the law in most legal matters and in the ways that citizens used the law.

The second conclusion to note is that Australian legal aid reflects the fact that legal aid does not develop in an evolutionary, linear and incremental

---

[60] Australia introduced 'no fault' divorce in 1975. The Commonwealth initially allowed citizens to apply for legal aid for divorce, but withdrew the provision for 'simple' divorces in the late 1970s. As a result the classes were developed by the LACs.

fashion. On the contrary, the study demonstrates the ongoing debate between the private profession and government over what legal aid services should be provided, who they should be provided by and for which citizens. The role of the public sector in particular has been decisive in ensuring that legal resources were available not only on the market. The early public provision of services through salaried lawyers meant that an exclusive priority was not given to legal representation in criminal and matrimonial matters. In addition the public schemes did not only adopt the priority of assisting the poor. Instead, the citizens' legal problems of daily life, especially if they were poor, were responded to by providing legal advice and assistance on a free, non means-tested basis, in marked contrast to other societies where this assistance is granted on the basis of means tests and fees. [61] The profession schemes, in contrast, emphasised representation in criminal and matrimonial matters and almost exclusively for the poor. To use the language of liberty once more, government schemes promoted citizens' liberty in both negative and positive senses, while the profession schemes emphasised protection of liberty for serious matters. At the same time the public schemes under-emphasised the protection of negative liberty by neglecting the importance of legal representation, and the profession neglected positive liberty by failing to provide legal advice and minor assistance. The Australian study therefore demonstrates that if citizenship is to be comprehensively promoted by legal aid both government and the profession should be actively involved in a partnership to provide legal resources. The public sector cannot just pay the bills; it must be involved in providing resources that would otherwise not be provided, or that would rely on a citizen's capacity to pay on the market. The public involvement also has the capacity to ensure that the profession's inclination to emphasise negative liberty only will be balanced by an emphasis on services that promote positive freedom. The public involvement also has the capacity to ensure that legal aid promotes equality before the law especially, but not only, for the poor.

Lastly, the Australian study presents a challenge to the accounts of the development of legal aid in the literature. It demonstrates in particular the

---

[61] In contrast the reforms in England in the Legal Advice and Assistance Act 1949 extended a right to legal representation to a high proportion of the citizens. Provision for legal advice was not introduced until 1955, and then on the basis of means test and fees. The UK reforms took place in the context of dramatic expansion of the welfare state in that society with the development of services which were typically characterised by generous levels of assistance, and with high proportions of the population eligible. See Goriely, *op. cit.* (1994), and chapter 2 of this volume. For discussion of the UK developments in the 1960s, see Dworkin, G., 'The Progress and Future of Legal Aid in Civil Litigation', *Modern Law Review*, 1965, vol. 28, p. 432. In Australia, legal representation was provided on a patchy basis under the private profession schemes and was not available in a national scheme until 1974. Even in the 1990s it is available only on a restricted basis due to funding limits and High Court decisions which have not guaranteed a right to legal representation in criminal trials.

danger of focusing upon one type of legal resource, such as representation. Australian legal aid may not have been comprehensive at all points in history, and services may not have been available for all citizens, but the danger of elevating the availability of legal representation as the benchmark for evaluating schemes has been demonstrated. The full range of legal resources must be identified and interpreted if we are accurately to assess legal aid's role in promoting citizens' equality before the law. Stressing both positive and negative freedom ensures that the other services are finally appreciated for their full worth.[62]

VI CONCLUSION

This chapter has demonstrated that legal aid's achievements may have been seriously underrated. Some schemes have been remarkable in the way that they have promoted citizenship by overriding the market. They have provided a comprehensive range of legal resources — including legal representation, advice and minor assistance, legal education and training — that promote the citizen's equality before the law in the ways that they use the law and in the types of law that they use. Legal aid does not have to be limited to providing legal representation in criminal matters — and it is better if it is not limited in this way — but if it is, then citizenship is promoted only weakly, and inadequately.

The discussion here also suggests, therefore, that there is an important future role for public legal aid in promoting citizenship. There can be little doubt that there is a need for provision of a wide range of legal resources for the citizens in the post-welfare state society. Public legal aid institutions will need to participate in this work, in particular by overriding the market allocation of legal resources. The private legal profession alone will never provide the range of resources that are needed and that can be provided by the public schemes. The private profession will almost inevitably give priority to promoting negative freedom through legal representation in criminal matters. If public legal aid is dismantled and citizens have to purchase all their legal services on the private market according to their capacity to pay, then equality before the law will decline. But it has been demonstrated here that legal representation in

[62] In this way the paradox of Swedish legal aid can be better understood. The Swedish scheme gives priority to legal representation and, to a lesser extent, to legal advice. However, because there is no provision for legal education, training and law reform, it does not promote citizenship to the same extent as the Australian scheme and does not promote citizens mobilising law for themselves without relying upon legal professionals. This suggests an insight into the paternalistic nature of the Swedish welfare state — that it has erected welfare provisions where things are primarily done for the citizens rather than at the same time promoting the capacity for citizens to do things for themselves.

criminal and matrimonial matters is not the only service which needs to be protected in the future.

A particular and immediate concern is therefore to ensure that in the future legal aid promotes citizenship in ways which are not limited to protecting negative liberty. The policy trend in many rich societies is increasingly to give priority to legal representation in criminal matters. It would be paradoxical if, at a time when we finally recognise the importance of legal aid in promoting citizens' equality before the law, in all areas of law and in all ways of using law, the priority reverts to protection of liberty in criminal matters. If criminal representation continues to grow in importance we would conclude that citizens' equality before the law is declining to the extent that other legal resources are not provided. Legal aid needs to do more than just promote negative liberty if it is effectively to promote citizens' equality before the law.

5

At the Heart of the Legal: The Role of Legal Aid in Legitimating Criminal Justice

Mel Cousins[1]

This chapter considers the role of criminal legal aid in relation to the criminal justice system in the Republic of Ireland.[2] It argues that, rather than providing 'access' to 'justice' within the system of criminal law, one of the main functions of legal aid is to provide legitimation for the criminal justice system. The growing need for legitimation — against a background of an increasingly busy and repressive criminal justice system — is seen as one of the main factors behind the increased use of legal aid in recent years. While the evidence relied on in this chapter relates mainly to the Republic of Ireland, the argument may also have a broader relevance for other common law countries.

I INTRODUCTION

Several explanations can be advanced for the rapid growth in criminal legal aid which occurred in both Ireland and the UK in recent decades. These include:

(a)   A principled recognition by the state that the increasing professional-isation of the prosecution required some counter-balancing.

---

[1] The author would like to thank the editors for their very helpful comments on an earlier draft.
[2] This chapter considers the operation of the criminal justice system in relation to those more serious offences for which criminal legal aid would normally be available; it does not consider 'minor' criminal proceedings. The focus is on the operation of the courts and thus the operation of the prisons or the police is not addressed.

(b)   The ideological need of the state (in particular the judiciary) to legitimate processes leading to state punishment.

(c)   The bureaucratic requirement of the courts for lawyers to facilitate the administration of criminal justice by sorting out contentious issues at a pre-trial stage and by managing defendants in court.

(d)   The influence of the legal profession in seeking to obtain a market for its services.

The difficulty is, of course, to come to some conclusions as to which factors — at any given time — are to be assigned most weight (and why). This author argues that the ideological need of the state (in particular the judicial branch of the state) and the influence of lawyers have had the greatest impact in shaping the Irish criminal legal aid scheme. In relation to the other possible explanations, history suggests that (even if one accepts that the state ever operates solely from 'principled' motives) principle on its own is rarely sufficient to justify the expenditure of significant amounts of public resources. The 'bureaucratic' argument perhaps holds more weight, and Tamara Goriely has argued that this factor largely explains the growth in criminal legal aid in England and Wales.[3] This author has not, to date, found significant evidence to support this thesis in the Irish context. However, there is no necessary contradiction between the various explanations, i.e., a criminal legal aid scheme may provide ideological justification for the criminal justice system, meet the bureaucratic requirements of the courts and provide an income for lawyers.

In support of the argument put forward here, evidence is relied upon concerning the development of the criminal legal aid scheme in the Republic of Ireland. The Irish scheme was introduced in 1962 at a time when there was no real increase in the number of criminal cases before the Irish courts. At that time there was no statutory provision for legal aid and the legislation appears to have been largely a measure intended to bring Irish legislation into line with that of other countries, in particular the United Kingdom. However, in the context of the sharply increasing levels of crime and criminal prosecution in the late 1960s and 1970s, the Supreme Court effectively transformed the legal aid scheme by recognising a right to legal aid under the Irish constitution. This had the effect of increasing sharply the number of people using the legal aid scheme. The argument is that the increased availability of legal aid was integral to the continued legitimacy of the criminal justice system.

---

[3] See Goriely, T., 'The Development of Criminal Legal Aid in England and Wales', at chapter 2 of this volume.

In putting forward this explanation as to the role of criminal legal aid, this author wishes to situate his argument within a broader discussion of what is described as the 'legal' — a discursive system which includes the legal profession, legal education, the courts and the judiciary — and its relationship to the law. These matters are discussed in the opening section of this chapter. In brief, the argument is that while the law, at least in theory, can be seen as a rule base intended to give empirical content to an abstract theory of justice, the legal operates so as to control the law for the economic and power benefits of dominant classes and groups. The criminal legal aid system may be seen as operating at the heart of the legal and its role — in legitimating criminal justice and reflecting the interests of the legal profession — as an exemplar of the way in which the legal operates.

This chapter continues with a brief discussion of the differences between criminal and civil legal aid and the role of the criminal justice system, before describing how the Irish criminal justice system has become increasingly legalised in recent decades. Given the explicitly repressive nature of the criminal justice system, there is a clear need for the operation of this system to be perceived to be 'fair' and 'legitimate'. It is argued that, given the increasing legalisation of those aspects of the criminal justice system considered in this chapter, the role of providing such legitimation has fallen on the system of criminal legal aid. In this context, the development of the criminal legal aid system in Ireland is described, particularly in the period of the mid-1970s when it underwent a rapid expansion. It is argued that the transformation of criminal legal aid in that period reflected a reaction to the challenges to the legitimacy of the criminal justice system caused by the sharp increase in case-load and the operation of repressive measures as a response to the troubles in Northern Ireland.

In conclusion it is argued that the development of legal aid has been influenced by the need to legitimate the criminal justice system and by the pressures of the legal profession, and that neither criminal legal aid nor alternative forms of dispute resolution actually challenge the existing criminal justice system.

II THE LAW AND THE LEGAL

This author has argued elsewhere[4] for the need to distinguish between the law and the legal.[5] The concept of the law from a legal (positivist) point of view

---

[4] Cousins, M., 'The Politics of Legal Aid — A Solution in Search of a Problem?', *Civil Justice Quarterly*, 1994, vol. 13, p. 111.

[5] The use of the singular in reference to the term 'the law' is subject to the qualification set out by Hunt, A. and Wickham, G., *Foucault and Law*, London: Pluto Press, 1994, p. 39, that 'Law is not and never has been a unitary phenomenon, even though the assumption that it is has played a central role in most legal discourses and theories of law'. This author follows those authors in adhering 'to the view that law is a complex of practices, discourses and institutions'.

(and from that of the legal profession) comprehends quite a narrow understanding of law and laws: 'Law consists of data — primarily rules — which can be recognised by relatively simple tests or "rules of recognition".'[6] One such test is that the rules have gone though 'certain formal stages of a legislative process'.[7] However, others have put forward a much broader understanding of 'the law'. Ehrlich, for example, sees the law as involving not just the norms created and applied by the state (which he refers to as 'legal provisions'), but also 'social order', i.e., the rules which are followed in social life: the real 'living law'.[8] As Ehrlich points out, 'The modern practical jurist understands by the word 'Law' generally only Legal Provisions because this is the part of Law which interests him primarily in his everyday practice'.[9]

Thus if one accepts this broader definition of law, there are many areas of law which have no direct relationship to the complex of discourses which will be described here as 'the legal', including the legal profession, legal education, the courts, the judiciary, etc.

The law can be seen as a rule base which has been partially colonised by the legal.[10] While the nominal role of the legal system is to facilitate access to the law and to act as an interface between the law and the community, in practice the legal system operates to control (part of) the operation of the law for the immediate financial benefit of the legal profession and for the economic and power benefits of dominant classes and groups. Thus the legal system serves to inhibit rather than to facilitate access to the law for those who are not part of these dominant groupings. This is not to suggest that the law in itself is an impartial forum. The law has always and, in a patriarchal and capitalist society, will always reflect inequalities in power and wealth. However, it is argued that the operation of the legal increases these imbalances.

III CIVIL AND CRIMINAL LEGAL AID

While not wishing to draw a rigid dividing line between the operation of the civil and criminal law, this author believes that the overtly repressive nature of the criminal justice system and the legalisation of the criminal justice system (which is examined in the next section of this chapter) mean that the roles which are to be played by criminal and civil legal aid are fundamentally different. He has argued elsewhere that the role of the civil legal aid system is not determined

---

[6] Cotterrell, R., *The Sociology of the Law*, London: Butterworths, 1992, p. 9.
[7] *Ibid.*
[8] Ehrlich, E., 'The Sociology of Law', *Harvard Law Review*, 1922, vol. 36, p. 130.
[9] *Ibid.*, p. 132.
[10] The relationship between the law and the legal — both of which can be seen as systems of discursive practices — is a complex one. In many areas the legal operates to control access to the law, yet in many other instances the legal partially constructs the law itself.

by functional factors such as industrialisation, development, religion, divorce or political unrest, although it may be (and frequently is) influenced by these factors.[11] He argued that the factors most likely to affect the development of civil legal aid were the role of the legal profession (either in influencing the expansion of legal aid in areas of benefit to its members (UK, France), or of resisting legal aid as contrary to the interests of the dominant sections of the legal profession (Ireland)) and that of the state administration. However, in contrast, it may be argued that there is a greater functional role for the criminal legal aid system in common law countries. It is noteworthy that spending on criminal legal aid equals or exceeds that on civil legal aid in many common law countries (in contrast to the situation in civil law countries, where it normally accounts for a relatively small proportion of the legal aid budget).[12] In both the US and Ireland, the courts have held that there is a constitutional right to criminal legal aid, although neither legal system has recognised a similar right to civil legal aid.[13] In Ireland, this recognition of a constitutional right to criminal legal aid corresponded with a period of sharp increase in the criminal case-load faced by the courts, increased use of repressive legislation and an increase in committals to prison.

IV   THE ROLE OF THE CRIMINAL JUSTICE SYSTEM

The function of the criminal justice system is largely to define people who have done certain (deviant) things as criminals and to punish them for their deviant behaviour in whatever manner is considered to be appropriate. The criminal justice system clearly represents one of society's most obvious uses of repressive force on the members of the population: Walter Benjamin speaks of the law's interest in the monopolisation of the use of legitimate violence (*Gewalt*).[14]

In practice, the criminal courts operate largely by constructing the accused person as a criminal through what Garfinkel has described as a degradation

---

[11] Cousins, *op. cit.*

[12] Legal Action Group, *A Strategy for Justice*, London: LAG, 1992; Conseil d'État, *L'aide juridique pour un meilleur accès au droit et à la justice*, Paris: La documentation française, 1991.

[13] The right to criminal legal aid was expressly recognised in the European Convention on Human Rights and this right has been developed in several cases by the European Court of Human Rights — see Ashworth, A., 'Legal Aid, Human Rights and Criminal Justice', at chapter 3 of this volume for further discussion. The European Court of Human Rights did establish a right to legal aid in some civil cases in *Airey* v *Ireland* (1979) 2 EHRR 305, but this appears to have been a one-off development and there has been no subsequent progression of the Court's jurisprudence in this area.

[14] 'Zur Kritik der Gewalt', quoted in Derrida, J., *Force de loi*, Paris: Galilée, 1994.

ceremony.[15] However, as Garfinkel shows, degradation ceremonies are quite complex, and the ideological and political role of the courts will not be carried out if the accused is seen as a helpless individual being persecuted by a powerful state system (rather than as an individual being fairly judged by an impartial system of criminal justice). Therefore, it is necessary that the system be seen to be 'fair' and 'legitimate'.

In common law countries, the exercise of coercion through the criminal justice system has been taken over more and more by the state and, in part, by the legal system. For example, in Ireland, the prosecution of criminal offences, which originally was left to private individuals, became more and more a function of the state, with the appointment of Crown Solicitors for each of the court circuits in 1801 and the appointment of Sessional Crown Solicitors to prosecute at quarter sessions in 1836.[16] In 1924, legislation provided that all criminal charges on indictment were to be prosecuted by the Attorney-General (the power has now generally been transferred to the Director of Public Prosecutions).[17] Thus, at present, only the state can prosecute in relation to indictable proceedings; and, of course, the people employed or retained by the state to exercise the prosecutorial function are lawyers.[18]

Similarly, in England and Wales, the perceived tension between the role of investigator and prosecutor led to the establishment of the Crown Prosecution Service (CPS) as a system of ensuring independent supervision of prosecutions and to take over all prosecutions initiated by the police forces in England and Wales.[19] The prosecutorial functions of the CPS are carried out by lawyers.

There has, therefore, in at least several common law countries, been a legalisation of the operation of the criminal justice system.[20] In the context of

---

[15] Garfinkel, H., 'Conditions of Successful Degradation Ceremonies', *American Journal of Sociology*, 1956, vol. 61, p. 420. See also McBarnet, D., 'Pre-Trial Procedures and the Construction of Conviction' in Carlen, P. (ed.), *The Sociology of Law*, Keele: University of Keele, 1976, p. 172.

[16] Ryan, E. and Magee, P., *The Irish Criminal Process*, Dublin: Mercier, 1983; McCabe, D., "That part that laws of kings can cause or cure': Crown Prosecution and Jury Trial at Longford Assizes, 1830–45', in Gillespie, R. and Moran, G. (eds), *Longford: Essays in County History*, Dublin: Lilliput, 1991. The tasks fulfilled by the Crown Solicitors were taken over by the newly appointed State Solicitors after Irish independence from the UK in 1922.

[17] Section 9 of the Criminal Justice (Administration) Act 1924. This position was confirmed in the current constitution of Ireland adopted in 1937, Article 30.3 of which provides that 'all crimes and offences prosecuted in any court ... other than a court of summary jurisdiction shall be prosecuted in the name of the People and at the suit of the Attorney-General or some other person authorised in accordance with law to act for that purpose'.

[18] It remains the case that the majority of criminal offences are prosecuted in the lower courts where private prosecution is allowed and where, in practice, the police rather than lawyers prosecute in many cases.

[19] Crawford, A., 'Access to Justice and Alternatives to Litigation in England and Wales', 1994, conference paper, Lille.

[20] As will be seen below, there has been an opposite tendency in relation to less serious offences with a growth in the disposal of cases outside the court system.

the discussion of the distinction between the law and the legal set out above, the aspects of the criminal justice system which are being addressed in this chapter operate almost entirely within the legal. Therefore, the criminal legal aid system — unlike at least some aspects of civil legal aid and advice — can be seen as operating at the heart of the legal. It is in that context that we must examine the developing importance of the system of criminal legal aid.

V THE ROLE OF CRIMINAL LEGAL AID

As discussed above, it is important for the role of the criminal justice system that its 'degradation ceremonies' work effectively and do not malfunction by presenting the accused in a favourable light as a helpless person persecuted by a Kafkaesque system. In common law countries, the criminal legal aid system plays an important part in ensuring that the criminal justice system generally is seen to be fair and legitimate. Thus this role of ensuring fairness has largely been captured by lawyers rather than by, for example, psychologists or social workers who play lesser roles in the system. This is not surprising given the important role played by lawyers generally in the criminal justice system in common law countries. What is surprising to someone from a common law background is that civil law countries apparently have adopted different methods of ensuring legitimacy in relation to their criminal justice systems, and criminal legal aid plays a much less important role in these countries. Unfortunately, a comparison with civil law countries must remain outside the scope of this chapter, but this issue raises interesting questions for future research.

VI CRIMINAL LEGAL AID IN THE REPUBLIC OF IRELAND

As a brief case study in this area, we will examine the development of criminal legal aid in Ireland. Unfortunately, the absence of comparative studies in this area means that it is not clear to what extent the Irish developments can be taken as broadly representative of developments in other common law countries.

In Ireland until the 1960s, legal aid was provided only in relation to murder cases (and even here it appears that there was no statutory basis for the practice).[21] A more comprehensive system of legal aid was provided for in the Criminal Justice (Legal Aid) Act 1962, although this legislation did not come into force until 1965 due to disagreement with the legal profession as to the fees to be paid. This Act provided for legal aid where a person's means were

---

[21] See generally, Carney, C., 'The Growth of Legal Aid in the Republic of Ireland', *Irish Jurist*, 1979, vol. XIV, pp. 61 and 211.

'insufficient to enable him to obtain legal aid' and where 'by reason of the gravity of the charge or of exceptional circumstances it is essential in the interests of justice that he should have legal aid in the preparation and conduct of his defence'.[22]

Decisions in relation to applications for legal aid are made by the courts. No means test is set out in the legislation and it appears that applications are rarely refused on this ground. The 'gravity' test is normally interpreted as meaning that the liberty of the individual may potentially be at risk should the facts alleged be proved, or as involving other exceptional circumstances (such as where a person might lose his or her job as a result of a successful prosecution).

The introduction of the legal aid scheme took place at a time when there was little indication of any serious increase in crime rates and appears to have been part of a tidying up exercise in relation to criminal justice and a move to bring the Irish legislation into line with that in other countries, in particular the United Kingdom.[23] In the early years of the scheme the number of persons availing themselves of legal aid was very low (c. 300 per annum in the period 1966–71), as was the cost of the scheme, which did not exceed £10,000 per annum until 1970–71.[24] However, the 1970s saw a transformation of the operation of the criminal legal aid system — although without any reform of the underlying legislation. This transformation led to a sharp increase both in the numbers using legal aid and in the costs of the legal aid scheme which was caused, first by a decision of the Irish Supreme Court recognising a right to legal aid under the Irish constitution, which led to a substantial increase in the numbers able to avail themselves of legal aid, and, secondly, by pressure from the legal professions which led to a sharp rise in the level of fees payable.[25] The first-mentioned factor increased the number of legally aided cases. The second increased the cost per case, and by making it more attractive for lawyers to take on such cases is likely to have increased the availability of legal aid and, indirectly, the numbers of applications for legal aid. As the number of persons qualifying for legal aid up to the mid-1970s was very low, and as the judiciary were bound to grant legal aid in appropriate cases, an increase in applications almost inevitably led to an increase in the number of cases in which legal aid was granted. Thus the second factor is also likely to have led to an increase in the number of legally aided cases.

While the original introduction of the criminal legal aid scheme appears to have been unrelated to any rise in crime, its transformation in the course of the

[22] There is no system of state-funded criminal legal advice in Ireland.
[23] There were two other Criminal Justice Acts in 1960 and 1964, and an Inter-Departmental Committee on the Prevention of Crime and Treatment of Offenders was set up in 1962.
[24] Carney, op. cit. p. 223.
[25] Criminal Legal Aid Review Committee, Report, Prl. 9986, Dublin: Stationery Office, 1981, p. 13.

mid-1970s must be seen in the context of several important developments in the criminal justice system. First, during a period which stretched from the Independence of Ireland in 1921 to the 1960s, there had been a level of reported crime substantially below that of most European nations and the level remained fairly static. However, there was a sharp rise in crime from the mid-1960s on: 'The mid-1960s in Ireland represented a watershed, breaking the long-standing pattern of stable levels of crime....'[26] This was reflected in a sharp increase in the level of criminal proceedings coming before the courts in relation to indictable offences. Such proceedings doubled in the decade after 1965, rising from 10,568 in that year to 21,028 in 1976.[27]

Secondly, there had been a series of repressive measures introduced in the light of the troubles in Northern Ireland, including the increased use of the powers to detain people in custody without charge for up to 48 hours under the Offences Against the State Act 1939, the revival of the non-jury Special Criminal Courts, and the introduction of the Emergency Powers Act 1976 which allowed detention without trial for up to seven days.

Lastly, in the mid-1970s there was considerable public disquiet about the maltreatment of persons in police custody (which ultimately led to the establishment in 1977 of a government committee to recommend safeguards for persons in custody).[28]

Thus the legitimacy of the Irish criminal justice system can be seen to have been under some pressure in the mid-1970s as a result of both the sharp rise in crime and the repressive response to the spin-off from the Northern Ireland situation.

It was against this background of an increasingly busy and repressive system of criminal justice that the case of *State (Healy) v Donoghue* [1976] IR 325[29] was heard. An 18-year-old youth had been charged with breaking and entering a building and committing a felony therein. He pleaded guilty and was sentenced to three months' detention. He did not apply for legal aid and was not informed of his right to apply for legal aid. Subsequently, he and a 16-year-old youth were charged with larceny. They both pleaded guilty, but later they applied for and were granted legal aid. However, they were

[26] Rottman, D., *The Criminal Justice System : Policy and Performance*, Dublin: National Economic and Social Council, 1985, p. 91. Between 1964 and 1975 police statistics indicate a 4.3 fold increase in housebreaking, an 11.4 fold increase in robberies, and similar increases in other areas of criminal activity.
[27] Source: *Statistical Abstracts* (Dublin: Stationery Office). The increase in non-indictable proceedings was even more marked, almost tripling over this period from 140,000 in 1965 to 395,000 in 1976.
[28] See MacBride, S. (ed.), *Crime and Punishment*, Dublin: Ward River Press, 1982.
[29] See also the decision of the Supreme Court of the USA in *Gideon v Wainwright* (1963) 372 US 335 (which overturned an earlier decision in *Betts v Brady* (1942) 316 US 415) which was referred to by the Irish court.

subsequently sentenced to six months' detention at a hearing at which the legal aid solicitor was not present.[30] The youths brought judicial review proceedings to challenge the legality of the convictions. The Irish Supreme Court held that article 38 of the Irish constitution (which provides that 'No person shall be tried on any criminal charge save in due course of law') imported the requirement of fair procedures which furnished an accused person with an adequate opportunity to defend himself or herself against the charge made. Accordingly, where an accused person faced a serious charge and needed the assistance of a lawyer, if the accused was unable to pay for that assistance, the administration of justice required that (i) legal aid should be made available under the 1962 Act, even if not applied for; and (ii) the trial should not go ahead against the accused's wishes without such assistance. Chief Justice O'Higgins held that:

> Where a man's liberty is at stake or where he faces a very severe penalty which may affect his welfare or his livelihood, justice may require more than the application of normal and fair procedures in relation to his trial. *Facing ... the power of the state which is his accuser*, the person charged may be unable to defend himself adequately because of ignorance, lack of education, youth or other incapacity. In such circumstances his plight may require, if justice is to be done, that he should have legal assistance. In such circumstances, if he cannot provide such assistance by reason of lack of means, does justice under the Constitution also require that he be aided in his defence? In my view it does.[31] (emphasis added)

The judgments of the other members of the Supreme Court also reflect the view that criminal trials must be seen to be fair.[32]

A Criminal Legal Aid Review Committee, appointed by the Minister for Justice in 1975 to review the operation of the criminal legal aid scheme, stated that the Healy case 'has had an enormous bearing on legal aid because it substantially altered what appeared to be a widely-held understanding of the rights of an accused person in regard to legal aid'.[33]

This was not the only decision at this time concerning the importance of legal representation for an accused person. The Court of Criminal Appeal held in

---

[30] Solicitors involved in the legal aid scheme were on strike at the time in a dispute over fees.

[31] [1976] IR 325 at 350.

[32] Henchy J at p. 354; Griffin J at p. 357; Kenny J at pp. 363–4.

[33] Criminal Legal Aid Review Committee, *op. cit.*, p. 15. Unfortunately, the Committee took a very narrow view of its remit and carefully refrained from setting out any principles by which to judge the operation of a criminal legal aid scheme or objectives for such a scheme. This reflected the fact that the Committee's establishment was largely a device to settle an ongoing dispute between the Government and the legal professions as to fees which had led to the professions withdrawing from the scheme.

People v Madden [1977] IR 336, that a person held in detention has a right of reasonable access to a legal adviser.

Thus, it may be argued that the decision of the Supreme Court in 1976 reflected the need to legitimate the functioning of the criminal justice system in the light of the challenges to that legitimacy caused by the developments outlined above.

VII   THE STRUCTURE OF THE IRISH SCHEME

There have, no doubt, been other factors involved in the development of criminal legal aid. Goriely has argued that the criminal legal aid scheme in England and Wales plays a role in assisting the processing of criminal cases before the courts and that this was a major factor in the growth of the legal aid scheme in that jurisdiction.[34] However, there has been no empirical study of this issue in the Irish courts and this author has discovered no significant evidence that this factor encouraged the Irish courts to increase the availability of legal aid. Indeed, there are many counter-arguments that the greater involvement of lawyers in fact slows down the operation of the courts.[35]

One factor which clearly has influenced the development of the legal aid scheme has been the views of the legal profession. In particular, the profession has influenced the costs and structure of the scheme. This is in line with the findings in relation to the development of civil legal aid.[36] As noted above, there were ongoing disputes between the legal profession and the state as to the level of remuneration to be paid. These delayed the implementation of the scheme from 1962 to 1965 and subsequently resulted in the establishment in 1975 of a Committee to review the operation of the scheme.[37] This Committee (chaired by a judge and consisting of three civil servants, two barristers and two solicitors) focused heavily on the question of the appropriate level of fees and produced an interim report on this issue in 1977 which allowed the settlement of the then 'breakdown' of the scheme. However, such disputes have continued to arise from time to time.

A second issue considered by the Committee was the appropriate structure for the provision of legal aid. The scheme operates on the basis of a panel system, whereby solicitors (and barristers) opt to undertake legal aid work. The accused is entitled to choose any lawyer on the area legal aid panel. The Review Committee examined the feasibility of introducing alternative systems of delivering legal aid, including a duty solicitor scheme (involving solicitors in

---

[34] See Goriely, *op. cit.*
[35] Criminal Legal Aid Review Committee, *op. cit.*, pp. 29 *et seq.*
[36] Cousins, *op. cit.*
[37] Criminal Legal Aid Review Committee, *op. cit.*

private practice being available on a rota basis to represent defendants in the lower courts) and a public defender system. The Committee recommended that a duty solicitor scheme should be introduced on a pilot basis, but this recommendation was never implemented. The Committee was unable to come to an agreed conclusion in relation to a public defender scheme. Some unnamed members (presumably civil servants) felt that such a system was an option which should be kept open, but other members were strongly against this proposal. They cited the lack of independence, including a 'very real danger' that a state employee would be less committed to the defence of accused persons than would an 'independent' private practitioner; the historical objection that accused persons would be particularly suspicious of defence lawyers who were on the state payroll and, therefore, part of the 'establishment' (particularly before the Special Criminal Court); the fact that it would not be an economic proposition to introduce such a system on a national basis; and the fact that the introduction of a limited public defender system would involve a severe curtailment of the accused's choice of lawyer. Not surprisingly, this option has not been pursued.

Interestingly, the Committee as a whole, in the context of its discussion of the duty solicitor scheme, did state that 'a limitation in choice of lawyer does not seem to us to be objectionable in principle'.[38] The Committee referred to the judgment of O'Higgins CJ in *Healy*, in which he stated *obiter* that

> ... I would be slow to hold that the Constitution requires the choice of lawyer which the statute gives. I can imagine circumstances in which, for one reason or another, the state cannot provide a choice of lawyer; in such cases the provision of a designated lawyer or lawyers, trained and experienced for the task, is an adequate discharge of the state's duty to provide legal assistance for the person without means.[39]

However, whatever may be the position in principle, sections of the legal profession and the higher judiciary have in practice been strongly opposed to any restriction on freedom of choice. This is indicated by the reservations expressed by some members of the Committee in relation to the restrictions implicit in a public defender scheme. The Committee sought the personal views of the Chief Justice on this point. The Chief Justice felt that a public defender scheme would discharge the state's duties under the constitution, but he thought that such a system should be introduced 'only if the panel system proved inoperative'. He would opt for a panel system rather than a public defender

---

[38] *Op. cit.*, p. 52.
[39] *State (Healy)* v *Donoghue* [1976] IR 325 at 352.

scheme 'because of the option and choice which it provides for the person charged'.[40]

The issue of the degree of choice required under the scheme arose in a High Court case in the late 1980s (*State (Freeman)* v *Connellan* [1987] ILRM 470). Faced with the fact that, in the Dublin city area, criminal legal aid work was dominated by six solicitors, and perceiving this to lead to disruption of the courts' workloads (due to the inability of these solicitors to be in different places at the same time), the district justices (who deal with all summary offences and initially with all more serious matters) had developed a practice of allocating legal aid solicitors on an alphabetical basis from the panel (in the absence of good reasons to the contrary). A defendant who requested the services of one of the six solicitors was told that he would have to take the solicitor appointed by the district justice. He challenged this decision by way of judicial review. The 1962 Act is silent as to any right to choose one's solicitor, but the Criminal Justice (Legal Aid) Regulations 1965 provide that the court 'shall, having taken into consideration the representations (if any) of the person … assign to him a solicitor'.[41] Barr J held that where an accused person nominates a particular solicitor, the judge should refuse to assign this solicitor only where there is good and sufficient reason for doing so and should state the reason for doing so and offer the accused a further choice. The judge should not choose a solicitor himself unless the accused does not nominate any solicitor, or where any nominated are not acceptable for good and sufficient reason. Barr J stated that this interpretation was in accord with the nature of the legal aid scheme, which included two important dimensions, i.e., the opportunity given to each person to nominate his or her own solicitor and the creation of panels of solicitors.[42]

A further issue concerning the structure of the scheme relates to the fact that the scheme applies to legal *aid* only (i.e., representation in court) and not to legal advice. This issue was considered by the Review Committee which received several submissions arguing that legal advice should be included in the scheme. While the introduction of a limited form of legal advice service was recommended by the Committee, this recommendation has never been implemented. In practice, it appears that legal aid lawyers will provide legal advice to persons on a gratuitous basis — particularly where a future grant of legal aid is likely to be made.

In summary, criminal legal aid is provided entirely on an individual basis in court by private solicitors. It thus is provided on the same basis as traditional legal services and does not involve any challenge to the status quo. Persons

---

[40] Quoted in Criminal Legal Aid Review Committee, *op. cit.* p. 58.
[41] Regulation 7(1).
[42] See also the similar decision in *Mulhall* v *O'Donnell* [1989] ILRM 367.

who are accused of 'serious' offences who cannot afford a lawyer are provided with one by the state which is, therefore, seen to be acting in a fair manner. If, playing within the existing rules of the game, the lawyer can secure the acquittal of the accused, the fairness of the system is seen to be enhanced; if he or she cannot then the chances of a successful degradation ceremony have been improved. This model of legal aid suits the state (in particular the judicial branch) by providing legitimation for the criminal justice system; and it suits the legal profession by providing funding for the profession and by operating within the model of traditional legal practice.

VIII ALTERNATIVE FORMS OF 'ACCESS TO JUSTICE'?

Criminal legal aid is often presented as a method of ensuring access to justice in the area of criminal law. It has been argued that this is not in fact the role that it plays in common law countries. To what extent can alternative forms of dispute resolution provide other (cheaper) methods of ensuring 'access to justice'? This approach would rely on resort to a notion of 'community' in order to legitimate its application in the area of criminal justice. However, Crawford has argued that rather than seeing these approaches as 'alternatives *to* litigation':

> we need to consider the extent to which they are part of a much larger set of disputing processes which supplement or assist the formal court in its work. In other words they may better be understood as 'alternative methods *of* litigation'.[43]

In particular, alternative dispute resolution in the area of criminal justice has been criticised on two grounds.[44] It is argued that, first, it is simply a method of dealing with the mass production of criminal cases which has created an overload in the court system and, secondly, that it is a way of extending social control into areas previously untouched by the criminal justice system. Thus one can argue that these methods constitute alternative forms *of* criminal justice rather than alternatives *to* criminal justice.

Bonafé-Schmitt's study of mediation in the US, UK, France and Canada has shown the way in which these types of systems have developed in the area of criminal justice in the US and France (promoted by the judiciary and also, in the US, by the legal profession).[45] However, in contrast to forms of alternative dispute resolution which have emerged in civil cases, there has been relatively

---

[43] Crawford, A., *op. cit.*, p. 3. See also chapter 15 in this volume.
[44] Bonafé-Schmitt, J.-P., *La médiation: une justice douce*, Paris: Syros-Alternatives, 1992.
[45] *Ibid.*

little development in the area of criminal justice in the UK and Ireland. In contrast, there has been a considerable growth in the administrative disposal of potential criminal cases (by way of police caution, caution plus, and fixed penalties).[46] However, the areas in which these types of procedures have been introduced are not generally ones in which the criminal legal aid system would have been involved in any case.

It may be argued that, currently in common law countries, there are few real 'alternative' approaches in the area of criminal legal aid, i.e., ones which attempt to use the law to challenge the existing approach. One example might be the work of some law centres in the 1960s and 1970s, where an attempt was made to go beyond working on an individual basis in relation to criminal cases and to try to develop a more policy based challenge to the existing criminal justice system and the way in which it impacted on specific groups of people. However, this type of work has not continued in any widespread way to date. Other alternatives, such as mediation services, are largely methods simply of managing the overload of the criminal justice system and they do not provide a real alternative to criminal justice. Their function is to provide a cheaper criminal justice system which also appears fair and legitimate. However, these 'alternatives' do not challenge the basic premises underlying the existing system.

IX CONCLUSION

The criminal justice system appears to be an exception to the general trend in the provision of social services away from the use of coercive power leading to incarceration and towards a greater reliance on indirect control by way of supervision and expertise. Carceral measures, which once were common in many areas of policy, have been replaced or transformed: workhouses have long disappeared from social security policy; lunatic asylums and industrial and reform schools have been abolished or transformed — the number of children and people with mental health problems in long-term residence in carceral institutions has declined sharply and there has been a shift from involuntary committal by the courts to 'voluntary' self-admission. If a similar tendency had occurred in the area of criminal justice, one would expect a decline in the number of cases before the courts and in the numbers committed to prison, with an increase in alternative methods of addressing this issue (including policies such as a comprehensive DNA register, policing of potential offenders by psychologists and social workers, non-judicial disposal of

---

[46] Crawford, A., 'Alternatives to Prosecution: Access to, or Exits from, Criminal Justice?', at chapter 15 of this volume.

offences, development of alternative forms of dispute resolution and a much greater dependence on non-custodial sentences). While many of these types of policies have developed, they have remained largely peripheral to the processing of more serious crime by the courts.

The reasons for the continued (and increased) operation of coercion in the area of criminal justice are outside the scope of this chapter.[47] However, these tendencies do emphasise yet again the need for legitimation of the criminal justice system. The more exceptional a mode of social control becomes, the greater the need for the appearance of fairness to be maintained. It has been argued that criminal legal aid plays an important role in this legitimation. It would appear that only a shift in the operation of the criminal justice system away from a reliance on the use of coercive force (or a decline in the need for legitimation of that force) will reduce the role of criminal legal aid. In that context any proposals for the reform of criminal legal aid which would significantly affect the degree to which the criminal justice system is seen to be legitimate may well be counter-productive for the state in the longer term.

---

[47] See Foucault, M., *Discipline and Punish: The Birth of the Prison*, London: Allen Lane, 1977.

6

Keyholders to Criminal Justice?: Solicitors and Applications for Criminal Legal Aid[1]

David Wall

Underlying the criminal legal aid system is a bureaucratic model of organisation which requires rational criteria to be applied efficiently at all stages. The conventional understanding is that solicitors possess both professional (legal) knowledge of, and practical experience gained from, applying for criminal legal aid,[2] which are combined to unlock the system by invoking the correct criteria to gain access to its resources. Simply put, if the courts are the gatekeepers to the criminal legal aid system, the Widgery criteria[3] are the keys and solicitors are its keyholders. The 'keyholding' role is to be institutionalised by recent policy initiatives, in particular, standard fees,[4] franchising[5] and block contracts.[6]

This chapter explores the solicitor's role in the applications process. By drawing upon empirical research findings, it will be argued that the solicitor's role is far more complex than the simple keyholding model suggests. It will

---

[1] The author is indebted to Richard Young and John Bell for their incisive and constructive suggestions and comments on previous drafts of this chapter.
[2] Unless stated otherwise, the term 'criminal legal aid' is used to refer to criminal legal aid in the magistrates' courts.
[3] A colloquial term for the legal merits test for criminal legal aid set out in s. 22(2) of the Legal Aid Act 1988.
[4] Legal Aid in Criminal and Care Proceedings (Costs) (Amendments) Regulations 1995 (SI 1995 No. 952).
[5] Legal Aid Act 1988, s. 4(4).
[6] Lord Chancellor's Department, *Legal Aid — Targeting Need: The future of publicly funded help in solving legal problems and disputes in England and Wales*, Cm 2854, London: HMSO, 1995, p. 24, para. 4.18 (subsequently referred to as the Green Paper).

also be argued that the operation of the application process is characterised by the competing rationalities that arise from the conflicting professional agendas of the groups involved in the process. These observations challenge some of the 'rational' assumptions that lie behind the policy initiatives.

The first part of this chapter looks briefly at why the role of the solicitor in the administration of criminal legal aid has become an important consideration. The middle section, divided into five parts, draws upon empirical findings in order to explore the nature of application practices and to look at when and why applications are made. The 'keyholding' hypothesis is tested by comparing solicitors' relative successes and failures in legal aid applications. The final part discusses the implications of the analysis for the recent policy initiatives.

I   RECENT POLICY DEVELOPMENTS IN CRIMINAL LEGAL AID

Before exploring the nature of solicitors' application practices it is important to look at why the role of the solicitor in the administration of criminal legal aid has become an important issue. The Legal Aid Board's franchising policy introduced in 1993–94 devolves much of the overall responsibility for administering legal aid to the solicitor. Similarly, the recent proposals in the Green Paper to contract out blocks of criminal legal aid cases will transfer responsibility for determining the legal merits and financial eligibility of many criminal legal aid applications from the courts to solicitors. Solicitors will effectively become the new administrators of criminal legal aid. However, this role will take place within the framework of policies that are designed to increase control over that part of the legal profession that provides publicly-funded legal services. Franchising, quality control mechanisms and the conditions under which block contracts are set out are employment conditions which provide a mechanism of governance and define a new type of legal professional, the 'hybrid public service professional'.[7]

II   APPLICATIONS FOR CRIMINAL LEGAL AID

There is very little literature, if any, relating to this specific area of legal practice, particularly regarding the profile of applications. This section looks at who applies for legal aid, when they apply for it and what they apply for.

---

[7] For further discussion of the 'hybrid public service professional' see Wall, D. S., 'Legal Aid, Lawyers and the Poor' (forthcoming).

(i) Making an application for criminal legal aid

The application form for criminal legal aid[8] has two parts. The first deals with administrative matters such as the personal details of the applicant and the case against him or her. A brief statement is also requested about the applicant's financial circumstances.[9] (The financial means test is not discussed in this chapter.) The second part of the application relates to the legal merits test, and it is constructed around the s. 22(2)[10] Widgery criteria. The first four questions[11] seek to ascertain the seriousness of the case against the applicant if convicted. These questions ask applicants if they are 'likely to lose their liberty,'[12] if they are presently subject to a suspended prison sentence or court order, if they are in real danger of losing their livelihood,[13] and/or if they are in real danger of suffering serious damage to their reputation.

The next five questions[14] seek information on both the complexities of the case and the consequences of the applicant not being able to participate adequately in the adversarial process. Applicants are asked if their case involves a substantial question of law, whether or not witnesses have to be traced on their behalf, whether they are unable to follow the court proceedings either because their English is bad or because they suffer from a disability, whether the case will involve expert cross-examination of a prosecution witness and whether it is in someone else's interests that they are represented.[15]

The procedure for completing the form is that applicants tick boxes relevant to the criteria they invoke and then give supporting details. The instructions to the applicant are as follows:

> If you [the applicant] need help completing this form, and especially if you have previous convictions, you should see a solicitor. He [sic] may be able to advise you free of charge or at a reduced fee.[16]

---

[8] 'Form 1', as prescribed by the Legal Aid in Criminal and Care Proceedings (General) Regulations 1995 (SI 1995 No. 542), regs 11 and 18, and sch. 2. Its format was changed with effect from 1 May 1995 and brought the questions it poses into line with the Legal Aid Act 1988 s. 22(2); the structure largely remains the same as before.

[9] Complete financial details are submitted on Form 5 as prescribed by the Legal Aid in Criminal and Care Proceedings (General) Regulations 1995 (SI 1995 No. 542), reg. 23.

[10] Legal Aid Act 1988.

[11] Relating to s. 22(2)(a) of the Legal Aid Act 1988.

[12] Formerly phrased as 'in real danger of custody'.

[13] Formerly 'in real danger of losing their job'.

[14] Relating to s. 22(2)(b)–(e) of the Legal Aid Act 1988.

[15] This question replaces 'the case is a complex one'.

[16] Legal Aid in Criminal and Care Proceedings (General) Regulations 1995, regs 11 and 18.

The implication here is that the applicant completes the form with help from, or under the guidance of, a solicitor. However, only a handful of the 5,500 applications for criminal legal aid studied by Wall and Wood,[17] and the 1,201 examined by Young et al.,[18] were completed by the clients themselves. For the most part they were made by the solicitor or an employee of the solicitor's practice. One court clerk told Wall and Wood that:

> In theory the defendant is supposed to complete the form but in practice the solicitor gets the defendant to sign the form to say that the information given in it is true.[19]

Young et al. confirm this picture:

> Although legal aid applications are in the name of the defendant, almost invariably they are completed by a legal adviser with the applicant merely appending his or her signature.[20]

The process of application is governed by the applicant's solicitor.[21] It is the solicitor who not only takes the initiative to apply for legal aid, but who also calculates whether or not the applicant falls within the relevant rules regarding financial eligibility[22] and will pass the merits test successfully. Observations of the application process, and interviews with practitioners, revealed that solicitors liked to exercise control over the application process for four main reasons. First, the legal aid certificate is an important source of income to the legal practitioner: 'that certificate is worth money to me'[23] one solicitor proclaimed. Secondly, clients are not always aware of the importance of the application form and, in the solicitors' experience, tend to leave the application to the last minute or to forget about it altogether. Thirdly, the clients prefer to leave the application to the solicitor because of the complex legal knowledge and legal expertise required to complete it. Fourthly, defendants are

---

[17] Wall, D. S. and Wood, A., *The Administration of Criminal Legal Aid in the Magistrates' Courts of England and Wales: Final Report to the ESRC*, Leeds: Centre for Criminal Justice Studies, 1994. This research was funded by the ESRC (awards nos. R000232673 and R000234528) and was carried out at the University of Leeds.

[18] See Young, R., Moloney, T. and Sanders, A., *In the Interests of Justice?: The Determination of Criminal Legal Aid Applications by Magistrates' Courts in England and Wales*, London: Legal Aid Board, 1992.

[19] Decision-maker DW CDM1 (Wall, observation and interview notes).

[20] Young et al., *op. cit.*, p. 81.

[21] See discussion later about the governance of the client.

[22] Legal Aid Board, *Legal Aid Handbook 1995*, London: Sweet & Maxwell, 1995, p. 459.

[23] Solicitor 7 – q. 11 (Wall, observation and interview notes).

encouraged by the information pamphlets — and also, as noted above, by the instructions on the legal aid form itself — to apply through a solicitor.[24]

(ii) Applications for criminal legal aid

Wall and Wood found that the majority (86 per cent) of all applicants were male, in their mid-20s (average age 26 years) and that the majority were unemployed (85 per cent). They were mostly adults (95 per cent), although the reorganisation of the juvenile courts into youth courts by the Criminal Justice Act 1991, which took the majority of 17-year-olds out of the adult courts, slightly reduced the percentage of applications made to the adult court.[25]

Just over half of applications (55 per cent) for criminal legal aid were made to the court before the first appearance of the case.[26] The remainder were submitted after the first hearing but prior to conviction.[27] It is estimated that between a fifth and a quarter of applications for criminal legal aid were made by the solicitor to the magistrates sitting in court. While most courts accept applications both before the first hearing and during a court appearance, it was apparent that court clerks made a conscious effort to 'steer' legal aid applications away from magistrates as they felt that the magistrates were not able properly to determine an application.[28]

Just under half (47 per cent) of the applications were for one offence only and the remainder (53 per cent) were multiple offence applications containing an average of three offences per application.

Since the purpose of each application is to demonstrate that legal aid should be granted 'in the interests of justice', it is to be expected that the majority of offences will be serious in nature. In fact, 70 per cent of applications were for either way offences and 4 per cent for offences triable only on indictment. However, the remaining quarter were for summary offences or for breach of a court order. These statistics are set out in Table 6.1.

---

[24] Legal Aid Board, *A Practical Guide to Legal Aid*, London: Legal Aid Board, 1993, section 5 (para. 5.5).
[25] Wall and Wood, *op. cit.*, para. 3.1.
[26] For example, the application was made to the court process department.
[27] While such applications could be for a wide range of circumstances, e.g., remand, trial etc., most tended to be at the first or second hearing.
[28] Wall and Wood, *op. cit.*, para. 3.1.2.

Table 6.1: Applications for criminal legal aid: type of offence cited in application

Offence types	No.	% of offences[29]
Indictable offences	456	4
Either way offences	7,784	70
Summary non-motoring	556	5
Summary motoring	1,865	17
Breach of court order	535	5
Total	11,196	101

When the offences for which the applications were made were broken down into generic types it was found that the most frequently cited type of offence was 'dishonesty'[30] (43 per cent), followed by driving related offences[31] (20 per cent), offences against the person (14 per cent) and public order offences (9 per cent). The remainder were for breach of a court order (5 per cent), criminal damage (5 per cent) and drug offences (3 per cent). Table 6.2 gives further details of this breakdown.

Table 6.2: Generic types of offence cited in legal aid applications

Offence types	No.	%
Dishonesty	2,323	43
Driving related	1,108	20
Offences against the person	759	14
Public order	517	9
Breach of court order	269	5
Criminal damage	269	5
Drugs	151	3
Other	65	1
Total (offences in applications)	5,461	102

---

[29] The percentages in this and other columns in this chapter are rounded to the nearest number and therefore may add up to a figure in excess of 100%.
[30] Theft, burglary, receiving, deception etc.
[31] Road Traffic Act offences, driving while disqualified, over the permitted limit, etc.

Tables 6.1 and 6.2 clearly indicate that applications contain many minor or 'less serious' offences that would not automatically attract legal aid by themselves.[32] There are four possible reasons for the inclusion of these offences in the applications. The first is that applicants include the less serious offences in the application in order to increase the perceived gravity of the case in question. A number of solicitors interviewed suggested that this was a common practice when they felt that the case might be borderline. However, for this assertion to hold water the analysis of single offence applications should show the marked absence of less serious cases. In fact the single offence applications did show a decrease in the less serious offences, but only by 8 per cent, much less than would be expected. A fifth (19 per cent) of the single offence applications were for summary non-motoring offences, summary motoring offences or for breach of a court order despite the fact that the chances of refusal are much greater than in the more serious cases.[33] While this finding does lend some weight to the theory that solicitors are increasing the perceived 'seriousness' of their applications, it does not provide a full explanation.

The second reason is far more mundane. It relates to the fact that the application form asks applicants to state 'what it is [they] are accused of doing' and suggests that in the section entitled 'case details' they describe 'briefly what [they] are accused of doing, e.g., ''stealing £50 from my employer'', ''kicking a door causing £50 damage''.' Applicants tend to list everything, regardless of its seriousness.[34]

A third reason is that the some applicants were trying to test, or possibly to influence, what the court decision-makers considered to be worthy of legal aid funding, effectively trying to influence their personal criteria for decision-making.

A fourth reason is that applicants were merely performing a bureaucratic exercise by submitting bulk applications in the knowledge that there is a high overall grant rate and therefore a high chance that their application may be granted.

The inclusion of less serious offences probably arises from a combination of the above.

(iii)   The quality of applications for criminal legal aid

Applicants are reasonably consistent around England and Wales in the types of offences for which they apply.[35] This is quite surprising given the differences

---

[32] See Young et al., *op. cit.*, Table 8, p. 41.
[33] *Ibid.*
[34] See the discussion of the single offence orientation of the criminal legal aid system in Wall and Wood, *op. cit.*, para. 4.1.
[35] Young et al., *op. cit.*, pp. 40–7 and Wall and Wood *op. cit.*, para. 3.1.4.

120

in grant rate[36] and the fact that there are regional differences in case mix.[37] This section explores solicitors' application practices and examines the features of the criminal legal aid system which might explain these consistencies when one could expect divergence. First the nature of the consistencies are examined and then the processes which sustain them are discussed.

The most common feature found in examination of the applications for criminal legal aid in the ten courts[38] studied by Wall and Wood and the six courts studied by Young et al., was the poor quality of reasoning to support or sustain applications. In fact it is estimated that, in relation to individual Widgery criteria, as many as 85 per cent of application forms are characterised by poor reasoning.[39] This lack of quality manifested itself in a number of different ways.

Many forms did not contain any substantive information to support the application, and appeared to rely solely upon the type of offence to signify the need for legal aid. As noted above, the legal merits section of the application form requires the applicant to tick boxes in response to a series of statements which relate to the Widgery criteria. It was common for applicants merely to tick the relevant boxes without giving any further details about the claim.

The applications which did have some added information or justification tended to be characterised by standardised wording. It was very common for applicants just to tick the relevant box and repeat the first part of the above statement in the section which asked for brief details or reasons.[40] For example, the first question in the legal merits section asks applicants to respond to the following statement: 'I am in real danger of a custodial sentence for the following reasons.' Applicants would often respond to this statement by stating simply: 'I am in real danger of a custodial sentence.'

Some applications were made to appear more serious or complex by the use of exaggerated claims which would allude to the strong likelihood of the defendant receiving a custodial sentence if convicted. The exaggeration was most noticeable where the offence was not very serious.

A few applications just did not make any sense; their wording was either contradictory or inconsistent, indicating a lack of quality supervision in their completion. Young et al. give some interesting examples of nonsensical claims. One applicant had stated: 'I am in real danger of suffering serious damage to my reputation because I am the son of God.'[41]

---

[36] Young et al., *op. cit.*, p. 13; Wall and Wood, *op. cit.*, para. 3.2.2. The exact extent of the differences depends upon whether the official statistics are used, see Wall and Wood, *op. cit.*, para. 4.1.3.
[37] See supplement to *Judicial Statistics 1991*.
[38] Ten courts were studied in all, of which four were used to collect detailed data.
[39] Young et al., *op. cit.*, p. 74.
[40] *Ibid.*, p. 72.
[41] *Ibid.*, p. 73.

Other applications contained statements that were legalistically written but unconvincing in terms of establishing that the interests of justice would be served. Young et al. found many unconvincing claims were made to support the serious question of law criterion. For example, 'the need to peruse the Theft Act' often appeared in the part of the form which addressed the existence of a serious question of law.

(iv)   Over-reliance upon the custody criterion

Dominating the application process was the consideration of the likelihood of the client receiving a custodial sentence. This was the key formal consideration for both applicants and court clerks, although not the key motivating consideration.[42] Some solicitors even complained about the emphasis on the custody criterion, as in the following example:

> There is too heavy an emphasis on the likelihood of custody. Other criterion [sic] are ignored or are given less weight to.[43]

Yet solicitors invoked the 'danger of custody' criterion in 80 per cent of cases (see Table 6.3), a statistic common to the studies by both Wall and Wood[44] and Young et al.[45] This estimate of the likelihood of custody may be contrasted with the findings of Wall and Wood and Young et al., who discovered that between a fifth (21 per cent) and a sixth (16.3 per cent), respectively, of cases where the custody criterion was invoked resulted in a custodial sentence or committal.[46]

III   SOLICITORS' APPLICATION PRACTICES

If the overall quality of legal aid applications is poor and the overall grant is high, then it is reasonable to assume that through a combination of their professional expertise and their experience of working in the court system, solicitors work out what is and what is not likely to be successful and, in effect, second-guess the decision-making of the court clerk. Many of the solicitors and court decision-makers said that they tried to anticipate the court's decision in this way.[47] This section tests the keyholding theory by drawing upon data collected by Wall and Wood before and after the Criminal Justice Act 1991.

---

[42] See Young, R., 'Will Widgery Do?: Court Clerks, Discretion, and the Determination of Legal Aid Applications', at chapter 7 of this volume.

[43] Solicitors 1 and 2 – q. 12 (Wall, observation and interview notes).

[44] Wall and Wood, *op. cit.*, para. 3.2.7.2.

[45] Young et al., *op. cit.*, p. 25.

[46] Wall and Wood, *op. cit.*, para. 4.2.2 and Young et al., *op. cit.*, p. 66.

[47] Wall and Wood, *op. cit.*, para. 4.2.3.1.

It will be remembered that s. 29 of the 1991 Act (with some qualifications) reduced the overall likelihood of defendants being given custodial sentences effectively by preventing sentencers from taking into consideration either a defendant's previous convictions[48] or the nature of any other offences committed in assessing the seriousness of an offence.[49] Since the likelihood of custody was apparently such an important issue in the determination of criminal legal aid, it was expected that these provisions would impact upon the decision-makers' gate-keeping behaviour by increasing the refusal rate for applications. On the basis of this, it was not unreasonable to expect applicants to adapt their application behaviour to the new decision-making rationale, either by an improvement in the quality of reasoning or by increasing the number of criteria invoked. It is possible to test this hypothesis by drawing upon Wall and Wood's[50] data and comparing decision-making from the spring quarters before and after the Criminal Justice Act 1991 came into force in October 1992.

Each time an application was determined in four target courts,[51] the decision-maker completed a questionnaire. These questionnaires gathered details of the criteria which the solicitor invoked in support of the application and the criteria which the decision-maker claimed were relevant to the decision.[52]

In the pre-Act applications survey, solicitors invoked an average of 2.5 criteria per application,[53] and the decision-makers claimed to have accepted an average of 1.4 of those criteria as being relevant to their decisions to grant or refuse the application. The post-Act survey revealed only a marginal change in the relationship between application and decision-making practice. Solicitors invoked 2.6 criteria, a slight increase, while the decision-makers accepted slightly fewer of those criteria (1.3) as being relevant to the decision. This latter figure represented in percentage terms a fall of 4 per cent from 55 per cent to 51 per cent.[54] While small, this finding suggests that decision-makers may have been influenced by something, possibly the effects of the legislation. Given that this deduction is based upon a broad range of data, it is likely that closer examination of specific criteria would better reveal the nature of any changes. Table 6.3 illustrates the percentage of Widgery criteria invoked in applications.

---

[48] This section was later repealed and replaced by the Criminal Justice Act 1993.
[49] Section 29(2) of the Criminal Justice Act 1991.
[50] Wall and Wood, *op. cit.*, Appendix One, Tables A1–A3.
[51] These courts were chosen because of the similarity of their case mix to the national average.
[52] For further details of the methodology see Wall and Wood, *op. cit.*, para. 1.6.
[53] Figures taken from table 3.2.6.1 in *ibid.*, para. 3.2.6.
[54] This figure can be found in *ibid.*, para. 3.2.7 and is not found in Table 6.1.

Table 6.3: Widgery criteria invoked in applications for criminal legal aid (as a percentage of applications) before and after implementation of the Criminal Justice Act 1991[55]

	Pre-Act	Post-Act	Change
Custody	80%	77%	−3%
Court order	24%	25%	1%
Lose job	8%	8%	0%
Damage to reputation	17%	20%	3%
Question of law	33%	41%	8%
Witnesses to be called	21%	26%	5%
Applicant had disabilities	6%	9%	3%
Cross-examination	33%	36%	3%
Complicated case	13%	15%	2%

Table 6.3 shows that there were some minor changes in the criteria invoked after the Criminal Justice Act 1991 came into force in October 1992. There was a small decrease in the use of the custody criterion and a slight increase in the other criteria, which might be interpreted as a business survival tactic by solicitors seeking to maintain their workload of legally aided clients in a diminishing market. The main observation here is that there was not a marked change in application practices, despite the fact that rumours circulating in the courts just before the Act came into force were predicting increases in the refusal rate of 10 to 20 per cent.[56] This suggests that solicitors felt that things after the Act were very much as they were before and that there was hardly any need to modify their application practices.

At this point it is necessary to compare the criteria invoked with the criteria felt to be important to the decision. The role of the Widgery criteria and the court decision-maker is discussed in greater detail in the next chapter. For the purposes of this discussion, Table 6.4 presents a comparison of the percentage of applicants' criteria found to be relevant by the decision-maker before and after the Criminal Justice Act 1991.

---

[55] Adapted from *ibid.*, Tables A1–A3, column C.
[56] These were the refusal rates anticipated by the senior court personnel. See *ibid.*, para. 4.5, n.161.

Table 6.4: Comparing the percentage of applicants' criteria found to be relevant by the decision-maker before and after the Criminal Justice Act 1991[57]

Pre-Act	Post-Act	Change	
Custody	80%	62%	−18%
Court order	90%	60%	−30%
Lose job	26%	26%	0%
Damage to reputation	29%	20%	−9%
Question of law	35%	32%	−3%
Witnesses to be called	15%	18%	3%
Applicant had disabilities	50%	39%	−11%
Cross-examination	58%	94%	36%
Complicated case	54%	50%	−4%

When the individual Widgery criteria were examined some interesting differences were found between the two sets of data. In the pre-Act data it is quite clear that the criterion found to be most important was that relating to custody. Solicitors had invoked it in 80 per cent of applications (Table 6.3), a figure almost identical to that found by Young et al.[58] Similarly, decision-makers felt that in 80 per cent of those applications (Table 6.4), this Widgery criterion was relevant to their decision. In the 1993 post-Act data, the percentage of all applications in which the custody criterion was invoked by solicitors remained more or less the same, falling by 3 per cent from 80 per cent to 77 per cent. This contrasts with a decrease of almost a quarter (see Table 6.4), from 80 per cent in the pre-Act data to 62 per cent post-Act, in the applications in which decision-makers felt the custody criterion to be relevant to the determination. Similarly with 'subject to a court order,' which is also related to the custody/liberty criterion, the percentage of applications stating that previous 'court orders' existed remained almost the same, but the relative importance accorded by the decision-maker reduced considerably. Table 6.4 shows that in the 1992 data, decision-makers claimed that 90 per cent of the criteria stating that the applicant was subject to a court order were relevant. However, a year later only 60 per cent were said to be still relevant to the decision. These changes were as expected and clearly suggest that the Criminal Justice Act 1991 had made an impact upon the decision-making but not upon

---

[57] Adapted from *ibid.*, Tables A1–A3, column F.
[58] Young et al., *op. cit.*, p. 25.

applications. It therefore follows that the significant reduction by a quarter in the relevance accorded to the custody criterion should translate into an equally marked increase in the refusal rate for criminal legal aid applications. The refusal rates are illustrated in Table 6.5.

Table 6.5: Comparing refusal percentages for 1992 and 1993 (from four courts)

	Official quarterly applications returns	Data from surveys
1992	5%	6%
1993	7%	10%

Table 6.5 shows an increase in the refusal rates calculated from both the official quarterly returns and the applications survey. The comparison of these two rates displays two interesting findings. First, there is a disparity between refusal rates calculated from the target courts' quarterly legal aid returns and those from the applications survey. This disparity was found to be created by inconsistencies in the way that the official legal aid statistics were gathered.[59] Secondly, and more importantly at this point, while both sets of data in Table 6.5 revealed an increase in refusals, neither increase was as great as was originally anticipated. In the applications survey data, the refusal rate rose by 4 per cent and the quarterly returns showed an increase of only 2 per cent. In fact the change is not outside the normal quarterly fluctuation of between 2 to 4 per cent that is often found in the legal aid returns.

The Criminal Justice Act's lack of impact upon the refusal rate begs the question as to what did happen. The answer lies in Table 6.4, which reveals that while the perceived importance of deprivation of liberty/likelihood of custody as grounds for granting legal aid decreased, there was a corresponding increase in the weight given to the expert cross-examination criterion. In 1992, solicitors invoked the 'need for expert cross-examination' criterion in a third (33 per cent) of applications, by 1993 there had been a marginal increase of 3 per cent. Yet when the perceived relevance of the criterion was examined it was found that there had been a considerable increase in the importance given to the criterion by the decision-makers. The criterion was seen as relevant by decision-makers in just over a half of cases (58 per cent) in the first applications

---

[59] Wall and Wood, *op. cit.*, para. 4.1.3.

survey, compared with nearly all (94 per cent) in the second survey; as if the decision-makers wanted to maintain the same grant rate as before the Act.

This action may be interpreted in a number of different ways. First, there genuinely was a massive increase in the need for the expert cross-examination of a prosecution witness, which is unlikely since the criterion was not invoked by the solicitors. Secondly, the greater use of the cross-examination criterion may have been a presentational strategy for the benefit of the researchers to justify what on the surface appears to be an unnecessarily high grant rate. This is possible, although researchers are not generally regarded by court decision-makers as people to whom they must account for their actions. A more plausible explanation is that 1993 was a year in which the Lord Chancellor proposed to remove responsibility for the determination of criminal legal aid from the courts to the Legal Aid Board, and the decision-makers were generally sensitive about their work and were keen to justify their decisions.

The most important observation from the above is that neither the existing rules[60] nor the changes caused by the Criminal Justice Act 1991 were 'internalised' by the decision-makers. Rather, local and personal traditions continued to prevail.[61] The decision-maker's rationale is discussed in greater detail by Richard Young in chapter 7. However, the main issue relevant to this discussion is that applicants were not in a position to receive any type of detailed feedback about the quality of their applications as the outcomes (grant rates) remained similar to those resulting before the Act. In addition, they had no need to seek such feedback, because from their perspective as applicants nothing appeared to have changed.

IV EXPLAINING WHY APPLICATION BEHAVIOUR DID NOT CHANGE

With little feedback being given to the applicants about their performance, the application process simply does not provide incentives to improve the quality of reasoning. Indeed, it is possible to identify a variety of 'disincentives' in this context. These fall into two groups: system related disincentives and occupation related disincentives.

---

[60] As expressed in s. 22(2) of the Legal Aid Act 1988.

[61] Wall and Wood, *op. cit.*, para. 3.2.5. Form 1, requires decision-makers to state their reasons for refusal. After 1 May 1995, they are also required to state the reasons for grant. Applicants receive the pro forma, Form 2, which notifies them as to whether they have failed either the financial test or the merits test.

(i) System related disincentives

High grant rate The main (system related) disincentive is the high overall grant rate, which exceeds 90 per cent in the majority of courts. Table 6.6 shows that there has been little overall change in the annual overall refusal rate since 1991.

Table 6.6: Grant/refusal rates for criminal legal aid in the magistrates' courts 1991–94 (inclusive)[62]

	Grant Rate	Refusal Rate
1991	91.3%	8.7%
1992	90.4%	9.6%
1993	90.3%	9.7%
1994	90.5%	9.5%

Applicants know that their applications have a very good chance of being granted as long as they fit within broad parameters, and therefore they feel that they do not have to make detailed applications. Moreover, if an application is refused, there exist various avenues for appeal against refusal, and applicants know from experience that if their applications are refused then they stand a good chance of being granted when represented to the court administration.[63] If they still fail to get a grant, applicants also know that they can make the application directly to the magistrates, who, as they know from experience, tend to be generous. These options make largely redundant the formal review procedure[64] of applying, after the first refusal, to the Area Legal Board for a review of the court's decision.[65]

'Unhelpful' clients and lack of advance disclosure A frequent complaint made by solicitors to justify not providing more detailed information on their applications, is that they receive poor quality information from the client and have to act upon it, as in the following example:

---

[62] Based upon statistics that were kindly supplied by Martin Brand of the Lord Chancellor's Department.

[63] See Wall and Wood, *op. cit.*, para. 3.3.

[64] On which see Wood, A., 'Administrative Justice Within the Legal Aid Board: Reviews by Caseworkers and Area Committees of Refusals of Criminal Legal Aid Applications', at chapter 8 of this volume.

[65] Wall and Wood, *op. cit.*, para. 3.3. and Young et al., *op. cit.*, pp. 90–91.

... one major problem is that we have to apply [for legal aid] straight from the outset and don't know the full weight of evidence at that time. We just have to take the client's word for it.[66]

Solicitors further claim that clients do not always tell the truth about their circumstances, or sometimes do not even realise the consequences of their actions, particularly in the early stages of a case: 'it's not that they always deliberately mislead us it's just that they tend to minimise them, though they do sometimes lie.'[67] The solicitors also complain that advance information is not usually available from the prosecution in the early stages of a case when the application is often made. This means that they cannot check the accuracy of any information that they are given by their clients.

Another common justification for poor quality applications by solicitors is that clients often wait until the last minute before seeking (their) legal advice. As one solicitor put it:

Between sixty and seventy per cent of all applications are made in court on the day of the case. They (defendants) just throw their charge sheet at you and just don't care. That's why some of the applications don't have much information on them. When you're in the corridor of the court you can have a queue of people waiting to see you. They know we are going to be in court because we are there each day so they don't bother to come and see us beforehand. They just expect us to be there.[68]

These complaints must be treated with caution, however. While the solicitors are quick to blame their clients for the poor quality information presented on application forms, McConville et al.[69] argue that it is the solicitors' own fault because they tend to concentrate on the case rather than on the client. It is often their perceived lack of interest in the client during the early stages of the investigation that causes the client to be unhelpful.

Laxity of decision-makers The applicants know that there is a tendency for court decision-makers to grant applications on the basis of an incomplete form. This is despite the fact that if applications are of poor quality then court decision-makers should return them to the solicitor. One of the court-based decision-makers stated that:

---

[66] Solicitor 12 – q. 12 (Wall, observation and interview notes).
[67] Solicitor 1 – YK (Wall, observation and interview notes).
[68] Solicitor 1 – YZ (Wall, observation and interview notes).
[69] McConville, M., Hodgson, J., Bridges, L. and Pavlovic, A., *Standing Accused: The Organisation and Practices of Criminal Defence Lawyers in Britain*, Oxford: Clarendon Press, 1994, ch. 11.

when a point of information is being sought or clarified the Lord Chancellor's Department says that the form should be returned to the applicant; it rarely is.[70]

Rather than return the form for further information, the decision-makers will often grant the application on the basis of incomplete information. Wall and Wood found that decision-makers rarely asked for additional information during the determination of an application. In only 7 per cent of the cases studied did decision-makers request additional information from the applicant's solicitor or court files.[71]

Even if the applicant has made a reasoned application and has completed the form properly, it is perhaps paradoxical that the decision-maker will ignore much of the information given. One of the more striking findings of both Wall and Wood and Young et al. in this respect, was that court decision-makers tend to discount approximately half of the claims made by applicants on the application form, including claims that involve the likelihood of receiving a custodial sentence if convicted (see above).

(ii) Occupation related disincentives

In addition to the system related disincentives there are various occupation related disincentives which sustain poor quality reasoning on the application form.

'Routinisation' The first disincentive arises from what McConville et al. refer to as the 'routinisation' of work, which many firms have adopted in managing their criminal case-loads. As legal practices tend to deal with cases rather than with clients, these cases become routinised so that clients can be processed through the system in a rapid and cost-effective manner.[72] As cases are routinised, so are applications.

Use of unqualified staff The second disincentive arises from the 'routinisation' of the management of the case and links up with the much broader issue of who completes the application form. It was found by both Young et al.[73] and Wall and Wood[74] that it was common practice for other, non-solicitor, staff to complete the application form. Only one solicitor out of 20 interviewed in Wall

---

[70] Decision-maker DW CDM1 (Wall, observation and interview notes).
[71] Wall and Wood, *op. cit.*, para. 3.2.1.
[72] McConville et al., *op. cit.*, p. 165.
[73] Young et al., *op. cit.*, p. 81.
[74] Wall and Wood, *op. cit.*, para. 3.2.2.

and Wood's research said that her firm insisted upon qualified solicitors filling out the form. She said that:

> normally, in about 90 per cent of cases, the form is filled in by the solicitor during the first interview with the client. We have maintained a solicitor driven practice here and make a point of turning out at the police station because it's the most important part of the case.[75]

More usually it was the case that:

> whomever sees the client fills in the application form, including the unqualified staff who attend the police station.[76]

In common with attendance at the police station, the completion of the application form is not something that most solicitors want to spend time on, because they earn more money through giving advice and, in particular, providing representation.[77] Both the former activities tend to be regarded by senior staff as a training rite, or as something that solicitors should not do. Therefore such senior staff naturally want to delegate this work to junior staff, typically the 'non-solicitors' or para-legals. More importantly, the work is not delegated to junior staff on the basis of their particular (legal) skills, rather delegation strategies are based upon the need to maximise profits.[78] Such actions are regarded as overheads rather than as fee-earning activities.

In most of the cases observed by Wall and Wood, application forms were completed by para-legals (trained and non-trained), and it was quite common in some of the very high volume firms for secretaries or administrative assistants to carry out this work. Few of the applications examined by Wall and Wood and by Young et al. appeared to have been supervised properly by a legally trained person. Those which did contain elements of reasoning were much more likely to receive grants than those which did not. Young et al. found that the unqualified staff were more likely than solicitors to make exaggerated claims and invoke criteria unthinkingly. They were also more likely than were trained personnel to have their applications refused.[79]

Preserving the status quo The third occupational disincentive to better quality applications is that the status quo largely suits the applicants and

---

[75] Solicitor 3 – q. 7 (Wall, observation and interview notes).
[76] Solicitor 10 – q. 7 (Wall, observation and interview notes).
[77] See McConville et al., *op. cit.*, pp. 37–40.
[78] *Ibid.*, p. 38.
[79] Young et al., *op. cit.*, p. 84.

decision-makers alike. Applicants know that if they were suddenly to engage in extensive legal reasoning on the application form, they might break the routine patterns of grants that has developed. This might serve to 'up the ante' by creating expectations of higher quality applications in future. This might mean harder work all around, especially in those courts which operate an 'administrative' ethos and which employ administrative staff to determine applications.[80] The tactical advantage of not providing full information on all application forms was alluded to by a number of those interviewed, as in the following example:

> Why don't we put more information on the form? Because we tend to save the embellishments for the ones on the borderline.[81]

Lack of communication with decision-makers The last occupationally related disincentive preventing applicants from engaging in legal reasoning on the application form is the lack of direct communication between applicants and the decision-makers about application procedures. While court user groups appeared to have been active in the target courts, there was little initiative by solicitors to discuss specific issues regarding the quality of application forms with decision-makers. If these issues had been discussed, nevertheless the discussion would have been largely redundant, since many of the solicitors who participated in the court user schemes did not have regular first-hand experience of completing the application forms.

V ASSESSING THE SOLICITORS' KEYHOLDING ABILITIES

It has so far been established in this chapter that the overall quality of reasoning in applications is inadequate, and that the dynamics of the current system contain a series of disincentives to improve the quality of that reasoning. Yet, if the applications are so poor and the grant rate is so high, then the question is begged why there are generally not more applications for minor offences (see Tables 6.1 and 6.2). This raises the issue of whether those who complete the application forms are actually exercising a limited keyholding function.

It is suggested here that solicitors do not second-guess the decision-maker by making 'shadow determinations' to the extent that is anticipated by the rational model which underlies legal aid. However, they do narrow the field of applications by filtering out what they believe are ungrantable applications, and this explains why the majority of applications profiled in Tables 6.1 and 6.2

---

[80] See the experience of Court A in Wall and Wood, *op. cit.*, para. 4.2.3.1.
[81] Interview with solicitor 3 (Wall, observation and interview notes).

were of the more serious types. This filtering process requires further explanation in order to determine whether it is a keyholding or a cost-cutting exercise.

Many solicitors claim to have an understanding of what would and would not get legal aid. Some look at the nature of the offence and/or plea: 'I wouldn't bother with shop-lifters who were giving a guilty plea.'[82] Others take a broader approach:

> I make a positive attempt to weed out any spurious cases. There is literally no point in trying with some cases but, if there are any grounds to do so, then I'll put an application in.[83]

This same solicitor claimed that through experience he and his colleagues:

> ... have been educated into what might or might not get legal aid. We are a very close group and we know what will get legal aid. And this is why this court has an unusually high grant rate. It's because we are keeping the bad applications out of the court.[84]

Those who make the basic assessment of whether or not to apply for criminal legal aid claim to operate two basic rules of thumb. They first consider the apparent seriousness of the offence and, secondly, look to see whether there are any complicating circumstances, such as a not guilty plea or the need for cross-examination of an expert witness. The application of these 'complicating circumstances' tends to be regarded by applicants not as a legitimate criterion upon which to base the application, but more as a means by which (they believe) the grant can be secured when there is an element of doubt over the seriousness of the offence. As the following solicitor explained:

> I've had legal aid for non-imprisonable offences, for example harassment, alarm and distress [Public Order Act 1986, s. 5]. In these cases I wouldn't ever put in a straightforward application for legal aid [i.e., one with no legal reasoning] but if there is anything about the offence that could attract legal aid then I'd use the 'other' category on the form. I got it once for an OPL [over the permitted limit] where the defendant claimed not to have been driving. I had to call an expert witness and got him off. If I hadn't represented him on legal aid then he would have been convicted.[85]

---

[82] Solicitor 6 – q. 6a (Wall, observation and interview notes).
[83] Solicitor 7 – q. 6a (Wall, observation notes).
[84] Solicitor 7 – q. 6a (Wall, observation and interview notes).
[85] Solicitor 7 – q. 6a (Wall, observation and interview notes).

But while the solicitors may express an understanding of the application criteria, it was established earlier that they are not necessarily the people who complete the application form. They may, however, be involved in the decision whether or not to apply for legal aid. The extent of this involvement depends upon the nature of the legal practice in which they operate and, more importantly, upon the overall level of legal training of those making the application. Where applications are subjected to some form of selectivity or basic supervision, the weaker cases tend to be weeded out. Wall and Wood examined the grant rates achieved by 16 firms of solicitors, representing the four most frequent applicants in each of the courts studied in detail.[86] It was found that of the 12 firms at which some selectivity was found, ten displayed refusal rates less than or equal to the overall refusal rate for the local court. Such selective firms tended to use articled clerks, trained legal executives or even solicitors either to complete or to oversee legal aid applications. Those with the refusal rates above the local norm tended to be the high volume firms[87] working on low profit margins in which applications for legal aid were made fairly unselectively. They would typically use anybody who was available to complete legal aid applications, preferably administrative staff, including secretaries and assistants.

VI WHAT HAPPENS WHEN LEGAL AID IS REFUSED?

Before concluding this chapter it is necessary to examine what happens when legal aid is not granted once all avenues, including appeal, have been exhausted. In practice it was found that there still were a number of options to be exercised. For example, the solicitor might negotiate a fee with the client, which might be less than the normal rate, or an easy payment scheme might be offered. In a number of cases observed, typically guilty plea road traffic offences which might have quite serious implications for the client's future employment, legal advice was given in the waiting area of the court under the green form scheme and the solicitor then represented the client in court by presenting mitigating circumstances. In other situations solicitors might represent established clients at no cost whatsoever in order to maintain their custom. This was often the case with drink driving offences.

Even if the solicitor refused to represent a client and the client entered court unrepresented, it is possible that the magistrates might suggest that he or she talk with the duty solicitor. In very rare circumstances the court clerk acts to

---

[86] See Table 3.2.2b in Wall and Wood, *op. cit.*, para. 3.2.2.
[87] *Ibid.*, para. 4.3. Practice 1 in Court C and Practice 1 in Court D were exceptions to the rule because they had developed in-house training programmes for their staff. In the latter case this was consciously based upon a para-medical model.

represent the defendant. The main problem with these 'half measures' is that they tend to occur for reasons that are in the interests of the provider. They suit the administration either of the legal practice or of the magistrates' court rather than the interests of the defendant or the interests of justice.

VII CONCLUSION

This chapter has questioned the keyholding concept which requires trained legal professionals to apply their professional legal expertise to invoke criteria that will convince decision-makers of the worthiness of their clients' application. Little evidence was found of the required legal reasoning, through the invoking of (Widgery) criteria, that related either to the seriousness or to the complexity of the case. Rather it was the case that some firms, but not all, filtered out very weak cases prior to application.

Applicants (solicitors) were not attuned to the rationale of the court decision-maker and application rationale bore little relation to decision-making rationale. But it was also found that within the present system it does not matter whether or not applicants are so attuned because of the high grant rate that exists and because of the other reasons documented above, few of which are related to the interests of justice.

The findings presented here raise questions about the viability of initiatives such as block contracts. Firms who standardise their procedures will wish to redefine non-standard cases as standard if they can, and to refuse to handle any which cannot be remoulded in this way.[88] This raises concerns about the administration of the proposed block contracts. If the policy is implemented, the rules and regulations surrounding block contracts will have to be tightly drawn if 'cherry-picking' is to be avoided.

Similarly, solicitors carrying out block contracted cases may not be prepared to take on the case of the 'difficult' client, who is the same person to whom court clerks are keen to grant legal aid in order to save time in court. Transferring decisions on legal aid to solicitors might thus make the administration of legal aid more efficient at the expense of court processes. After all, solicitors would have an interest in court efficiency only with regard to the cases they were dealing with. While some of these defendants are picked up by the duty solicitors in court, they nevertheless tend to have quite complex legal needs which require preparation time.

The findings in this chapter raise broader questions about the nature of the criminal legal aid system itself, and in particular about the bureaucratic process model upon which it is designed. To be effective the system requires rational

---

[88] See discussion in McConville et al., *op. cit.*, pp. 164–165.

predetermined criteria to be applied efficiently at all stages, and it is therefore dependent upon rational decision-making, rational applicants and rational delivery. The system's practical operation is the antithesis to this ideal. While an individually determined rationale underpins the actions of those operating the application and determination processes, those processes are certainly not rational in the sense of complying with the bureaucratic model.[89] In addition, the applicants/defendants/clients are far from being the organised, informed and self-aware rational beings which this model demands. Rather, they tend to possess the opposite characteristics and further complicate the rational delivery of legal services. The result is a classic bureaucratic muddle which somehow works because those who have to work within the system make it work.

More specifically, the above analysis raises some important questions about the viability of using the Widgery criteria to test for the 'interests of justice'. The analysis also suggests that any attempt to change the existing procedures would have to be carefully engineered to take account of the working practices of legal advisers and the courts, and also the needs of the defendant.

---

[89] See Young et al., *op. cit.*, for discussion about the rationality of legal aid decision-making.

7

Will Widgery Do?: Court Clerks, Discretion, and the Determination of Legal Aid Applications

Richard Young[*]

This chapter is concerned with criminal legal aid for proceedings in the magistrates' courts. The great majority of applications for this form of legal aid are made by solicitors on behalf of their clients, and are determined by magistrates' court clerks as a paper exercise. Court clerks must determine whether it is in 'the interests of justice' to grant legal aid.[1] In doing so they are obliged to take into account the 'Widgery criteria'.[2] These comprise a number of factors relating primarily to the gravity and complexity of the case. This chapter will analyse the practical operation of the Widgery test and question whether the broad discretion it allows to court clerks is defensible. In short, will Widgery do?

The chapter falls into five main sections. In the first, the historical and political context within which analysis of the Widgery test may be located is outlined. The second section explores the legal complexity of that test. The third sets out details of the two research studies on which this chapter is largely based, and comments on the methodological problems of studying discretion. The fourth section forms the central core of the chapter. It explores the way in

---

[*] The author is grateful to John Baldwin, Andrew Sanders and David Wall for their valuable comments on earlier drafts of this chapter.

[1] Section 21 of the Legal Aid Act 1988.

[2] These criteria are the progeny of the *Report of the Departmental Committee on Legal Aid in Criminal Proceedings*, Cmnd. 2934, London: HMSO, 1966, chaired by Mr Justice Widgery (hereinafter the Widgery Report). The criteria were put on a statutory footing by s. 22(2) of the Legal Aid Act 1988.

which court clerks use the Widgery test in practice and seeks to explain patterns of grants and refusals. In the conclusion, the implications of this analysis for policy-making are examined. This author's contention is that the interests of justice test amounts to a hypocritical pretence and should be dropped.

I HISTORICAL AND POLITICAL BACKGROUND

Legal aid has, in fits and starts, colonised the criminal justice process over the course of the twentieth century.[3] There have remained, however, pockets of resistance to the encroachment of publicly-funded defence lawyers. Whereas virtually all of those appearing before the Crown Court or the Court of Appeal are nowadays legally aided, many defendants facing summary trial are unrepresented,[4] even though the eligibility conditions are identical. Defendants must pass two tests: one on means, one on merits. The application by court clerks of the means test is non-discretionary and falls outside the scope of this chapter. Turning to the merits test, this stipulates that legal aid may be granted only if it is in the interests of justice to do so. It is now generally accepted that it is nearly always in the interests of justice to grant legal aid in the higher courts, but this is not the case as far as magistrates' courts are concerned.

The modern history of the merits test dates from the mid-1960s with the setting up of an official committee on legal aid chaired by Mr Justice Widgery. The Widgery Committee concluded that there should be no automatic right to legal aid in the magistrates' courts, but that it should continue to be granted on a discretionary basis when the 'interests of justice' so required.[5] It did, however, stipulate factors which should be taken into account in assessing this issue. These Widgery criteria were meant to promote a modest increase in the granting of legal aid, together with a greater consistency of approach. However, since the criteria were introduced there has been an enormous increase in both the number and proportion of defendants receiving legal aid for proceedings in the magistrates' courts — a phenomenon sometimes referred to as 'Widgery drift'.[6] In 1964, one legal aid grant was made for every nine defendants facing a non-summary charge, whereas by the mid-1990s the vast majority of such

---

[3] See Goriely, T., 'The Development of Criminal Legal Aid in England and Wales', at chapter 2 of this volume.

[4] See Astor, H., 'The Unrepresented Defendant Revisited: a Consideration of the Role of the Clerk in Magistrates' Courts', *Journal of Law and Society*, 1986, vol. 13, p. 225.

[5] The Widgery Report, *op. cit.*, para. 56.

[6] See Young, R., Moloney, T. and Sanders, A., *In the Interests of Justice?*, London: Legal Aid Board, 1992, pp. 9–10.

defendants were legally aided.[7] Moreover, legal aid is now often granted to those charged with summary offences, something that would have been almost unthinkable a few decades ago.[8]

A number of factors prompted a questioning by the Government of whether the discretionary system endorsed and refined by the Widgery Committee could survive into the twenty-first century. First, its open-ended nature had allowed costs to spiral dramatically.[9] Secondly, there was concern that decisions were made on the basis of inadequate information. Thus, every year from 1992 to 1995, the Comptroller and Auditor-General expressed formal reservations about whether magistrates' courts were discharging their duties properly when deciding whether or not to grant legal aid, in respect of applying both the means test and the interests of justice test.[10] Lastly, there were concerns about inconsistencies of approach. While most magistrates' courts maintain high grant rates of 90 per cent or above, a significant minority grant much less frequently. Using the 1990 figures covering 384 courts, for example, there were eight courts which refused at least a quarter of all applications, whereas, at the other extreme, 97 refused no more than one in 20.[11] Statistical analysis of the official legal aid figures indicates that the explanation for differing rates of grant by magistrates' courts lies not in differences in their legal aid case-loads but in their processes of decision-making.[12] Put simply, like cases are not being treated alike. This raises the issue of differential access to legal aid funds.

The Lord Chancellor responded to the Comptroller and Auditor-General's concern by issuing what amounted to an ultimatum:

> Unless there is a very marked improvement, very soon, in the way in which the courts carry out their functions, alternative arrangements will have to be implemented.[13]

---

[7] See McConville, M., Hodgson, J., Bridges, L. and Pavlovic, A., *Standing Accused: The Organisation and Practices of Criminal Defence Lawyers in Britain*, Oxford: Clarendon Press, 1994, pp. 209–300, and Goriely, *op. cit.*, for fuller discussion and supporting references.

[8] 15% of legal aid grants in 1989 were for summary offences: McConville et al., *op. cit.*, p. 300.

[9] In 1990 prices, the cost of legal aid in the magistrates' courts grew from £16.9 million in 1970 to £169.1m in 1990 — a ten-fold increase: *ibid.*, p. 299.

[10] National Audit Office Report by the Comptroller and Auditor-General, *The Administration of Legal Aid in England and Wales*, London: HMSO, 1992, and subsequent reports. See also Public Accounts Committee, *LCD: The Qualification of Audit Opinion and Alleged Fraud on the Green Form Scheme*, HC 282, 1994–5, London: HMSO, 1995.

[11] Young et al., *op. cit.*, appendix 2, p. 111.

[12] See *ibid.*, at p. 10 and pp. 62–3.

[13] Lord Chancellor's Department, *Legal Aid – Targeting Need: The future of publicly funded help in solving legal problems and disputes in England and Wales*, Cm 2854, London: HMSO, 1995, p. 73, para. 10.11 (hereinafter the Green Paper).

The options considered in the 1995 Green Paper included a simple transfer of responsibility for making decisions about legal aid either to solicitors or to the Legal Aid Board.[14] The course which the Government appeared to favour, however, was to dispense with the Widgery criteria altogether in favour of a new set of interests of justice criteria that would be easier to apply and to audit.[15] The following caveat was added:

> The Government does not favour a simpler definition if it would have the effect of extending the scope of criminal legal aid to more cases than at present. It does not believe that is necessary.[16]

Others disagree. Ashworth, for example, has demonstrated that there are strong due process arguments for establishing a right to legal aid for any person accused of a criminal offence.[17] This aspect of the legal aid scheme has thus become a controversial pressure point, with the Government determined to resist the arguments for any further colonisation of the magistrates' courts by publicly-funded lawyers.

This chapter examines how magistrates' courts exercise their discretionary power to grant legal aid against this background of controversy about the merits test as bequeathed by the Widgery Committee. It explores the factors lying behind decisions to grant or to refuse legal aid and attempts to explain the disparity in grant rates identified above. Such an analysis bears directly on questions of policy. Unless the factors influencing the determination of legal aid applications are understood, attempts to control the discretion of court clerks are likely to fail and produce unintended and undesirable consequences. Furthermore, if responsibility for granting legal aid is to be transferred either to solicitors or to the Legal Aid Board it is important that problematic aspects of the current system are not simply replicated in a new setting.

The following section outlines the legal framework within which court clerks are meant to operate. The use of this starting point does not imply that the law

---

[14] The idea of transferring decision-making to the Legal Aid Board is evaluated in Young, R. and Sanders, A., 'A wise and sensible move ?', *New Law Journal*, 1992, vol. 142., p. 1409.

[15] The Green Paper, *op. cit.*, p. 74, para. 10.16. This document leans in favour of making solicitors responsible for applying this simplified test on the basis that transferring responsibility to the Board would cause unacceptable delay and bureaucracy (*ibid.*, para. 10.14). See the concluding section of this chapter for discussion of this simplified test.

[16] *Ibid.* For a critique of the Green Paper proposals, see Bridges, L., 'The Reform of Criminal Legal Aid', at chapter 13 of this volume.

[17] Ashworth, A., 'Legal Aid, Human Rights and Criminal Justice', at chapter 3 of this volume.

is necessarily the most important factor in structuring decision-making.[18] Rather, legal norms are best regarded as but one form of constraint on (or resource for) court clerks. These norms, however, provide a yardstick by which to assess the legitimacy of the decision-making behaviour of court clerks. An analysis of the legal framework will also be of help in developing an understanding of that behaviour. For reasons to be explored below, the more complex the decision-making process prescribed by law, the more likely it is that the business of taking decisions will be simplified in practice.

II THE LEGAL FRAMEWORK

Discretionary power has been described by Galligan as:

> powers delegated within a system of authority to an official or set of officials, where they have some significant scope for settling the reasons and standards according to which that power is to be exercised, and for applying them in the making of specific decisions.[19]

Under this definition, it is clear that court clerks are provided with such power. Section 21 of the Legal Aid Act 1988 incorporates the long-standing test that legal aid may be granted where it appears desirable 'in the interests of justice' to do so. The 'interests of justice' are undefined, leaving court clerks significant scope for setting standards by which to assess whether legal aid should be granted or not.

This broad power is subject, however, to a number of legal constraints. Court clerks are public officials, and as such their actions are judicially reviewable. They must act in good faith, use their powers for the purpose they were given, take into account relevant matters and disregard the irrelevant, and avoid acting in a way so unreasonable that no reasonable court clerk could have so acted.[20] This begs the question of what constitutes a relevant or irrelevant matter. The Widgery criteria, given legal force by s. 22 of the 1988 Act, provide guidance here. Section 22(2) specifies that these criteria must be taken into account in the determination of legal aid applications. Three are concerned with the consequences of conviction, in that regard must be had to whether the

---

[18] As Bell, J., 'Discretionary Decision-Making: A Jurisprudential View', in Hawkins, K. (ed.), *The Uses of Discretion*, Oxford: Clarendon Press, 1992, p. 110, argues, law is best viewed not as a set of normative directions, 'but as a scheme of legitimating values operating within specific institutional frameworks in conjunction with other social schemes of value'.

[19] Galligan, D., *Discretionary Powers: A Legal Study of Official Discretion*, Oxford: Clarendon Press, 1986, p. 21.

[20] *Associated Provincial Picture Houses Ltd* v *Wednesbury Corpn* [1948] 1 KB 223. See, generally, Craig, P., *Administrative Law*, 3rd ed., London: Sweet & Maxwell, 1994, ch. 11.

defendant is likely to lose liberty, or livelihood or suffer serious damage to reputation. The remainder concern the incapacity of the defendant effectively to present a case in person, either because of some personal characteristic of the defendant (such as inadequate English, or physical or mental disability) or because of the complexity of the case itself. Thus consideration should be given to whether the defence is such that witnesses will need to be traced and interviewed, that expert cross-examination is required, or that a substantial question of law is involved. Lastly, court clerks must consider whether it is in the interests of someone other than the accused that legal aid be granted. This might arise, for example, if it would be inappropriate for the accused to cross-examine in person, as where an offence involving child abuse has been alleged.

The fact that standards have been provided in law for court clerks to follow can be seen as an attempt to constrain or structure their discretion. Yet such legal standards inevitably introduce a need for new forms of discretion to be exercised. For example, the s. 22 criteria require interpretation, and their relative weight needs to be assessed. Court clerks also exercise a form of discretionary judgment in deciding whether the facts recorded in a legal aid application fall within the s. 22 criteria. Lastly, court clerks must decide how much credence or weight to give to the information provided in legal aid applications. If, having considered all these matters, a court clerk is in doubt as to whether legal aid should be granted, the law requires that doubt to be resolved in favour of the applicant.[21]

Since the factors to be taken into account by court clerks are specified in law, it follows that their interpretation is also ultimately a matter of law. Another form of legal constraint to which court clerks are thus subject is judicial guidance as to the meaning of the s. 22 criteria. The Divisional Court, in *McGhee*,[22] decided, for example, that defendants who are likely to receive community service orders if convicted should not be regarded as at risk of losing their liberty within the meaning of s. 22. The court also held, contrary to the view of many magistrates' court clerks,[23] that the need for expert cross-examination of a witness as referred to in s. 22 might arise even if the witness in question was not an expert.

The wording of s. 22 precludes any attempt by the judiciary to transform the power to determine legal aid applications into a mechanical exercise. The section does not contain an exhaustive definition of the interests of justice, it merely provides indications of matters bearing on this question. In a series of

---

[21] Section 21(7) of the Legal Aid Act 1988.
[22] *R* v *Liverpool City Magistrates ex parte McGhee* [1993] Crim LR 609.
[23] See the commentary to this case in the *Criminal Law Review*, 1993, p. 610, and Young et al., *op. cit.*, pp. 21–2.

cases, the Divisional Court has made it plain that those taking decisions on criminal legal aid have a very wide discretion when applying the interests of justice test.[24] Factors other than those in s. 22 may be taken into account.[25] Even when the circumstances of a case fall squarely within the statutory criteria, legal aid need not be granted.[26] Moreover, there are many points of interpretation concerning the s. 22 criteria which have yet to be resolved by the higher courts, and such rulings as have been laid down must always be interpreted themselves. In law, court clerks have, therefore, considerable freedom for manoeuvre.

It follows that what at first sight may seem to be a simple question, 'Would a grant of legal aid be in the interests of justice or not?', can be broken down into a number of discrete and discretionary steps. Court clerks have the following kinds of decisions to take:

— how much credence to give to information or claims provided on the application form;
— how to interpret the s. 22 criteria;
— what other criteria, if any, to take into account;
— which types of facts or situations are covered by the statutory and non-statutory criteria;
— how much weight to give to each of the relevant criteria;
— what is meant by the 'interests of justice';
— whether granting legal aid would (or might) serve those interests.

This highly legalistic exploration of legal aid decision-making demonstrates the potential complexity of the process even when attention is confined to the determination of a single application by a single court clerk. The reality is that cases are not dealt with as isolated entities, but as part of wider organisational processes and within specific situational and social contexts. In consequence, court clerk decision-making bears little resemblance to the legalistic model discussed above. The remainder of this chapter will be devoted to illuminating the behaviour of court clerks through the development of an account of the factors operating on them when determining legal aid applications. It is necessary first, however, to give brief details of the empirical work which informs this account.

---

[24] See, in particular, *R v Macclesfield Justices ex parte Greenhalgh* [1980] 144 JP 142; *R v Cambridge Crown Court ex parte Hagi* [1980] 144 JP 145, and *R v Havering Juvenile Court ex parte Buckley*, Lexis CO/554/83, 12 July 1983.
[25] *R v Havering Justices ex parte Buckley, op. cit., per* Forbes J; *R v Liverpool City Magistrates ex parte McGhee, op. cit.*
[26] *R v Cambridge Crown Court ex parte Hagi, op. cit.*; *R v Stratford Magistrates' Court ex parte Gorman*, Lexis CO/687/89, 12 June 1992.

III METHODOLOGICAL ASPECTS OF STUDYING DISCRETION

The following discussion draws upon the results of two empirical studies into legal aid decision-making conducted in the early 1990s. The first was carried out by Young et al.,[27] and the second by Wall and Wood.[28] Theoretical work on the nature of discretion is also drawn upon.[29] This literature emphasises the need for sensitive methodological strategies when attempting to study discretionary power. As Hawkins notes, 'producing a more sophisticated understanding of how discretion is used is a very complex task, because decision making is itself extremely complex, and discretion is a dynamic and adaptable phenomenon'.[30] An illustration of the problems involved is that those whose behaviour is being studied may be unable or unwilling to articulate why decisions were reached. As will be seen below, court clerks in the studies undertaken were quite willing to talk about their decision-making norms. While it is helpful to know what decision-makers think influences them, they may not always be able to identify accurately all the factors which have a bearing on their behaviour. Thus, for example, they may not be conscious of the organisational pressures on them to take legal aid decisions in a particular fashion. Interviews with decision-makers must therefore be supplemented by other methods, such as examination of paper records and comparisons between courts and over time. Moreover, any study of decision-making must embrace the wider processes and broader contexts within which this activity takes place.

The two research studies, on which this chapter is largely based, adopted similar research strategies. It is not claimed that these strategies were ideally suited to probing all the complexities of legal aid decision-making, since neither study was truly ethnographic in nature. Nonetheless, the various techniques adopted did allow the researchers to gain a more in-depth understanding of this aspect of the criminal process than has previously been obtained. Young et al. investigated the factors underlying the apparent disparity in grant rates amongst magistrates' courts.[31] The fieldwork was carried out between March and June 1992 and data were collected in two distinct stages. In the first, a weighted sample of 200 legal aid applications in each of six courts

---

[27] Young et al., op. cit. For summaries of the main findings, see Young, R., 'Court clerks, legal aid and the interests of justice', New Law Journal, 1992, vol. 142, p. 1264, and Sanders, A. and Young, R., 'Swings and roundabouts', Law Society Gazette, 2 December 1992, vol. 89, no.44, p. 23.

[28] Wall, D. S. and Wood, A., The Administration of Criminal Legal Aid in the Magistrates' Courts of England and Wales: Final Report, Report to ESRC, March 1994.

[29] See, in particular, the collection of essays in Hawkins (ed.), op. cit., n. 18.

[30] Hawkins, K. 'The Use of Legal Discretion: Perspectives from Law and Social Science', ibid., p. 45.

[31] For a full description of the aims of this research and the methodology employed, see Young et al., op. cit., pp. 5–8.

(three with high grant rates, three with low) was examined in order to establish patterns of decision-making. The issues identified as a result of this analysis were then pursued in the second stage. This involved semi-structured interviews with two court clerks from each court, as well as with representatives from busy firms of solicitors, two in each court's catchment area. In addition to being questioned at length about their handling of legal aid applications, court clerks were asked to complete an 'offence rating form' designed to test the relationship between the offence charged and the perceived need for legal aid. They were also asked to consider six 'dummy applications' constructed on the basis of real applications.

In the time available, Young et al. were unable to sit with court clerks as they determined 'live' legal aid applications, neither were they able to achieve much more than a snapshot of decision-making at a particular point in time. Another limitation of the study is that it focused on the perceived problem of disparity in grant rates. While this involved an examination of a wide range of factors that might affect these rates, more in-depth study of legal aid decision-making in general was not possible. Such an inquiry was undertaken by Wall and Wood in a two-year project funded by the ESRC.[32] Four courts were studied: two large, two small. The principal research technique was to ask court clerks to complete a self-administered questionnaire each time they determined a legal aid application. This produced data regarding the s. 22 criteria as invoked by the applicant and as portrayed as influential by the clerk in reaching a decision to grant or refuse legal aid. This survey of applications covered the complete workload of each court for the period 1 April to 30 June of 1992 and 1993.[33] This enabled comparisons to be drawn across time as well as between courts. In addition, interviews were conducted with solicitors and court clerks in each of the courts studied and observations of practice were made. Lastly, a controlled decision-making experiment was conducted which involved 70 court staff considering 11 'dummy' legal aid applications.[34]

IV THE DECISION-MAKING BEHAVIOUR OF COURT CLERKS

The following analysis will be broken down into a number of thematic sections. In the first, the use of the Widgery criteria by both applicants and court clerks will be documented. In the second, the poor quality of legal aid applications

---

[32] Again, for a fuller account see Wall and Wood, *op. cit.*, pp. 12–15.

[33] In one court, concerns raised by the clerks about the time needed to complete the questionnaire resulted in the taking of a 50% sample.

[34] Six of the 'dummies' used by Wall and Wood were identical to those devised by Young et al. This came about because the two research teams shared information and ideas as the respective studies progressed.

will be examined. The remaining sections will explore the factors which bear on court clerks when taking decisions on legal aid.

(i) The use of the Widgery criteria by applicants and court clerks

The standard legal aid application form is divided into a number of sections, each corresponding to one of the s. 22 factors.[35] As noted by Wall,[36] defendants leave the completion of this form to their legal advisers. These advisers manage the process of application and may be regarded as *de facto* applicants. Solicitors (or, more usually, their representatives) tick a box for each section which they claim to be applicable and give supporting reasoning in the space provided. The design of the form serves to focus the attention of court clerks on the factors which the law states must be taken into account. But which factors are invoked by legal advisers, and how much credence is placed on the information given in the legal aid application form?

Taking the second quarter of 1992, Wall and Wood compared the criteria invoked by applicants and those which court clerks said they had thought relevant in reaching their decision.[37] This exercise revealed the dominance of the custody criterion. In four out of five applications, the claim was made that applicants were at risk of losing their liberty. The next most frequently ticked criteria, 'cross-examination' and 'question of law', were invoked in only one third of applications. It also revealed that court clerks frequently discount claims made by solicitors on behalf of their clients. The extreme case concerned the criterion that legal aid should be granted so as to enable the defence to trace and interview witnesses. Only one in seven of such claims was accepted as valid. But for nearly all the criteria, less than half of the claims made by solicitors were accepted. The notable exception concerned 'danger of custody' which court clerks saw as relevant in 65 per cent of all cases, amounting to 80 per cent of the cases in which it had been invoked by solicitors.

The dominance of the custody criterion was also noted by Young et al. This study showed that legal aid applications which resulted in grants did not have a radically different profile from those which were refused; most of the s. 22 criteria were invoked by applicants in roughly the same proportion in both granted and refused cases. There was an association, however, between an

---

[35] It is worth noting, however, that the wording of the prompts on the form varies from the statutory language in a number of respects. See further, Young et al., *op. cit.*, pp. 22–4; and Wall and Wood, *op. cit.*, p. 47.

[36] Wall, D. S., 'Keyholders to Criminal Justice? Solicitors and Applications for Criminal Legal Aid', at chapter 6 of this volume.

[37] Wall and Wood, *op. cit.*, pp. 68–9. A separate survey of 1,201 application forms produced strikingly similar percentage figures as regards the criteria invoked by applicants: Young et al., *op. cit.*, p. 25.

applicant invoking the danger of custody criterion and a decision to grant legal aid.[38] Most of the court clerks interviewed acknowledged that the danger of custody was the most important criterion in the minds of those taking decisions on legal aid. 'We would put this at the top of the list,' stated one clerk, and continued, 'if there was any likelihood of a custodial sentence being imposed we would grant legal aid.'[39] In contrast to the Wall and Wood study, however, Young et al. concluded that court clerks discounted claims made by solicitors about the risk of custody in most cases. The risk of losing one's liberty has to be assessed within the context of the various legislative efforts of recent years to curb custodial sentencing.[40] As one clerk said in interview:

> It's not as significant [a criterion] as it was because there aren't that many custodial sentences now.... That's one of the problems, solicitors put that on applications willy-nilly almost.[41]

Young et al. found that only 16.3 per cent of cases where the danger of custody criterion was invoked resulted in a custodial sentence or committal to the Crown Court. Almost half of such cases resulted in a fine, a conditional discharge or a compensation order.[42] This suggests that the risk of custody is frequently exaggerated by solicitors. Interview material indicated that solicitors and court clerks alike were well aware of this.[43] How then can the finding of Wall and Wood, that court clerks accepted 80 per cent of the claims made by solicitors about custody, be explained? It seems likely that, when court clerks in the latter study recorded that they had been influenced by a claim that an applicant was at risk of custody, they were often seeking to rationalise or justify a decision which had been made on other grounds.

Further evidence for this conclusion is provided by Wall and Wood's discussion of the impact of the Criminal Justice Act 1991 on legal aid decision-making.[44] In its original form this Act reduced the likelihood that convicted defendants would be sent to prison, and therefore also reduced the significance of the custody criterion in the 'interests of justice' test. In advance of the Act's implementation, court clerks had claimed that the refusal rate could rise in consequence by as much as 10 to 20 per cent, whereas in the event it

---

[38] Young et al., *op. cit.*, p. 26.

[39] *Ibid.*, p. 27.

[40] The present Home Secretary, Michael Howard, has reversed this trend since taking office, and this may be having an effect on the grant of legal aid.

[41] Quoted in Young et al., *op. cit.*, p. 28.

[42] *Ibid.*, p. 66.

[43] For the comments of solicitors on this point, see *ibid.*, p. 27 and pp. 69–71. For the views of court clerks, see *ibid.*, p. 28.

[44] Wall and Wood, *op. cit.*, pp. 34–5. For further elaboration see Wall, *op. cit.*

rose by a mere 0.6 per cent.[45] This is so despite the fact that prior to the Act court clerks regarded 80 per cent of claims made by applicants that they were at risk of custody as valid, compared with 62 per cent following the Act. How, then, did court clerks justify such a small increase in the overall refusal rate? They did so by accepting much more frequently claims by solicitors that there was a need for expert cross-examination. Prior to the Act, court clerks said they were influenced by this criterion in 58 per cent of applications in which it was invoked. After the Act this figure leapt to 94 per cent.[46]

It is implausible that the courts studied by Wall and Wood were suddenly flooded with cases in which there was a clear need for expert cross-examination. Rather, it appears that court clerks wished to maintain a particular level of grant, but to do so in a way which would seem legitimate both to themselves and to outside observers. When they were unable to justify their pattern of grants by reference to the custody criterion, they simply switched to another criterion. This raises the question why court clerks wish to maintain a high level of grant. Before turning to this, however, it will be helpful to look more closely at the raw material — legal aid application forms — out of which court clerks supposedly fashion their decisions.

(ii) The poor quality of information on application forms

As noted above, court clerks express great scepticism about the information provided on legal aid application forms and frequently reject claims made by solicitors. A good illustration of this concerns the criteria relating to expert cross-examination, the need to trace witnesses, and a substantial question of law, all of which apply only if there is a genuine intention to contest the charges in court. As Wall and Wood's 1992 survey suggests,[47] and as interviews confirmed,[48] court clerks are cynical about the prospect of defendants maintaining not guilty pleas. It is their experience that a claim on an application form that guilt will be denied is often a ruse to secure a grant of legal aid. As one clerk said when asked about the weight given to the need to trace witnesses:

> This is one of those things where one gets 'Seven defence witnesses to be interviewed'. Very rarely in fact does the case turn out to have seven defence witnesses. That, I always feel, is just a try-on.[49]

---

[45] See Wall, D. S., *Policy into Practice: The Impact of Changes in Policy upon Discretionary Decision Making in the Magistrates' Courts*, paper delivered to Socio-Legal Studies Association conference, Leeds, England, on 27 March 1995, p. 7.

[46] See Wall, *op. cit.*, n. 36.

[47] Op. cit., pp. 68–9.

[48] See Young et al., *op. cit.*, pp. 30–31 in particular.

[49] Quoted in *ibid.*, p. 30.

They are also unimpressed by the level of detail given on applications. Since the fact that there is to be a contested trial is not a relevant factor *per se* under s. 22, the clerks tend to look for something exceptional in the circumstances of the case that marks it out as requiring a grant of legal aid. Scrutiny of application forms confirmed that solicitors rarely specify exactly what is the substantial question of law raised by the case, or precisely why tracing of witnesses or expert cross-examination is necessary. It also confirms that standard wording is often employed in completing the forms, and this is another reason why court clerks treat what is written on applications with suspicion.[50] One clerk summed up the prevailing attitude amongst decision-makers to legal aid applications:

> I could not say that I have come across one where they have told me out-and-out lies. I have not the slightest doubt that I have seen hundreds where the truth has been gilded or the facts blurred. What does cause me suspicion, and in fact devalues the actual applications themselves, is that they use the same phrase in answer to the same question on every application. And I just look at it and say 'Oh Christ, not again'. When I see the two thousandth application from a solicitor in a year and I see under 'question of law' that he still has a 'need to consider and peruse the Theft Act', it's a bit pathetic isn't it?[51]

(iii) Decision-making horizons

One way to conceptualise these findings is by reference to decision-making 'horizons'. Decision-making horizons refer to the variable and shifting contexts relevant to particular decisions. Context, in other words, is not seen as comprised of fixed factors but as emerging through interaction in specific situations. Thus, Emerson and Paley argue that, to understand a decision, one needs to examine its context 'as known and understood by decision makers as they confront and grapple with some current decision task'.[52] The horizons of court clerks include knowledge of a legal aid application's 'organisational history'. By this is meant that the interests of those who have initiated a legal aid application are taken into account in disposing of it. Court clerks appreciate that a grant of legal aid is in the solicitor's interests at least as much as in the

---

[50] On the quality of reasoning provided on application forms see *ibid.*, pp. 72–80 and Young, R. and Sanders, A., 'Boxing in the defence: the Royal Commission, disclosure, and the lessons of research', *The Criminal Lawyer*, November 1994, no.50, p. 3.

[51] Quoted in *ibid.*, p. 30.

[52] Emerson, R. and Paley, B., 'Organizational Horizons and Complaint-Filing', in Hawkins (ed.), *op. cit.*, p. 233.

applicant's. They are also aware that the business of completing legal aid applications is routinely delegated by many solicitors to unqualified staff. They therefore expect legal aid applications to contain exaggerated and poorly constructed claims concerning the need for legal representation. As one clerk explained:

> What we do find here is that you have the same clerk at a solicitor's office filling in a pile of forms with the same line of application. Two applications for two totally different offences could come in, and they'll be the same all the way through.... A lot of them are done quickly and it reads like absolute rubbish sometimes. It's not so much the solicitors. But a lot of the firms in this area operate with clerks who aren't qualified. They're the ones you've got to watch.[53]

Applications also have 'organisational futures'. Court clerks anticipate the consequences that will flow from a refusal or grant of legal aid, and their horizons are shaped by an intimate knowledge of how similar cases have been disposed of in the past. They know, for example, that at least 90 per cent of all defendants in the magistrates' courts ultimately plead guilty and that many applicants who start by claiming innocence will subsequently admit guilt. They also know that relatively few defendants are at risk of receiving a custodial sentence. Similarly, they take into account other methods by which defendants might be assisted if legal aid were refused. A common argument employed by clerks in explaining why little weight is given to many of the s. 22 criteria is that, save in cases of particular difficulty or complexity, they can themselves adequately protect a unrepresented defendant's interests.[54] They claimed that the clerk in court on the day could deal with any points of law that the case raised, and carry out any necessary cross-examination of an expert on the defendant's behalf.

Another illustration of how the organisational future of a case is taken into account comes from the following interview in which a court clerk was asked to decide one of the dummy applications:

> I think this is a duty solicitor job myself. I think with a bit of sensible advice that would be a plea. So, because in real terms the duty solicitor would get him to plead, we would refuse that one. I'm doing these from a practical point of view you'll realise.[55]

---

[53] Quoted in Young et al., *op. cit.*, p. 83.

[54] Note that such an argument was deployed by the judiciary in the nineteenth and much of the twentith century to resist the spread of legally-aided lawyers into the higher courts: Goriely, *op. cit.*

[55] Quoted in Young et al., *op. cit.*, p. 53.

An important methodological point prompted by this quote is that organisational horizons as understood by the decision-maker are not as difficult for researchers to uncover as one might imagine. This is because, as Emerson and Paley note, 'decision horizons are not simply experienced, but are specifically invoked by decision makers to present and establish the orderly, practically rational character of their decisions'.[56] Court clerks see their decisions as based on rational considerations, albeit ones not embedded in law, and they appear quite prepared to talk openly about the factors they see as influential in determining legal aid applications.

Another factor within a court clerk's horizon of future possibilities is the impact of a grant or refusal on courtroom efficiency. Young et al. asked court clerks whether they would ever grant legal aid in the court's interests. Most conceded that this happened. One clerk answered as follows:

> Yes, certainly you would grant sometimes for efficiency, that is when you exercise your discretion. You know that certain defendants will be a nuisance. A section 5 [Public Order Act 1986] which on the face of it wouldn't attract legal aid, would then be granted. The court is assisted and you have saved court listing time as an unrepresented defendant takes much longer. So yes, it is in the interests of everybody and I think the cost to the Legal Aid Board is justified.[57]

Court clerks were not prepared, however, to admit to a general policy of granting legal aid in order to aid court efficiency.[58] Rather, they said that they relied on their local knowledge in order to identify applicants likely to pose special problems for the court if left unrepresented. Applicants with a reputation for being obstreperous or aggressive in court were more likely to be granted legal aid than are those known to be submissive and passive. This illustrates the theoretical point that the context of decision-making should not be regarded as fixed and external to decisions. It would be mistaken to regard 'the need for courtroom efficiency' as anything other than part of the process of reaching particular decisions. That 'need' is determined according to the specific decision-making task at hand. Its meaning and influence will vary from decision to decision based on such factors as knowledge of the applicant's behavioural propensities and the court clerk's confidence in managing unrepresented defendants in court.

Lastly, court clerks may be influenced by the future possibility that a refusal of legal aid may be overturned. An application for legal aid may be renewed at

---

[56] Op. cit., p. 246.
[57] Quoted in Young et al., *op. cit.*, pp. 35–6. See also Wall and Wood, *op. cit.*, p. 44.
[58] Whether there is in fact such a policy is further discussed below.

any stage in the proceedings, either to the court clerk or to the magistrates in open court. On a renewal, the clerk cannot refuse the application but must grant it, or else refer it to the magistrates. In addition, the applicant can apply to a Legal Aid Board area committee (made up of practising solicitors and barristers) for a review of a refused application in certain circumstances.[59] There may seem little point in refusing an application if it is believed that this refusal will be overturned either by a magistrate or by an area committee.

It is difficult to gauge the extent to which this factor influences court clerks, although some adjustment in their behaviour is apparent. Thus, Wall and Wood found that court clerks were more likely to grant a legal aid application if it involved co-defendants. This was in part because of the evidential complications raised by such cases, and in part because previous experience indicated that magistrates rarely refused such applications if renewed in open court.[60] It might be thought that magistrates rely so heavily on their clerks for advice in court that there would be little risk that they would grant a previously refused application. As against this, solicitors are able to put magistrates under pressure to grant in open court by parading an obviously 'inadequate' defendant before them.[61] As one of the solicitors interviewed by Young et al. put it: 'The magistrates are more sympathetic. It's a much more emotional level, particularly with disadvantaged defendants. If you have them in the dock going, 'whoaar, where am I?', it does bring it home.'[62] A refusal of legal aid in these circumstances may undermine the due process pretensions of the magistrates' courts. Court clerks thus know that there is a strong possibility that refusals of legal aid in other than a 'trivial' case will be overturned in open court.

A different set of considerations apply to review by area committees. These committees work outside of court processes and are not subject to any form of directive control by court clerks, and they are made up of people who may well be predisposed towards the grant of legal aid. As with magistrates, they may substitute their decision for that of the court clerk and are not confined merely to examining whether the original decision was patently irrational.[63] But since they have no jurisdiction over summary offences, their potential influence on first-tier decision-making is limited to either way and indictable matters.

Wall and Wood found that only 3 per cent of refused applications concerning non-summary offences were appealed to the area committee.[64] From this it

---

[59] For details, see Wood, A., 'Administrative Justice Within the Legal Aid Board: Reviews by caseworkers and area committees of refusals of criminal legal aid applications', at chapter 8 of this volume.

[60] Wall and Wood, *op. cit.*, p. 31.

[61] *Ibid.*, p. 19.

[62] Quoted in Young et al., *op. cit.*, p. 62.

[63] For the importance of this distinction see Bell, *op. cit.*, p. 94.

[64] *Op. cit.*, p. 35.

might be inferred that the review process is of marginal significance. On the other hand, court clerks may have already adjusted their decision-making to take account of the possibility of this type of review and, as a result, granted in many more cases than they would otherwise have done. What can be said as a minimum is that any right of appeal in any context reduces the likelihood of decision-makers flouting the law, or, to put it another way, it effectively reduces their discretion to do so.[65]

(iv) The offence-based nature of decision-making

The above examination of the factors that influence court clerks in determining legal aid applications demonstrated that the Widgery criteria are used more to justify than to guide decisions about legal aid. It appears that many (perhaps most) grants of legal aid are made in situations where the s. 22 criteria are regarded either as inapplicable, or as applicable but not that influential. Yet the reality is that the great majority of legal aid applications are granted (as noted above, most courts maintain grant rates of 90 per cent or more).[66]

This does not mean that grants of legal aid are arbitrary. Clear patterns of grants and refusals emerged from the Young et al. study, but these patterns related to the offence charged rather than to the s. 22 criteria themselves.[67] For certain offences, such as indecent assault, robbery and burglary of a dwelling, legal aid is almost automatically granted; for others, such as summary motoring offences, it is almost automatically refused. In the middle lies a grey area in which the legal aid decision cannot be predicted with any certainty. The lack of regard paid to the Widgery criteria is implicit in the following extract from an interview with a court clerk:

> What are the most important criteria I apply in looking at a legal aid application? I think the most important is the seriousness of the offence and whether or not it's a guilty plea. Even with a serious offence, if it's a guilty plea, I wouldn't necessarily grant it. I also wouldn't grant for a serious offence if it was doubtful that the magistrates would impose a custodial sentence, or any kind of serious sentence. But I think that the first thing I would look at is the nature of the offence and how serious it is.[68]

---

[65] See Lempert, R., 'Discretion in a Behavioral Perspective: The Case of a Public Housing Eviction Board', in Hawkins (ed.), *op. cit.*, pp. 195–8 for further discussion.
[66] In 1994, the grant rate for all legal aid applications was approximately 90.5 per cent: unpublished figures supplied by the Lord Chancellor's Department.
[67] See Young et al., *op. cit.*, pp. 34–5 and 40–7.
[68] Quoted in *ibid.*, p. 35.

A solicitor working in the same court as this clerk confirmed this account:

> I don't think, quite honestly, that they have any regard to the Widgery criteria at all. They look at an application and think that it should be granted without looking at the specific points that are made. I'm sure they work on a crude rule of thumb basis.[69]

Wall and Wood came to much the same conclusion. Having noted that determining a legal aid application might take court clerks only a minute or two, they continued:

> Rather than view the facts that were before them, they would tend to make a quick decision based upon the offence and plea, relying upon their previous experience of this combination of factors to support their decision if it were ever brought into question. Many determinations were found to be little more than snap judgments.[70]

It is the perceived seriousness of the defendant's position before the court that forms the basis for these quick decisions. The dominance of the custody criterion in the thinking of both court clerks and solicitors reflects a shared understanding that legal aid should be granted for serious matters. The custody criterion most closely reflects this idea of seriousness. That is why it is almost invariably invoked notwithstanding that both occupational groups know that a custodial outcome is unlikely. As one solicitor told Young et al.:

> In practical terms, custody is very rare before the magistrates. So you are using that criterion more to say that it is a serious matter. I think that provided people are charged with a reasonable offence, and offences which are either-way must fall within that category, they should get legal aid.[71]

The phenomenon of Widgery 'drift' suggests that court clerks broadly agree with this assessment. The focus on seriousness rather than custody was evident in the way that some of the dummy applications were decided. For example, one of these applications concerned a s. 47 assault in which the claim was made that the defendant was at risk of custody due to the nature of the offence and because he was subject to a bind-over for a similar offence. No other Widgery criteria were invoked. One clerk responded as follows:

---

[69] Quoted in *ibid.*, p. 34.
[70] Wall and Wood, *op. cit.*, p. 51.
[71] Quoted in Young et al., *op. cit.*, pp. 69–70.

He's charged with s. 47, so obviously it could be serious. The previous conviction is a bind-over, which is not a conviction, but it was for whacking his wife. He's not necessarily in real danger of custody. It's a tough one. There was actual injury caused. I think I'd have to grant it. If you are in doubt you've got to come down on the defendant's side.[72]

Court clerks were presented by Young et al. with a list of offences and asked to indicate (on a scale of 1–5) how likely it was that someone charged with a particular offence would be granted legal aid.[73] That they had no difficulty in completing this exercise with great rapidity provides further evidence of their offence-based approach to granting legal aid.

In summary, court clerks have developed a series of standardised responses to legal aid applications which represent a considerable simplification and distortion of the decision-making process prescribed by law. Because little credence is placed on information provided on application forms, each application is skim-read and the s. 22 criteria are presumed not to apply. Moreover, the pronounced tendency to grant in 'serious' cases and to refuse in 'non-serious' cases, means that court clerks rarely ponder the mysteries of the phrase 'the interests of justice'. These standardised responses are not invariably applied, however, and a well argued legal aid application form will sometimes produce a more considered decision. But so few applications are well argued that deviation from the decision-making norms described above is rare indeed.

(v) Accounting for the rule of law by rule of thumb

What lies behind the decision-making practices of court clerks as described above? One possible explanation is that such an offence-based approach has been encouraged officially. The Justices' Clerks' Society guidelines in force at the time of the research did little more than list those offences which it was felt should attract grants and those which should not. Similarly, one of the courts studied by Young et al. had developed its own set of guidelines which set out its own embedded tariff-based approach. In reality, however, such guidance is rarely consulted by court clerks.[74] It is fair to say that the guidelines represented a summary of existing practice rather than having any independent effect.

In understanding the behaviour of court clerks it is important to recognise that their decision-making is quasi-judicial and adjudicative in nature. That is to say, they have little or no control over the production or presentation of the facts contained in the legal aid application, and their decision is of the same

---

[72] Quoted in *ibid.*, p. 49.
[73] *Ibid.*, p. 45 and p. 110.
[74] Wall and Wood, *op. cit.*, p. 31.

dichotomous nature as that of an adjudicator. Either the application is granted or it is refused.[75] Moreover, court clerks operate within a judicial setting and are familiar with courtroom procedures and styles of decision-making.

The significance of viewing court clerks in this way stems from the body of socio-legal knowledge concerning those who occupy a quasi-judicial role.[76] Apparently wide discretionary powers are often subject in practice to detailed rules, albeit not necessarily legal rules. Decision-makers commonly use a grant of discretion not so much in the making of individual decisions, but in the creation and use of general standards or working rules which then guide or even dictate those decisions.[77] Similarly, adjudicators possessed of broad discretion will often in practice constrain themselves to a narrow range of options and produce predictable patterns of decision-making behaviour. This is particularly likely to occur where the decision-maker is faced, as court clerks are, with an endless stream of similar cases. As Lempert neatly puts it, familiarity breeds precedent.[78] By precedent here is meant informal working rules which govern the way in which cases are categorised and disposed of. These informal rules serve to simplify considerably the decision-making process.

We saw above how court clerks are engaged in a process of stereotyping in which a few features of each case, most notably the offences with which an applicant was charged, are seen as the basis for categorisation and subsequent decision-making. The individualised and complex acts of discretion prescribed by the law are replaced by rules of thumb.

This kind of simplification of decision-making may partly be a result of self-interest, since it makes the adjudicator's job easier, and partly a result of pursuing an organisational goal of efficiency, since cases can be disposed of far more quickly. Another factor is the adjudicator's desire to treat like cases alike. The specific organisational context within which court clerks work is also important. Magistrates' courts operate with large case-loads and are expected to dispense summary justice.[79] Time is always at a premium and business is conducted briskly with a minimum of formality. Yet, as has been seen, the law prescribes a complex and open-ended process for taking decisions on legal aid. The desire to simplify this task may be overpowering for hard-pressed bureaucrats.

---

[75] Another possibility is that further information will be sought from the applicant or from court files. Wall and Wood, *op. cit.*, p. 7, found that this happened in 7% of cases.

[76] See, for example, Hawkins, *op. cit.*, at p. 38.

[77] Lempert, *op. cit.*, p. 226. This observation holds true in non-adjudicative settings, such as policing on the street: McConville, M., Sanders, A. and Leng, R., *The Case for the Prosecution*, London: Routledge, 1991, pp. 22–35.

[78] Lempert, *op. cit.*, p. 208.

[79] See Sanders, A. and Young, R., *Criminal Justice*, London: Butterworths, 1994, pp. 249–53.

(vi)   Accounting for the particular rules of thumb employed

While the repetitive nature of decision-making may explain why simplification takes place, there is still a need to account for the particular forms it takes. Why, for example, has the band of offences for which legal aid is granted become so wide, and why does its size differ from court to court? Each court's pattern of grants and refusals (and the size and location of any 'grey area') depends on its clerks' views on the value of legal aid and the weight given to the notion that a greater involvement of solicitors will serve to oil the wheels of justice. As one court clerk conceded when interviewed: 'I am a believer that anyone who comes before the court should have a solicitor.'[80] In other words, the personal and bureaucratic values held by court clerks are of key significance in understanding their decision-making behaviour.

Previous studies have portrayed court clerks as liberal bureaucrats, interested in efficiency and saving court time but also in ensuring that the legitimacy of the court is not called into question.[81] How does the power to grant legal aid mesh with this analysis? McConville et al. have suggested that the widespread granting of legal aid is functional for court clerks on two levels.[82] First, it relieves them of the responsibility of helping unrepresented defendants, allowing them to concentrate on the more prestigious role of advising the bench. Secondly, it allows much of the processing of summary cases to be conducted by prosecution and defence lawyers outside of the courtroom through negotiation and compromise. The defendant and his or her case can then be served primed and 'oven-ready', so that the court need do little more than rubber-stamp decisions formulated by the lawyers over such matters as bail, mode of trial, plea and so on. It may be added that the greater involvement of defence lawyers in open court adds an air of fairness to the proceedings and thus serves to legitimate the processes leading to punishment.[83] Legal aid is thus a useful resource for liberal bureaucratic clerks since it helps them achieve both efficiency and legitimacy in court.

A factor which such analysis overlooks, but which may be influential, is a genuine belief in due process as a good in itself. The theoretical basis of the adversarial system rests on there being equality of arms between the prosecution and defence.[84] Now that the prosecution is always legally

---

[80] Quoted in Young et al., *op. cit.*, p. 35.

[81] See Bottoms, A. and McClean, J., *Defendants in the Criminal Process*, London: Routledge & Kegan Paul, 1976, p. 228, and Astor, *op. cit.*, n. 4. For a critique of this view of clerks as liberal bureaucrats, see Sanders and Young, *op. cit.* (1994), pp. 296–9.

[82] *Op. cit.* n. 7, pp. 6–7.

[83] See Cousins, M., 'At the Heart of the Legal: The Role of Legal Aid in Legitimating Criminal Justice', at chapter 5 of this volume.

[84] See Ashworth, *op. cit.*

represented there is a strong case for saying that legal aid should be automatically available for defendants in the magistrates' courts. This was clearly the view of the solicitors interviewed in both the studies discussed here. As one put it:

> I think that the purpose of involving solicitors is to ensure that the system operates fairly to balance in some way the power and resources that the police have. To that extent I think we should be involved in what I term serious offences.[85]

Solicitors were aware, however, that some courts were more sympathetic to this reasoning than others. The above solicitor, working in a court with a below average grant rate, continued:

> ... in this court the ideal of the clerk to the justices would be to have as few solicitors as possible in court with the clients numbered and lined up at the back with a conveyor belt to push them through. And I think he feels that, if someone appears in person, it takes five minutes, whereas if a solicitor is involved it takes twenty. He seems obsessed with throughput and I think the defendants suffer. All he's concerned about is statistics, how many defendants can he get through in the least number of court days.

This suggests that there is no simple relationship between the grant of legal aid and the achievement of efficiency gains. If those operating the court believe that the apparent and/or substantive fairness of proceedings is paramount, they are likely to grant legal aid on the grounds that they can achieve their objectives more efficiently by doing so. Deploying the court clerk to assist unrepresented defendants would be seen as second-best and potentially long-winded justice. But proceedings may actually be quicker if the defendant is unrepresented. This will be so as long as the help offered to unrepresented defendants is kept to a minimum and tight control is maintained in court. As the above quote illustrates, such a policy was evident in one of the courts studied by Young et al. The main decision-maker in this court asserted that the need for expert cross-examination was not a strong ground for granting legal aid, because in 90 per cent of cases it could be done by the defendant or the clerk. He immediately conceded that 'I know that isn't true, but that's what I'm told by my boss, and that's what I apply'.[86]

---

[85] Quoted in Young et al., *op. cit.*, p. 37.
[86] Quoted in *ibid.*, p. 38.

What should by now be clear is that there is no blanket policy of granting legal aid in order to aid courtroom efficiency. There are too many refusals of legal aid applications for this to be true, and in some courts efficiency appears to be pursued by other means. Nonetheless, court clerks would have been unlikely to sanction Widgery drift if a greater involvement of solicitors slowed down the business of the courts, and there can be little doubt that the analysis by McConville et al. is essentially correct.

(vii) Court cultures and variation in approach within a court

This discussion leads naturally to the observation that the culture of magistrates' courts varies enormously. These courts remain in essence decentralised institutions. Each strikes its own balance between such values as providing a service to court users, minimising delays, maximising the effective use of court time, controlling costs, achieving the appearance of due process and so forth.[87] Where court clerks value legal aid and have good relationships with local defence lawyers, a higher than average grant rate is likely to obtain than where relationships are poor and clerks are more doubtful about the need for solicitors in and out of court.[88]

Local court cultures are not monolithic, however, and there may be failures to transmit expectations and policies down the managerial line from the senior Clerk to the Justices to subordinate officers with day-to-day responsibility for determining legal aid applications. Furthermore, while those taking decisions on legal aid believe themselves to be in tune with their colleagues, this is not always so. For example, one of the dummy applications administered by Young et al. was based on a possession of cannabis charge. One clerk granted this peremptorily: 'He's had probation, he's had CSO — possession of cannabis does carry six months' imprisonment so there must be a risk of custody.' This clerk commented that his colleague approached legal aid applications in the same way and added that, 'We often discuss things if I think something's on the borderline and we seem to think pretty much the same way when we have those discussions'. Yet the determination of the same application by his colleague displayed a distinct lack of such uniformity: 'refused — it would be taken by the court as a small amount, class B drug, personal use, does not have a risk of a custodial sentence despite his previous'. Since neither clerk saw this as a borderline case, there would have been no reason to confer over it, and the

---

[87] See Raine, J. and Wilson, M., 'Organizational Culture and the Scheduling of Court Appearances', *Journal of Law and Society*, 1993, vol. 20, p. 237, and Wall and Wood, *op. cit.*, pp. 51–2.
[88] Courts with a positive attitude towards legal aid also tend to interpret the Widgery criteria more widely. See further Young, R., 'The Merits of Legal Aid in the Magistrates' Court', *Criminal Law Review*, 1993, p. 336.

opposing rules of thumb would have remained undetected.[89] Thus, while variation within a court is undoubtedly less than that which exists between courts, it is arguable that courts do not have policies on legal aid other than those pursued in a rather idiosyncratic fashion by individual clerks.

(viii) Widgery 'drift'

As noted above, since the Widgery Committee reported in 1966 there has been a massive increase in the number and proportion of defendants in the magistrates' courts who are granted legal aid. There are few better illustrations of Hawkin's observation that discretion is an adaptable and dynamic phenomenon.[90] It is unlikely that there is any simple explanation for what McConville et al. rightly call the major transformation of the position regarding the availability of legal aid under the Widgery criteria.[91] Many of the factors identified above will have played a part. In addition, Goriely points to the growth in the business handled by the magistrates' courts as fuelling the need for courtroom efficiency and the growth of lawyers' pre-trial 'informal justice'.[92] Another reason may have been the growing professionalisation of the prosecution function, which culminated in the mid-1980s with the creation of the Crown Prosecution Service. To have failed to respond through a greater readiness to grant legal aid would have threatened both the appearance and substance of justice in the magistrates' courts.

Yet the Widgery drift may cease, or even be reversed, because of broader economic and political pressures. The Government has repeatedly expressed its belief that court clerks are too lax in granting legal aid and has taken steps to ensure that that message is taken seriously. The President of the Justices' Clerks' Society warned its 1995 annual conference that the Lord Chancellor's Department had made it clear to him that, unless greater care was taken in determining legal aid applications in future, the power to do so would be transferred to some other agency. He added that this would lead to 'horrendous delays' in the throughput of criminal cases.[93] Since avoiding delay is a central concern of the magistrates' courts, one can well imagine that court clerks might take the hint and begin to decide legal aid applications more carefully and restrictively.

---

[89] For further discussion of variation in approach within a court, see Young et al., *op. cit.*, pp. 58–61.
[90] Hawkins, *op. cit.*, p. 45.
[91] McConville et al., *op. cit.* (1994), p. 9.
[92] Goriely, *op. cit.*
[93] *The Lawyer*, 9 May 1995. As noted in the first section of this chapter, the Lord Chancellor has repeated this warning in the Green Paper, *op. cit.*

V CONCLUSION

The way in which court clerks determine legal aid applications bears little resemblance to the model of decision-making implicit in the law. In this final section, the implications of this analysis are considered.

One problem with such a discretionary system as flows from the 'interests of justice' test is that it allows irrelevant considerations to come into play. Whether an applicant receives legal aid can depend as much upon the personal views and whims of court clerks as upon the need for professional advice and representation. Virtually identical applications for legal aid may be granted in one court and refused in another, or granted in one court by one clerk and refused by another clerk in the same court.

As the Widgery Report recognised, complete uniformity of practice cannot be achieved so long as the responsibility for considering applications is shared by a large number of separate authorities exercising a wide discretion. That report nonetheless favoured the retention of court-based decision-making on the ground that determining whether legal aid was in the interests of justice involved a delicate balancing of many considerations and that, therefore, those responsible for determining legal aid applications 'should have an intimate knowledge of the working and atmosphere of the court in which proceedings are to take place'.[94] The position taken by the Widgery Committee on this important issue needs to be reassessed in the light of the empirical findings discussed above. The tariff-based nature of current legal aid decision-making does not suggest great delicacy of approach, but rather the operation of somewhat crude rules of thumb.

Official guidance on the interests of justice test, issued since the conclusion of the two studies summarised here, attempts both to reassert the need for individualised judgment and to structure decision-making in terms of the s. 22 criteria.[95] But these new guidelines are unlikely to affect the informal working rules of court clerks unless broader contextual and structural features of their activities are addressed. Chief amongst these is the simple human expedient to simplify a complex task.

If such simplification is unavoidable, it may be preferable for it to take place at the democratic level rather than be left to the idiosyncrasies of individual court clerks operating within particularistic court cultures. There is a case, in other words, for Parliament to substitute for the discretionary 'interests of justice' test, detailed prescriptions of when legal aid should be granted and when refused. This contention is not based on the naive assumption that rules

---

[94] Widgery Report, *op. cit.*, para. 67.
[95] *Guidance on the Interests of Justice Test for the Grant of Criminal Legal Aid*, London: Lord Chancellor's Department, Justices' Clerks Society, Legal Aid Board, May 1994.

are good and discretion bad. Rather it stems from the position that rule-application always involves the exercise of discretion, just as discretion is invariably rule-bound. The real question concerns the right mix of rules and discretion. This cannot be determined *a priori*, but depends on the specific decision-making context with which one is dealing.[96] The argument here is that the discretion of court clerks is currently less rule-bound by law than is desirable.

Hard and fast legal rules would produce hard cases and fast decision-making, just as hard and fast working rules currently do. The difference would lie in the legitimacy of the source of the rules and the degree of open debate which surrounded their introduction and subsequent development. To that extent, the proposal in the Green Paper to replace the Widgery criteria with a simpler interests of justice test may be given a qualified welcome.[97] Under the new test, the interests of justice would be deemed to require an automatic grant of legal aid in three situations: first, where the applicant was charged with an either-way offence or with one triable only on indictment; secondly, where he or she would be unable to understand the proceedings or act in person because of inadequate knowledge of English, mental illness, or other mental or physical disability; thirdly, where an allegation is made of serious abuse of power by the police.[98] For summary offences where the last two situations did not apply, legal aid would remain discretionary and a range of factors would be taken into account, much as is supposed to happen now, in deciding whether a grant would be in the interests of justice. This would represent a great simplification as far as indictable offences are concerned (in law if not in practice) and would certainly promote greater consistency. But it would lead to a higher level of grant in many courts while doing nothing to address the problems of the existing discretionary test as far as summary offences are concerned. As the Green Paper observes, 'there might be difficulties with auditing the summary offences test, and the criteria for automatic grant of legal aid might be too broad'.[99]

No further attempt will be made here to develop a view as to what should replace the current legal framework beyond the making of a simple observation: if legal aid is to continue to be denied to large numbers of defendants facing criminal charges, the pretence that decisions are based purely on a

---

[96] See Schneider, C., 'Discretion and Rules: A Lawyer's View', in Hawkins (ed.), *op. cit.*, at p. 88.
[97] This is discussed in the Green Paper, *op. cit.*, pp. 74–5, paras 10.16–10.18.
[98] The Green Paper is clumsily expressed on this issue and does not make it clear that any one of these situations in isolation will prompt an automatic grant of criminal legal aid, although that does appear to be the intention.
[99] *Ibid.*, pp. 74–5, para. 10.18.

conception of what the interests of justice require should be abandoned.[100] Instead, one might build a new set of rules around an express (and more honest) legislative aim of directing limited legal aid funds to those defendants whose legal need is the greatest. To some extent, the Green Paper possesses the virtue of this kind of honesty. Although the interests of justice test is to be retained, the advocacy of a fixed pre-determined budget for legal aid implies that considerations of cost may override the interests of justice on occasion. Ultimately, however, the Green Paper ducks the real issue of principle by failing to specify the situations in which the Government considers that leaving defendants unrepresented, when faced with the might of the state in an adversarial setting, is in the interests of justice.

---

[100] Paradoxically, because the European Convention on Human Rights embodies a right to legal aid when the 'interests of justice' so require, the Government cannot simply legislate the phrase away. For discussion of the Convention, see Ashworth, *op. cit.*

8

Administrative Justice within the Legal Aid Board: Reviews by Caseworkers and Area Committees of Refusals of Criminal Legal Aid Applications

Adrian Wood[*]

In his influential study of official discretion Galligan noted that:

> The expanded role of the modern state has brought with it, for reasons not always made clear, an increase in discretionary powers, in the sense that control over a wider range of matters is delegated to officials with varying degrees of guidance as to the policy goals to be achieved or the standards by which they are to be achieved.[1]

This chapter explores the dynamics of criminal legal aid decision-making by officials at the area committee level of the Legal Aid Board of England and Wales. It argues, first, that the Board's procedures for reviewing magistrates' court refusals of legal aid are inadequate and, secondly, that the decision-making approaches by individual Legal Aid Board personnel are so seriously flawed that gross inconsistencies are created in decision outcomes. It is suggested that recent empirical research on criminal legal aid decision-making demonstrates a need seriously to consider alternative mechanisms for allocating legal aid assistance in the criminal justice system.

[*] The author would like to thank Richard Young, and his colleagues John Bell, Dave Wall, Brian Hogan, and Michael Cardwell for their helpful comments and suggestions.
[1] Galligan, D., *Discretionary Powers: A Legal Study of Official Discretion*, Oxford: Clarendon Press, 1986, p. 2.

164

I INTRODUCTION

When a criminal legal aid application is refused by the magistrates' court, in practice one of two routes is available for reconsideration of the application: either a re-application is made directly back to the court, and usually dealt with orally before magistrates, or the applicant may seek a review before the area committee of the Legal Aid Board within 14 days of the date of notification of the original refusal.

To be eligible for review the application must relate to an either way or purely indictable offence and no rehearing of the legal aid application must have taken place at court before the review has been determined by the Board.[2] On receipt of the review application at the Legal Aid Board Area Office (henceforth Area Office) a Legal Aid Board administrator acting under delegated powers (known as a caseworker) may either grant the application or refer it to an area committee of the Board composed of a minimum of three solicitors nominated by local Law Societies. This committee may either grant or refuse the application. No appeal lies from the decision of the area committee, although an unlimited number of further re-applications can be made back to the magistrates' court.[3]

Richard Young's assessment of criminal legal aid determinations in the magistrates' courts reveals decision-makers to be subject to a huge range of situational and occupational influences impacting on the decision-making process.[4] Based on an analysis of recent studies,[5] he argues that the final determination may rely heavily on the personal judgement and individually constructed standards of individual court decision-makers. However, equally important was the finding that the occupational culture of the courts tempered these personal idiosyncrasies. Common standards (or rules of thumb) for decision-making emerged, which in turn sustained relatively consistent discretionary decision-making.

The following account of Legal Aid Board decision-making practices focuses on many similar discretion-related themes. This chapter aims, first, to

---

[2] Since a change in Legal Aid Board policy in 1993, summary offences may also be joined to the application as long as the either way/purely indictable criterion is satisfied. A further prerequisite to seeking a review is that the original application to court must have been made at least 21 days before the date set for trial. See Legal Aid in Criminal and Care Proceedings (General) Regulations 1989 (SI 1989 No. 344), regs 15–16.

[3] *Ibid.*, regs 14 and 17.

[4] See Young, R., 'Will Widgery Do?: Court Clerks, Discretion, and the Determination of Legal Aid Applications', at chapter 7 of this volume.

[5] Particularly Young, R., Moloney, T. and Sanders, A., *In the Interests of Justice?*, London: Legal Aid Board, 1992, and Wall, D. S. and Wood, A., *The Administration of Criminal Legal Aid in the Magistrates' Courts of England and Wales: Final Report*, Leeds: Centre for Criminal Justice Studies, 1994.

unravel the factors taken into account, consciously or unconsciously, at Board level in formulating any decision-making standards, secondly, to determine whether Legal Aid Board decision-makers operate any consistent decision-making standards, and, thirdly, to discover any pre-eminence attached to particular standards. How these Board administrators operate the relevant statutory provisions will facilitate an understanding of the impact of procedures on substantive decision outcomes. The assessment is timely because it may throw some light on the consistency of decision-making in criminal legal aid at a time when the Government is considering the transfer from the courts to the Legal Aid Board of the administration of criminal legal aid.[6]

The discussion and evaluation of decision-making practices incorporates findings from Young et al.'s[7] study on legal aid, but is based principally on previously unreported research which builds on Wall and Wood's study[8] into magistrates' courts' decision-making. A total of six Area Offices (out of 13 nationally) of the Legal Aid Board were studied and 6,200 criminal legal aid review decisions, covering the period January 1992 to June 1994, were analysed. In addition, 2,716 criminal legal aid review files were read fully to obtain information on the following: the name of the original court, the applicants' solicitors, the basis of the application, the offences involved, plea, how long it took to process the application, who was the decision-maker, what criterion/criteria was/were used by the decision-maker, and any special procedural or substantive circumstances. A total of eight area committee meetings were observed and the decision-making of 17 caseworkers analysed. Semi-structured interviews and decision-making exercises were conducted with key decision-makers.

For the purposes of this chapter much of the relevant theoretical discussion on discretionary decision-making in this field, together with a full account of the statutory framework applicable to criminal legal aid decision-making, have been examined already by Richard Young in the context of legal aid determinations at court level.[9] Thus the same statutory provisions in s. 22 of the Legal Aid Act 1988, as applied by court clerks, are used by caseworkers and area committee members, and in principle the same guidance on the application of those criteria, whether judicial or administrative in origin, should be invoked at Board level.

In this discussion of Legal Aid Board procedures, it will become apparent that caseworkers exercise a crucial role in the determination process, and this raises questions about their accountability. Galligan has observed that:

---

[6] Lord Chancellor's Department, *Legal Aid – Targeting Need: The future of publicly funded help in solving legal problems and disputes in England and Wales*, Cm 2854, London: HMSO, 1995.
[7] *Op. cit.*
[8] *Op. cit.* The research was funded by the ESRC: award nos. R000232673 and R000234528.
[9] See chapter 7 of this volume.

In the context of delegated powers, accountability branches off in two directions, one towards the political process, the other towards the legal system. [I believe] ... legal accountability ... should be seen as not self-contained and independent of political morality, but as constituting the application and working out of that morality within the context of relations between citizens and state.[10]

While helpful as a guide, Galligan's definition does not adequately embrace the full extent of the role of the caseworker, who both represents the state and stands between it (in its executive role as paymaster) and the citizen (as applicant for public funding). In addition, although strictly speaking an 'appeal' to the Area Office ought to be viewed as *de novo*, the impression cannot be avoided of an administrative body reviewing a quasi-judicial or magisterial decision. This places the Board decision-maker in a distinctive situation in which difficult choices must be made. For example, in the formulation of decision-making standards, what weight should be given to Legal Aid Board policy? Applications for legal aid may be refused by magistrates' courts at first instance on the basis that the applicant is not likely to receive a custodial sentence if convicted.[11] Should any presumption exist that courts know their sentencing policy better than any other external body; and would it intrude on perceptions of judicial independence for the Legal Aid Board to gainsay a decision on a matter about which the courts should be expert? Or do such priorities as creating a national uniform decision-making standard for criminal legal aid justify Board decision-makers marginalising the often strongly expressed views of court officials? How these conflicts are allowed to impinge on the formulation of standards in decision-making is essentially a matter of personal choice, but the exercise of that choice raises tensions between political will and judicial independence.

The structure of the chapter is as follows. In section II, the historical background of the review system is charted. Section III examines the pattern of applications for review, and section IV looks at the way in which professional interests dominate the system. Section V explores the complex relationship between caseworkers and area committees, and section VI evaluates Area Office decision-making overall in the light of a theoretical model of administrative justice. In the conclusion, the main occupational, situational and legislative factors impinging on Legal Aid Board decision-makers are summarised and placed into the context of current reform initiatives.

---

[10] Galligan, *op. cit.*, p. 4.

[11] See s. 22(2)(a) of the Legal Aid Act 1988 and the exposition of the statutory framework by Young, *op. cit.*

II THE POLITICAL AND HISTORICAL CONTEXT OF THE REVIEW MECHANISM

In order to develop an understanding of the relationship between the different tiers of legal aid decision-making, it is instructive to consider the background to the implementation of the review procedure in 1984. The creation of a mechanism to challenge criminal legal aid refusals was the product of an Opposition sponsored amendment by Lord Elwyn-Jones to the 1982 Legal Aid Bill. The amendment originally stated that 'an appeal shall lie against the refusal by a magistrates' court to make a legal aid order', and was born of concern that serious unexplained discrepancies were appearing in the decisions of magistrates' courts on legal aid. An all-party consensus existed that refusal rates at courts had got out of hand, to the extent that refusal rates in neighbouring courts might differ by a factor of eight. Of the need to create a mechanism to challenge first-tier decisions, Lord Mishcon observed that:

It was an utmost necessity if justice is to be given to people to whom this matter of legal aid in criminal matters is of such great importance.[12]

Initially, due to arguments over costs and delay, the Government had been sceptical of the value of a new procedure. Lord Hailsham summarised its view:

Ever since the Widgery Committee, it was always held to be doctrine that it was impracticable to introduce a system of appeals against refusals of legal aid.[13]

The Government's objections were eventually overcome by considerations of natural justice. As Lord Elwyn-Jones noted:

I cannot repeat too emphatically that this right of appeal is an essential need in the whole legal aid set-up. My noble and learned friend Lord Gardiner has indicated its unique position as an important branch of social welfare and the only part of it where there is no form of recourse.[14]

Once the principle of a review had been accepted, the House of Lords wrestled at length with the problem of how to implement an appropriate delivery mechanism. The original amendment had referred to the creation of an 'appeal against refusal to a court or body' and the Opposition proposed the

---

[12] Hansard (HL) vol. 429, col. 242.
[13] Hansard (HL) vol. 435, col. 234.
[14] Hansard (HL) vol. 429, col. 531.

Crown Court as a suitable vehicle. Lord Hailsham, the then Lord Chancellor, could not accept that an 'appeal' was appropriate terminology, because a subsequent decision might be based on a premise or information wholly unrelated to the facts surrounding the original application. He thus preferred the phraseology of 'recourse' to that of 'appeal'. Stronger objections also existed; that the Crown Court was already overburdened with the effects of the Criminal Justice Act 1982, and it would be impracticable to encourage shuttling to and from courts on minor issues. Lord Hailsham suggested that an appeal to the Crown Court:

> Would then turn out to be a fifth wheel to the coach if there had to be two resorts to the Crown Court, one appealing against refusal of legal aid and the other appealing against the verdict when it comes.[15]

Others, however, noted that it would also be inappropriate to subject the decisions of the judiciary to a non-judicial body. As Lord Campbell of Alloway observed:

> Would your Lordships not think that it would be wrong, on any showing, notwithstanding such discrepancies as may exist, to have a re-hearing *de novo*? This subjects the magistrates to a type of revisory procedure which does not obtain in other courts. It would mean substituting the discretion of the revisory court for that of the magistrates and that, in my submission, would be undesirable as reflecting on the competence of the magistrates, and would be wrong.[16]

In the course of the 18-month delay in deciding which body would re-examine refusals, the question of how any such body should approach an application was lost and no guidance appeared in the implementing legislation. Regulations eventually provided for the creation of a 'review to the appropriate criminal legal aid committee' of the Law Society, modelled on the existing civil legal aid committee.[17] When the Legal Aid Board took over the administration of legal aid from the Law Society in 1989, reviews were to be directed to 'appropriate area committees'. In practice, civil and criminal matters were dealt with alongside each other in a civil legal aid orientated committee and the specific criminal legal aid expertise which had hitherto existed was lost.

---

[15] Hansard (HL) vol. 429, col. 528.
[16] Hansard (HL) vol. 429, col. 526.
[17] The Legal Aid in Criminal Proceedings (General) (Amendment) Regulations 1983 (SI 1983 No. 1863).

The reaction of magistrates to the review mechanism was initially mistrustful, heightened by a perception that the role of the non-professional judiciary was under threat.[18] By offering greater flexibility for applicants to test the merits of their eligibility for public-funded assistance, the courts were made to feel that they were not always best placed to appreciate the subtleties of an application. However, the relatively modest take-up of reviews served to allay any fears among court administrators that the judicial process would be invaded by bureaucratic structures.[19]

III PATTERN OF APPLICATIONS

The problems associated with determining the precise numbers of grants and refusals made by magistrates' courts[20] impose some constraints on assessing the exact use of the review system. Quantitatively, the review applications amounted to less than 1 per cent of all applications (civil and criminal) processed by the Board. Table 8.1 charts the historical throughput of reviews in the first column.[21] Those figures are then expressed in the second column as a percentage of all court refusals.[22] The third column details the cumulative caseworker and area committee grant rate at Board level.[23]

---

[18] The propriety of a Legal Aid Board committee adjudicating legal aid refusals featured on the agenda of the 22nd AGM of the Magistrates' Association in 1984. See *The Magistrate*, 1984, vol. 40, p. 146.

[19] The rapid growth in legal aid grants in magistrates' courts since the middle 1980s has been attributed by some commentators to the provision of a review route. The argument made was that court decision-makers assumed that Area Office administrators would grant most reviews and thus sought to short-circuit the process by granting more applications. A court culture more sympathetic to applications was thus created. See Bazell, C., 'Casenote on *R* v *Bury Magistrates, ex. p. N (a minor)*', *Journal of Criminal Law*, 1987, p. 119. For a contrary view, see Law Society and LCAC, *Legal Aid: 38th Annual Reports of the Law Society and the Lord Chancellor's Advisory Committee (1987–1988)*, HC 134, London: HMSO, 1989, p. 6, paras 43–44.

[20] See Wall and Wood, *op. cit.*, pp. 45–46 for a discussion of these problems.

[21] Source: Legal Aid Board, *Annual Report (1994–95)*, HC 526, London: HMSO, 1995, p. 76.

[22] Applications for review are expressed as a percentage of all magistrates' courts refusals (including refusals ineligible for review). From Lord Chancellor's Department, *Judicial Statistics*, Cmnd 9599, London: HMSO, 1984, ch. 10; Lord Chancellor's Department, *Judicial Statistics*, Cmnd 1990, London: HMSO, 1991, ch. 10; and also unpublished data supplied by the Lord Chancellor's Department.

[23] Source: Legal Aid Board, *op. cit.*, p. 76. Figures have been rounded to the nearest whole number.

Table 8.1: Applications for review of refusal of criminal legal aid

	Applications received	Take-up rate	Grant rate
1984–85	4,476	9.2%	69%
1985–86	5,418	10.9%	71%
1986–87	6,138	13.0%	72%
1987–88	6,359	13.2%	69%
1988–89	5,791	12.1%	67%
1989–90	4,025	8.5%	68%
1990–91	3,831	8.5%	66%
1991–92	3,890	8.2%	60%
1992–93	5,767	11.0%	53%
1993–94	4,957	10.5%	59%
1994–95	4,860	9.9%	61%

Several points can be made about this Table. First, when the review files were manually checked against the returns made by Area Offices to Board Head Office, it was discovered that significant variations existed in the true grant (success) rates. So, for example, in the 1992–93 period, the official overall grant rate was 53 per cent,[24] which corresponds to the average of the grant rate figures sent to Head Office by the six Area Offices surveyed.[25] However, when the true grant rate was computed from the actual files, the average grant rate was found to be 67 per cent across the six Area Offices. This discrepancy is due in large part to the Legal Aid Board practice of including all applications (including invalid ones typically relating to purely summary offences such as driving with excess alcohol) in the gross figure, which is then further inflated by a common practice among some caseworkers of withdrawing applications from the computer and relisting them as new applications in order to present a better set of fortnightly disposal statistics to Head Office. Since 1993, the Legal Aid Board has set targets for turning around applications and any remaining undetermined for over 14 days from receipt undermine the perceived efficiency of the Area Office.

Secondly, while the criminal legal aid application rate to courts increased by only 2 per cent in the period 1991–92 to 1992–93, in volume terms the review application rate increased in 1992–93 by 48 per cent over 1991–92. That

---

[24] Legal Aid Board, *op. cit.*, p. 76.
[25] Data kindly supplied by the Legal Aid Board.

increase is also mirrored in the take-up rate, which rose from 8 to 11 per cent over the same period. At the same time the national court refusal rate increased by only 0.9 per cent to 9.6 per cent. It is clear from the content of applications that the main cause of the rise in reviews stems from the difficulties encountered by solicitors in persuading court decision-makers that a defendant's record aggravated the present offence under s. 29 of the Criminal Justice Act 1991.[26] The significance of this lies in s. 22(2)(a) of the Legal Aid Act 1988, which provides, in essence, that the greater the risk that the defendant will be given a custodial sentence if convicted, the stronger the case for granting legal aid. It is noticeable that the number of firms using the review procedure increased significantly during the period immediately following the implementation of s. 29 and during a period that showed a national increase in magistrates' courts refusals.[27] This suggests that there was widespread discontent amongst the practitioners about the impact of the Act on legal aid income generation and that the area committee structure served a purpose as a useful reference point for an alternative interpretation of the Act.

Thirdly, when the pattern of review applications is charted over a 24-month period, a remarkably consistent correlation is found between Area Offices in terms of peaks and troughs of monthly review activity. As might be expected, increased review activity occurred shortly after the implementation of the Criminal Justice Act 1991, in October 1992, as lawyers sought to make sense of the Act and bring their applications within its strictures. Quiet periods mirrored lower police charging rates around holiday periods. Although care must be taken not to extrapolate too much from a set of figures about whose accuracy reservations have already been made, it is noticeable that since 1984 other peaks of activity occurred shortly after the introduction of the Police and Criminal Evidence Act 1984 and the Prosecution of Offences Act 1985. Review applications are also sensitive to judicial developments. So for example, when the Divisional Court ruled in *McGhee*[28] that community service orders were not custodial sentences within the meaning of s. 22(2)(a) of the Legal Aid Act 1988, a drop occurred in the number of review applications. This decline in throughput was hastened when the Criminal Justice Act 1991 was amended from 15 August 1993, restoring to sentencers the ability to have regard to previous convictions.

---

[26] Section 29 of the Criminal Justice Act 1991 provided that courts were not, subject to limited exceptions, to use a defendant's previous convictions as a reason to increase the appropriate sentence for the offence.

[27] Wall, D. and Wood, A., 'Buying time for the debate over criminal legal aid', *New Law Journal*, 1993, vol. 143, p. 324.

[28] *R* v *Liverpool City Magistrates ex parte McGhee* [1993] Crim LR 609.

While each Board Area Office has one or two high-volume practices which maintain a bureaucratic practice of seeking reviews as a matter of course, the majority of review applications are made by small to medium-sized general practices. Busy court solicitors are less likely to use the Legal Aid Board process, and where they seek reconsideration of the refusal, applications are usually made orally to the court. Re-applications are not made as a matter of course, however, and experienced criminal practitioners appear to have a strong sense of realism about whether a refusal is within the accepted court norm for a given situation.[29] Solicitors from smaller or less local practices appear less frequently in court and therefore have fewer opportunities to re-present refused applications. This may explain why they turn to the review process so often. They are also less familiar with the accepted court norms for granting legal aid and so are more likely to regard refusals as unjustifiable and susceptible to a successful challenge through an external review.

IV PROFESSIONAL DOMINATION OF THE SYSTEM

Whereas the initiative for making an initial application for legal aid is taken by the solicitor,[30] when it comes to the post-refusal situation, interviews with solicitors revealed that the initiative for reconsideration comes frequently from the defendant. This turnaround in pro-active thinking is due to the latter's receipt of the court refusal notice, this being the first formal contact in practice with the legal aid process. From this point on, however, a striking feature of the review process is its focus on lawyers and its dependency on practitioner involvement in the minutiae of the process. This illustrates well the extent to which lawyers have 'captured' the legal aid scheme.[31]

The statutory legal aid application form, a copy of which is supposed to be returned to the applicant by the refusing court, is deemed insufficient for Board purposes and the Board produces its own review application form, known as the Crim 9. It is clear from the documentation used for the appeal process that the area committee review system is designed to be used by professionals for the benefit of professionals. First, Crim 9 is available only from the Board and not from courts. Failure by the applicant to supply this form is viewed as fatal to the application, even though the statutory application form is arguably more important for confirming the fact of a court refusal. Secondly, the Crim 9 form is premised on the basis that the applicant is a solicitor. So, for example, the

[29] Wall, D. and Wood, A., 'An endangered species: The experienced criminal practitioner', *Solicitors' Journal*, 1992, vol. 136, p. 796.
[30] See chapter 6 of this volume.
[31] See generally, Hansen, O., 'A Future for Legal Aid?', *Journal of Law and Society*, 1992, vol. 19, p. 85 at p. 86.

form states 'attach your client's statement' and refers to the Widgery criteria, a reference which would be meaningless to anyone but a lawyer engaged in criminal practice. Thirdly, every instance of a defendant applying alone for review is met by the Board with a computer-generated request for a catalogue of detailed information from the applicant. This request is aimed at, and is usually only comprehensible by, a solicitor. In short, Legal Aid Board terminology promotes confusion and discourages further application. With Green Form assistance exhausted and rarely extended, the applicant is unable to obtain further advice from the solicitor and the review process for such solo applicants effectively terminates at this point, unless the duty solicitor can be persuaded to undertake the task. The participation of a solicitor in the process, even though not a *de jure* requirement, becomes a *de facto* necessity for defendants. From the client's perspective, the success of a review application hinges on the willingness of the solicitor to engage in the process.

The importance of the solicitor to the review process is reinforced when procedures are observed. On receipt of a review request the caseworker registers the application, checks that the appropriate documentation has been supplied and, if necessary, will request further information from the applicant's solicitor. As no formal contacts exist between the Legal Aid Board and the courts, the solicitor acts as a conduit for the supply of information from court level. The Crim 9 review application form requires disclosure of plea, a summary of the prosecution case, and an outline of the defence or mitigation. Under regulations,[32] the applicant has to provide a copy of the original application form and notice of refusal from the court. Legal Aid Board procedures require a copy of the Advance Disclosure,[33] if available, and a copy of the applicant's statement. Such demands impose significant burdens on solicitors and contributed to the lack of enthusiasm among lawyers for the system. As one solicitor commented:

> I get nothing but hassle from them [caseworkers]. I dread a DX[34] from the Legal Aid Board because they invariably ask me questions I cannot answer, or which cost me much time in obtaining when they could get the information themselves if they wanted to. The fuller I make the application the more they seem to want. But what is galling is the pernicketiness of their requests. I would not bother with the system were it not for the fact that court clerks can be worse.

---

[32] Legal Aid in Criminal and Care Proceedings (General) Regulations 1989 (SI 1989 No. 344, as amended), reg 17(2).

[33] That is, information provided by the prosecution to the defence in advance of trial.

[34] Short for document exchange, but in practice has come to mean in 'solicitor-speak' any delivery received through this private postal system.

The costs of initiating the procedure are outweighed for some practitioners in some cases, however, by the economic benefits of applying for a review. From interviews with solicitors it is abundantly clear that the review process serves to maximise financial reward. The process of seeking a review serves to extinguish any residual claimable time under the Green Form scheme.[35] As one solicitor commented:

> Hard times mean squeezing what you can from the system. After all, I see no harm in getting the state to pay something towards the work I otherwise do for free.

Another experienced practitioner was just as explicit:

> If the truth be told, by the time I clock up the real time I spend on a case on Green Form in getting it reviewed, I am looking for assistance as much as my client.

In a system so dominated by professional interests, it is perhaps not surprising that it is sometimes operated purely or mainly in the interests of those professionals.

V THE DYNAMICS OF THE CASEWORKER/AREA COMMITTEE RELATIONSHIP

Having examined how reviews are initiated, we turn now to the handling of reviews within Area Offices. The caseworker is the linchpin in this regard. Decisions about whether the application is within the Board's jurisdiction, can be granted forthwith or should be referred to the area committee lie initially with the caseworker who remains effectively unaccountable for such actions. Legal Aid Board internal procedures provide for audit and appraisal of caseworker decision-making. Two such appraisals were observed and it was clear that the appraisers concentrated solely on procedural issues rather than factors relevant to how decisions had been arrived at. At one Area Office, a caseworker admitted that he had reviewed his own decisions.

Where a caseworker is not prepared to grant an application, the file is forwarded to the clerk of the area committee. This person is usually an Area Office solicitor, but senior administrators sometimes perform the same function. The review application is then placed before the next available

---

[35] This head of the Legal Aid Scheme funds initial advice and assistance to defendants.

meeting of the area committee, together with a short agenda note prepared by the caseworker.

Area committees are supposedly comprised of experts who retain sufficient links with court culture to provide the necessary guidance for proper decision-making on legal aid applications. As Lord Hailsham observed: '[Area] committees ... consist of experienced practising lawyers who bring an independent professional judgement to bear on their work.'[36] However, enquiries with Area Offices revealed that no more than approximately 30 per cent of panel members have current experience of a criminal case-load, and in a number of hearings observed no criminal practitioner was present. Area committee meetings are closed to the public and no instance of an applicant being invited to attend the hearing was discovered, even though attendance at civil legal aid hearings is relatively common. In practice most committee adjudications are unstructured, and if a criminal practitioner is present discussion is frequently led by that person, who adopts the line of what would be expected at that practitioner's local court for a similar matter. The committee clerk usually remains passive throughout the hearing. One clerk commented:

I do not see it as my job to try and steer the committee towards a solution unless they are completely on the wrong tack. They tend to steer the discussion themselves. They make a decision and I often have to remind them that they should declare a ground under s. 22. In reality it is often left to the clerk to choose a ground because the committee either won't find one or can't find one.

Committee members do not see the papers before the actual committee hearing and the reviews are placed at the end of the agenda. Each review rarely took longer than 45 seconds to consider.

The difficulties associated with the composition of the committee were starkly drawn by one committee clerk (a solicitor):

The problem is that they are basically civil practitioners and may have no grounding in current issues of criminal law. They tend to grant through ignorance. They certainly come up with odd decisions ... I guess a real problem is that they are unaccountable, and by the time they deal with the criminal stuff they are knackered from the rest of the list.

The problem of area committee composition has long been recognised by the Legal Aid Board. Its submission to the Lord Chancellor's Department on the question of the Legal Aid Board take-over of criminal legal aid notes that:

---

[36] Hansard (HL) vol. 427, col. 753.

The area committee members who deal with criminal cases are not at present necessarily criminal practitioners. It would be more equitable if area committees were expanded to contain more criminal practitioners, with a view to the area committees being divided into civil committees and criminal committees accordingly.[37]

The role of the area committee in criminal matters is to determine those cases which the Area Office (i.e., caseworker) is not willing to grant.[38] The committee is dependent for its work on a reference from the caseworker. Research indicates that caseworkers hold different views as to when the area committee route should be invoked. One caseworker commented:

They [area committee members] are the experts. They ought to know what is the going rate for the offence. I would only grant those applications which I was sure ought to get legal aid.

A different perspective, from an Area Office in which area committees played only a minor role in criminal reviews, was offered by another caseworker:

Put it this way. Sometimes they help. A lot of the time it is a lottery what they do. I might float one to the committee as a test case to cover my back but I prefer not to bother them if I can.

On the relationship between caseworker and committee the same caseworker noted: 'I suppose we are second-guessing the committee, but it is difficult when they come up with such crap decisions.'

The use of the referral power has potentially important consequences for applications. Those caseworkers who take the view that a committee of professionals is the proper forum for such considerations tend to refer borderline applications to the committee instead of there and then invoking the provision of s. 21(7) of the Legal Aid Act 1988. This section states that 'where a doubt arises whether representation . . . should be granted to any person, the doubt should be resolved in that person's favour'. That the area committee might nevertheless refuse the application is not seen as a concern by willing referrers. This line of thinking leads to potential refusals by the area committee of those legal aid applications which ought otherwise to have been granted in accordance with the Legal Aid Act 1988, s. 21(7). This deference shown by

---

[37] Legal Aid Board, *The Legal Aid Board's Advice to the Lord Chancellor on the implications of its taking over responsibility for criminal legal aid in the magistrates' courts*, London: Legal Aid Board, January 1993, para. 148.

[38] See Legal Aid Board draft guidance to area committees, dated August 1995.

caseworkers to the professionals' experience clouds the potential for caseworkers to exercise an objective evaluation of the merits of the application.

VI   EVALUATING AREA OFFICE DECISION-MAKING

We have seen how relationships between caseworkers and area committees vary from office to office. In this section we examine how these differences translate into different patterns of decision-making, thus raising questions about the inherent fairness of the system. Six core offences[39] provided each Area Office with between 72 to 75 per cent of its reviews and the frequency of all (core and non-core) offence types was similar at each Area Office. The consistency of throughput at Area Office level allowed meaningful comparisons to be made. In Table 8.2, information drawn from 2,716 review files is presented so as to reveal the grant rate[40] in each Area Office before and after the implementation of the Criminal Justice Act 1991.

Table 8.2: Area Office grant rates

Area	Grant rate pre-CJA 1991 %	Grant rate post-CJA 1991 %
A	75	79
B	51	61
C	70	55
D	50	67
E	73	70
F	*	66

* Data not available.[41]

In parenthesis, we may note that the high success rate obtaining in all Area Offices should not be taken to mean that court clerks and magistrates frequently come to the wrong decision in refusing these applications, as like is not being compared to like. As we have noted, Legal Aid Board procedures require the

[39] The offences are criminal damage (Criminal Damage Act 1971, s.1), theft (Theft Act 1968, s. 1), assault occasioning actual bodily harm (Offences against the Person Act 1861, s. 47), handling (Theft Act 1968, s.22), deception (Theft Act 1968, s.15) and burglary (Theft Act 1968, s. 9).
[40] Grant rates are expressed as a percentage of all valid applications for review.
[41] Although computer printouts of the results for this Area Office pre-CJA 1991 were available, the files had been destroyed. As it was impossible to cross-check the accuracy of the computer data, the column has been left blank.

solicitor to produce a range of information and the Board decision-maker is usually provided with the prosecution and defence versions of the offence. By contrast, court decision-makers have only spartan information available to them, normally no more than a poorly completed application form (Form 1).[42] The importance of good quality information was confirmed in a decision-making experiment undertaken with court clerks. A total of 12 legal aid applications, originally refused by court clerks but granted by caseworkers, were placed before 35 court clerks together with all the documentation made available at the review stage to caseworkers. The great majority of applications were granted by a high percentage of court clerks and the main reasons offered for grant centred on the fullness of information provided in the application.

Table 8.2 discloses a variation in Area Office grant rate of between 50 per cent and 75 per cent pre-implementation of the Criminal Justice Act 1991, changing to a range of 55 per cent to 79 per cent post-implementation. In considering apparent differences in approach between Area Offices, it is important to construct a model of what a good system of administrative justice should achieve. Sainsbury provides a helpful guide when he states that:

> The qualities that a decision process ought to exhibit, which provide arguments for the acceptability of its decisions, are the ability to provide accurate decisions and the ability to produce them in a manner which is fair by being prompt, impartial and allowing claimants to participate and receive accountable decisions. An administrative agency should hold the promise of administrative justice in its structures and procedures, and be able to demonstrate the achievement of administrative justice in its practices.[43]

In developing his model, Sainsbury suggested the adoption of two broad tests, these being accuracy and fairness. Using Mashaw's definition of accuracy,[44] Sainsbury suggests the notion denotes a relationship between the decision outcome and the true facts concerning the applicant's situation. Fairness is said to comprise promptness, lack of bias, participation and accountability. This last component requires the addressee of the decision to understand the reasons underpinning the exercise of discretion.

Although an excellent foundation for evaluating the workplace practices of administrators, Sainsbury's model was designed around an analysis of the UK

---

[42] See chapter 6 of this volume.

[43] Sainsbury, R., 'Administrative Justice: Discretion and Procedure in Social Security Decision-Making', in Hawkins, K. (ed.), *The Uses of Discretion*, Oxford: Clarendon Press, 1992, p. 295 at p. 305.

[44] Mashaw, J., 'The Management Side of Due Process: Some Theoretical and Litigation Notes on the Assurance of Accuracy, Fairness and Timeliness in the Adjudication of Social Welfare Claims', *Cornell Law Review*, 1974, vol. 59, p. 772, cited in Sainsbury, *op. cit.*, p. 302.

social security system. For the purposes of legal aid decision-making at Legal Aid Board level, the definition might usefully be extended to add two further requirements for an effective review process: first, that decisions on review be accepted at all levels by those charged with exercising the same functions and, secondly, that the review system generates sufficient guidance for those operating the processes. These notions are closely related to issues of accountability and so they will be included in a later discussion under that heading.

(i) Accuracy

The accuracy of decision-making places the decision-maker under an obligation to have clear standards which can be applied to the facts. The creation of normative standards, or at the least the creation of accepted parameters within which standards may be created, should be viewed as a prerequisite to accurate decision-making. In assessing the level of performance shown by Board decision-makers two indicators have been selected for close examination: first, the degree of diligence shown by caseworkers in placing before the area committee relevant and accurate information relating to the application and, secondly, the use made by Board decision-makers of the criteria in the Legal Aid Act 1988, s. 22(2).

Diligence shown by caseworkers The implementation of the Criminal Justice Act 1991 during the period of research facilitated a close examination of the effect of changes in legislation on the workplace practices of administrators. Table 8.2 reveals that Areas A, B, and D show an increase in the grant rate over the period of between 4 to 17 per cent, while Areas C and E record a decrease in grants of 15 and 3 per cent respectively. As noted earlier, the national refusal rate by magistrates' courts for legal aid increased by about 1 per cent over the same period.

Observations of how the caseworkers reacted to the changes brought in by the Act were of help in explaining the divergences. At Areas C and E, the caseworkers provided to the area committee members a detailed agenda note reminding them of some of the main changes effected by the Criminal Justice Act 1991. Two typical agenda notes in Area C are set out below:

> The Area Committee is reminded that the Criminal Justice Act restricts the powers of the Magistrates to impose a custodial sentence. Before passing a custodial sentence, the Magistrates must adjourn the cases for the preparation of a pre-sentence report. The Magistrates must also reconsider the question of legal aid and afford a defendant the opportunity of being legally aided before passing a custodial sentence.

The area committee will be aware that by virtue of s. 29 CJA 1991 which came into force on 1/10/92 the applicant's convictions are only relevant if they aggravate the present offence.

In Area E the following style of agenda note was common:

Whilst details of this conviction were revealed to [X] magistrates' court, it may be noted that by CJA 1991 the court cannot impose a more severe sentence simply because of that conviction, which the court feels would not lead to a custodial sentence.

Neither formula properly summarises the full extent of the pre-amended s. 29 of the Criminal Justice Act 1991, but both serve to convey an impression to the area committee that a significant break has occurred with past court practices on the imposition of imprisonment.

In the remaining areas, either no reference to the Criminal Justice Act 1991 was made on the agenda note, or, where a reference occurred, the effect of the Act was not explained or was presented in a misleading fashion. As an example of the former, a caseworker's agenda note in Area F would typically continue post-Criminal Justice Act to state blandly:

The area committee is asked to consider granting legal aid on review following the Magistrates' Courts refusal of legal aid.

It was clear from an analysis of the post-Criminal Justice Act refusals in Areas C and E, that the area committee turned down more applications based on the risk of custody than had been the case pre-Criminal Justice Act; and it must be a reasonable assumption that some connection existed between the type of information provided on the agenda note and the decision outcome. As one caseworker in Area C phrased it:

They need help. Basically they are civil practitioners and you have to help them out sometimes. After a while you get to know whether they are on the ball or not. But I give them a reminder of the changes to cover my back if they drop a howler.

The increase in grant rates in Area Offices B and D appeared to be connected closely with an increase in the number of grants based on the custody criterion in s. 22(2)(a) of the Legal Aid Act 1988. So, for example, the frequency of use of the custody criterion in all grants in Area D increased from 42 to 65 per cent after the implementation of s. 29 of the Criminal Justice Act 1991. This stands in stark contrast to the pattern found in Areas C and E, where, as we have seen, the grant rate decreased due to less weight being given to this criterion. A decision-making exercise carried out by the author in Area D indicated that caseworkers there had found the new legislation too complex to apply and that they were basically ignoring it. It was not possible, however, to isolate the reason(s) for the *increase* in grant rate in these two offices.

Another factor which helps explain variation in grant rates in Area Offices is the selective way in which information is placed by caseworkers before the area committee on occasions. Some caseworkers rarely supply the full advance information as disclosed by the prosecution to the defence, preferring to summarise it in a fashion which might result in the drawing of misleading inferences by the area committees. For example, in Area F, if a defendant seeking review was pleading guilty, the (often voluminous) advance information was not provided to the committee. In cases of not guilty pleas, only the police summary of the case went before the committee members, who were thus denied the opportunity of reading the defendant's interview statement.[45]

The problem of information being held back from the area committee was exacerbated after the implementation of the Criminal Justice Act 1991. Caseworkers varied immensely in their approaches to the provision of previous convictions. On the agenda note some caseworkers offered to provide them if required, others selected convictions close in type to the present offence, and still others (particularly in Areas B and D) supplied the whole list of previous convictions to the area committee.

Use by board decision-makers of the criteria in s. 22 of the Legal Aid Act 1988 A brief survey below of the use made by decision-makers of the criteria in s. 22 demonstrates that no uniformity of decision-making standards exists within the Legal Aid Board. The custody criterion in s. 22(2)(a) provides a ready example of the difficulties involved. Many caseworkers interpret this section as meaning that custody would be the only possible court sentence, while others feel that if custody fell realistically within a range of probable options then it would be correct to grant legal aid. The risk of a community service order being imposed was still viewed by most Area Offices as a reason *per se* to grant legal aid, even after the Divisional Court had ruled otherwise in *McGhee*.[46]

---

[45] Since research by Baldwin, J., *Preparing the Record of Taped Interview*, Royal Commission on Criminal Justice Research Study No. 2, London: HMSO, 1992, has shown that police summaries exaggerate the strength of the prosecution evidence, area committees might believe that the applicant has less of a chance of avoiding conviction than is in fact the case, and, as a corollary, be less willing to grant legal aid.

[46] *Op. cit.*

At Area Offices where the turnover of personnel handling reviews was high, the frequency of grants based on s. 22(2)(b) (the case involves a substantial question of law) was much higher than where the same decision-maker had been involved throughout the whole study period, and in both cases far higher than at court decision-maker level where only 32 per cent of s. 22(2)(b) based applications were accepted. One Area A caseworker commented 'for substantial question of law you might as just well read question of law — anything seems to go here'.

Some consistency between Board decision-makers did exist. Legal aid was nearly always granted to first-time offenders and to those pleading not guilty to shoplifting (irrespective of previous convictions). Related to this, applications based on a risk to lost reputation were viewed in a favourable light.

Generally speaking, however, little evidence of consistency was detected. Confirmation of the widely differing approaches to s. 22 was found in exercises involving dummy review applications undertaken with caseworkers. Within Area Offices no uniformity of approach was detected in, *inter alia*, the attitude towards such issues as the relevance of a possible election for Crown Court trial, a claim that the sole prosecution witnesses were police officers, or whether *mens rea* in criminal damage amounted to a substantial question of law. These findings support those of Young et al., where in comparing the uniformity of decision-making in courts and area committees, the authors stated that 'current decision-making at area level is equally inconsistent and, on average, more generous'.[47]

What explanations are to be found for the wide discrepancies in approach? Some clues came from the caseworkers' response to questions about their general approach to decision-making. The majority of decision-makers acting under delegated powers saw their function as being one of re-examining the application *de novo*. As one caseworker in Board F succinctly put it:

I tend to look at the case as if I were the Clerk to the Justices hearing it for the first time. I look at the case before I look at the reasons for refusal.

A smaller number interpreted review as being synonymous with judicial review, in which the decision-maker would be required to assess whether the original decision was one which a reasonable magistrates' court could reasonably reach. Still others took the pragmatic view that the courts would have greater knowledge of the defendant's circumstances and that a presumption that the court was correct should be rebutted only if either the court had not offered detailed reasons for finding that the statutory criteria did not apply,

---

[47] *Op. cit.*, p. 99.

or new information was available at review that had not been considered at court. These variations in approach owe much to the historical creation of the area committee. Unlike the position pertaining to civil legal aid reviews, statute provides no indication that the review constitutes an appeal, to be dealt with by way of full reconsideration of the merits. The *Legal Aid Handbook* pronounces that the review function is an appellate one, but offers no guidance on how a Board decision-maker should approach an appeal.[48] Recently circulated draft guidance to area committees merely states the function of the committee as being to hear those applications which the Area Office caseworker has declined to grant.[49]

Another problem lies in the civil law orientation of the area committee, which provides great scope for confusion in the application of tests, particularly as civil and criminal matters are being heard together. Caseworkers are in the same dilemma, in that they switch repeatedly to and from civil and criminal matters. Controlled decision-making experiments with caseworkers revealed a strong tendency for the less experienced to import the civil legal aid 'reasonable grounds for defending' criterion into criminal review decision-making. So, for example, the agenda note of a relatively new caseworker stated 'none of criteria would appear to be satisfied and it would also appear that the defendant has no defence'.

This emphasis by the decision-maker on whether the defendant would succeed in securing an acquittal potentially serves to reverse the burden of proof by requiring a defendant either to prove innocence, or to establish a defence. In relation to the former, the ultimate burden to prove guilt remains on the prosecution throughout the trial. In relation to the evidential burden cast on a defendant to establish a defence, it would appear that caseworkers are requiring a higher standard of proof from a defendant at legal aid application stage than might otherwise be required at trial. This approach by decision-makers has serious potential for prejudicing the interests of the defendant. Armed with Advance Disclosure, the decision-maker is in possession of all the prosecution evidence, but for practical and/or tactical reasons, the applicant may not be able to reveal the full extent of the defence, even if it is available. That the Legal Aid Board has not eradicated this forbidden line of reasoning in its decision-makers is much the most serious indictment of its present administration of the criminal review process.

---

[48] Legal Aid Board, *Legal Aid Handbook 1995*, London: Sweet & Maxwell, 1995, p. 51.
[49] Legal Aid Board draft guidance to area committees, dated August 1995.

(ii) Fairness

Turning to Sainsbury's second element of a just decision-making process, several illustrative pointers to the absence of a fair review structure were detected in the research.

Promptness and participation These components of the definition can be dealt with briefly. Delay is a strong feature of Board processes. Whereas in 1993 courts took only one day to determine a legal aid application, average Legal Aid Board time in Areas A to F ranged from nine to 21 days over the same period, although greater efforts were made at the end of 1993 to expedite the process. As for participation, unlike the position in civil review matters, the attendance of the applicant was not encouraged, even though regulations do not appear to preclude an oral application for criminal review. And, as discussed above, the applicant is marginalised within the review process as a whole, and is forced to put the matter in the hands of professionals.

Accountability This notion demands slightly more extensive treatment. At its core it relates to the transparency of decision-making, but it also includes concerns centring on the acceptability at large of a decision-making function for the Board.

The issue of transparency is premised on clarity of reasoning in reaching the decision. At the time of the survey, full and detailed reasons for granting or refusing legal aid were advanced in only two out of the 2,716 files perused. In all other cases decision-makers merely invoked a statutory criterion without further explanation to the applicant.

Reasons should be arrived at on the basis of the best information available to the decision-maker. In terms of information gathering, caseworkers fail to achieve the requisite standards. Internal Board policies handicap the caseworker by restricting the amount of guidance a decision-maker could seek. In interview, decision-makers reported it to be a disciplinary offence[50] to accumulate material other than that provided by the Board, and such limited guidance that did exist either had not permeated down to caseworker level or was not used in practice. In response some caseworkers have developed their own guidance to compensate for the lack of training and direction.

With regard to the acceptability of the Board's role as decision-maker, interviews with relevant Board personnel and court decision-makers revealed strong perceptions about a lack of legitimacy attaching to the Board's role in reviewing refusals. Hostility to the Board was found to be endemic at court

---

[50] Mashaw, *op. cit.*, would characterise such a rule as 'internal administrative law'.

level. Typical of the tenor of comments was the following from one court decision-maker:

> What do they [the Legal Aid Board] know about the way we run our courts. They grant reviews in the most hopeless of cases and make us look foolish in front of solicitors. We are supposed to be guardians of the public purse but they [the Board] seem to be protecting the interests of solicitors. They claim they have more information than we do. That may be so for some cases, but I can't see that it's relevant when it comes to deciding whether someone is going to go down [to prison]. We know the going rate for our courts and we stick by it. I find it an affront for a non-lawyer to tell me whether a defendant is facing custody.

Some personnel within the Area Office tended to be critical about the roles of other Board decision-makers. As noted earlier, negative perceptions exist among caseworkers about the quality of area committee decision-making. Indeed, one comment from a caseworker questioned the whole basis of the area committee structure:

> You need solicitors involved somehow [in the review process] for their expertise. However, I'm not too taken on solicitors judging their peers as the basis of jurisdiction. It just does not smell right to the ordinary person.

Within the same Area Office, a former clerk to the area committee commented on the role of caseworkers as follows:

> I admire solicitors doing this work.... They [solicitors] might not be quite the same as they used to be. In the past they used to be real wordsmiths. But I think it impertinent that some young people [caseworkers] can pass judgement on cases [reviews].

At the heart of this mistrust, and intimately connected to the issue of transparency of decision-making, is the lack of communication existing between different levels of decision-making. The acceptability of a ruling at area committee level appears to be closely related to an understanding of why decisions had been made at that level. Area committees rarely discover the reasons for referral from caseworkers, caseworkers rarely discover the reasons for an area committee's decision from committee clerks and, at the time, courts were never told the detailed reasons for the Board granting a review request. Furthermore, it did not seem to be part of Legal Aid Board philosophy to deal directly with the courts. One caseworker in Area C phrased the policy as 'the need to keep each other at arm's length'.

In consequence, a lack of communication between different tiers of decision-maker contributed to a lack of guidance circulating within the administration of the criminal legal aid system. It came as no surprise that, in general, caseworkers viewed their criminal review function as thankless, of no promotion value and as something of a Cinderella activity to the Board's main functions in the civil legal aid field. The high turnover of personnel dealing with criminal reviews reflected that perception. In its many facets, the review structure was unaccountable, and the automatic right to make a subsequent re-application to the court serves to undermine the perceived utility of the review system.

Impartiality The issue of impartiality is a more difficult notion in this context. Caseworkers have to adapt to Board policy, and the Board's insistence on the use of form Crim 9 may be seen as biasing the process against the applicant in favour of a professional domination of the system. On the other hand, solicitors typically advanced their clients' cases forcefully to secure a grant of legal aid. Observations and decision-making exercises showed that many caseworkers adopt an uncritical approach to the statements advanced by solicitors on the review application form. For example, such statements as 'my client advises me that he is not guilty of the allegation' and 'the defendant feels he is in grave risk of a custodial sentence' were accepted rather too readily by inexperienced caseworkers as reasons to grant legal aid. Moreover, it may be argued that caseworkers are, if anything, likely to be biased towards the applicants' interests since the easy option is to grant, as this brought the application for review to a close. By contrast, a refusal to grant would mean that the case would have to be passed on to the area committee, and this involves the caseworker in further paperwork.

In searching for reasons to explain why caseworkers did not adopt a more forensic approach to applications, it became apparent that caseworkers in particular regret the absence of contact with a court culture capable of keeping them abreast with developments in law and practice. They had no way of knowing, for instance, whether a solicitor's claim that a client would receive a custodial sentence if convicted was well-founded or not. Only two of the 17 caseworkers interviewed had visited a magistrates' court and only three had a law degree. No formal channels of communication between the Legal Aid Board and the courts are provided for in statute. It is true that the original application form forwarded to the Board by the applicant should contain the court's reasons for refusing to grant legal aid. But the quality of reasoning evident on the face of the application form is so poor that the educative value of this paperwork is minimal and it does little to ameliorate the caseworker's sense of isolation from the courts.[51]

One consequence of this isolation was that caseworkers had a shaky understanding of how to apply the legislation governing reviews. All Area Offices had granted reviews illegally, both at caseworker and at area committee level, usually for applications revealing only summary offences such as driving with excess alcohol, driving without due care and attention, and possessing a blade in a public place without reasonable excuse. In Area F, which had the highest number of illegal grants in volume terms, 17 per cent of all review applications in 1993 were invalid, suggesting that local practitioners believed Area Office decision-making procedures to be so lax that it was well worth making such applications. One firm applied repeatedly for s. 5 of the Public Order Act 1986 reviews, even though it had previously received 'no jurisdiction' notices from the Board.

During the period of application of the unamended s. 29 of the Criminal Justice Act 1991, many caseworkers wrote to solicitors requesting provision of the applicants' previous convictions in cases where solicitors had not provided them because of their irrelevance to sentencing. The astute practitioner would have realised that the Board and the courts were not working to the same script and that applications which would be automatically refused in the courts might achieve grants in the Area Office. Although a matter of speculation, this factor may help to explain why a high level of review activity was maintained at Board level during the period 1 October 1992 to 15 August 1993.

VII CONCLUSION

There is no doubt that the review system has met the basic need identified by Parliament of providing a mechanism by which courts with low legal aid grant rates could be subjected to external review.[52] But whether the proper function of the area committee be review or appeal, it is incumbent on its administrators to operate the system in such a way as to make its decisions acceptable. The function of any such body should be to create a flexible, accessible and comprehensible delivery mechanism, which is not only capable of offering transparent decision-making of high quality within accepted parameters of discretion, but which also integrates fully with other decision-making tiers and

---

[51] The regulations in force at the time of the research here reported were remarkably opaque on the need for reasons to be given. For analysis, see Young et al., *op. cit.*, pp. 92–3. As discussed in the concluding section of this chapter, court clerks have since been directed in clearer terms as to their duty to give reasons. Whether this makes any difference in practice remains to be seen.

[52] Research has shown that low grant courts produce a disproportionately high number of applications for review in comparison to high grant courts. See Young et al., *op. cit.*, p. 94.

provides them with appropriate feedback and guidance. The area committee structure fails miserably on all these tests. Through poor prioritising of criminal reviews and insufficient training, the system has become tainted with irrelevant considerations and has created significant potential for injustice. Examples given above included the emphasis by some caseworkers on the applicant needing to establish a successful defence and the tendencies amongst caseworkers to make referrals to the area committee rather than giving applicants the benefit of the doubt as required by s. 21(7) of the Legal Aid Act 1988.

At a time when the Government is considering whether the Legal Aid Board should administer the criminal legal aid system in the future, the failings of the Board cast significant doubt on its ability to discharge its duties properly. Even were solicitors to be given the power to grant criminal legal aid under block contracts, the Legal Aid Board's role in reviewing the refusals of solicitors would presumably still continue and, unless corrected, similar problems would arise.

The research reported here demonstrates the importance of engaging in a wide-spread evaluation of the working practices of those involved in operating the legal system.[53] The area committee structure is an example of the criminal justice process being compromised by a managerial ethos which focuses on internal procedural concerns rather than substantive decision-related issues. The findings from the research support Sainsbury's contention that supposed procedural improvements are related to decision outcomes but do not necessarily improve the quality of those outcomes.[54]

As with any research into the criminal justice system, the dynamics of the processes require a detailed assessment of the interaction of its main players, and the separate agendas they bring to courts. In the case of the area committee structure, the rights and expectations of applicants fall victim to an open-ended exercise of discretion. A caseworker from Area F neatly summarised the statutory position as being one in which any decision may be justified by any criterion: '. . . the criteria are not over embracing but I think that you can find anything out there to fit into the criterion you want.'

The situation demands effective guidance and clearly worked out decision-making standards. Since the study was undertaken, moves have been underway to strengthen the system at first-tier and review levels. Thus, since 1 May 1995, both courts and area committees have been required to offer reasons for their

---

[53] This echoes the lessons of other research. See, for example, Ashworth, A., *The English Criminal Process: a Review of Empirical Research, Centre for Criminological Research*, University of Oxford, 1984, ch. 14 for cautionary observations about the different perspectives brought to the same legislative tools by different actors.

[54] Sainsbury, *op. cit.*, p. 327.

decisions in support of the criteria invoked for grant or refusal.[55] This innovation follows the issue in May 1994 of joint guidance on the interpretation of s. 22 of the Legal Aid Act 1988.[56] Such overdue measures emphasise the difficulties caused to decision-makers by continued reliance on the Widgery criteria.[57] They represent, however, mere tinkering at the edges of an unhealthy system. Until the structural issue is addressed of determining the correct approach by decision-makers to a review application, and in consequence the precise relationship between court refusals and Board reconsiderations, the fundamental problem of achieving quality decision-making at Board level will remain. Lord Hailsham's opinion on the merits of a review or an appeal function have come to haunt the Legal Aid Board. In stating that 'there is not too much between them [appeal or review]'[58] he was not to know that Parliament's failure to grasp the nettle was to lay the foundation of much confusion for decision-makers in later years.

The purpose of the research was not to determine whether individual decisions are made better in the courts than at the Board, nor is it possible to compare the actual decisions of courts with those of the Board and draw conclusions about whether a fundamentally judicial or administrative system of legal aid determination is better suited to the exigencies of criminal legal aid decision-making. But it remains unsatisfactory that three levels of decision-maker (courts, caseworker, and area committee) are evidently working to different agendas. The potential for inconsistency is perhaps as important as actual inconsistency. No amount of guidance will be effective until the two occupational cultures of court and administrative bureaucracy are brought closer together by mutual recognition of each other's role.

The only fail-safe mechanism to ensure the transparent distribution of legal aid, and one canvassed in the recent Green Paper,[59] would be to consider allocating criminal legal aid by label of offence. The choice for the future appears to lie between a rigid offence-type system capable of addressing the needs of specified categories of defendants, and an expensive individualised model founded on a Sainsbury-type decision-making process. The former option would create certainty, but would no doubt hand over to the executive

---

[55] Legal Aid in Criminal and Care Proceedings (General) (Amendment) Regulations 1995 (SI 1995 No. 542).

[56] Issued jointly by the Lord Chancellor's Department, The Legal Aid Board and Justices' Clerks Society, and reproduced in Legal Aid Board, op. cit., p. 550.

[57] As long ago as 1981, Lord Hailsham acknowledged that the Widgery criteria 'are now getting a bit long in the tooth, but they are all we have, and that being so, we must use them'. Speech to Surrey magistrates at Kingston on Thames on 27 March 1981, reproduced in The Magistrate, 1981, vol. 37, p. 151.

[58] Hansard (HL) vol. 428, col. 532.

[59] Legal Aid – Targeting Need, op. cit., p. 74, para. 10.16. See chapter 7 of this volume for further discussion of the reform initiative.

complete power to determine legal aid eligibility, while the latter solution would have the merit of flexibility to meet unforeseen circumstances. It is to be hoped that the obvious failings of all current decision-making structures for criminal legal aid do not produce a knee-jerk reaction by policy makers, when the potential for reorganising the system on the lines of Sainsbury's model has not yet been fully explored.

9

Controlling Lawyers' Costs through Standard Fees: An Economic Analysis[1]

Alastair Gray, Paul Fenn and Neil Rickman

I INTRODUCTION

The rise in expenditure on criminal legal aid in recent years is well documented,[2] and an important justification for the introduction of standard fees, particularly in magistrates' courts, has been to control expenditure. Two characteristics of standard fees might assist in this control. First, the fact that, in principle, standard fees are administratively less complicated than paying by fee-for-service. Second, standard fees might be expected to place a check on the size of legal aid bills. To our knowledge, however, little information has so far been presented to indicate how successful these fees have been in achieving effective cost control.

In the absence of such information, the purpose of this chapter is to consider some aspects of standard fees which might prevent them from providing effective control of legal aid fees. In particular, we ask how lawyers might react to the financial incentives inherent in the currently existing standard fee structures and whether these reactions might have adverse consequences for the size of legal aid bills, as well as for the quality of work done on legal aid cases. Although a lack of current data prevents us from testing our predictions,

[1] The authors are grateful to the Legal Aid Board for funding the assembly of a database on legally-aided criminal cases in magistrates' courts, and to the Lord Chancellor's Department for funding some modelling work on the application of standard fees. The views expressed in this work are solely those of the authors.
[2] Gray, A., 'The reform of legal aid', *Oxford Review of Economic Policy*, 1994, vol. 10, no.1, p. 51.

we use data from a sample of legally-aided criminal cases in magistrates' courts from 1988–90 to simulate some possible effects if the behaviour we predict were to occur. The chapter also highlights the types of information required in order to test for the effects we identify.

The background to standard fees may be stated quite briefly. Until 1986, solicitors and barristers performing legal aid work on criminal cases were remunerated on a fee-for-service basis. Under this scheme, they would itemise their inputs on the case, submit the completed bill to the court clerks and — depending on whether the bill was assessed as being reasonable — be paid for the inputs recorded. In 1986, this method of remuneration was replaced in some categories of proceedings in the Crown Court by a system of standard fees. Under this system, lawyers are paid a set fee for their work on a case. Unlike the fee-for-service, this standard fee is unrelated to lawyers' inputs on the case, except in so far as two threshold levels of inputs exist: the first triggering a higher standard fee, the second allowing payment to revert to a fee-for-service basis. As of March 1994, standard fees were applied to 69 per cent of solicitors' bills and 73 per cent of counsels' bills. However, these standard fees apply only to relatively straightforward and short cases (usually of less than three days' duration). In consequence, only 22 per cent and 37 per cent respectively of Crown Court legal aid expenditure is covered by the standard fee system, the remaining bills usually being set on a fee-for-service basis by the clerks to the court.

A similar system of graduated standard fees was introduced for criminal cases in magistrates' courts in 1993. There is a lower and a higher standard fee, with cases involving more work than is covered by the higher standard fee being paid on a fee-per-item basis. Three types of proceedings are covered and these encompass a much larger percentage of magistrates' courts' work than in the Crown Court. Thus, by March 1994, 77 per cent of bills were lower standard fee claims, 9 per cent were higher standard fee claims, and 6 per cent were above the upper limit of the higher standard fee and paid on a non-standard basis.

Our discussion of standard fees is structured as follows. The next section uses economic theory to predict how a move from fee-for-service to standard fees may influence the number of hours a lawyer chooses to devote to a given case, assuming that lawyers respond to the financial incentives provided by the fee scheme they face. The third section introduces our data set and discusses how it might be used to calculate an appropriate standard fee level. The fourth section simulates our predictions to estimate their potential importance for the size of legal aid bills. A concluding section discusses the data which would be needed in order to test our predictions and the implications of being able to do so.

II   STANDARD FEES AND ECONOMIC THEORY

The arrangements by which individuals are paid for the work they do has long been a focus of attention for economists. This is particularly the case when it is difficult to monitor either the quantity or quality of the work being done. In such situations, payment schemes can provide incentives to ensure that appropriate levels of both are supplied. For this reason, a large literature has developed to analyse the optimal form of payment contract between different individuals, depending on the types of work being done and the degree to which inputs such as effort are observable.[3] Although our purpose is not to discuss the optimal form of contract which might be used to govern lawyers' work on legally-aided criminal cases, we can draw upon this literature to predict some of the consequences of moving from fee-for-service contracts to standard fee ones. To do this, we introduce a framework for looking at the amount of time which individuals will devote to their work.

(i)   A labour supply framework

The starting point for the analysis is the general observation that individuals make choices amongst available alternatives in order to maximise their utilities subject to the constraints they face. The choices we are interested in concern how much labour to supply. In particular, how much labour (or effort) will a lawyer supply on a given legally-aided criminal case when faced with either a standard fee or a fee-for-service?

To address this question, assume that a lawyer derives utility from income (Y) and leisure time (L), so that the lawyer has a utility function $U(Y,L)$, which translates quantities of income and leisure into levels of utility. We assume that both income and leisure make lawyers happier: they increase a lawyer's utility. Further, assume that the lawyer either works on the legally-aided case at hand, or does no work at all. This is an extreme simplification which can easily be generalised to circumstances where lawyers also have the choice of working on other, perhaps non legally-aided, cases. The lawyers face a clear trade-off: in order to earn income they must work, but in doing so they sacrifice valuable leisure time. They therefore face a constraint on the choices of Y and L that can be made. (Of course, a lawyer also faces a physical constraint on the amount of leisure time that can be taken.) This constraint is captured by the lawyer's 'budget constraint' which, in turn, is clearly dependent upon the remuneration

---

[3] See the surveys by Rees, R., 'The Theory of Principal and Agent, Parts I and II', *Bulletin of Economic Research*, 1985, vol. 37, p. 3 and p. 77; and Sappington, D.E.M., 'Incentives in Principal–Agent Relationships', *Journal of Economic Perspectives*, 1991, vol. 5, p. 45.

scheme which the lawyer faces. We begin by looking at the lawyer's optimal choice of leisure time and income when facing a fee-for-service budget constraint.

(ii) Labour supply decisions under fee-for-service remuneration

When paid on this basis, the lawyer receives fees for each task reported to the court clerk/legal aid office. If we suppose, without loss of generality, that each of these tasks is remunerated at the same rate, say w, and that the lawyer can choose to devote H hours to the case, then the income available on any given day is $Y = wH = w(24-L)$, where the second equality comes from the physical constraint on the hours of leisure and work that can be taken in a day. We can represent this budget constraint diagrammatically, as in Figure 9.1.

Figure 9.1: The fee-for-service budget constraint

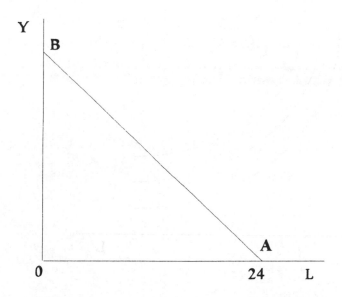

The budget constraint, AB, shows the combinations of income and leisure available to the lawyer given the prevailing fee scheme and fee level. Points below AB are available, while points outside it are not. Its negative slope indicates that the lawyer sacrifices income by taking more leisure. In order to determine which point on the budget constraint the lawyer will select, we need to represent the lawyer's preferences over income and leisure. To do this, we introduce the concept of 'indifference curves'. An indifference curve is the locus of income-leisure combinations which yield the lawyer the same utility (i.e., which make the lawyer indifferent between these income and leisure combinations). Accordingly, for each level of utility, there is a separate indifference curve. The set of indifference curves for an individual is called an 'indifference map'. Representative curves from one such map are depicted in Figure 9.2.

Figure 9.2: An individual's indifference curves

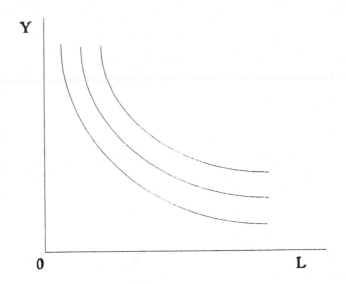

Several properties of the indifference curves depicted in Figure 9.2 will be important below.[4] First, assuming that the lawyer wants more of both income and leisure (they are both 'goods'), utility is increasing as the lawyer moves to curves which are further to the north-east. This also explains their negative slope: if we take a unit of income away, the lawyer must be given an extra amount of leisure in order to be made as well off as before (i.e., in order to return to the same indifference curve).

Secondly, the slopes of the curves indicate how the lawyer is willing to trade income for leisure: the steeper the curves, the more the lawyer is prepared to give up income in order to gain a unit increase in leisure, while keeping utility constant. Therefore, different lawyers' preferences over income and leisure will be represented by different indifference curve slopes. These differences are also represented by the degree of curvature of the indifference curves. Their shape in Figure 9.2 (convex to the origin) reflects the principle of diminishing marginal utility: the more of either income or leisure the lawyer has, the more of it he is willing to sacrifice in order to receive a unit of the other.

Lastly, indifference curves in any indifference map cannot intersect. The reason for this is that each indifference curve represents a unique level of utility. Therefore, if two were to intersect at a given Y–L combination, this would imply that two different values were placed on that combination. Such behaviour is assumed, perhaps not surprisingly, to be unreasonable. The main result of this discussion is that each individual will have his or her own indifference map, expressing his or her preferences over, in this case, income and leisure.

Having represented the lawyer's preferences and the constraints faced, we can bring these two together in order to see what quantity of leisure the lawyer will choose (and, therefore, the amount of time directed into the case) to solve the problem:

$$\text{Maximise } U(Y,L)$$
$$\text{subject to } Y = wH$$

Figure 9.3 shows the solution to this problem. In the figure, the optimal amount of leisure time is L^*, implying an income of Y^*. The reason for this is that this combination provides the lawyer with the highest level of utility (i.e., places the lawyer on the highest indifference curve) given the budget constraint faced. Clearly, different points would be optimal for different lawyers with different preferences over income and leisure.

---

[4] These properties depict several of the 'axioms of consumer choice' upon which economists base the microeconomic theory of individual choice and behaviour. See any intermediate microeconomics text, such as Varian, H. R., *Intermediate Microeconomics: a modern approach*, 3rd ed., New York: Norton, 1993.

Figure 9.3: The individual's choice of income and leisure

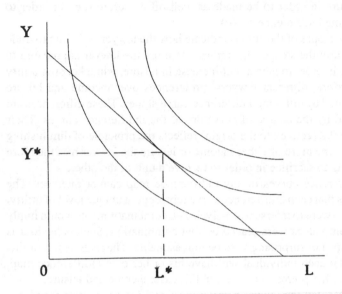

(iii) Introducing standard fees

We can now compare the lawyer's behaviour under a fee-for-service with that under a standard fee. For simplicity, and in contradiction with current practice under standard fees, we shall begin by assuming that only one standard fee is in operation. In accordance with the current system, however, we shall assume that there is a threshold level of work on the case which, if it can be proved to have been performed by the lawyer, allows the lawyer to be paid on the old fee-for-service basis. Calling the associated threshold level of leisure time L_0 and the standard fee F, the lawyer's problem is now

$$\text{Maximise } U(Y,L)$$
$$\text{subject to } Y = F \quad \text{if } L > L_0$$
$$wH \text{ if } L < L_0.$$

Figure 9.4: The standard fee budget constraint

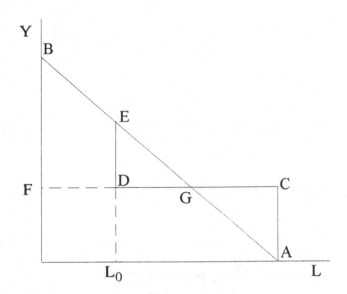

The problem has been altered by the new remuneration scheme, which is reflected in the new budget constraint in Figure 9.4. Here, the old fee-for-service scheme is again represented by the line AB. Introducing the standard fee creates a 'step' in the budget constraint. In particular, the lawyer now receives a fee of F regardless of the work done on the case until the lawyer's daily input of hours becomes $24-L_0$. At this point the lawyer's fee reverts to the fee-for-service. Therefore, the standard fee budget constraint is given by ACDEB. Notice that this makes some income-leisure combinations available which were not before (i.e., those in the triangle ACG), while removing others (those in triangle GDE). These represent the way in which the new fee structure alters the lawyer's opportunities to trade income for leisure.

To illustrate this argument with a practical example, suppose the standard fee is £320 for anything up to eight hours' work on a case. Thus, in the notation used above, $F = 320$ and $L_0 = 16$. If more than eight hours are performed, however, the lawyer is remunerated at a rate (W) of £40 an hour, so that an input of nine hours will yield an income of £360.

We can use the fee-for-service and standard fee budget constraints to predict how lawyers, motivated solely by economic incentives, will react to the change in regime. As might be expected, the results here depend on their preferences for income and leisure, as expressed in their indifference curves. Given this, we demonstrate the possible outcomes which may occur in Figures 9.5a, 9.5b and 9.5c.

Figure 9.5a

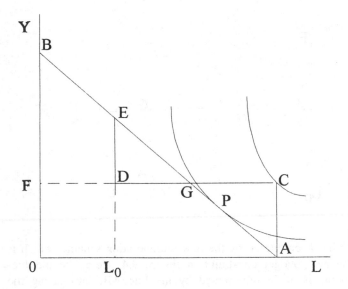

In Figure 9.5a, the lawyer originally chose to work at point P, on portion AG of the fee-for-service budget constraint. In this case, the standard fee allows the lawyer a higher fee with less input and the optimal response is therefore to move to the 'corner solution' at point C, where the lawyer puts the minimum quantity of effort into the case. The lawyer's utility is increased as a result. In Figures 9.5b and 9.5c, however, the standard fee removes the portion of the budget upon which the lawyer chose to operate under the fee-for-service. The result is a move from the original equilibrium at point Q to another indifference curve. The two possibilities are at the 'corners' C and E. Which is chosen will depend on whether the utility derived at C is above that derived at E. In particular, if

$U(C) > U(E)$ then point C will be chosen, as lawyers seek to minimise their inputs given that these will not affect the fee they receive (Figure 9.5b). If, however, this inequality is reversed point E will result as lawyers attempt to boost their input levels in order to qualify for the higher fee available above the threshold (Figure 9.5c).

Figure 9.5b

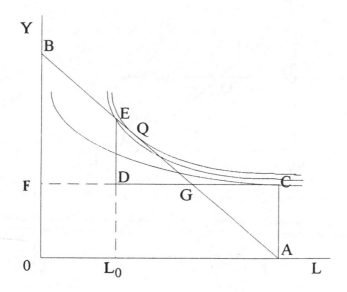

Figure 9.5c

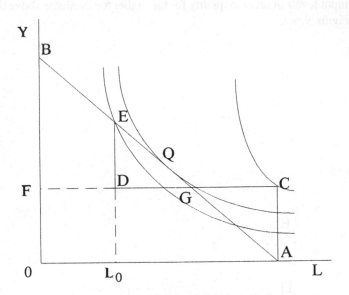

Two predictions emerge from this analysis:

(a) If lawyers are principally motivated by economic incentives, we would expect to observe their effort levels clustering around the threshold levels introduced by the standard fee.

(b) If lawyers are principally motivated by economic incentives, we would expect to observe a pattern to these clusters: cases which would have received a fee below the standard fee will display minimum input levels under the standard fee, while cases which would have received a higher fee will either display these minimum levels or will display higher input levels under the standard fee.

202

It is worth noting that these predictions isolate a trade-off faced by the state in introducing standard fees: that between cost control and quality of service. To the extent that we observe clustering around minimum effort levels, this may be beneficial from the perspective of cost control but may also imply a diluted quality of service (if input levels and output qualities are related), with ultimate consequences for standards of representation and justice.

Before we move to our empirical analysis, it should be clear that the discussion so far can be easily adapted to incorporate two standard fee levels (as actually exist under the current legal aid scheme). The resulting budget constraint is shown in Figure 9.6, with F_0 representing the 'lower standard fee' and F_1 representing the 'higher' one. Clearly, none of the predictions above is altered by this added realism.

Figure 9.6: 'Lower' and 'higher' standard fees

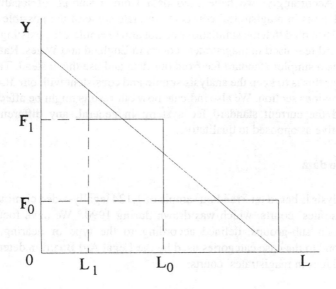

(iv) Other incentive issues

In addition to the incentive effects identified here, it is possible that targeting one aspect of the solicitor's activity — the bill submitted for a case — might then lead to effects on other activities. For example, it is possible that ways will be found of redefining what constitutes a case, so that more bills are submitted for essentially the same volume of work. Similarly, it is possible that only large firms will be able to diversify the risk associated with taking on fixed-fee cases, while firms prepared to perform small volumes of legal aid work on a fee-for-service will be deterred by uncertainty and withdraw from the legal aid market. These and other possible consequences of legal aid are explored in the following section.

III SIMULATION STUDY

As mentioned in section I, no data are yet available to test for all of the above effects. Accordingly, we have used data from a sample of legally-aided criminal cases in magistrates' courts to simulate some of the possible effects. It should be noted that the simulations do not aim to emulate the existing system of standard fees used in magistrates' courts in England and Wales. Rather, we formulate a simpler standard fee from our data and use this instead. The main reason for this is to keep the analysis simple and consistent with our discussion in the previous section. We also indicate how our results might be affected had we used the current standard fee system: in general, any differences are quantitative as opposed to qualitative.

(i) The data

The analysis is based on a random sample of 1,124 legally-aided criminal cases in magistrates' courts, which was drawn during 1990.[5] We have focused on three main sub-groups, defined according to the type of hearing, which correspond to the case categories used by the Legal Aid Board in determining standard fees in magistrates' courts:

(a)   summary hearings where a guilty plea was entered;
(b)   summary hearings where a not guilty plea was entered; and
(c)   committals under s. 6(2).

---

[5] Gray, A. and Fenn P., 'The rising cost of legally aided criminal cases', *New Law Journal*, 1991, vol. 141, p. 1622.

The main analysis focuses on single-defendant cases, but the multi-defendant issue is also examined below. Table 9.1 shows the mean values of some key variables for the complete sample of single-defendant hearings for 1990, and similar information for each of the three main sub-groups.

Table 9.1: Mean and median values and number of observations in sample: single-defendant hearings, 1990 (n = 1053)

Variable:	All	Summary trial, guilty plea	Summary trial, not guilty plea	Committal s. 6(2)
Attendance & preparation:				
Hours in attendance	2.05	1.59	2.19	2.54
Cost for attendance	£77.47	£60.52	£82.81	£95.07
Hours preparing	1.40	1.09	1.58	1.61
Cost for preparation	£52.85	£41.04	£59.12	£60.54
Hearing:				
Hours waiting	1.88	1.51	2.85	1.96
Cost for waiting	£39.19	£31.65	£58.85	£40.83
Hours of advocacy	1.15	0.99	1.52	0.92
Cost for advocacy	£53.78	£46.99	£70.70	£43.51
Length of case (days)	58.37	43.38	79.82	67.82
Solicitor's fees net of				
travel and disbursements	£275.40	£226.02	£305.85	£308.31

The table shows, as expected, that a summary trial in which a guilty plea is entered is the least costly of the hearing types, with less attendance time, preparation time, waiting time and advocacy time than the other sub-groups.

(ii) Constructing a standard fee

In order to arrive at a standard fee for our data, we have used several principles. The first, inclusivity, states that the fee should cover a large number of cases. The second, fairness, states that the fee should be closely correlated with (at least) some of the inputs lawyers actually invest in the case. In this way, they are partially assured of an income in the region of that received under a fee-for-service. Of course, the more input-types used here, the closer the correlation will be. Using too many inputs would, however, conflict with our next two principles: simplicity and objectivity. The former of these means that the fee should not be too complicated to calculate. The latter addresses the concern that, when lawyers are able to choose the inputs they invest in a case, it is possible that they will not choose an appropriate quantity. This would mean that a standard fee conditioned on such input levels would be unnecessarily high. Therefore, we wish to condition the fee on inputs which are capable of objective monitoring by third parties. Lastly, we have assumed that the fee is chosen to maintain a constant expenditure level on criminal legal aid. Whether or not the magistrates' court standard fee scheme adhered to this principle of expenditure neutrality was vigorously contested immediately prior to the scheme's introduction.[6]

Using these principles, we are able to construct an appropriate standard fee from our data. We note that one other principle might also have been added: economic efficiency. Here we mean that the standard fee mechanism adopted should not be economically more inefficient than the present system. In particular, it should not provide fewer services for the same level of resources, or the same services for a higher level of resources. From an economic perspective we would be interested in the net resource cost to society as a whole and not just to the Legal Aid system: a solution which simply passed on costs to the courts, the prisons or the clients would not in our view represent a net gain in efficiency. Our data do not allow us to address wider issues relating to the courts and legal system itself. However, the chapter's objective is to highlight potential inefficiencies in the way the standard fee might work in terms of its influence on lawyers' inputs (and, in consequence, case outcomes and cost control). Therefore, we do not impose economic efficiency when constructing our standard fee but, rather, judge the resulting fee from this perspective.

To summarise our method of constructing a standard fee: we first calculate the distribution of cases by size, length, cost, and the time input to various components of the case, such as preparation, attendance, and advocacy. We then calculate the proportion of cases that would be included or excluded in a standard fee system when different criteria, trigger points and upper limits are applied, and use sensitivity analysis to illustrate the consequences of adjusting these criteria/trigger points in terms of changes in the numbers of cases included/excluded. From the distribution and aggregate cost of bills, it is then possible to compute the levels at which standard fees would leave overall spending unchanged (all else remaining unchanged).

---

[6] See, for example, comment and correspondence in the *New Law Journal*, 1992, vol. 142, pp. 149, 309, 1309, 1401, 1403.

Simplicity, fairness and objectivity   One attribute of a simple mechanism would be a single selection criterion which was closely related to the likely total cost of the case. To examine which individual components of the total bill seem to be the best predictors of the total solicitor's fees net of travel and disbursements (the net cost), Table 9.2 reports the correlations between the net cost and other variables in each of the sub-groups.

Table 9.2: Correlations between the net cost and selected components of the bill, single-defendant cases, by hearing type, 1990 (Pearson correlation coefficients)*

Variable:	Summary guilty	Summary not guilty	Committal s. 6(2)
Total hours in attendance	0.810	0.787	0.743
Total hours preparing	0.761	0.811	0.638
Total hours of advocacy	0.799	0.800	0.648

* All significance < 0.001

The three items which are highly correlated with the net cost of a case are total hours in attendance while preparing the case, total hours preparing the case, and total hours in advocacy during hearing(s), and there is little to choose between them within each sub-group. However, all three variables have a significantly lower degree of correlation with the net cost in s. 6(2) committal proceedings. In terms of the objectivity principle, although all three items are self-reported, it could be argued that the time spent in hearing is most amenable to third-party corroboration, and therefore the remainder of the analysis concentrates on the implications of using a selection criterion based on total hearing time to trigger the standard fee for the case. (This is in line with the system introduced by the Legal Aid Board to magistrates' court cases in 1993.)[7]

This relationship between total hearing time and the net cost of the case is not, however, stable across all sizes of case. Analysis of the data shows that the variability in net cost increases as the hearing time increases, suggesting that it is less easy to predict the cost of a large case than a small one on the basis of the total hearing time. This confirms the need to have an upper limit to the standard fee system, above which lawyers are recompensed on a fee-for-service basis.

---

[7] Legal Aid in Criminal and Care Proceedings (Costs) (Amendment) Regulations 1993 (SI 1993 No. 934). For full details of the legal aid scheme see Legal Aid Board, *Legal Aid Handbook 1995*, London: Sweet & Maxwell, 1995.

Inclusiveness The criteria set out earlier suggest that the selection criteria should embrace a reasonably high proportion of all bills presented. In the context of the distributions observed above, it is necessary to identify a specified total hearing time below which the standard fee mechanism is activated, but above which point the case will be deemed to be too complex to apply standard fees to, and will be separately assessed. Figure 9.7 shows the distribution of each sub-group according to the total hearing time: in each case the total hearing time has been divided into 10-minute intervals, and the cumulative percentage of cases within each sub-group falling below each interval has been calculated.

Figure 9.7: Cumulative percentage of criminal cases by total hearing time

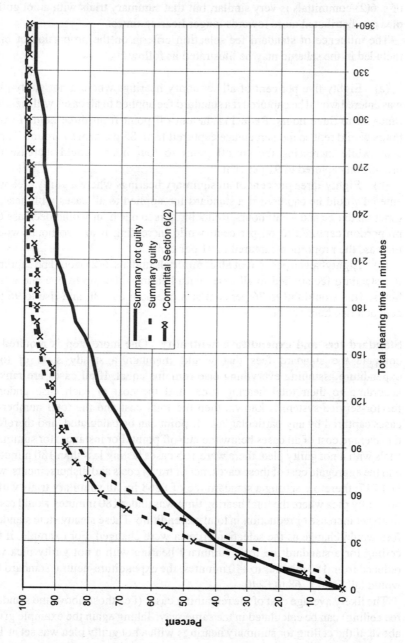

It can be seen that the distribution of summary trials with a guilty plea and of s. 6(2) committals is very similar, but that summary trials with a not guilty plea are distributed more towards longer hearing times.

The influence of standard fee selection criteria on the proportion of bills included in the scheme may be illustrated as follows:

(a)   Eighty-five per cent of all summary hearings where a not guilty plea was entered would be captured if a standard fee applied to all cases with hearing times up to three hours. Reducing the cut-off point from three hours to two hours would reduce the percentage captured from 85 per cent to around 74 per cent, while increasing the cut-off point to four hours would increase the proportion captured to 91 per cent.

(b)   Eighty-three per cent of all summary hearings where a guilty plea was entered would be captured if a standard fee applied to all cases with hearing times up to one and a half hours. Reducing this to one hour would decrease the proportion captured to 66 per cent, while increasing it to two hours would increase the proportion captured to 91 per cent.

(c)   Eighty-seven per cent of all committals under s. 6(2) would be captured if a standard fee applied to all cases with hearing times up to one and a half hours. This would fall to 76 per cent at a one hour cut-off, and rise to 96 per cent at a two hour cut-off.

Standard fees and expenditure neutrality   One more step is required to compute the standard fees that would maintain a steady state of total expenditure assuming everything else remains equal. If all cases are ranked according to their total hearing time, and the cost of each case under a fee-for-service system is known, then the total cost and the total number of cases captured by any particular cut-off point can be calculated, and therefore the average cost of all cases below the cut-off point. For instance, for summary trials with a not guilty plea, there were 165 cases lasting less than 180 minutes, and the aggregate cost of these cases, net of travel costs and disbursements, was £44,217; therefore setting a standard fee of £268 for all summary trials with a not guilty plea where the total hearing time was under 180 minutes would result in no net increase or reduction in total expenditure. These steady state standard fees would change as the selection criteria were changed. For example, if the ceiling for a standard fee for a summary hearing with a not guilty plea was reduced from 180 minutes to 110 minutes, the expenditure-neutral standard fee would fall from £268 to £240.

The likely average cost of the remaining cases (i.e., those above the standard fee ceiling) can be calculated in the same way. Taking again the example given above, if the ceiling for summary hearings with a not guilty plea was set at 110 minutes, so that cases below this figure were paid a standard fee while those above were not, the average cost of those cases would be approximately £560.

IV   STANDARD FEES AND SOLICITOR BEHAVIOUR

Having illustrated how a standard fee can be set on the basis of the principles set out earlier, we can proceed to our simulations of the incentive effects discussed in section II. First, it should be noted that the steady state assumptions referred to above are plausible only if it is not possible for solicitors to determine the total hearing time of a case. Where there is some control in the hands of solicitors, the introduction of standard fees could present an incentive to minimise inputs to cases where such behaviour will not affect the fee received (Figure 9.5(b)), or to boost their input levels in order to get above a threshold point for a higher standard fee (Figure 9.5(c)) or above the standard fee ceiling and back into the realm of fee-for-service. The reasons for this are intuitively clear as well as theoretically straightforward: those cases which fall just below a threshold will have most to lose relative to existing remuneration practice, and a marginal increase in inputs would avoid this loss.

It is clearly impossible to predict with any precision the extent to which such behaviour might occur. However, we have attempted to show what effect it might have on total costs given certain assumptions about the degree to which hearing time could change. Figure 9.8 shows for one particular subgroup — summary trials with a guilty plea — how total costs could be affected after the introduction of a standard fee with different ceilings. The lower line shows the impact if 50 per cent of all cases in the 10-minute band just below the ceiling were to push above the ceiling and therefore receive a non-standard fee. The upper line shows the effect if 50 per cent of cases in the two 10-minute bands just below the ceiling were similarly to push above the ceiling. Given the latter assumption, the total cost of legally aiding all summary trials with a guilty plea would increase by around 8 per cent in real terms, assuming a standard fee with a 90-minute hearing time ceiling.

Figure 9.8 Simulated effects of changes in lawyer behaviour on total costs

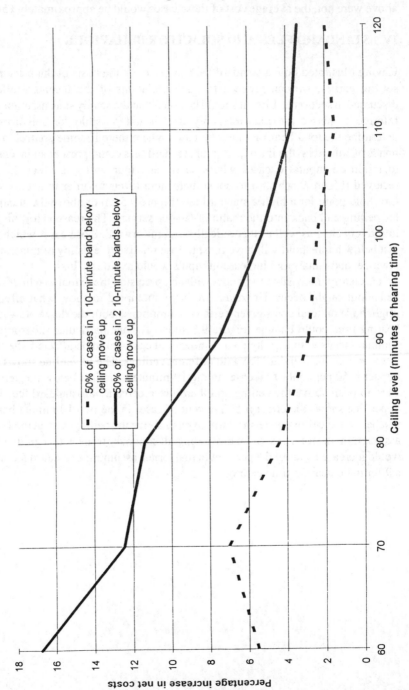

It must be emphasised that these estimates are illustrative only, in the absence of detailed empirical information about the actual impact of standard fees. However, they serve to demonstrate the caution which needs to be exercised in forecasting the cost implications of such schemes. Moreover, even if hearing time, and consequently costs, were to be unchanged, it could not be assumed that other dimensions of solicitors' work would remain unchanged. For example, a standard fee based on a bill in respect of each case performed may provide an incentive to split work that previously would have been defined as one case, so that standard fees are received for two or more cases. There is some suggestion that this may indeed be occurring. The Legal Aid Board reports a rising volume of criminal aid bills submitted following the introduction of standard fees — a reversal of the previous trend.[8] There is also quite strong evidence that solicitors who previously may have included some element of advice and assistance within an overall fee-for-service claim have responded to the introduction of standard fees by claiming separately for this work under the green form scheme (in line with the incentive to minimise inputs to standard fee cases hypothesised in section II). Thus, between the third quarter of 1993 and the first quarter of 1994 (the six months after standard fees were introduced), use of the green form scheme increased by approximately 25 per cent.[9]

Similar incentive or disincentive effects may arise in relation to other aspects of a case, which may influence the actual cost to the solicitor of conducting a case and thereby make it less or more attractive in relation to the standard fee on offer. For example, our data indicate that the cost of a case is clearly related to the number of defendants: an additional defendant on average increases the cost of a case by 60 per cent. Moreover, this effect remains even after standardising for hearing time. Consequently, a standard fee based on hearing time but with no extra fee for additional defendants (the actual position at present) may provide solicitors with disincentives to perform these cases.

Volume of legal aid work Another principle set out in section III above was that of fairness: that a standard fee system should give solicitors on average over a number of cases a sum approximately equivalent to the sum they would have received had they been paid on a fee-for-service basis. This is most likely to be the case if solicitors are doing a reasonable volume of legal aid work; and is less likely to be the case if solicitors are doing only a few cases each year, as small numbers of cases will increase the probability of emerging a 'loser' or 'winner' in relation to the work actually performed.

---

[8] Legal Aid Board, *Annual Report 1993–94*, HC 435, London: HMSO, 1994, paras 7.7–7.9.
[9] Ibid., para. 7.10.

This can be illustrated by drawing a number of random samples from the data set (using the largest sub-group, consisting of summary trials where a guilty plea is entered). First, ten random samples of 50 cases were drawn, then ten samples of 25 cases, and lastly ten samples of five cases. The results are shown in Table 9.3.

Table 9.3: The average net value of work done per summary trial with a guilty plea over 10 samples when the sample size is varied.

Sample No.	Average net value of work done in sample comprising		
	50 cases	25 cases	5 cases
Minimum	£150	£143	£87
Maximum	£224	£213	£282
Average	£191	£183	£174
Standard deviation	£20	£22	£49

The table shows that, when the sample consists of 50 cases, the average value of work performed in ten different samples (that is, ten hypothetical solicitors doing 50 cases of this type) varies between £150 and £224. The average across all the ten samples is £191, compared to the actual average value for the entire sample of 332 cases on which this experiment is based of £187. The standard deviation is £20, suggesting in crude terms that the majority of solicitors who performed 50 cases on a standard fee basis might expect to finish up with an amount per case within £20 one way or another from the value of the work actually done.

When the sample size is reduced from 50 to 25, the table shows that the standard deviation increases slightly. Thus one solicitor doing 25 cases might find it necessary to perform an average of £213 of work across these cases, while another might only perform £143 of work on average over 25 cases. If both were paid a standard fee for each of these cases, the former would lose substantially but the latter would gain.

When the sample size is reduced to five, these effects become even more pronounced. There is a very large increase in the standard deviation and also a large increase in the range between the minimum and the maximum values. Thus one hypothetical solicitor in this final scenario might perform five cases requiring an average of £282 in inputs from the solicitor: if remuneration, however, is based on a standard fee, the reward for doing these cases will be much less than the actual effort expended.

Thus, everything else being equal, our work would predict that the introduction of a standard fee system is likely to have least effect on the overall payments to solicitors doing larger volumes of legal aid work. Conversely, solicitors doing small amounts of legal aid work would be much less likely to find that their overall payments remained equivalent to the earnings they would have received for the same cases under a fee-for-service system. This is likely to discourage solicitors doing small amounts of legal aid work from participating in the scheme, a possibility anticipated in the recent Green Paper on Legal Aid.[10]

V CONCLUSIONS

In this chapter, we began by setting out a framework within which the behaviour of solicitors who respond to financial incentives can be analysed and predicted when a fee-for-service payment system is replaced with a standard fee system. The assumptions required for this analysis were standard assumptions which are commonly made and have frequently been empirically verified in the economic analysis of a wide range of occupational groups.[11]

The results of this economic analysis led us to two main predictions. First, solicitor effort levels will cluster around the threshold/ceiling levels introduced by the standard fee. Secondly, cases which would have received a fee-for-service below the standard fee will display minimum input levels under the standard fee, while cases which would have received a higher fee-for-service will either display these minimum levels, or will display higher input levels under the standard fee.

It is possible to build on these basic predictions in a number of ways. For example, if lawyers are influenced by economic incentives, we would also expect to observe higher inputs (i.e., movements towards point E in Figure 9.5) in geographical regions where alternative earnings opportunities are limited.

These predictions may have some important implications if realised in practice. For example, a reduction by the solicitor in the quantity or quality of work expended on a standard fee case may have an adverse effect on the outcome of the case, and hence be damaging to the client. Conversely, if lawyers play the system effectively — by pushing more cases over the thresholds or by splitting cases — the costs of legal aid will continue to rise,

---

[10] Lord Chancellor's Department, *Legal Aid — Targeting Need: The future of publicly funded help in solving legal problems and disputes in England and Wales*, Cm 2854, London: HMSO, 1995, para. 6.12.

[11] See, for example, Fallon, P. and Verry, D., *The Economics of Labour Markets*, Oxford: Philip Allan, 1988, chs 1 and 2; Hamermesh, D. and Rees, A., *The Economics of Work and Pay*, New York: Harper & Row, 1988, ch. 2.

resulting in a higher burden on taxpayers or, perhaps, further cuts in eligibility or in the scope of the scheme.

We then performed a series of simulation exercises to demonstrate the way in which solicitor behaviour might respond to the introduction of standard fees, noting that relatively conservative assumptions about changes in inputs to cases around the ceiling points might push up the aggregate costs of a standard fee system. We also simulated the effects of different volumes of legal aid work to demonstrate that, at lower volumes of legal aid work, individual solicitors will face substantial uncertainty over whether they are over- or under-rewarded for their inputs by a standard fee scheme. This uncertainty is likely to deter solicitors from doing small amounts of legal aid work.

There is circumstantial evidence to support some of the predictions made here: evidence of a surge in green form claims following the introduction of standard fees, and of more bills being presented in possible consequence of case-splitting to increase the number of standard fees payable for a given amount of work, was noted.

An improved quantity and quality of information would allow us to move on from circumstantial evidence to more rigorous hypothesis testing. Ideally, such information would consist of data from before and after the introduction of standard fees on the actual inputs to a sample of individual cases. However, one paradox of the introduction of standard fees is that much less information is now recorded on the inputs to criminal cases, particularly when a claim is made within the lower standard fee range. This in itself is a predictable outcome, in that a supposed benefit of standard fees was lower administrative costs. But our analysis suggests that any such reductions in administrative costs must be set against a substantially increased need for close monitoring to ensure that unwanted incentive effects arising from standard fees do not undermine the economic efficiency of the system.

10

Criminal Legal Aid Expenditure: Supplier or System Driven? The Case of Scotland

Elaine Samuel

I INTRODUCTION

This chapter examines the issue of spiralling legal aid costs. In particular, it considers the theory of supplier-induced demand which holds that lawyers are to blame for this upward spiral. It argues that the theory is based on an overly simplistic model of human behaviour which fails to take account of the institutional settings and social structures within which defence agents work. The criminal justice system is examined for ways in which the system itself constrains lawyer (supplier) and defender (user) behaviour so as to drive up criminal legal aid costs. Examples will be drawn from a recent study of criminal legal aid and criminal proceedings in Scotland.[1]

Public debate on legal aid has been dominated by the issue of rising public expenditure. Legal aid costs in Scotland have more than doubled in the past six years, rising to £132 million in 1994–95. The Scottish rate of increase has been equalled in England and Wales where the annual cost of legal aid is ten-fold greater, and expenditure is expected to exceed £1.6 billion by 1997–98. This has not gone unnoticed by the Government. The most recent attempt to limit the rate of increase of public expenditure on legal aid was taken in 1993, when eligibility criteria were considerably reduced. Since this appears to have made

---

[1] The author wishes to thank Richard Young and Michael Adler for their helpful suggestions in the preparation of this chapter.

little or no impact in cost terms, the search to find new measures to curb expenditure has been resumed with greater intensity.

The use of eligibility criteria to control legal aid costs was, by the Lord Chancellor's own admission, a blunt instrument, applied under pressure and aimed at the scope of the scheme.[2] While brutal surgery may have removed many persons from the remit of the scheme, it has done little to stop the seemingly exponential growth of legal aid expenditure. A radical alternative was clearly desired, and one which was based upon some understanding of the forces driving legal aid costs on to ever greater heights. Policy-makers did not have to wait long before such a theory of growth arrived to inform their policy. It appeared in 1994 as a Social Market Foundation Memorandum, and was based on a theory of supplier (i.e., lawyer) induced demand.[3]

The theorists of supplier-induced demand offered both an explanation for rising criminal and civil legal aid expenditure, and a panacea. Though the Lord Chancellor found the explanatory power of the argument most compelling, the remedy was received with less enthusiasm, and especially for criminal case work.[4] With his eye perhaps on Article 6 of the European Convention on Human Rights,[5] the Lord Chancellor found it 'more difficult to foresee the operation of a cash limit where criminal legal aid is concerned,'[6] and has rejected a proposed 'fund-holders for justice' scheme. Nonetheless, the theory of supplier-induced demand appears to have been accepted without reservation, constituting a more or less uncontested official view of how legal aid operates and why legal aid expenditure has been driven ever upwards.[7] If this theory has found its opponents, it has been amongst lawyers, but outrage emanating from these quarters has done little to rupture the paradigmatic assumptions on which the theory is based. It thus remains intact, providing a framework out of which future Government policies with relation to the criminal justice system and legal aid are likely to emerge. As such, the theory merits empirical testing.

The remit of the particular research project which now informs this discussion of supplier-induced demand was to examine the relationship between criminal legal aid and court proceedings. It was undertaken between

---

[2] The Lord Chancellor, Speech to the Social Market Foundation, 11 January 1995.
[3] Bevan, G., Holland, T. and Partington, M., *Organising Cost Effective Access to Justice*, Memorandum No.7, Social Market Foundation, July 1994.
[4] The Lord Chancellor, *op. cit.*
[5] For discussion, see Ashworth, A., 'Legal Aid, Human Rights and Criminal Justice', at chapter 3 of this volume.
[6] The Lord Chancellor, *op. cit..*
[7] But see Bridges, L., 'The Reform of Criminal Legal Aid', and Goriely, T., 'The Development of Criminal Legal Aid in England and Wales', at chapters 13 and 2 of this volume respectively.

1992 and 1993 by a team at the University of Edinburgh.[8] The project was one of four separate projects commissioned by The Scottish Office Legal Studies Research Group as part of a programme of research on various aspects of the operation of criminal legal aid in Scotland. This followed the completion of a programme of research on legal aid in civil proceedings, and constituted the second stage of a general review of legal aid by the Government which had been undertaken separately for Scotland by The Scottish Office Home and Health Department.

The Scottish review of criminal legal aid was conducted against a background of costs which were rising in Scotland at almost twice the rate of civil legal aid costs. Moreover, the baseline for criminal legal aid expenditure was considerably higher than for civil legal aid. Indeed, in contrast to England and Wales, where civil legal aid expenditure is more than twice that of criminal legal aid, their relative positions are reversed in Scotland. In 1994–95, for example, criminal legal aid payments in Scotland totalled £76.2 million, in contrast to £30.2 million in civil legal aid payments.[9] Prior to the commission of the research, the increasing rate of growth in criminal legal aid expenditure had already been identified as representing an increase in both the number of applications for criminal legal aid and the average cost of legally-aided cases.[10] Between 1988–89 and 1992–93, for example, the number of applications to the six major legal aid schemes comprising criminal legal aid in Scotland rose by 29 per cent, while the number of persons proceeded against in the courts over the same five-year period fell by approximately 5 per cent. At the same time, the average cost per case rose from £535 in 1988–89 to £820 in 1992–93, that is, by 53 per cent. Why costs per case were rising well over the rate of inflation, and why the number of applications was growing when criminal proceedings in the Scottish courts were stabilising and even falling in number, were questions which could not be ignored in a programme of research undertaken with the ultimate objective of providing more efficient and cost-effective methods of delivering legal aid in criminal cases. Thus, while the research programme's remit was broader than an enquiry into the growth of criminal legal aid expenditure, its long-term objective could not be achieved without addressing the ever-spiralling public expenditure on criminal legal aid in Scotland.

---

[8] The research was located in the Edinburgh Centre for Social Welfare Research at the University of Edinburgh. It was made possible by a grant from the Scottish Office Home and Health Department to Michael Adler, at the University of Edinburgh's Department of Social Policy. This author is indebted to Michael Adler for his contribution to the research report, as well as to Alan Alexander and Cathy Cooke for their conduct of the surveys.

[9] Scottish Legal Aid Board, *Annual Report 1994/5*, Edinburgh: Scottish Legal Aid Board, 1995.

[10] Machin, D., Ward, S. and Millar, A., *Applications for Criminal Legal Aid*, Edinburgh: Central Research Unit, 1994.

The idea that legal aid makes an impact upon criminal case proceedings by providing an opportunity to prolong criminal cases was one of many working hypotheses employed during the course of the research. As we shall see, the hypothesis sits squarely within a broader theory of supplier-induced demand. During the course of the project, the relationship between criminal legal aid and criminal case proceedings was investigated through three discrete exercises. First, criminal court business in Scotland was charted by carrying out a census of 1,554 individuals who made a plea on summary charges, and who faced a trial under solemn procedure, in a sample of courts over a specified period. Their cases, where appropriate, were followed up over a period of nine months. Secondly, a postal questionnaire was sent to all individuals recorded by the census and facing summary charges, for their perceptions as to the paths their cases took, and the impact of legal aid upon these paths. Lastly, a series of in-depth and case-specific interviews were conducted with defence agents to identify different patterns of case trajectories, to examine the processes by which these patterns could be accounted for, and to consider the impact of legal aid on them. In the following discussion, reference is made to the data collected by means of the census and the postal surveys, as well as by in-depth interviews with defence agents.

II SUPPLIER-INDUCED DEMAND AND CRIMINAL LEGAL AID

According to the supplier-induced theory of demand, the recent rapid growth in legal aid expenditure is the responsibility of the suppliers of legal services, namely, lawyers.[11] Legally-aided consumers of legal services exercise no control over the type and amount of legal services which lawyers offer them because, as in most other professional/client relationships, there is an asymmetrical power relationship based on inequality of access to information. The services that are required by clients are largely, so the theory goes, the services their lawyers say they need. Moreover, because the costs of legal services are underwritten by a third party (the Legal Aid Board, or, in England and Wales, the Lord Chancellor's Department), there is no incentive on the part of legally-aided clients to exercise control over the type and amount of legal services their lawyers provide. There is, however, every incentive for lawyers to deliver as high a volume of services as possible, regardless of the needs of their clients and regardless of the costs of these services which, in any case, are the responsibility of a third party. Nor does the legal aid system offer any resistance to lawyers as to the volume of services they deliver. Since the legal aid budget is uncapped except where standard fees have been introduced,

---

[11] Bevan et al., *op. cit.*, pp. 5-9.

lawyers may tap it without limit once the financial and 'interests of justice', eligibility criteria have been satisfied. Lastly, lawyers have fully exploited the legal aid scheme during this past recessionary period as alternative sources of income have dried up. In sum, the theory asserts that the present system of publicly-funded legal services provision presents lawyers with the opportunity to drive up the demand for these services, while the recession has given them every incentive to do so.

How rising criminal legal aid expenditure may be explained in terms of this theory has been less clearly articulated than for civil legal aid. The number of acts of assistance and the cost per act of assistance have both increased dramatically in recent years in legal aid for civil proceedings. As far as criminal legal aid in the higher courts in England and Wales is concerned, the number of acts of assistance has decreased, though overall legal aid expenditure has increased because of a surge in the average cost per case which is largely the responsibility of those cases not covered by standard fees. At the same time, both the number of acts of assistance and the cost per act of assistance in criminal cases heard at magistrates' courts have increased. Both patterns are used to support the supplier-induced theory of growth, since magistrates' courts presumably offer more scope for increasing the number of supplier-driven acts of assistance than do the higher criminal courts. The argument, however, is never fully spelled out.

What is inadequately formulated, however, may be less problematic than what is omitted from the argument altogether. Patterns of legal aid expenditure are introduced and the theory of supplier-induced demand is invoked to explain them, but no enquiry is made as to whether these patterns may find a fuller or more convincing explanation elsewhere. Support for the explanatory power of the supplier-induced demand hypothesis appears to have taken precedence over what needs to be explained.

In particular, the explanation which is offered makes no recognition of the extent to which the growth in legal aid expenditure may be attributed to consumer-driven or system-driven demand. The former is surprising in view of the extensive programme of education which potential consumers of legal services have been receiving as to their rights over the past few years. The latter is less surprising in view of the model of man on which the theory of supplier-induced demand rests. It is essentially a model of man (and who better to typify it than lawyers?) as self-interested, in which actions are driven only by those interests, and which exists outside the social world where interests and actions are shaped and modified by institutions and organisations. In other words, the model has no regard for the social context in which case-related decisions are taken or for systemic constraints upon those decisions. Grounded in this model of human behaviour, the theory of supplier-induced demand appears simplistic and may be expected to provide explanations of a limited and partial nature. Let us consider this further by examining the institutional and organisational settings within which Scottish criminal lawyers work.

III THE CRIMINAL JUSTICE SYSTEM AND LEGAL AID IN SCOTLAND

The Scottish legal system has developed separately from that of England and Wales and is based on different principles and traditions.[12] The prosecution of crime in Scotland is under the control of the Lord Advocate, and crimes are reported by the police to procurators fiscal who, as the Lord Advocate's local representatives, are responsible for investigating the report and for deciding whether to prosecute, in which court to proceed and under what criminal jurisdiction or procedure. Procurators fiscal are also responsible for the prosecution of all cases, except for those tried in the High Court which are prosecuted by Advocate Deputes.

Scotland has three levels of criminal court: the district court, the sheriff court, and the High Court of Justiciary. There are district courts in all local authority district and islands areas of Scotland, and their jurisdiction is limited to offences committed within their area. Criminal cases in the district courts are conducted by lay justices and stipendiary magistrates, and though they primarily handle minor offences, there has been a growing tendency for fiscals to relieve the pressure on the sheriff courts by diverting cases to the district courts. This has been accompanied by the expansion of the district court's jurisdiction as to power and competence. Criminal proceedings in the sheriff court are conducted by sheriffs who have jurisdiction over crimes committed in their respective sheriffdoms, and whose jurisdiction as to power and competence is considerably broader than that of lay and stipendiary magistrates. Cases may also be remitted by sheriffs to the High Court, which has territorial jurisdiction over crimes committed anywhere in Scotland, possesses unlimited powers of imprisonment and has exclusive jurisdiction over certain crimes such as murder, rape and treason.

There are two types of criminal jurisdiction or procedure in Scotland — solemn and summary. Under solemn procedure, the sheriff or judge sits with a jury of 15, the trial proceeds on the basis of charges contained in a document called an indictment, and severe penalties are available on conviction. Under summary procedure, lay justices, stipendiary magistrates or sheriffs sit alone,

---

[12] For further information, see Walker, D. M., *The Scottish Legal System*, Edinburgh: W. Green, 1992; Gordon, G. H., *Scots Criminal Law*, Edinburgh: W. Green, 1992; Paterson, A. A. and Bates, T. S. N., *The Legal System of Scotland: Cases and Materials*, Edinburgh: W. Green, 1993; and *The Royal Commission on Legal Services in Scotland*, Cmnd. 7846, London: HMSO, 1980.

prosecution proceeds on the basis of charges contained in a summary complaint, and limits are placed upon the severity of penalties which may be imposed. It is important to note, if only because it is not known by those unfamiliar with the Scottish system, that fewer than 3 per cent of all prosecutions in Scotland are brought under solemn procedure. The High Court of Justiciary exercises solemn jurisdiction only; district courts exercise summary jurisdiction only; while sheriff courts exercise both. In fact, over 75 per cent of all cases brought under solemn procedure are tried in sheriff courts.

Charges are brought against accused persons either after they have been arrested and taken into custody, or while they are at liberty. Under summary procedure, accused persons taken into custody tender a plea at their first court appearance, at which time they may either be remanded in custody or liberated on an undertaking to appear in court. Persons who are charged while at liberty are cited to appear in court at a pleading diet, and this constitutes their first court appearance. The opportunity for accused persons to review and change their pleas prior to their trial under summary procedure was made possible by the introduction of intermediate diets (pre-trial reviews) into some sheriff courts in the 1980s. Under the Criminal Justice (Scotland) Act 1980, however, solemn trials are no longer preceded by pleading diets and accused persons whose cases are brought under solemn procedure are provided with no opportunity to tender a plea until the trial diet.

While the legal profession in Scotland has long accepted the defence of poor persons on criminal charges as a public duty, the legal aid system began to emerge in its present form only after the Second World War. Civil legal aid was introduced in 1950, criminal legal aid in 1964, the duty solicitor scheme in 1967, and preliminary advice and assistance in 1972. Up until 1986, the administration of the legal aid fund was the responsibility of the Law Society of Scotland; civil legal aid applications were handled by local committees, and criminal legal aid applications by the courts. Much inconsistency as to practice was noted. For example, because the views of sheriffs on legal aid varied enormously, the success rate of legal aid applications depended significantly upon the sheriffdoms in which applications were made. There was also concern that the governing body of the legal profession was responsible for supervising the payment of public funds to its own members.

Under the Legal Aid (Scotland) Act 1986, the Scottish Legal Aid Board was established as a non-departmental public body with primary responsibility for the administration of legal aid and the introduction of standardised practices into the administration and disbursement of legal aid funds throughout Scotland. Applications are still made to the courts for criminal legal aid in solemn proceedings, while Advice and Assistance, and ABWOR, are administered by solicitors. But the two largest schemes, civil legal aid and summary criminal legal aid, are administered by the Scottish Legal Aid Board. All applications for legal aid under these schemes are made to the Board and all accounts for professional fees and expenses are sent to it.

The 1986 Act also adjusted the scope of criminal legal aid by targeting it upon accused persons pleading not guilty. Criminal legal aid is currently available under six different schemes, depending on plea, custodial status and the criminal procedure under which charges are brought.[13]

Advice and Assistance

Advice and Assistance, known as the 'green form' in England and Wales, and the 'pink form' in Scotland, is available for advice and assistance on any matter of Scots law, including criminal matters, but is not available for representation in court. The scheme is administered by solicitors, the initial payment is restricted to £70, and solicitors must apply to the Scottish Legal Aid Board for any increase. Applicants are required to meet strictly defined financial criteria and may be required to pay a contribution, though few solicitors ask clients on criminal charges to do so.

ABWOR

Assistance by Way of Representation (ABWOR) is available for accused persons who plead guilty to summary criminal charges, and is restricted to charges which commence with a citation.[14] Accused persons who wish to change their plea to guilty may also apply for ABWOR, as long as they do so within 14 days of the pleading diet. ABWOR is administered by solicitors and is initially limited to £70 for advice, assistance and representation, though solicitors can themselves certify an increase of up to a maximum of £150 where, for example, a second or subsequent diets have been ordered by the court. Remuneration for services provided under ABWOR is therefore set at the same level as for Advice and Assistance, except that follow-up obligations subsequent to first appearance are remunerated, albeit at a low level. Applicants must satisfy the same financial eligibility criteria as is the case with Advice and Assistance, but the 'interests of justice' eligibility criteria are more restrictive.

Before solicitors may grant ABWOR, they must be satisfied that the court will impose a sentence that is likely to deprive the accused of liberty or lead to the loss of livelihood, or that the accused is unable to understand the

---

[13] For further information, see Scottish Legal Aid Board, *The Scottish Legal Aid Handbook 1992*, Edinburgh: Ritchie, 1992.
[14] A citation, like the summons in England and Wales, is used to call people before the court to answer charges laid against them.

proceedings or make a plea in mitigation because of some incapacity. Legally-aided representation is therefore available for those pleading guilty only in very limited circumstances.

The Duty Solicitor Scheme

The Duty Solicitor Scheme provides free advice and representation to accused persons who are taken into custody to await their first appearance in a district or sheriff court. No means or merits (interests of justice) tests are applied. A rota is set up in each sheriff and district court, and solicitors who have both indicated their willingness to serve and been approved by the Scottish Legal Aid Board are put on the duty roster. Accused persons charged under solemn procedure may receive free legal services from the duty solicitor, or from a solicitor of their own choosing. Under summary procedure, however, accused persons are entitled to free legal services from the duty solicitor only. If they plead guilty, they are entitled to the services of the duty solicitor up until the conclusion of the case, including any diets to which the case is adjourned for reports or otherwise deferred for sentence. If they plead not guilty, they may go on to make an application to the Scottish Legal Aid Board for summary criminal legal aid, and select a solicitor of their own choosing to do so on their behalf. Duty solicitors are paid by the number of clients on whose behalf they make an appearance, up to a maximum of £96.25 per session. Remuneration for all follow-up obligations incurred by duty solicitors is set at a ceiling of £64.55.

Summary criminal legal aid

Summary criminal legal aid is available to accused persons charged under summary procedure, and only after a plea of not guilty has been tendered. The Scottish Legal Aid Board must be satisfied that the expenses of the case cannot be met without undue hardship and that it is in the interests of justice that legal aid be granted. Unlike Advice and Assistance and ABWOR, summary criminal legal aid is not a contributory scheme. The Board received 66,529 applications for summary criminal legal aid in 1993–94, of which 92 per cent were granted either at first instance or after review. Approximately 50 per cent of refusals were on 'interests of justice' grounds, while just over 20 per cent of refusals were on financial eligibility grounds — constituting less than 2 per cent of all applications. Applicants refused summary criminal legal aid may have their applications reviewed by an independent practising solicitor who played no part in the initial decision. Summary criminal legal aid is Scotland's single most expensive legal aid scheme.

Solemn criminal legal aid

Solemn criminal legal aid is available for accused persons prosecuted under solemn procedure. They must apply for legal aid to the court in which they first appear. Because of the serious nature of the crimes which are prosecuted under solemn procedure, no interests of justice criteria need be met, and applicants must satisfy the court only that they cannot meet the expenses of the case without undue hardship. Unlike summary legal aid, solemn legal aid is also available to those who plead guilty. Unlike the Duty Solicitor Scheme, accused persons in custody may be represented by a solicitor of their choosing from the initial stages of criminal proceedings. In 1993–94, 12,426 grants of legal aid under this heading were made by the courts.

Legal aid for criminal appeals

Legal aid for criminal appeals exists for accused persons who wish to appeal against their conviction, or to oppose an appeal by the prosecution against acquittal or sentence. Applicants must satisfy the Scottish Legal Aid Board that there are substantial grounds for the appeal and that they cannot meet the expenses without undue hardship.

IV CRIMINAL LEGAL AID AS SYSTEM DRIVEN: LATE CHANGES OF PLEA

Having provided an outline of the Scottish legal (and legal aid) system, we can now explore the extent to which the system itself drives up legal aid costs. One issue with which the Scottish review of criminal legal aid was especially concerned was that of late changes of plea — the practice whereby accused persons plead not guilty at the initial pleading diet, only to change their plea to guilty on the day of their trial some weeks or months later. Meanwhile, considerable financial burdens are frequently incurred by the procurator fiscal (in respect of the costs of prosecution), by the Scottish Courts Administration (in respect of court costs), by the police (in respect of police witnesses attending court), and by the legal aid scheme (in respect of defence costs). Case trajectories characterised by late changes of plea therefore have cost implications which reach far wider than the legal aid scheme.

When legal aid is under review, there is a temptation to attribute the frequency with which accused persons plead not guilty in the first instance, and only much later change their plea to guilty, to their defence agents. The temptation is an easy one to understand and lies at the heart of the theory of criminal legal aid expenditure growth as supplier-induced demand. Indeed, the late guilty plea has been viewed by proponents of the theory as a crucial mechanism by which lawyers drive up criminal legal aid expenditure. According to this view, defence agents have an interest in stretching out cases for as long as possible. Because the Legal Aid (Scotland) Act 1986 was instrumental in targeting the provision of criminal legal aid towards accused persons tendering a not guilty plea, it is in the interest of lawyers that clients enter a not guilty plea and adhere to it for as long as possible. It is further assumed that because late changes of plea are costly to the legal aid scheme, they are therefore profitable for solicitors. Parenthetically, this takes no account of the opportunity costs to defence agents of continuing cases.

Even if it were self-evidently in the interest of defence agents to continue cases for as long as possible, however, this could not account for the appearance of systematic variations between cases in late changes of plea in our census of criminal court proceedings. Striking differences in the rates of late changes of plea were found between courts, geographical areas and types of charges, as well as between accused persons making their first appearance from custody and those whose cases were initiated by citation. Structural and institutional factors operating in and around the criminal justice system were clearly of some importance in explaining the prevalence of plea changes following initial not guilty pleas. While it may be the case that individual defence agents are driven by the profit motive, and while this may manifest itself in drawing out cases for as long as possible in some instances, the appearance of patterns of late changes of plea could be understood only in terms of systematic pressures upon the conduct of criminal proceedings and the decision-making process. Raw, invariant, self-interest alone would not suffice to explain them.

In the following sections, some exemplifications of the institutional and structural factors responsible for shaping criminal case trajectories in Scotland are presented. These pertain both to the rules governing the criminal legal aid scheme in Scotland, and to the structural context within which criminal cases proceed. They suggest that the opportunity and power available to lawyers to drive legal aid expenditure, and their responsibility for doing so, is misrepresented and exaggerated by the supplier-induced theory of demand.

V CUSTODY COURTS

In our census of criminal proceedings, the proportion of accused persons making their first appearance from custody under summary procedure varied greatly between specific courts; between 0 per cent and 21 per cent in district courts, and between 23 per cent and 45 per cent in the sheriff courts. This variation between the courts has crucial implications for the volume of business in the criminal justice system and its concomitant court and legal aid costs, because of the different patterns of pleading which are generated by the custody courts. Thus, 71 per cent of all accused persons pleading from custody in summary cases were found to have pleaded not guilty to some or all charges, compared to 44 per cent of all cited cases. Custody courts not only generate a far higher percentage of not guilty pleas, but also generate a higher rate of plea changes. Indeed, more than a third (34 per cent) of all accused persons pleading not guilty in the custody courts went on to change their plea to guilty, whereas only 15 per cent of cited persons pleading not guilty went on to change their plea. Thus, though custodial cases constituted only 21 per cent of all summary cases in the census, they comprised 37 per cent of all cases for which there was information about changes of plea. Where first appearance is from custody, therefore, cases are more costly in legal aid terms because they are more likely to be continued. On the face of it, they also appear to be a waste of public resources since many accused persons eventually do plead guilty.

The disproportionate contribution of custody courts to the criminal legal aid bill may be located in the operation of the custody court, and particularly in the way it structures pleading decisions. Solicitors interviewed during the project reported that delays in serving papers on accused persons in custody were increasing over the years, and this they attributed to a shortage of staff in the procurator fiscal's office. Until such time as they know what charges have been made against their client, they obviously can neither advise as to pleading decisions, nor negotiate a plea with the procurator fiscal. By the time papers are served, the court is often about to sit, thus reducing their ability to confer with their clients or with the procurator fiscal. Once court finally commences, the speed of throughput is terrifying. In the absence of a full discussion with their clients over charges, a plea of not guilty in the custody courts is often seen as the only responsible course of action, to be followed at some later point by more careful consideration. This is even more likely to be the case with duty solicitors since, under these same conditions, they must attend to all accused persons who have not nominated their own defence agent. Once a plea of not guilty has been tendered, however, accused persons may then go on to seek legally-aided advice and representation by making an application for summary criminal legal aid. In other words, pleading not guilty is a threshold over which accused persons in custody must pass if they wish to gain access to adequate legal advice and assistance.

Another factor which contributes to the high rates of continued cases generated by the custody courts is to be found in the fact that the pressures to which procurators fiscal are subject provide little opportunity for the negotiation of pleas. A minimum knowledge of the case is clearly a basic requirement of negotiation, and yet fiscals rarely have time to acquaint themselves with individual cases because of the sheer number of cases allocated to them at each session, and often at the eleventh hour. Neither is it in their immediate interest to negotiate partial pleas at first appearances, since pleas in mitigation and sentencing are very likely to slacken the speed of throughput in the custody courts. Furthermore, it was also reported that many recent and relatively inexperienced recruits to the procurator fiscal service are unable to negotiate under the pressure of custody court conditions.

Neither should one ignore the potential of the consumer-driven theory for explaining patterns of pleading in the custody courts. There is every incentive for accused persons to plead not guilty in the first instance, even where pleas are likely to be changed at a later date. Not only is the quality of legal advice likely to be improved by pleading not guilty and applying for summary criminal legal aid, but there is the additional incentive of delaying sentencing. Where bail is granted, of course, defenders (= defendants) acquire their freedom too. Only where bail is likely to be opposed do the custody courts provide accused persons with some incentive to tender a guilty plea. This is because the conditions which prevail in Scottish prisons for those remanded in custody are such that accused persons were reported to be pleading guilty to avoid them. For some, custody under sentence was preferable to custody on remand.

In addition to these structural pressures on pleading decisions, the legal aid rules pertaining to the provision and remuneration of legal services for accused persons in custody who are facing charges under summary procedure also provide a consistent series of incentives to both defence agents and accused persons to continue their cases by pleading not guilty in the first instance. The legal aid scheme operating for accused persons pleading from custody is the duty solicitor scheme. While solicitors may complain about their remuneration for sessions served on the duty rota, they go into the duty scheme voluntarily and with a guarantee that their time spent on the rota is predictable, even if it may be written off financially in the short term. The same cannot be said of any follow-up obligations which may be incurred should they advise a guilty plea at first appearance. Repeated deferral of sentencing was a particular source of grievance amongst solicitors on the duty rota, largely because it is beyond their control, as when, for example, required social enquiry reports are unavailable. The problem is exacerbated by the amount of time wasted by waiting for cases to be called, often long after the sessional fee ceiling for duty solicitors has been reached. Indeed, the remuneration of duty solicitors for follow-up work subsequent to guilty pleas was described by many on the duty scheme rota as derisory, and was felt to constitute a strong disincentive against supporting accused persons who wish to plead guilty. It provides duty solicitors with every incentive to advise a not guilty plea in the first instance, allowing accused persons to make application for summary criminal legal aid through a solicitor out with the duty scheme. Duty solicitors will occasionally pick up clients this way, and take them on under summary criminal legal aid. For the main part, however, duty solicitors have no direct interest in prolonging the cases of accused persons whom they advise under the duty scheme. They do have an interest, however, in avoiding the follow-up work which may accompany guilty pleas. How the self-interest of duty solicitors manifests itself, therefore, can be understood only in terms of the organisation and remuneration of the duty scheme. Any attempt to address the growth of criminal legal aid expenditure arising out of the proportion of applications to summary criminal legal aid generated by the custody courts must look at the way in which the self-interest of duty solicitors is structured by the very rules and remuneration levels to which duty solicitors are subject.

Legal aid rules also provide strong disincentives to plead guilty when accused persons charged under summary procedure nominate a solicitor of their own choosing to represent them at their first appearance from custody rather than the duty solicitor. The census shows marked variations between courts in the proportions of accused persons making their first appearance from custody who choose to be represented by a nominated solicitor rather than by the duty solicitor. This ranged from 55 per cent in the smallest of the sheriff courts sampled, to 84 per cent in the largest. The majority of accused persons making their first appearance from custody in Scotland's sheriff courts, therefore, dispense with the services of the duty solicitor and nominate their own. Nominated solicitors receive no remuneration for waiting or for representing clients in the custody courts, though they are eligible to receive fees for 15–30 minutes of services rendered under the Advice and Assistance scheme. More than a few solicitors found the work involved in claiming these fees to be hardly worth the effort. Where a plea of not guilty is entered, however, there is the prospect of some future pay-off, and this makes the enterprise attractive. Where a plea of guilty is entered, on the other hand, there are neither future nor present pay-offs for nominated solicitors. This is to be contrasted with cited cases, where solicitors may at least apply for ABWOR should their client tender a guilty plea. It may also be contrasted with duty solicitors who receive some, albeit minimal, remuneration for follow-up work subsequent to a guilty plea. The system of legal aid which operates in the custody courts, therefore, generates a strong incentive towards not guilty pleas because it discounts and all but ignores the much more common presence of nominated solicitors in these courts. It may certainly be in the interest of nominated solicitors to advise their clients to plead not guilty and apply for summary criminal legal aid. Their self-interest is structured by the legal aid rules to which custody cases are subject, however, and may be understood and explained in terms of them.

230

The sad paradox is that nominated solicitors might more adequately deal with pleas in mitigation and deferred sentences than solicitors who happen to be on the duty rota, both because they are more likely to have greater knowledge of their client's history and because they have more time available at their client's first appearance from custody. Certainly, their potential for securing a guilty plea is probably higher than that of duty solicitors, in that accused persons place greater trust in them and have greater confidence in their advice and their ability to present an effective plea in mitigation. What the duty solicitor scheme attempted to introduce was a streamlined and cost-effective approach to the public funding of legal services for those initially pleading from custody. Because of the organisation and resourcing of the custody courts in which the duty scheme now operates, however, and because of the restrictions which the duty scheme imposes on the remuneration of legal services, the duty scheme has generated a set of incentives to plead not guilty in the first instance. As a result, applications are then made for summary criminal legal aid in order to deal with what might otherwise have been undertaken at an earlier and less costly stage in the life-history of a criminal case.

VI   ASSISTANCE BY WAY OF REPRESENTATION

Assistance by Way of Representation (ABWOR) is the only legal aid available to persons who wish to tender a guilty plea, and it is limited to individuals whose cases are initiated by citation. Even then, the eligibility criteria are most restrictive and the remuneration for legal services rendered is minimal. This supports the Legal Aid (Scotland) Act 1986 in its aim of targeting the most needy by concentrating resources on those pleading not guilty.

The restriction of ABWOR to cited cases has important implications for accused persons on bail. Those who plead not guilty in the custody courts may be inclined to make an early change of plea once on bail if, on consideration of the case, their own solicitor advises them that there is no case to fight. Accused persons may also have greater confidence in their own solicitors to make an effective plea in mitigation on their behalf. As we have already seen, accused persons on bail are more likely to change their plea than those at liberty. There is every reason to believe, then, that they do not have the same commitment to adhering to their not guilty plea. Any inclination to change their plea at an early stage, though, will be tempered by the rules governing legally-aided representation of accused persons on bail which leaves them outwith the scope of ABWOR. Under these circumstances, only two options are left open to accused persons on bail who wish to change their plea — either to return to the duty solicitor, or to adhere to their original not guilty plea in order to access the assistance of their own solicitor through summary criminal

231

legal aid, and plead guilty or negotiate a plea later. The denial of ABWOR to accused persons on bail therefore has the following consequences:

(a) it creates an incentive to adhere to a not guilty plea where otherwise there may be good reason to change it at an early stage;

(b) it exerts a strong pressure on those requiring legal assistance to apply for summary criminal legal aid by adhering to a not guilty plea; and

(c) it inflates the number of 'late guilty' pleas, thus driving criminal cases along trajectories which are both longer and costlier for the administration of criminal justice and legal aid.

Cited cases, unlike custody cases, are eligible for ABWOR. This is not a generous scheme, however. The Scottish Legal Aid Board warns solicitors that the most stringently limiting interpretation of ABWOR's eligibility criteria should be employed in their administration of the scheme. Though some scope for interpretation obviously still exists because solicitors vary so much in their use of ABWOR, criteria of eligibility such as 'loss of livelihood' are regarded by almost all solicitors as unnecessarily inflexible and restrictive — especially in areas and amongst age groups where there is already high unemployment and from amongst whom a high proportion of all applications for criminal legal aid are likely to be received. If young unemployed people wish to be represented to tender a guilty plea, they may, therefore, have no option but to plead not guilty in the first instance and apply for summary criminal legal aid, even if they have little intention of adhering to their not guilty plea. While ABWOR is also available to accused persons who plead not guilty at their first appearance but wish to change their plea, they must make application within 14 days of their initial plea. This takes no account of the fact that many who plead not guilty at their first appearance do so without legal representation, and often wait more than 14 days before they consult a solicitor. After 14 days, they must adhere to their not guilty plea if they wish to be eligible for legally-aided representation. Here again the legal aid rules are responsible for structuring pleading decisions by generating strong incentives amongst accused persons to opt for, or to adhere to, a not guilty plea.

As for solicitors, ABWOR is perceived by many to be something of a 'loss leader'. Though fees may be increased for attendance at second or subsequent diets, the very low level at which ABWOR is remunerated does not begin to cover meetings with the client, preparation of the plea, travel to and from court, waiting in court, and representing the client. Indeed, many solicitors argued that ABWOR's present ceiling does not always allow them to do sufficient preparation so as to be confident about advising a guilty plea. The opportunity to collect enough evidence under ABWOR so as to negotiate a plea with the

232

fiscals prior to the pleading diet is, *a fortiori*, out of the question. ABWOR therefore provides solicitors with strong professional, as well as financial, inducements to advise their clients to tender a not guilty plea and apply for summary criminal legal aid.

When guilty pleas are tendered, legal representation is still of benefit to accused persons since solicitors know what mitigating circumstances may be called upon and can ensure that their clients are able to meet the terms of their disposal. Legal representation is also of benefit to the courts since it 'oils the wheels' on which the day-to-day business of the court runs.[15] The successful disposal of cases at their first appearance also has knock-on effects for the courts and criminal legal aid expenditure by reducing the volume of criminal business in the courts, as well as the cost per case. By targeting resources on those who plead not guilty, however, the personal and public value of legally-aided representation for those pleading guilty remains formally unacknowledged. Instead, the legal aid system generates incentives to plead not guilty, and to adhere to that plea until such time as access to legal representation is obtained through summary criminal legal aid.

VII INTERMEDIATE DIETS

According to the supplier-driven theory of legal aid expenditure, cases are prolonged by lawyers in the interest of lawyers. A late change of plea, then, should be understood as a device by which the thirst of suppliers of legal services is quenched by milking a more or less bottomless legal aid fund until it is no longer possible to adhere to a not guilty plea. Interestingly, most lawyers have no hesitation in proposing a counter-theory by attributing the 'late guilty plea' phenomenon to the consumers of their services: accused persons are characterised by their commitment to one goal above all else, namely, 'putting off the evil day'. What neither view considers is whether or not the criminal justice system presents any opportunity to change pleas earlier rather than later. Our study indicates, indeed, that when such an opportunity does present itself, it is often taken.

A crucial site for observing this is at intermediate diets. Intermediate diets, or pre-trial reviews, were first introduced into Scotland in 1983, with the aim of reducing the frequency of adjourning costlier trial diets, as well as providing an opportunity to change or negotiate pleas earlier rather than later. Lawyers interviewed during the research project were unanimous in agreeing that the initial introduction of intermediate diets had been disastrous, and blamed poor

---

[15] See further, Young, R., 'Will Widgery Do?': Court clerks, discretion, and the determination of legal aid applications', at chapter 7 of this volume.

organisation, under-resourcing and inadequate direction from the bench for their failure. Because of past experience, therefore, their re-introduction by some sheriff courts in the early 1990s was greeted with hostility and grave doubts as to their effectiveness. When the census of criminal business was undertaken in 1992, only one of the five sheriff courts sampled (sheriff court A) was setting intermediate diets for a majority (78 per cent) of all cases where pleas of not guilty had been tendered. Another court (sheriff court B) was setting them for just 30 per cent of all such cases, and a third court (sheriff court C) was setting them for a small minority (3 per cent). What the census of criminal business shows is that when intermediate diets are set, however, pleas are more likely to be changed at an earlier stage of the proceedings than when they are not. The figures are presented in Table 10.1.

Table 10.1: Use of intermediate diets in three sheriff courts and their effect on the timing of plea changes

	Percentage of all cases proceeding to trial for which intermediate diet set	Percentage of plea changes	
		Before trial	At trial
Sheriff court			
A	78	50	50
B	30	24	76
C	3	13	87

Thus, for example, in court A, where intermediate diets were set for 78 per cent of all accused persons pleading not guilty, only 50 per cent of those who eventually changed their plea waited until the trial diet to do so, while the other 50 per cent changed their pleas before the trial. On the other hand, in court C, where intermediate diets were set for only 3 per cent of all accused persons pleading not guilty, 87 per cent of those who changed their plea waited until the trial to do so. Where intermediate diets had been set for the majority of accused persons pleading not guilty, then, the proportion of those changing their pleas at a later and more costly stage in the life-history of a criminal case was substantially reduced. Solicitors working in the court A area admitted that their initial anxieties over the re-introduction of intermediate diets had been proved wrong. They reported that intermediate diets were now enabling accused persons, fiscals and defence agents to negotiate pleas at an earlier stage of the proceedings by providing an opportunity for solicitors and their clients to review the case together. They also claimed that intermediate diets were providing solicitors with an earlier opportunity to ascertain the case against their clients, and to negotiate with fiscals in the presence of their clients.[16] Since partial or amended pleas were now being negotiated some weeks prior to the trial, there was time to countermand any witnesses who might have been cited. Intermediate diets also indicated where there may be no merit in going to trial: 'It's a way of concentrating the mind and making sure that clients realise that by adhering to their not guilty plea, they are only putting off the evil day.'[17]

The impact of intermediate diets on pleading decisions strongly suggests that neither theories of supplier-induced demand nor of consumer-induced demand can fully explain the rising costs per case of criminal legal aid. The assumption that lawyers and defenders are driven by the wish to continue cases for as long as there are prospects of remuneration, or for as long as the day of judgment may be postponed, has no regard for the context in which criminal cases proceed. The research indicates that where there are socially structured opportunities for doing so, criminal cases may be brought to an earlier conclusion. Intermediate diets provide one such opportunity, albeit not one which may be implemented cheaply or easily. To succeed in their objectives, as intermediate diets have apparently done in court A, adequate resourcing of court and fiscal services, improved organisation of court proceedings, and firm and consistent direction from the bench are all required. Much responsibility rests upon the criminal justice system, its procedures and its management, therefore, for providing the opportunities to structure the decisions of accused persons and their defence agents.

VIII CONCLUSION

Under the Legal Aid (Scotland) Act 1986, criminal legal aid was targeted on the most needy, who were identified by the Act as those protesting their innocence by pleading not guilty. On the face of it, this may appear to be beyond reproach. The eligibility rules around which the various criminal legal aid schemes are administered, and the remuneration levels around which publicly-funded legal services are provided, were thereby directed in favour of

---

[16] The presence of defenders at intermediate diets is mandatory in Scotland. For an evaluation of pre-trial reviews in England and Wales, see Brownlee, I. D., Mulcahy, A. and Walker, C., 'Pre-Trial Reviews, Court Efficiency and Justice: A Study in Leeds and Bradford Magistrates' Courts', *The Howard Journal*, 1994, vol. 83, p. 109, in which the authors argue that the presence of defendants is required to achieve substantive as well as procedurally efficient justice. Interestingly, the professionals interviewed in this English study were in agreement that pre-trial reviews are more effective if conducted in the absence of defendants. In our Scottish study, defence agents pointed to the value of the presence of defenders in all but exceptional circumstances.
[17] Interview with defence agent operating in court A area.

those who tender not guilty pleas. This is reflected in the focus of criminal legal aid disbursements upon the funding of trials, which lie at the costlier end of the life-cycle of criminal case proceedings. By contrast, legal aid eligibility is limited and remuneration is restricted at the pleading stage, that is, at the earlier and cheaper end of criminal case trajectories. The legal aid system therefore provides accused persons with the incentive to plead not guilty and to apply for summary criminal legal aid in order to access legal advice, assistance and representation which might otherwise not be available. It thereby provides them with the incentive to access costlier forms of assistance when their needs might adequately be met by accessing legal services in the earlier and less costly phases of criminal case proceedings. By targeting those who protest their innocence, therefore, the rules governing criminal legal aid eligibility generate perverse incentives which drive criminal cases along a course which incurs increasing rates of expenditure as they go. While both accused persons and their defence agents may undoubtedly act out of self-interest, where these self-interests lie and what direction these self-interests take are shaped by institutional features of the legal aid system to which criminal cases are subject.

Self-interest is also shaped by structural constraints upon pleading decisions. While specific eligibility criteria and remuneration rules in the criminal legal aid system provide defence agents and their clients with incentives to prolong cases by pleading not guilty, these incentives are reinforced by the opportunity structure which faces defence agents and their clients in the criminal justice system. Given the congestion and rate of throughput in many custody courts, the decision to plead guilty at first appearance cannot be reached with any degree of security, plea negotiation with the fiscal service cannot be undertaken with any degree of satisfaction, and pleas in mitigation cannot be made with any degree of effectiveness. The possibility of entering into negotiation over pleas in the initial stages of case proceedings is further reduced by an understaffed and under-resourced fiscal service, and limits the opportunity for both cited and custody cases to reach an early conclusion. The scarcity of institutionalised procedures between pleading and trial diets for bringing cases to an earlier and less costly conclusion, such as preliminary hearings or intermediate diets, drive criminal case trajectories on an inexorable journey downstream, where expenditures rapidly accumulate and assume deeper and ever-widening proportions.

According to the supplier-induced theory of demand, explanations for the growth of legal aid expenditure are located within a legal aid system which allows the appetites of defence agents to run rampant. The remedies which this theory suggests all deal with the appetite by employing different mechanisms for withdrawing the supply of food. The appetite itself is invariant and not subject to manipulation. This chapter suggests, on the contrary, that the self-interests of defence agents are shaped by the institutions and social structures in which legally-aided criminal case work is conducted. Both criminal legal aid rules pertaining to eligibility and remuneration, and the procedures of the criminal justice system, shape the interests of defence agents and accused persons alike, and conspire to drive criminal cases downstream to where the costs of proceeding are at their highest point. The targeting of legal aid on accused persons who plead not guilty was intended as a measure of economy. It has proven to be a false economy, however, because it has led to more, and more protracted, contested cases. Thus, what savings might have been made upstream are likely to have been lost many times over by driving cases further downstream. The same may be said of those economies made by poor resourcing of the fiscal service, court facilities, and court procedures such as preliminary hearings in civil cases and intermediate diets in criminal cases.

Some of these processes were officially recognised in the 1994 White Paper, *Firm and Fair*,[18] which set out the Government's proposals for changes to the criminal justice system in Scotland. These proposals have been translated into action in various ways. Thus, for example, work is currently being undertaken on a system of standard fees for legally-aided cases which acknowledges the potential of such a system for influencing the structure of criminal case trajectories, and for reducing built-in incentives to continue cases.[*] Under the Criminal Justice (Scotland) Act 1995, intermediate diets are to be made mandatory in all summary and solemn cases in the sheriff courts from April 1996. Changes to criminal legal aid eligibility criteria are also being planned which may go some way to counteracting the unintended consequences of targeting legal aid on those pleading not guilty. Thus, access to legal representation for those wishing to tender a guilty plea is to be broadened by abolishing the '14 day rule' which has restricted ABWOR to accused persons intimating a change of plea within 14 days of pleading not guilty. It is now proposed to extend the time limit for intimating a change of plea up to the intermediate diet.

In many ways, then, we are in an enviable position in Scotland in seeing some of the findings produced by a large and systematic programme of research commissioned by the Scottish Office make their way into official policy documents, consultation papers and recommendations.[19] The recognition that criminal legal aid rules, and the criminal justice system itself, bear some responsibility for driving the volume and cost of business in the criminal courts is just one of them.

---

[18] Scottish Office, *Firm and Fair*, White Paper (Dd 0287999 C10), Edinburgh: HMSO, June 1994.
[*] At the point of going to press, the Secretary of State for Scotland, Michael Forsyth, announced that standard fees are no longer under consideration.
[19] See, in particular, Scottish Office, *Criminal Legal Aid Review: A Consultation Paper*, (MAB00624.073), November 1993.

11

Legal Firms, Lawyers' Attitudes and Criminal Legal Aid in Scotland

Karen Kerner

I INTRODUCTION

Throughout the United Kingdom, both policy-makers and legal practitioners have had to contend with increased demands both for the provision of criminal legal aid and for the containment of its spiralling costs. This chapter examines the criminal legal aid system in Scotland from the perspective of the legal profession. The many suggestions for improving the delivery of justice and containing legal aid costs are discussed. Recent changes to the criminal legal aid system in Scotland (proposed or implemented) are noted where relevant. The implications of the effects of these changes on the market structure and types of business undertaken by Scottish legal firms are also discussed.

The chapter discusses the results of two surveys. The first, conducted between 1991 and 1992, looked at the involvement of a random sample of Scottish partners and sole practitioners in legal aid work.[1] The second, conducted between 1992 and 1993, examined solicitors' attitudes towards and experiences with the then current Scottish criminal legal aid system.[2] An outline of the various legal aid programmes (and their escalating costs) that make up that 'system', together with a description of the Scottish court system, is provided by Elaine Samuel in the preceding chapter. Accordingly, we will concentrate here upon the views of defence agents.

---

[1] Kerner, K., *Specialism in Private Legal Practice*, Edinburgh: Scottish Office Central Research Unit, 1995.

[2] Kerner, K., *Defence Agents' Attitudes and Experiences of Criminal Legal Aid*, Edinburgh: Scottish Office Central Research Unit, 1993 (unpublished manuscript).

This chapter is divided into six parts. In the next section the details of the two research surveys on which this chapter draws are set out. Section III examines how legal aid work is allocated between and within firms of solicitors. Section IV discusses solicitors' views on the best and worst aspects of the criminal legal aid system, and section V examines changes desired and implemented in criminal legal aid in Scotland. The chapter concludes by summarising the level of agreement and disagreement between policy-makers and the providers of legally-aided services as to the way forward for the legal aid scheme.

II   THE RESEARCH SAMPLES

It is important to set out details of the research samples upon which the remaining discussion in this chapter is largely based.

The 1991–92 survey of principals (partners and sole practitioners) in Scottish law firms comprised a randomly selected sample of 135 solicitors in 124 firms drawn from throughout Scotland. The first such survey undertaken in Scotland, it was designed to provide baseline information on the solicitor profession in Scotland prior to the implementation of the sweeping changes enacted in the Law Reform (Miscellaneous Provisions) (Scotland) Act 1990. That survey looked at both the work and characteristics of Scottish partners and sole practitioners, and the structure and organisation of their firms.[3] Information on legal aid from this survey formed only a small part of the data collected in the course of the research and was not its primary focus.

The central core of the 1992–93 legal aid study, a census of court cases conducted in five areas of Scotland — Airdrie, Dumfries, Dundee, Edinburgh, and Glasgow — during the week of 11–15 May 1992, was the first such census undertaken in the Scottish courts, and was conducted by Michael Adler, Alan Alexander, Cathy Cooke and Elaine Samuel.[4] This author's part of the research, the investigation of solicitors' experiences with and attitudes toward the then current criminal legal aid system, surveyed the views of 41 criminal legal aid practitioners. Of these, 26 of the solicitors interviewed were specialists in criminal representation and criminal legal aid. Fourteen solicitors were more general practitioners who dealt with a smaller number of criminal legal aid applications, and who were surveyed for comparative purposes. One was a specialist consultant. In addition, 11 advocates (criminal court specialists) were interviewed about their experiences with and opinions of the current criminal legal aid programmes.

---

[3] Kerner, *op. cit.* (1993) and Kerner, *op. cit.* (1995).
[4] Some of the results of that census are discussed in Samuel, E., 'Criminal Legal Aid Expenditure: Supplier or System Driven? The Case of Scotland', at chapter 10 of this volume.

The defence agents interviewed included solicitors from Edinburgh, Glasgow, Dundee, Airdrie, and Dumfries. Respondents were selected from Scottish Legal Aid Board records and compiled from lists of specialists and generalists assembled by the Scottish Legal Aid Board. Because respondents were selected from the Scottish Legal Aid Board's records, they formed a representative, rather than a random, sample and their responses must be considered in the light of that fact. Nonetheless, as solicitors experienced in undertaking legal aid work, their opinions can responsibly inform the ongoing debate on legal aid.

III WHO DOES LEGAL AID WORK IN SCOTLAND?

In this section we examine the question of who is carrying out which kinds of legal aid work. A preliminary point is that the great majority of criminal defence work undertaken in Scotland is legally-aided. Nearly half the defence agents (criminal defence practitioners) in the 1992–93 attitudinal survey reported that 99 per cent or more of their criminal work was legally-aided, while 1 per cent or less was private case work.[5] Even at the lower end of the scale, three of the criminal defence practitioners interviewed reckoned that legally-aided work comprised at least 70–75 per cent of their criminal business. Interestingly, both the highest and lowest amounts of legally-aided work were claimed by full-time criminal defence practitioners in specialist criminal practice firms. Even for specialist criminal lawyers who deal with specific types of cases, such as drug-related or juvenile offences, the vast majority of criminal business is paid for by criminal legal aid.

Yet, despite an overall increase in legal aid expenditure, many of Scotland's larger firms have ceased involvement in legal aid work for new clients, while specialist firms of defence agents have come increasingly to dominate the market for legally-aided criminal defence work.[6] Criminal legal aid work is increasingly the province of small (two to four partner) specialist firms, located in the big cities and Central Belt of Scotland.[7]

In multi-practices (legal firms offering a range of legal services), legal aid is frequently delegated to younger, less experienced solicitors. Rural multi-practices, in general, conduct a low volume of criminal legal aid business, but often feel obliged to offer criminal legal aid services to clients in their areas. Thus, according to the 1992 random survey of legal principals in Scotland,

---

[5] Kerner, *op. cit.* (1993), p. 10.
[6] Kerner, *op. cit.* (1995), pp. 15–16.
[7] Kerner, *op. cit.* (1993), p. 12.

nearly 58 per cent of country partners dealt personally with legally-aided cases, but only 37 per cent of city partners did so.[8]

Ten firms in Scotland earned more than £1 million in legal aid fees during 1994–95, although just over 17 per cent of Scottish law firms undertook no legal aid work at all. Table 11.1[9] indicates legal aid fee levels earned by Scottish legal practices in 1994–95.

Table 11.1: Fees earned by Scottish law firms 1994–95 for civil and criminal legal aid and advice and assistance

Amount earned	Number of firms	Fees earned as percentage of total legal aid bill
Over £1 million	10	13.4
£750,000–£1 million	9	7.2
£500,000–£749,999	21	11.7
£250,000–£499,999	84	25.9
£100,000–£249,999	157	22.9
£50,000–£99,999	170	10.8
Under £50,000	541	8.1
TOTAL	992	100.0

In 1994–95, the highest fee earners comprised only 1 per cent of all legal aid practices, but earned more than 13 per cent of the total legal aid bill. The majority of legal aid practitioners earned less than £50,000, and represented just over 8 per cent of the total legal aid bill. A similar bifurcation can be found in England and Wales.[10] Although Scottish solicitors in general reported long working days — a ten-hour working day is the norm[11] — criminal defence practitioners interviewed in 1992–93 varied greatly in the amount of time they spent each day on legally-aided criminal defence work. Solicitors in Edinburgh and Glasgow reported the highest number of hours worked daily on criminal legally-aided work, while those in Dumfries and Dundee reported the fewest

---

[8] Kerner, *op. cit.* (1995), p. 15.
[9] Source: Scottish Legal Aid Board, *Annual Report 1994/95*, Edinburgh: Scottish Legal Aid Board, 1995. See also *Glasgow Herald*, 28 July 1995.
[10] See McConville, M., Hodgson, J., Bridges, L. and Pavlovic, A., *Standing Accused: The Organisation and Practices of Criminal Defence Lawyers in Britain*, Oxford: OUP, 1994.
[11] Kerner, *op. cit.* (1995), p. 14.

hours worked. Not surprisingly, practitioners in specialist criminal firms reported the highest numbers of daily working hours on legally-aided work, while solicitors in multi-practices reported the lowest numbers of hours worked each day on legally-aided cases.[12]

Legally-aided criminal work in Scotland, like that in England and Wales, tends to be a high volume business. Because of this, it is extremely unusual for Scottish criminal defence practitioners to prepare and conduct legally-aided criminal cases without delegating some or most of the work involved to one or more other individuals. Over 90 per cent of the defence agents in the 1992-93 sample delegated at least some of their work in the preparation of a criminal case. The vast majority of delegated work (over 90 per cent) in Scotland is represented by work contracted out to precognition agents, who are employed to obtain witness statements.[13]

Delegated work is also performed by assistants, or by trainees. To a lesser extent, secretaries or assistants may be responsible for routine correspondence during a case; most solicitors maintain a bank of styles, or sample letters, to be sent to the client, the court, the Scottish Legal Aid Board, the police, and so on. With the introduction of new forms by the Scottish Legal Aid Board in 1995, now available on disk, maintaining a bank of application styles has been made easier for criminal legal aid practitioners.[14]

Senior partners typically reserve the most complicated criminal cases for themselves, leaving routine criminal matters for younger, less experienced solicitors. In addition, solicitors frequently delegate work to other solicitors as their agents in cases in other jurisdictions. As one solicitor in the criminal practitioner sample explained: 'This is a high volume business, or we'd never survive financially. We have to delegate some of the work on each case or we couldn't maintain the volume.'

The criminal legal aid programmes most commonly used by the 1992–93 survey defence agents were criminal advice and assistance and summary criminal legal aid, followed by solemn criminal legal aid.[15] Solicitors in the sample dealt less frequently with ABWOR (Assistance by Way of Representation) and with criminal appeals. More than 77 per cent reported having had experience in self-certifying for ABWOR. Although three solicitors complained that they did not understand the programme at all, the most common complaints made about the ABWOR programme in 1992–93 were that the self-certification limits were too low and the eligibility criteria too restrictive.

[12] Kerner, op. cit. (1993), p. 10.
[13] Ibid., p. 12.
[14] The Scottish Legal Aid Board Reporter, spring 1995.
[15] See Samuel, op. cit., for discussion of the various Scottish legal aid programmes.

All of the solicitors in the 1992–93 sample told clients whether they were likely to be eligible for legal aid or not. 'It is,' as one solicitor commented, 'an integral part of the initial interview.' The great majority (65.9 per cent) of the solicitors provided information about legal aid to their clients before a decision was made about whether the client would plead guilty or not guilty, and nearly 20 per cent explained legal aid after a plea was decided. As clients are more likely to obtain legal aid if they plead not guilty,[16] it is perhaps not surprising that solicitors generally explained the legal aid rules prior to discussing plea.

Indeed, the majority of Scottish defence agents interviewed used the legal aid application forms as the basis for the structure of an interview. Thus, all of the solicitors in the sample inquired about their clients' financial circumstances, although more than a third of those interviewed suggested that it was pointless to explain about possible financial contributions (for criminal advice and assistance and for ABWOR), 'because the client wouldn't pay it anyway.'

Consequently, the vast majority of defence agents offered an initial interview to clients free of charge to the client, even if they did not qualify on financial grounds for fully paid criminal Advice and Assistance or ABWOR. One solicitor commented that 'my clients don't understand that they can qualify for advice and assistance one time, and not be eligible at another, so I just don't bother to explain it and I don't charge them'.

According to their defence solicitors, the great majority of criminal clients know that legal aid exists, but they are less familiar with the specifics of particular legal aid programmes. 'One of my clients thought legal aid was like the NHS; you signed on with a solicitor, like you sign on a GP's panel, and legal advice and representation would be free to you at point of use just like medical care,' said one of the defence agents interviewed. If clients were aware of their eligibility for a particular legal aid programme or programmes, it was because they had previous experience of receiving such legal aid, although, as the solicitors above pointed out, many think such an entitlement is automatic, which is true only for those individuals on income support.

Nearly all of the solicitors questioned in 1992–93 sent in legal aid applications routinely, even if they questioned whether a client was eligible, because they said that the precise eligibility criteria remained a secret to persons outside the Scottish Legal Aid Board. 'It is up to the Scottish Legal Aid Board to decide,' said one solicitor, 'not me'.

The Scottish Legal Aid Board has a statutory obligation to evaluate whether it is in the interests of justice to grant legal aid in summary criminal cases. To aid the staff of the Board in such evaluation, a panel of solicitors and advocates serve as Reporters to the Board, scrutinising applications and rendering

---

[16] See *ibid.* for explanation.

opinions as to their suitability for support. Of the solicitors serving on the Reporters' panel, many are in multi-practice firms. Most full-time criminal defence practitioners in the 1992–93 interview sample said that they would not have the time to serve as a Reporter, but that a reliance on solicitors who are not full-time criminal defence practitioners may mean that decisions are being made by people who have less criminal court experience than do many of the solicitors they are evaluating.[17]

Summarising the opinions of defence solicitors interviewed in 1992–93 about the different criminal legal aid programmes, the ABWOR programme was seen as overly restrictive (and therefore somewhat under-utilised) both financially and situationally (it could be used only in a limited number of circumstances), leaving an appreciable number of potential clients outside its eligibility requirements. Moreover, the fee differentials between the criminal advice and assistance programme and that of ABWOR in 1992–93 puzzled defence agents (these have now been harmonised), many of whom followed the example of the solicitor who claimed that 'I never use ABWOR; I have my clients apply for advice and assistance, plead not guilty, and then apply for regular criminal legal aid'.[18] In contrast, the summary criminal legal aid programme in 1992–93 appeared to be serving the large majority of clients, in the opinion of defence agents.

IV DEFENCE AGENTS' OPINIONS AND ATTITUDES

It tends to be assumed by policy-makers that solicitors are simply out to profit from the legal aid system. Interviews with defence agents reveal this to be too simplistic. Indeed, as will be seen in this section, many defence agents are concerned about cost control and the quality of service provided under legal aid.

Defence agents in the 1992–93 attitudinal survey were asked to indicate what they thought of the then current criminal legal aid system, with particular attention to what they thought were the best and worst aspects of the system. It is interesting to note that many of the same aspects of the system were both lauded and criticised, although not by the same person, depending on the individual solicitor's personal experience. The main points raised by defence agents are highlighted here.

---

[17] Kerner, *op. cit.* (1993), p. 24. The problem of practitioners with insufficient experience of criminal work determining legal aid issues on behalf of the Board is replicated within the review procedure operated by the Legal Aid Board in England and Wales: Wood, A., 'Administrative Justice Within the Legal Aid Board: Reviews by Caseworkers and Area Committees of Refusals of Criminal Legal Aid Applications', at chapter 8 of this volume.

[18] See further Samuel, *op. cit.*, on how the legal aid rules condition the behaviour of legal aid lawyers.

(i) Best aspects of the system

'It exists'   More than 60 per cent of those interviewed in 1992–93 thought that the best thing about the then current criminal legal aid system was that it existed. As a solicitor from a specialist criminal defence firm observed:

> ... the system allows the client to choose the solicitor, which means that the person in the street controls the market. It's a good thing that the system exists at all. Because it does exist, it keeps the quality of justice high: a high standard of defence keeps a high standard of prosecution.

Another solicitor agreed, saying that 'the best thing about the current legal aid system is that, by and large, a person can choose his own lawyer and have his defence funded for him'. A solicitor from a multi-practice stated that 'the current criminal legal aid system is the best attempt in the world to make justice available to the ordinary citizen. I can't conceive of running the criminal justice system without it'. Another multi-practice solicitor agreed: 'From a moral point of view, the best thing about the system is that it exists at all.'

'It is efficient'   More than 43 per cent of those interviewed thought that one of the best things about the then current legal aid system was its comparative efficiency, resulting in a reasonably rapid payment of accounts. Nine solicitors from criminal defence firms mentioned the Scottish Legal Aid Board's efficiency and speed of payment, as did nine from the multi-practices. Comparing the current situation with that of the past, one solicitor from a specialist criminal defence firm mentioned that 'the grant of legal aid has increased,' and another said that, 'the best thing is the speed with which accounts get processed and paid. The system is working very well.' Solicitors in other specialist criminal defence firms agreed: 'I'm happy with the system. It works quickly and efficiently, and there are a lot of people making reasonable money.' A practitioner in a multi-practice firm stated:

> The current system is relatively good from the point of view of administration to get legal aid or sanctions. In fact, the Scottish Legal Aid Board probably operates a good deal better than most regulatory bodies, and the granting and application rates are pretty good.

Another said that, 'If you compare it with civil legal aid, it's efficient and fast — much better than civil'. Another solicitor, from a multi-practice, liked 'the guarantee of payment, if timeous — and I also like the ability to explore avenues of investigation'. Advocates noted that the introduction of form CR33

245

(which permits a portion of fees to be paid directly by the Scottish Legal Aid Board to the advocate, rather than waiting until the instructing solicitor has been paid) has speeded up payment of fees, 'although it depends on whether the instructing solicitor remembers to give you the form'.

'It provides independent representation' Two solicitors, one from a criminal defence practice and one from a multi-practice, noted that one of the best things about the then current criminal legal aid system was that it provided independent representation to the accused, unlike a salaried public defender system.

'The grant rate is good' One solicitor from a multi-practice commented that the grant rate for the criminal legal aid programmes was good. In 1994–95, 71,405 applications were made for summary criminal legal aid, of which 67,020 were granted (a grant rate of nearly 94 per cent).[19] It should be remembered that one of the major reasons the Scottish Legal Aid Board was organised was to eliminate on-going disparities in the provision of criminal legal aid throughout the country. With the establishment of a centralised authority, the grant rates are now the same throughout Scotland.[20]

(ii) Worst aspects of the system

Even those respondents most negative about the then current criminal legal aid system and its operations in 1992–93 noted that its very existence was a credit to the system of justice in Scotland. However, there was no shortage of complaints about the system, particularly in relation to levels of fees.

'The levels of remuneration are appalling' Nearly 70 per cent of the defence agents and all of the advocates interviewed identified what they perceived to be very low fee levels as the worst aspect of the criminal legal aid system. Certainly, the fee levels provided for criminal legal aid representation approximated only half of what the Law Society of Scotland recommended in 1992–93 as an hourly fee scale. Remuneration at the recommended scale rate would, however, have immediately doubled the criminal legal aid bill without allowing for an increase in numbers of applications. The current level of

---

[19] See Scottish Legal Aid Board, *op. cit.*
[20] Contrast this with the continuing problem of disparity in England and Wales: see Young, R., 'Will Widgery Do?: Court Clerks, Discretion, and the Determination of Legal Aid Applications', at chapter 7 of this volume.

remuneration, though, necessitated long hours and a very high volume of work in order to guarantee a profit, and, in some cases, the survival of the criminal legal firm, according to the defence agents interviewed.

Government proposals to introduce standard or block fees for criminal legal aid cases, regardless of their length and complexity, were therefore unpopular with defence agents. Some of the more experienced criminal defence specialists in the survey suggested that this cost-containing exercise would lead ultimately both to increased specialisation in criminal law (for the most efficient practitioners) and to limitations on the total numbers of criminal legal aid practitioners, leading to a diminution in choice for the client. It would also, they asserted, maximise the delegation of the work involved in any criminal case, in order for the legal firm to contain costs and maintain a high volume of cases.

'There is a lot of administrative hassle'   Nearly 27 per cent of the solicitors interviewed described what they perceived to be cumbersome and unwieldy administrative procedures as one of the worst things about the criminal legal aid system. Two advocates also suggested that Scottish Legal Aid Board procedures could be simplified and improved. Many of their complaints have been addressed with the implementation of a simplified system introduced in early 1995, including the provision of forms on disk. The 1994–95 Annual Report for the Scottish Legal Aid Board reports that all criminal applications are now turned around within two weeks, with almost 60 per cent of all criminal applications turned around within two days.[21]

'There are problems with representation for the guilty'   Nearly 15 per cent of the solicitors interviewed in 1992–93 mentioned significant difficulties with the ABWOR scheme, including what they perceived to be very restrictive limitations on its use and funding, as one of the worst problems with the then current criminal legal aid system. One solicitor noted that 'people who have received a past custodial sentence and wish to plead guilty don't qualify for legal aid'. This situation followed from the Legal Aid (Scotland) Act 1986, which specifically targeted legal aid towards accused persons who plead not guilty. The Government has subsequently recognised the difficulties which have arisen in the wake of the 1986 Act, and proposals to extend the use of ABWOR, as in the case of pleas in mitigation, are designed to augment remedies available to those who plead guilty at an early stage.[22]

---

[21] Scottish Legal Aid Board, *op. cit.*
[22] See further Samuel, *op. cit.*

'There are problems with the duty scheme' Nearly 15 per cent of the defence agents interviewed in 1992–93 pointed to difficulties with the duty solicitor scheme as being one of the worst things about the then current criminal legal aid system. Among their major complaints was the fact that only duty solicitors were paid for the initial advice and representation of accused persons held in custody, even though much of that work was actually performed, according to the client's request, by nominated solicitors.

Levels of pay for the duty follow-up scheme were described as 'outrageously low' by two defence agents. Some solicitors also complained about the quality of service provided by duty solicitors 'who were inexperienced in dealing with criminal matters'. As the duty scheme is presently organised, any solicitor from any firm may apply to join the rota (although in Edinburgh, solicitors may not serve on the duty rota for the Sheriff Court unless they have served for at least two years on the rota for the district court).

'Payments are late' Just over 12 per cent of the solicitors interviewed in 1992–93 complained that payments for legal aid were often late, and one solicitor in a specialist criminal defence firm said that this had resulted in arguments about fees. Three of the advocates explained that their payments were customarily six months in arrears; one noted that 'The amount I'm owed varies between £18,000 and £30,000 at any given time'. The Scottish Legal Aid Board Annual Report for 1994/95 reports that there has now been an 11 per cent improvement in the turnaround of criminal accounts, rising from 77 per cent processed within four weeks to 88 per cent processed within four weeks, compared with a target of 80 per cent.[23]

'The extent of the scheme is too limited' Two solicitors, one in a specialist criminal defence firm and one in a multi-practice firm, thought that the extent of eligibility for the criminal legal aid system was too limited, particularly for accused persons in the district courts.

'The forms need simplification' Two solicitors, one in a criminal defence firm and one in a multi-practice, thought that the application forms for the criminal legal aid system in 1992–93, particularly those for summary criminal legal aid, should be simplified. Of all the forms, those for solemn legal aid applications, which comprised only a single page, were considered easiest to complete by all the solicitors. As noted above, this issue has now been addressed by a complete redesign of the applications system, including the

---

[23] See Scottish Legal Aid Board, *op. cit.*

issuing of a personal identifier or individual reference number, which will apply to all applications, regardless of programme, from one person.

'The system requires additional quality control'   Scottish Legal Aid Board officials were not the only individuals concerned about the quality of criminal legal aid representation in 1992–93; two solicitors in criminal defence firms both suggested a need for much greater control over the quality of legal representation paid for by the Scottish Legal Aid Board. Both solicitors commented that, particularly with regard to the duty scheme, many accused persons were not receiving the quality of representation that they required.

One of the advocates interviewed said:

> ... we know from our own observations of legal aid that many client firms have limited standards of professional skills and competence, but are being paid by the Scottish Legal Aid Board regardless. In terms of their abilities, many practitioners are overpaid. Sadly, there are many firms which are doing legal aid work which are grossly underpaid in terms of the quality of service they deliver.

Another well-known criminal defence practitioner, not part of the survey sample, has noted that

> competent, experienced defence agents take one-quarter of the time in court that is taken by inexperienced and incompetent lawyers, who consequently get paid by the Scottish Legal Aid Board four times as much. This is not right. Experienced senior defence agents should be rewarded for their competency by higher fees — and the system of justice would ultimately save money.

His comments were echoed by a senior counsel, who pointed out that there is little differential in fees for junior and senior counsel, despite the increased competency and efficiency offered to the criminal justice system by the latter.

There are at present no Government proposals to introduce a system of quality assured suppliers (QAS) in Scotland along the lines of the franchising system introduced in England and Wales by the Legal Aid Board. If such a system were to be introduced in Scotland it would, on the one hand, increase administrative control over records and money by the designated QAS firm. On the other hand, defence agents surveyed in 1992–93 believed that if legal aid work were to be restricted only to QAS firms, clients in less populous and rural areas, which at present support only a limited number of generalist firms, would ultimately be deprived of access to legal aid and advice in criminal matters.

The suggested provision of law centres empowered to conduct legally-aided criminal work, as in England and Wales, while augmenting the total availability of service providers in Scotland, would be problematic. At present, the nine existing Scottish law centres are concentrated in the most densely populated areas of Scotland. A rural law centre would face the same difficulties as rural solicitors: a limited client base, a lack of sufficient cases for specialisation in any particular type of law, and problems of location (because of client travelling needs).

'The system is open to abuse'   Three solicitors interviewed in 1992–93 pointed out that the criminal legal aid system is open to financial abuse because of 'the greed of some practitioners'. Each suggested that this could be counteracted by a very rigorous scrutiny of accounts, and, in particular, by altering the bases for payments such as remunerating solicitors the most for what solicitors think is most important (i.e., court appearances), and lowering fees for incidental expenses like photocopying and the taking of precognitions. As one solicitor noted:

> the worst thing is that, for all the expertise in pleading that a criminal lawyer has, either in the process of examination of witnesses or consecutive speaking, he's not as well paid for that as for the ridiculously mechanical process of sending out a list of witnesses for precognitions. That is bad for the Scottish Legal Aid Board and bad for the paymaster.

A highly publicised case involving two solicitors now struck off for their conduct has resulted in the implementation of tighter and more effective monitoring of the criminal legal aid accounts system, and the Audit and Investigations Department of the Scottish Legal Aid Board have conducted a 'Fraudit' exercise

> to identify and minimise the extent to which the Legal Aid Fund may be open to fraud and abuse by solicitors or their clients. . . . That work has continued during the year and while there were very few instances of actual fraud (and these have been vigorously pursued) there is, nevertheless, given the nature of legal aid, a potential exposure.[24]

The Scottish Legal Aid Board is also analysing and examining payments made to some of the highest earners, including the top ten earning firms, each of whom earned more than £1 million during the year (see Table 11.1 above).

---

[24] *Ibid.*

'There are problems with obtaining sanctions'   Several solicitors in the 1992–93 sample said that they had experienced difficulties in obtaining sanctions, particularly in obtaining them timeously, for instructing counsel or expert witnesses.

V CHANGES DESIRED AND IMPLEMENTED IN SCOTTISH CRIMINAL LEGAL AID

We turn now to more general issues concerning the Scottish legal aid system. Many defence agents in the 1992–93 sample complained that they did not understand the necessity for applying and reapplying to so many different criminal legal aid programmes for the same accused person. Simplifying procedures and minimising the number of times application is necessary would alleviate the Scottish Legal Aid Board's administrative burdens and those of the defence agents, they said, and the introduction of an individual reference number should help to diminish administrative complexity. It should be remembered that some, if not all, defence agents in the sample observed and appreciated what they perceived to be existing improvements in the administration of the criminal legal aid system in 1992–93.

As it was then constituted, sample practitioners observed that the duty scheme was unsatisfactory to many defence agents, including many of those who served on the duty rota. Defence agents in the 1992–93 sample claimed that they did not make very much money from the duty scheme because recidivists tend to have their own family lawyers, leaving the first-time offenders and the mentally distressed to the duty solicitor. Nominated solicitors, who were paid for initial advice and court appearances prior to the introduction of the Legal Aid (Scotland) Act 1986 and were no longer paid for them after its introduction (even though they frequently did advise and represent clients at initial court appearances), were also unhappy about the duty scheme, according to sample defence agents. Practitioners in rural areas had specific complaints about the amounts of time they are required to serve as duty solicitors, and the consequent impact on their other business.

At a time of increased competition for all legal services, criminal practitioners in the 1992–93 sample said that they were dealing with a younger population of clients who were increasingly willing to change their defence agents. Anecdotal evidence suggested that the 'poaching' of clients, particularly of those in custody, was known to occur. Despite the high rate of competition amongst defence agents, however, the existence of the Scottish criminal legal aid system enabled many sole practitioners and small firms to set up independently more rapidly than they would have been able to do in other forms of legal business. It appeared, however, that difficulties in the business climate

251

were causing increasing numbers of solicitors to abandon or curtail legal aid work, particularly in larger, more general practices.

Virtually all the defence agents in the 1992–93 sample argued that additional resources should be directed toward the procurator fiscal service to facilitate the efficient operation of the whole criminal justice system. A better resourced fiscal service, they said, would enhance throughput of cases through the courts and might lead also to an earlier negotiation of pleas.

One defence agent in the 1992–93 survey said that 'defence work should be seen to be honourable'. This is doubly meaningful: not only should criminal defence practitioners be seen to behave (as the majority of them do) in an honourable way, but also those who deal with them should treat them in an honourable manner. Sometimes defence agents are not so regarded and treated, several of the sample respondents said. In terms of the status hierarchy within the legal profession in Scotland, criminal defence practitioners do not rank as highly as commercial and corporate lawyers. On the other hand, defence agents probably actively enjoy their work more than any other lawyers, according to sample respondents.

Notwithstanding the high level of satisfaction felt by most criminal defence practitioners ('if we didn't enjoy it, we wouldn't continue to put up with all the problems'), they noted that it should be recognised that defence agents work very long hours, often under difficult conditions. The intrinsically stressful nature of a job on which someone else's liberty or livelihood may depend has been compounded by increasing competition and by recession, which affects legal practices as well as other businesses. Stress-related illnesses were not uncommon among defence agents in 1992–93, despite the fact that the majority of defence agents were relatively young at the time of interview.

Since the 1992–93 survey was conducted, numerous changes in procedures have been introduced by the Scottish Legal Aid Board, including the publication of a very useful *Handbook*, which provides a single source of information about the legal aid programmes and how to apply for them. Applications for civil legal aid have continued to fall since changes in eligibility were introduced in April 1993, while the number of criminal applications has increased. The Scottish Legal Aid Board has also been assisting the Scottish Office in considering the possible introduction of standard fees and has instituted a pilot project for funding mediation in matrimonial cases.

Research undertaken by the Scottish Legal Aid Board early in 1994 identified a number of areas in which further improvement was required, including better and more open communications and information, more accuracy and consistency in decisions, greater flexibility, an improved strategic and planning role, and more emphasis on management development and a clarification of the roles of senior management in the Board.[25] Actions taken to improve all these areas are underway and include: establishing a strong senior management team, giving full reasons for refusal for all civil applications (but not, to date, criminal applications), circulating information to solicitors in a clearer and more helpful format, and a redesigned applications system and format.

VI CONCLUSION

The 1992–93 survey of Scottish defence agents' opinions and experiences with criminal legal aid suggested that defence agents shared with policy-makers a desire to facilitate the timeous, efficient and cost-effective delivery of justice in Scotland. However, they appeared to disagree in certain instances on how to achieve this. In addition to maintaining a broadly based system of justice, and providing support for legal counsel and representation for those unable to pay for their own defences, the Government is concerned to develop and maintain the most cost-effective and efficient system of providing criminal legal aid. While sharing this desire for increased efficiency, defence agents, who are also business people, appeared to believe that measures which restrict the availability of criminal legal aid will ultimately affect the viability of criminal legal aid practices. The debate has just begun about the ways in which shared aims and conflicting desires with regard to the various participants in the criminal legal aid system can best be reconciled. It will be interesting to see what compromises will be reached, and which policies will ultimately predominate in Scotland's criminal legal aid system.

---

[25] See *ibid*.

12

Access to Justice in the Police Station: An Elusive Dream?

Andrew Sanders[*]

This chapter examines the nature and quality of the legal advice provided to suspects detained in the police station. The legal aid scheme appears to recognise the fundamental importance of the police–suspect encounter. No means or merits test is applied to those who ask for legal assistance, and there are administrative arrangements to ensure that legal advisers are always available to attend suspects who request help. Yet many problems remain, for access to justice is dependent on quality legal services being made available to suspects. This chapter will document these problems, chart the reforms that have been made since the scheme's inception through the 1991 and 1995 revisions to the law, and analyse the reasons lying behind both the problems and the limited success of the reforms. It concludes that the achievement of balance and fairness between police and suspects through legal aid, however generous, is an elusive dream.

I INTRODUCTION: THE THEORETICAL AND HISTORICAL BACKGROUND

Never has the nature and quality of the criminal justice system in this country been so hotly debated as it has in the 1980s and 1990s. Two Royal Commissions covering similar ground in 13 years (1981 and 1993) is testimony to that.[1] Yet

---

[*] The author would like to thank Richard Young for his contribution to an earlier draft of this chapter.
[1] Royal Commission on Criminal Procedure, *Report*, Cmnd 8092, London: HMSO, 1981; Royal Commission on Criminal Justice, *Report*, Cm 2263, London: HMSO, 1993.

few would argue, either normatively or descriptively, against two key propositions: the presumption of innocence and the adversarial character of the English system.[2] The implications for police powers of arrest and detention are that suspects should not be disadvantaged by refusing to assist the police and that suspects should not be placed in a disadvantageous bargaining position *vis-à-vis* the police.

Traditionally these twin assumptions meant that, following arrest, the police could not interview suspects. Instead, they had to bring them before a court as soon as possible where, it was assumed (or asserted), they would be treated fairly. It was not regarded as safe to allow the police to exercise power over anyone with whom they had an adversarial relationship. As the police came to rely more and more on confession evidence and other information from suspects, this position became increasingly difficult to sustain. The myth that suspects spent hour after hour in police detention voluntarily 'helping with enquiries' before being formally arrested was not difficult to see through.

To maintain the twin assumptions of adversarialism and presumed innocence, the system either had to revert to the *status quo ante*, or it had to equalise the relationship in some other way. The obvious way to secure the latter position was to provide suspects with the knowledge and support they needed to behave in the way anyone presumed innocent would wish to behave — for instance, to refuse to answer questions, if they wished, without fear of adverse consequences. The provision of legal advice is one way of transmitting this knowledge, and the presence of legal advisers in interviews is a way of providing support. Thus the Judges Rules (which used to govern police station detention) provided that suspects were, in general, to be allowed to secure legal advice when detained. Few suspects actually secured advice, though, so the reality in most cases was an imbalance of power.

The Royal Commission on Criminal Procedure (Philips Commission) therefore argued that a clear legal right to free legal advice was needed, along with administrative arrangements to ensure that all suspects who requested advice and assistance actually secured it. This, to the Conservative Government's great credit, is what the Police and Criminal Evidence Act (PACE) provided for in 1984. Although this chapter will show that PACE has failed dismally in this objective, this is not the fault of the Government. We shall see that the failure is neither one of law nor of resources, but is instead a product of the nature of this country's criminal justice system.

The remainder of this chapter is structured as follows. In the next section we examine the structure of the PACE scheme and review the findings of research

---

[2] Actually, this author does argue, with Richard Young, that in many respects English criminal justice does not live up to these ideals, although it does not entirely abandon them either. See Sanders, A. and Young, R., *Criminal Justice*, London: Butterworths, 1994.

on basic aspects of its operation. Section III looks at what influences suspects in deciding whether or not to request legal advice. Sections IV and V form the heart of the chapter: the former examines the nature and quality of the legal services currently on offer to suspects; the latter addresses the scope for improving the quality of these services. In section VI it is asserted that the Achilles' heel of all attempts to improve the suspect's position through legal aid lies in the structural domination of the pre-trial process by the police.

II SECURING LEGAL ADVICE

PACE 1984, s. 58(1), provides that 'A person arrested ... shall be entitled, if he so requests, to consult a solicitor privately at any time.' There are no exceptions to this rule, although the police are allowed to delay access in exceptional circumstances. This now hardly ever occurs.[3] Code of Practice C, which is made under the authority of PACE, provides that this right applies equally to persons in the station voluntarily.[4] It should be noted that not only is the right to advice absolute, but also it is not time-limited; the right is to consultation *in private*, and the suspect may consult any solicitor of his or her choice.

None of this would be any use without a means — financial and administrative — of securing delivery of legal services to suspects. This PACE did in s. 59.[5] It provided for a nation-wide network of locally organised duty solicitor schemes paid for by government via the legal aid scheme. Solicitors on duty (busy schemes have a rota system which pays one or more solicitors to be on duty all or most of the time) are obliged to give advice, or arrange for advice to be given, when it is requested. Duty solicitors can apply for their para-legals (articled clerks or legal executives) to be accredited for this work. Solicitors contacted directly can send anyone to the station, whether legally trained or not.[6] Whether the adviser is the suspect's own solicitor, a duty solicitor, or a representative (as a para-legal or other employee is known in this context) of one or the other, payment is from the Legal Aid Fund. Through these mechanisms the availability of legal advice of some sort can be almost, although not wholly, guaranteed for all suspects.

How well has the legal aid scheme worked? Unlike other aspects of legal aid, the police station scheme has been the subject of rigorous, if *ad hoc*,

---

[3] Brown, D., Ellis, T. and Larcombe, K., *Changing the Code: Police detention under the revised PACE Codes of Practice*, Home Office Research Study No. 129, London: HMSO, 1992, pp. 68–9.
[4] Home Office, *Code of Practice for the detention, treatment and questioning of persons by police officers*, London: HMSO, 1995, para. 3.1 (hereinafter Code of Practice C).
[5] Now see the Legal Aid Board Duty Solicitor Arrangements 1992 (made under the Legal Aid Act 1988).
[6] This is now changing. See section V below.

evaluation from its inception. The first research into the operation of these provisions was funded by the Lord Chancellor's Department and carried out by this author and colleagues in 1987-89.[7] We found that around 25 per cent of all suspects requested advice and 19 per cent (i.e., three-quarters of all who requested it) received it. This research uncovered many problems with the working of the legal advice scheme and also established something of a baseline from which to chart subsequent developments.

In 1991, Code of Practice C was revised, substantially strengthening the legal advice provisions. The revision was intended to correct a number of defects in the legal advice scheme which had become apparent in the light of the above research and the experience of those working within the system. For example, we had found that suspects were rarely informed of their rights in anything other than a grudging and discouraging way. Paragraph 3.1 of the revised Code required that suspects be told explicitly that the legal advice on offer was free of charge, and para. 6.3 stipulated that in the reception area of police stations posters must be displayed advertising the right to advice.[8] Home Office-funded research by Brown et al. examined whether the revisions had any practical effect. One important effect uncovered was a substantial increase in the proportion of suspects requesting legal advice in 1991: around 32 per cent of all suspects requested advice in that year, and 25 per cent (again, three-quarters) received it.[9] In terms of raw figures, the number of suspects assisted jumped from 397,000 in 1990–91 to 549,000 in 1991–92 (an increase of nearly 30 per cent).[10]

The rise in the number of those requesting advice following the 1991 revision indicates that legal reforms can produce real change in practice. Now that, in 1995, the Code has been revised and strengthened again (as discussed later), we may see a further rise in the percentage of suspects requesting and securing legal advice. But requesting advice is one thing, receiving it quite another. For those suspects who received advice, around half of all contacts are made within 30 minutes, and three-quarters within one hour.[11] These are, however, phone contacts between the suspect (or even just the police) and the solicitor. Where advice is given in person, the average gap between request and consultation during the day is two hours (with a median of one hour); during the night it is

---

[7] Sanders, A., Bridges, L., Mulvaney, A. and Crozier, G., *Advice and Assistance at police stations and the 24 hour duty solicitor scheme*, London: Lord Chancellor's Department, 1989.
[8] For a detailed analysis of the changes made in 1991 to Code of Practice C, see Wolchover, D. and Heaton-Armstrong, A., 'The Questioning Code Revamped', *Criminal Law Review*, 1991, p. 232.
[9] Brown et al., *op. cit.* Note that all the research has found great variations in rates of requests and advice received between police stations and different offence types.
[10] Legal Aid Board, *Annual Report, 1993–4*, London: HMSO, 1994, p. 88, Table 9.
[11] Brown et al., *op. cit.*, pp. 61-2.

three and a half hours (the median being 1 hour and 40 minutes).[12] Contact with a legal adviser is not synonymous with consultation: consultations do not occur in around 10 per cent of cases where contact is made, largely because in those cases the suspect had already been dealt with by the police by the time contact was made, and so there was no point in having a consultation.[13] In 13 per cent of Brown et al.'s 1991 cases, no contact was made at all.[14]

We have seen that around one quarter of requests 'fail'. This is partly a product of non-contact, which occurs in around 5 per cent of duty solicitor requests but a higher proportion of 'own' solicitor requests. [15] It is also a result of cancellation by the suspect, sometimes because of delay in making contact and sometimes because the suspect would deal only with his or her own solicitor. In an example given by Brown et al. there was no duty solicitor available, neither were any of the solicitors on a list provided for suspects without their own solicitor. The suspect was self-employed and anxious that the delay was losing him income. Despite being advised by the custody officer that being interviewed without legal advice was not in his best interests, he decided, albeit reluctantly, to agree to be interviewed nonetheless. [16]

According to Brown et al., problems of delay (although not the overall contact rate) were exacerbated by the increase in demand for advice which occurred in 1991, presumably because there were no mechanisms established to cope with that increase in demand. If the latest revision to the Code has the effect of the previous revision, and increases the request rate again, we might expect the gap between request and advice rates to increase further.

In themselves, none of these figures provides conclusive evidence of either the success or the failure of the advice scheme in PACE. We need to ask why most suspects still do not request advice; and what is the nature and quality of that advice when it is provided. We shall then go on to evaluate the reforms which aim to deal with the current failures of the system.

III INFLUENCES ON REQUEST RATES

Obviously the prerequisite for securing advice is that the suspect knows that he or she has a right to it (presupposing, that is, that advice be provided only on request, which we shall return to in section VI). When the LCD research was

---

[12] *Ibid.*

[13] *Ibid.*, p. 64.

[14] *Ibid.*, Table 4.1. The figures in this section are all highly approximate, for they are derived from research studies (Brown et al., *ibid.*, and Sanders et al., *op. cit.*). There are no national figures providing percentages of suspects requesting or receiving advice or on the time intervals between requests and contact.

[15] Brown et al., *op. cit.*, p. 60.

[16] *Ibid.*

carried out in the mid-1980s, the right to free advice was new and not widely known. At least some suspects failed to request advice for this reason. Most suspects now probably have a reasonably good appreciation of their rights. Even if, as previously, custody officers still fail clearly to inform suspects of their full rights (and in 1990 and 1991, when Brown et al. did their research, this was still the case),[17] this is no longer likely, in itself, substantially to depress request rates. Indeed, para. 6.5 of the 1995 version of the Code of Practice now requires custody officers to ask suspects who decline to request advice why this is so, and to record these reasons.

The behaviour of the police can influence suspects' decisions in other ways, through the use of 'ploys' or the presentation of discouraging information. It is not intended to attempt to disentangle how far the manner in which information is presented can justifiably be presented as a 'ploy', how often ploys are used, or precisely how much they influence suspects; these matters have been extensively debated, although not resolved, elsewhere.[18] What is clear is that there is an 'elasticity of demand' for legal advice, and the more elastic the demand the more susceptible to influence the suspect is.[19]

The strongest influence on suspects is the anticipated length of time to be spent in the police station.[20] Objectively, time spent waiting for a solicitor could mean more time in the station; as we have seen, there is often a long delay between request and actual consultation. But in any given case legal advice might not create a delay, for the police may not be able or willing to interview the suspect immediately anyway, and the time lag between requests and consultations sometimes occurs because the solicitor comes to the station only when the police are ready to interview. Brown et al. believe that this explains the long time lag at night, when the police avoid interviewing. Only the police themselves can estimate how long any one suspect is likely to be in the station, and so what they tell suspects about this can be a crucial influence. The police also have a good idea of how long a suspect is likely to have to wait for a

---

[17] *Ibid.*, ch. 2.

[18] Sanders and Bridges, *op. cit.*; Dixon, D., 'Legal Regulation and Policing Practice', *Social and Legal Studies*, 1992, vol. 1, p. 515; McConville, M. and Sanders, A., 'The Case for the Prosecution and Administrative Criminology', in Noaks, L., Levi, M. and Maguire, M. (eds), *Contemporary Issues in Criminology*, Cardiff: University of Wales Press, 1995.

[19] Maguire, M., 'Effects of the PACE Provisions on Detention and Questioning', *British Journal of Criminology*, 1988, vol. 28, p. 19. Sanders et al., *op. cit.*, sought to test the influence of the police by comparing cases in which ploys were and were not used, and by comparing request rates in cases which we did, and did not, observe (thinking that the police might press their ploys more strongly when not being scrutinised). Neither comparison produced significant differences. However, Brown et al. did find that their 'observed' sample had a higher request rate than their non-observed sample, although they do not speculate about why this might be so.

[20] See, for instance, Sanders et al., *op. cit.*, and the example given above taken from Brown et al., *op. cit.*

solicitor. As we have seen, this can be substantial, but will vary according to the station and the time of day and day of the week.

Brown et al. found that nearly half of all suspects who did not request a solicitor immediately would have done so had one been readily available.[21] This calls for further comment. When suspects request advice, either their solicitor is phoned direct or a duty solicitor (obtained via a national service) will phone in. Either way, the suspect's first contact can be, and usually is, on the phone. The delay is usually less than one hour, as stated earlier. Suspects therefore have little to lose by requesting advice and making telephone contact, even if they decide that they will not wait for the solicitor to attend if he or she cannot do so quickly. Some suspects doubtless realise this, but obviously many do not, and in none of the research reported by Sanders et al. or Brown et al. were the police ever observed advising suspects of this obvious fact.

Now that para. 6.5 of the 1995 version of the Code of Practice requires custody officers to advise suspects of the possibility of receiving advice over the telephone, we may see a change of police practice and increased request rates. This would be expected if this revision has the effect of the previous revision, but only up to a less than optimum point. For in some respects — particularly regarding the clarity with which suspects' rights were explained to them — the police breached the revised Code in 1991 more often than the (less demanding) original Code.[22] So while legal changes can lead to changes in police practice, anything even approaching complete compliance is rare.[23]

Many suspects are not, and will never be, greatly influenced either by the police, or by the length of time it would take to see a solicitor. These suspects, whose demand for solicitors is inelastic, are sometimes so confident that they believe they do not need the help of a solicitor; or so fatalistic that they do not believe a solicitor can help them; or simply distrustful of solicitors. Overall, the belief that advice 'would not assist' was the most common reason given to Brown et al. for not requesting it.[24] Where suspects are right in these evaluations, the absence of legal advice does not greatly undermine the principles of even-handed adversarialism and the presumption of innocence. Often, though, they are wrong. This should not be surprising, for a lawyer is usually needed to evaluate the legal predicament in which suspects find themselves. As most suspects need lawyers to advise them on whether they need the services of a lawyer, it would seem to follow that all suspects should automatically be put in touch with a legal adviser without the necessity for

---

[21] Brown et al., *op. cit.*, p. 53.
[22] *Ibid.*, Table 2.5.
[23] This is the heart of the debate between Dixon, in particular, and McConville, Sanders and Leng. See references in n. 18.
[24] *Op. cit.*, Table 3.6.

making a formal request. But we should not assume that lawyers would necessarily provide advice of sufficiently high quality were the advice scheme to be amended in this way. As will now be seen, research provides us with ample material on which to assert the contrary.

IV THE NATURE AND QUALITY OF LEGAL ADVICE AND ASSISTANCE

One of the most striking findings of the original LCD research was that so much of the advice and assistance provided was unsatisfactory. This was particularly true of duty solicitors, but it was not confined to them; and it was particularly true of solicitors' representatives, but it was, again, not confined to them. Quality is not dependent on the professional standing of the adviser or on that adviser's professional relationship with the suspect, although it will sometimes be influenced by these matters. The reality of legal advice will be explored by looking at four closely related issues: mode of delivery; attendance and support at interview; the content of advice and assistance; and advising suspects to exercise their right to remain silent.

(i) Mode of delivery

The LCD research found that much advice — around 30 per cent of it — was delivered over the telephone alone.[25] This is not always inappropriate. Some legal situations are generally simple (e.g., breathalyser cases), or intractable (e.g., drunks). Some suspects are clearly guilty, wish to confess and can provide such details as are necessary for the lawyer to advise accordingly. However, many cases are not this straightforward. Not only will a proper exchange and discussion require face-to-face communication, but it will usually require privacy. Fear of being overheard by the police, and sometimes uncertainty about who exactly is on the other end of the phone, is very inhibiting for many suspects.

What solicitors should do, and what some claim to do, is to judge the appropriate mode of delivery according to various criteria. One is the bald facts, in so far as they can be assessed. Another is the seriousness of the alleged offence (which may not complicate the law as such, but can impact, for instance, on the question of bail and extended detention). Another is the suspect's intended response to the police interview: most suspects find it very difficult to maintain silence unaided. Another is the nervous and emotional state of the suspect. All the research in this area has found that in large numbers of

---

[25] Sanders and Bridges, *op. cit.*, p. 48.

cases decisions are not made on the basis of these criteria (we, for instance, found that, even in serious cases, phone advice was provided around 20 per cent of the time[26]). Decisions were made either on the basis of the general stance of the firm (some always attend, some avoid it wherever possible, some are more inclined to do it for their own clients than when acting as duty solicitors),or on the basis of whether anyone who could easily be spared was available at that time.[27]

This has all been recognised by the Law Society, the Legal Aid Board and the Home Office. In 1991, the Legal Aid Rules were altered to create a presumption that solicitors attend in person (or send a representative) unless there was a positive reason not to do so. Although the number of police station visits increased, this was in line with an underlying trend of more suspects being assisted each year.[28] The *percentage* of advised cases in which someone attended did not increase.[29] The 1995 revision to the Code of Practice recognises one of the consequent problems by providing in Note 6J that:

> Where a person chooses to speak to a solicitor on the telephone, he should be allowed to do so in private unless this is impractical because of the design and layout of the custody area or the location of telephones.

The problem, though, is that securing privacy on the telephone nearly always is impractical.

(ii)   Attendance and support at interview

We have seen that one reason why phone advice is often inappropriate is that even-handed adversarialism is not possible for many suspects without support, particularly if the advice is difficult to follow — advice to remain silent in interview being the best example. There are also other reasons why legal advisers should attend interviews. For example, there should be no 'pre-interview interviewing', but the suspect may not know this. Also, interviewing practice should not be 'oppressive' or 'unfair' — this includes lying, hectoring,

---

[26] *Ibid.*

[27] Similar considerations should apply in respect of sending representatives. See Law Society, *Advising a Suspect in the Police Station*, London: Law Society, 1991. Again, the claims of solicitors that such considerations are taken into account are frequently at odds with the facts: see McConville, M., Hodgson, J., Bridges, L. and Pavlovic, A., *Standing Accused*, Oxford: Clarendon Press, 1994.

[28] See Legal Aid Board, *op. cit.*, p. 88.

[29] See *ibid.* Brown et al., *op. cit.*, Table 4.3, found that 31% of advised cases in the 1991 sample were by phone only (compared with 30% in 1987–89 according to the sample taken by Sanders et al., *op. cit.*).

threats or inducements — but the law on this is unclear and suspects do not know where the lines are drawn.[30] It follows that attendance at the station will usually be worth little unless the solicitor attends the interview too. This is recognised by para. 6.8 of the Code, which makes the right of an adviser to attend absolute. Yet many legal advisers do not stay to help their clients, but leave them to face their interrogators alone.

The LCD research found that, of interviewed suspects whose advisers attended the station, around one-fifth had no adviser in the interview.[31] This meant that, overall, only about 14 per cent of all interviewed suspects had an adviser in the interview. Brown's 1991 sample, moreover, showed a dramatic fall in the percentage of advised cases in which there was interview attendance: over two-fifths of interviewed suspects whose advisers attended the station had no adviser in the interview. The result was a similar overall percentage of interviewed suspects who had an adviser present in 1991, after the changes to the duty solicitor rules and the Code of Practice, as compared to 1988. In the place where the inequality between police and suspect is greatest, only about one-seventh of suspects have that power imbalance redressed in this way.[32]

However, simply to attend the interview is in turn of little value unless the adviser provides advice and support where required, and ensures that the police behave legally and fairly. There have been some remarkable examples of cases where lawyers allowed the police to breach numerous sections of PACE and Code C with little or no protest.[33] These examples are not isolated. Baldwin's research for the Runciman Commission found that the legal adviser did nothing in two-thirds of the interviews with an adviser present which he examined. When they did intervene it was nearly as often to help the police as it was to help their clients.[34] Sometimes, however, there is nothing to do. The important question is how often advisers did nothing, or too little, when they should have done more. Baldwin makes no attempt to evaluate this. Thus, as Roberts points out, 'Nowhere does Professor Baldwin create a model of what he thinks should

---

[30] Indeed, lawyers, police officers and judges have only a vague idea and the law is something of a moving target. See Sanders and Young, *op. cit.*, pp. 158–70.

[31] Sanders and Bridges, *op. cit.*, p. 50.

[32] Brown et al., *op. cit.* In contrast to all the other research, McConville et al., *op. cit.* (1994), found that most advisers who attended the station attended the interview. Lawyer behaviour could have been affected by the effect of the researchers' presence alongside them.

[33] The 'Cardiff Three' case is the most notorious. The lawyer allowed the police to engage in behaviour which the Court of Appeal unhesitatingly condemned as 'oppressive'. See Sanders and Young, *op. cit.*, pp. 166–7.

[34] Baldwin, J., *The Role of Legal Representatives at the Police Station*, Royal Commission on Criminal Justice, Research Study No. 3, London: HMSO, 1993.

be the professional solicitor's role'.[35] Nonetheless, both Baldwin and McConville et al. give numerous examples of interrogations where the legal advisers made no attempt to intervene in clearly improper questioning.[36]

The root of the issue is how far the solicitor should adopt an adversarial stance. One might have thought, in the light of the context in which the advice scheme was introduced, that adversarialism was central to the solicitor's role. This was the, admittedly vague, yardstick by which Baldwin implicitly evaluated the performance of solicitors. Roberts, though, who shared responsibility for the original Law Society guidance to police station advisers, regards adversarialism as appropriate only when the police behave improperly. Otherwise, he argues, 'Interviews run better if the solicitor is able to establish a working relationship with the interviewer . . . co-operating to do it'.[37] Baldwin argues, in his reply to Roberts, that the interests of the client should be paramount to the lawyer, not whether or not interviews run well or badly.[38] This position flows naturally from the twin assumptions of adversarialism and presumed innocence, but the disagreement illustrates the ambiguity at the heart of the solicitor's role. Equally important, we shall see that Baldwin's position fails to take account of the structural realities of the system.

One of these realities is that the law with which defence advisers have to work is vague and uncertain. As we said earlier, there is no clear law on what constitutes 'unfairness' and 'oppressiveness'. This puts defence advisers at a disadvantage as it is difficult for them to judge when police officers have overstepped the mark and intervention is called for. The Law Society attempted to address this by advising lawyers that:

> If questions are improper or improperly put, you should intervene and be prepared to explain your objections. If improprieties remain uncorrected or continue, advise the suspect of his/her right to remain silent.[39]

Apart from some examples, though (such as questions being threatening, insulting or based on a false premise), what is and is not 'proper' is left open. Matters have certainly improved, however, as far as the establishment of a model of what role defence advisers are meant to play is concerned. Previous to the 1995 revision, Code of Practice C gave little clue to police officers or defence advisers as to the latter's proper role in interviews with suspects. Note 6D now states that:

---

[35] Roberts, D., 'Questioning the suspect: the solicitor's role', *Criminal Law Review*, 1993, p. 368 at p. 369.
[36] McConville et al., *op. cit.* (1994), ch. 5.
[37] Roberts, *op. cit.*, p. 370.
[38] Baldwin, J., 'Legal advice at the Police Station', *Criminal Law Review*, 1993, p. 371.
[39] Law Society, *op. cit.*, 1991 ed.

The solicitor's only role in the police station is to protect and advance the legal rights of his client. On occasions this may require the solicitor to give advice which has the effect of his client avoiding giving evidence which strengthens a prosecution case. The solicitor may intervene in order to seek clarification or to challenge an improper question to his client or the manner in which it is put, or to advise his client not to reply ... or ... give his client further legal advice.

However, the adviser has to be careful. If his intervention 'is such that the investigating officer is unable properly to put questions to the suspect' — and 'proper' questioning is, as we have seen, a moving target — he or she can be removed from the interview and reported to the Law Society.[40] It thus remains to be seen whether the welcome clarification of the solicitor's role in police interviews will have a significant effect on the behaviour of defence advisers.

(iii)   The content of advice and assistance

Whether advice is provided over the phone or in person, and prior to an interview or in it, ensuring that the content of that advice is appropriate to the particular case is crucial. This may require advisers to try to find out what the police know or believe about the case (although some are wary of this because they fear 'contamination').[41] It certainly requires them to find out what the suspect knows or believes. Solicitors should also ensure that suspects are aware of their rights, and of what powers the police can exercise over them (such as the permissible length of detention, the right of the police to interview suspects, and so forth). They should then generally spell out suspects' options — basically to answer questions fully, partially, or not at all — and advise them on what course of action is best for them in the light of what they know of the case. The interview process sometimes changes solicitors' understanding of the case, which sometimes leads them to wish to change the advice. Solicitors are entitled to ask for a break in an interview for this purpose, and the police themselves often break off when they believe that, because of a damaging admission, for instance, fresh advice from the solicitor would expedite matters.

While some solicitors advise according to these considerations, many do not. McConville et al. found that one firm in particular, which specialised in criminal work, simply gave advice over the phone to 'Tell the truth, son, you won't go far wrong on that advice'.[42] This 'advice' was not confined to that firm or to telephone advice, though, but was commonly given. Empty advice is often

---

[40] Code C, paras 6.9 and 6.11.
[41] McConville et al., *op. cit.* (1994), ch. 4.
[42] *Ibid.*, p. 8.

provided because the adviser knows too little about the suspect's story to do anything else. In one in six of McConville et al.'s cases the adviser was not concerned at all with the client's account. Thorough knowledge of this was secured in little more than one-quarter of all cases.

(iv) Advising silence

The police used to claim that many solicitors simply advised 'no comment' routinely and that they are usually obstructive.[43] Silence is actually advised surprisingly infrequently, although probably more frequently than it is exercised (estimates of the extent of its use vary from less than 3 per cent to 16 per cent of cases).[44] It is difficult to maintain silence in the face of determined police questioning even with the support of a solicitor, and McConville and Hodgson observed many cases where suspects began answering questions within minutes of agreeing to remain silent. When silence is advised by a solicitor who is not present in the interview, as often happens, it is more difficult still.

Also, the police may hold a suspect in detention for up to 24 hours if they believe that this is necessary in order to obtain evidence by questioning.[45] The detention of suspects who do not answer police questions in an initial interview must be continued if those suspects are to be persuaded to speak, for questioning is not allowed at any other time or in any other place.[46] Thus the exercise of silence is likely to bring about the most feared of all the consequences of arrest — prolonged detention. The police know this. As they told one suspect: '... don't think we'll just let it go because in one interview you make no replies — we're just starting'.[47]

Why is silence advised rarely? Sometimes it is not in the best interests of the suspect: in some cases suspects will best convince the police of their innocence by answering questions, and in other cases their guilt is so obvious (or they are

[43] See, e.g., Baldwin, J., *The Role of Legal Representatives at the Police Station, op. cit.*
[44] Sanders et al., *op. cit.*; Leng, R., *The Right to Silence in Police Interrogation: A Study of Some of the Issues Underlying the Debate*, Royal Commission on Criminal Justice, Research Study No. 10, London: HMSO, 1993. See also McConville et al., *op. cit.* (1994). Where advisers attended the station, McConville et al. found that silence was advised in 22.5% of cases. This, of course, overstates the extent to which silence is maintained, since advice is not always followed, it is advised more often in person than on the phone, and silence is rarely maintained without the presence of a legal adviser.
[45] PACE, s. 37. For a serious arrestable offence they can detain up to 36 hours, and longer in exceptional circumstances: PACE, ss. 41–44.
[46] Code C, para. 11.1. See Sanders and Young, *op. cit.*, pp. 150–8, 176–82.
[47] McConville, M. and Hodgson, J., *Custodial Legal Advice and the Right to Silence*, Royal Commission on Criminal Justice, Research Study No. 16, London: HMSO, 1993, p. 124. Clients are often advised that this will happen if they 'refuse to cooperate': McConville et al., *op. cit.* (1994), p. 112.

so keen to admit to it) that silence is at best time-wasting and hinders suspects' attempts to distance themselves from the most serious potential charges. In many cases, though, where the best advice would be silence, it is not advised; and where suspects might best be advised that they should be silent if police questions become unfair (in the sense discussed earlier), they are often not so advised. There are a number of explanations for this. First, sheer neglect: the job of the solicitor is at its easiest when all that is required is that they watch what the police do and do not actively participate.

Secondly, a non-adversarial ideology is shared by many legal advisers. In particular, para-legals are less adversarial than qualified solicitors. This is often a matter of background (many para-legals are ex police officers) and often a matter of lack of knowledge and confidence among this largely untrained and poorly regarded group. But all lawyers doing police station work have to establish some kind of working relationship with the police, on the police's own territory, which is difficult alongside an overtly adversarial stance.[48] McConville et al., for instance, show that where solicitors have no working relationship with the police, the latter refuse to disclose their case to the solicitor prior to the solicitor seeing the client. An important change since this study was conducted is that para. 2.4 of the 1995 version of the Code of Practice now provides solicitors with the right to consult the custody record as soon as they arrive at the police station. This may serve to weaken the negotiating position of the police a little, and reduce the perceived need amongst defence advisers to 'keep in' with the police. On the other hand, a custody record usually provides only a scanty outline of the police case and it is as yet unclear how useful this new defence right will prove to be.

Third, the cooperation of the police is often wanted in order to best serve the client. For example, if a lawyer is not immediately available the police can (subject to certain legal constraints in the Code)[49] require the suspect to choose another lawyer, if one can be found, or forgo the right to have the lawyer present in the interview. A cooperative solicitor, though, will usually be able to persuade the police to await his or her arrival. Similarly, cooperative solicitors will find the police informing them of the planned times of interviews, helping them to avoid wasting time in the station.[50] In these and other ways solicitors find themselves entering into negotiation with the police although, as Dixon says, this is not on the basis of equality of power.[51] Other areas of negotiation include the police telling advisers the nature and substance of their case; decisions to, and levels of, charge; bail decisions; and treatment of the suspect

---

[48] Dixon, D., 'Common Sense, Legal Advice, and the Right of Silence', *Public Law*, 1991, p. 233.
[49] See Code of Practice C, *op. cit.*, para. 6.6.
[50] Dixon, *op. cit.* (1991), pp. 237–9.
[51] *Ibid.*

while in custody. But the police will not negotiate with lawyers whom they perceive as un-cooperative. Moreover, Dixon points out, suspects and their advisers have only one resource to trade with the police — information. Thus where silence is advised it is often precisely when the defence knows little of the police case and wants to discover more.[52]

The situation is now complicated by the erosion of the right of silence by the Criminal Justice and Public Order Act 1994.[53] Section 34 provides that a court hearing a case of a suspect who, when being questioned:

> failed to mention any fact relied on in his defence ... being a fact which in the circumstances existing at the time the accused could reasonably have been expected to mention when so questioned ... may draw such inferences from the failure as appear proper.

In other words, when a suspect fails to mention something to the police which he or she relies on in court, the court may draw the inference that the suspect is lying. Section 35 provides that a court

> may draw such inferences as appear proper from the failure of the accused to give evidence or his refusal, without good cause, to answer any question [asked in court].

Section 34 might have a major impact on suspects in police stations. The new caution which the police have to read to suspects states:

> You do not have to say anything. But it may harm your defence if you do not mention when questioned something which you later rely on in court. Anything you do say may be given in evidence.[54]

This might lead more suspects to speak where they need not do so which, of course, could lead to more convictions. But the new caution is so opaque that it could lead many more to seek advice from solicitors where they would not otherwise have done so. Whether this would lead to more or less silence than now we cannot guess. In so far as silence hitherto has not been enthusiastically

---

[52] McConville and Hodgson, *op. cit.*, pp. 90–3.
[53] These provisions came into operation in April 1995. Sections 36 and 37 have similar provisions in respect of the effect, in court, of exercising the 'right' of silence on the streets.
[54] Code of Practice C, *op. cit.*, para. 10.4.

advised by solicitors seeking police cooperation, these provisions are likely to encourage them still further to advise clients to answer questions.[55]

Roberts, however, maintains that legal advisers will continue to have to balance the advantages of maintaining silence against its disadvantages. He also points out that, under s. 34, some suspects would be well advised to speak about matters about which they have not been questioned. Many suspects not currently requiring advice will do so in the future, and many more suspects than hitherto will require advice up to the point of charging — requiring more extended attendance at the station than is now common.[56] If past practice is any guide to the future, though, it is not likely that the extra needs inadvertently created by this legislation will be met by a positive response from the legal profession.

V ADDRESSING THE QUALITY ISSUE

Without a high quality legal advice service in the police station, even-handed adversarialism and the presumption of innocence cannot be achieved for most suspects. Much police station advice does little to redress the power imbalance inherent in the police–detainee relationship. But the problem goes even beyond this. In so far as suspects are aware of being let down by their advisers, they are more likely to refuse advice in the future or be more susceptible to pressure not to wait for a solicitor. Many suspects realise that it is duty solicitors who let them down and, thereafter, refuse to see duty solicitors when their own are unavailable, not realising that duty solicitor performance is variable. This accounts for a proportion of the non-contact rate. Addressing the quality issue is therefore necessary if the request rate and contact rate are to be improved.

The quality problems discussed above show that criminal legal defence work is far from what 'common sense' and professional ideology would lead us to expect.[57] If this arises from the failure of personnel to comply with their firms' professional ideology, the answer lies in better training and control of personnel. But if it arises from the implementation of solicitors' work policies, the problem lies with those policies and the socio-economic environment in which they are shaped. The previous section discussed the police environment, to which we will return. That environment does not, however, determine any particular response, although it does create many of the benefits and disbenefits which ensue from the choices which are made. A further element playing a part

---

[55] Fenwick, H., 'Curtailing the Right to Silence, Access to Legal Advice, and Section 78', *Criminal Law Review*, 1995, p. 132.

[56] Roberts, D., 'Legal Advice, the Unrepresented Suspect and the Courts', *Criminal Law Review*, 1995, p. 483.

[57] See Dixon, *op. cit.* (1991), for the contrast between 'common sense' and reality.

in shaping the nature of the services provided must therefore be identified. That element is the working ideology of the solicitor's firm.

McConville et al., based on an extensive study of defence practices, identify four types of firm. The 'classical' type (which puts the client first but has no professional ideological commitment to either suspect or state), and the 'political' type (which is committed to the client) would be those from which these prevalent practices would represent clear deviation. However, out of 48 firms studied by McConville et al., only three conformed to the classical model, and four to the political model. Prevalent practices would also be inconsistent, in many ways, with the third, 'managerial', model; but only one firm in McConville's sample was managerial. The overwhelming majority of firms, then, were 'routine', for which the practices described above are natural. Solicitors in routine firms have a low opinion of their clients, and spend much of their time rushing around from office to court and from dictaphone to interview engaged in intellectually undemanding but physically exhausting activity. This, and maximal delegation,[58] is the only way to make legal aid work pay at the rates which most solicitors expect. In order to delegate the work has to be routinised. Cases are processed in standardised ways, as Sudnow observed many years ago.[59] Thus clients' files often contain little or no evidence from the clients, but are simply the records of court appearances and so forth needed for billing purposes.

The form of delegation which is most important for the purposes of this chapter is the use of representatives in the police station. McConville et al. found that only 25 per cent of visits to the station were by qualified solicitors, an even smaller proportion than found in earlier research.[60] The rest were by representatives: para-legals, articled clerks, and completely unqualified secretarial staff or self-employed 'runners'. As noted above, many are ex police officers. There is nothing wrong, in principle, with the use of representatives if they are well-trained and used only in cases where the seriousness and complexity is suitable to their level of professionalism. This is what happens in 'classical' and in 'managerial' firms. A well-trained para-legal can provide a better service than a qualified solicitor who does not specialise in the area and who does not keep up to date. In a good firm delegation is structured and

---

[58] McConville et al., *op. cit.* (1994), pp. 37–45, reject the use of the term 'delegation' in this context since it implies a measure of thought and control on the part of those directing work to their juniors. Rather, they argue that work is routinely 'allocated' to non-qualified staff. The term 'delegation' will nonetheless be adopted in the text for convenience.

[59] Sudnow, D., 'Normal Crimes', *Social Problems*, 1965, vol. 12, p. 255.

[60] McConville et al., *op. cit.* (1994); Sanders et al., *op. cit.* Bridges, L. and Hodgson, J., 'Improving Custodial Legal Advice', *Criminal Law Review*, 1995, p. 101, suggest that these differences are a product of the different sampling procedures used in different studies, and that probably 40–50 % of all attendances at the station are by non-solicitor staff.

training is provided. 'Routine' firms, however, can do neither while operating policies of maximal delegation. Work is delegated to whoever is available, whenever that person is available.

It is not surprising that advisers behave in the ways described earlier, failing to ensure adherence to the law and failing to adopt adversarial stances. Many advisers either do not know the law or have little confidence in their dealings with the police. McConville et al. occasionally even had advisers appealing to them, the researchers, to help them out. Ex police officers are generally assumed to need no training as they know the relevant law anyway; but the outlook of an ex officer is completely different to that of the professional solicitor, and so a non-adversarial stance towards the police is natural.

The problem of quality was addressed in the LCD research of the mid-1980s. But only now, in the mid-1990s, is serious action being taken. It is true that the need for training of representatives was recognised when the duty solicitor scheme was introduced in the mid-1980s. A duty solicitor could use accredited representatives only, and then only when the case was delegated by the solicitor (on the basis that it would be screened and its suitability for the representative evaluated). But little more was required. And a suspect asking for his or her own solicitor might find a representative who not only had no training at all, but who received the case directly without the initial involvement of any solicitor at all. And, of course, an attending solicitor may be as poorly trained as an unqualified runner. The Runciman Commission recognised the problem in part.[61] It recommended that solicitors and their representatives, whether 'own' or 'duty', should have to satisfy the Legal Aid Board that they are 'fit and proper' before being allowed to undertake this work on the legal aid scheme; and, in the longer term, 'the training, education, supervision and monitoring of all legal advisers who operate at police stations should be thoroughly reviewed'.[62]

The Law Society and Legal Aid Board have responded with an accreditation scheme for representatives, beginning in 1995, which, however, exempts not only persons already approved as duty solicitor representatives, but also trainee solicitors and qualified solicitors. It therefore falls far short of even Runciman's minimalist recommendations, although consideration is being given to plans to cover these last two groups.[63] Accreditation is to be awarded after a 12-month probationary period and involves practical and written examination-type

---

[61] Royal Commission on Criminal Justice, *op. cit.* The Commission's approach was nonetheless inadequate: Bridges, L., 'The Royal Commission's Approach to Criminal Defence Services — A Case of Professional Incompetence'; Cape, E., 'Defence services: What should defence lawyers do in police stations?', and Hodgson, J., 'No defence for the Royal Commission', all in McConville, M. and Bridges, L. (eds), *Criminal Justice in Crisis*, Aldershot: Edward Elgar, 1994.

[62] Royal Commission on Criminal Justice, *op. cit.*, p. 194, recommendation 68.

[63] For a detailed discussion see Bridges and Hodgson, *op. cit.*

elements. Key background for the probationary adviser will be the Law Society's resource book, which was written by the psychologist who promoted the concept of 'ethical interviewing' for police officers.[64] In some ways this was an inspired development. The book details various 'unethical' police interrogation tactics with a view to the adviser monitoring and responding to them when used in interviews. Not only should the suspect be protected directly by this monitoring and intervention, but that should also create additional pressure on the police to move away from adversarial interviewing and further towards 'ethical' interviewing.

This appears paradoxical. Shepherd is at one and the same time trying to discourage the police from adversarialism while trying to promote adversarialism in defence advisers: the mirror image of current practice. We can argue, though, that our natural tendency to seek even-handedness — that both police and defence adopt 'truth-seeking' practices, or that both be adversarial — would be misguided. The presumption of innocence should mean that the defence can be 'obstructive' while requiring the police to be non-adversarial, especially in the light of the erosion of the right of silence. More fundamentally, even-handedness in the police station is illusory. The idea that, in conditions of compulsory detention, the suspect would not feel pressurised and that the defence can stand on its rights with impunity, is naive. Ethical police interviewing and adversarial defence tactics are ideals which these developments will bring nearer, but which will never be even close to achievement in most cases.

Accreditation and training developments, then — that is, this particular scheme and any other that could be devised — even if extended to all police station advisers, could only ever have a limited impact on the power imbalance inherent in the PACE regime. Thus *Becoming Skilled* itself suggests that when officers use unfair tactics the adviser should engage in 'principled negotiation', rather than simply asserting the client's rights. But what are these 'rights'? There is no legal right to insist on 'ethical interviewing', and, as argued above, the legality or otherwise of a whole range of adversarial police tactics is unclear.[65]

The question of who can exercise whatever rights do exist has been clarified, however. The rights of para-legals, as opposed to defence solicitors, was at best hazy under the pre-1995 PACE regime. That year's revision to Code of Practice C stipulates that for the purposes of PACE, the term 'solicitor' includes trainee solicitors, a duty solicitor representative, or an accredited representative. But

---

[64] Shepherd, E., *Becoming Skilled: A Resource Book*, London: Law Society, 1994.
[65] Sanders and Young, *op. cit.*, pp. 158–70; Bridges and Hodgson, *op. cit.* As Bridges and Hodgson point out, *Becoming Skilled* is as much a statement of what the law *should* be as it is descriptive of what the law actually *is*, a distinction that is not always clearly made out.

until the law regulating the PACE regime is clarified and made to incorporate protections for suspects against misleading and oppressive questioning, there will be limited mileage to be gained by training advisers to ensure adherence to the law.[66] Even with the new training scheme, applicable as it is to such a restricted group of para-legals, most police station advice will not secure sufficient adversarialism and presumed innocence to bring the reality of the system into line with its rhetoric.[67]

VI CONCLUSION

We have seen that it is still a minority of suspects who request and receive legal advice. A smaller minority actually see a legal adviser in person and receive advice and support when interviewed by the police. They often have to wait a long time for this, about which the police are all too eager to warn. Even then, up to half of those advisers will be para-legals with little or no training. The nature of that advice and support is a long way away from the adversarial ideal of fighting for suspects' rights, advising silence wherever that would help the suspect, and intervening when questioning gets rough.

It would be easy to blame this on the negligence of the profession and its desire to avoid antagonising the police, on an ideological commitment to crime control values by most criminal firms, or on poor legal aid rates which only reward routinised responses.[68] But it is fair criticism only up to a point. For it is in the interests of suspects that they are not kept waiting for a solicitor longer than necessary, and this is something which the police can facilitate, if they wish. But they will do so only for cooperative solicitors. It is in the interests of suspects that solicitors be told about the police case; again, this is up to the police. In all sorts of ways the police can make life difficult for solicitors and thus, directly and indirectly, for suspects. And so we find a catch-22: if solicitors wish to do their best for suspects they have to compromise by becoming acceptable to the police; and if they wish to help their clients by retaining their adversarial purity, they forfeit cooperation and fail to do their best for their clients.

It is not just chance that the police can do this to solicitors who are perceived as overly adversarial. It flows from their structural power to dictate when, where, and how interviews and detention take place. They have the legal right to do this, and it all takes place on their own territory, which puts the lawyer at a disadvantage. At every point, it is police power which ensures that, whatever the suspect does, adversarialism and the presumption of innocence is

---

[66] Cape, *op. cit.*
[67] See McConville et al., *op. cit.* (1991), on rhetoric and reality in the criminal justice system.
[68] These are the broad messages of McConville et al., *op. cit.* (1994).

undermined. Why do suspects mind waiting for their lawyer? If they were at home or at work they would not mind. It is because they are in police custody that they mind. And the decision to take suspects into custody is that of the police and the police alone. Why do solicitors sometimes give phone advice or send clerks? Because at certain times nothing else can be done or no one else is available. If solicitors or suspects, rather than the police, were to choose the time this problem would be much reduced. As it is, the police can ensure that the process of detention is so unpleasant that 'standing on one's rights' only produces more suffering.[69]

As has been emphasised throughout, the 'PACE regime' can uphold the presumption of innocence and adversarialism only if genuine legal services are provided to suspects. It is therefore strange that suspects are given important choices to make by solicitors and by the police. The police ask suspects (as the legislation requires) if they want legal advice; and solicitors often ask if they want them to come to the station, or if they wish to remain silent. These are not choices most suspects can sensibly make. If it were otherwise, the equality of resources which advice and support is meant to secure would already exist. These choices promote an illusion and rhetoric of equality which runs through the criminal process but which is utterly false.[70] To create the conditions whereby a proper legal service can be provided in police stations it would be necessary to require suspects to receive advice and support — which would run counter to our liberal legal ideology.

This is not to suggest that it is wrong for the police to determine when, where and how interviews with suspects take place. But we have to recognise that the fact that they do means that proper legal services cannot be provided in the police station. Only if the time and circumstances were dictated by lawyers or courts could anything else be true. Thus we noted earlier that the latest version of Code C now obliges the police to provide legal advisers with a copy of the custody record. This was a recommendation of the Runciman Commission. The Commission also recommended that the police 'inform the suspect's solicitor of at least the general nature of the case and the prima facie evidence against the suspect' (p. 53). This would go a long way to reducing the dependence of solicitors on the police and thus to reducing police power. The opportunity not taken to undermine police control in the station is therefore as significant as the reform which *was* made.

---

[69] The situation alluded to here is similar to that analysed in an American lower court by Feeley, M., *The Process is the Punishment*, New York: Sage, 1979.

[70] This is argued in a more general way, to the effect that the Rule of Law fails to operate in the pre-trial process as a whole, in Sanders, A. and Young, R., 'The Rule of Law, Due Process, and Pre-Trial Criminal Justice', *Current Legal Problems*, 1994, p. 125. See also McConville et al., *op. cit.* (1991).

Thus most solicitors adopt the ideological position identified by McConville et al., that most suspects are guilty and that therefore the police are generally right. It is not that solicitors necessarily will always believe this. It is that the structural facts of the system require them to behave in the ways described, and this set of beliefs provides a justification for this which enables the profession to feel less impotent when it fails to provide the necessary level of service. No particular solution is advocated here. For until we recognise the reality as has been described we will not understand the nature of the problem to which the solution is ostensibly addressed.

What are the implications for legal aid more generally? Clearly the argument is that legal aid is a necessary condition for suspects to achieve access to justice in an adversarial system. Equally clearly, this chapter demonstrates that legal aid is not a sufficient condition. The working practices of the police and defence advisers alike need to be addressed if legal aid is to achieve its full potential. Much research has been done, and many seemingly important reforms have been implemented. But the structural imbalance between suspects and police created by the law sanctioning coercive and extended detention for interrogation means that legal aid will generally achieve only an amelioration of injustice, and even then in only a minority of cases. The system is loaded in favour of the police to such an extent that access to justice at the all-important pre-trial stage of the criminal process is doomed to remain an elusive dream.

13

The Reform of Criminal Legal Aid

Lee Bridges

I   A CAUTIONARY TALE

Imagine a situation in one of Britain's inner city areas in the late 1990s. The area has a large ethnic minority population with a long history of conflict between the police and the local black community, the former seeing it as a 'high crime' area and the latter arguing that they are the victims of racist policing targeted on their young people in particular.

Within this area there are several firms of solicitors operating in the field of criminal defence work. One of these firms (which we shall call Firm X) has a reputation among the local black population as being 'fighters' for its clients and as 'standing up to the system'. The firm has taken a policy decision to employ local black people on its staff in order to build its links with the community and also to instruct ethnic minority barristers. (Its rivals, the police and some local magistrates, tend to see this more as a cynical ploy to attract business from young black criminals.) Firm X's solicitors spend most of their days in court and many of their evenings and nights in police stations advising clients. They do not have much time to devote to management or training: case-work is organised on-the-hoof and staff pick up their skills on the job.

In line with its reputation, Firm X has resisted moves over recent years within the criminal justice system — in the form of restrictions on the right to silence and on prosecution disclosure, formal sentence discounts, and related changes to the procedure on mode of trial decisions — to induce its clients to plead guilty and to have their cases dealt with in magistrates' courts rather than at the Crown Court before juries. In any event, many of the firm's black clients have an instinctive distrust of both the police and the local magistrates' court: they usually want to remain silent under police interrogation and to get their cases

276

out of the magistrates' court as soon as possible. As a result, a higher proportion of the firm's criminal cases end up at the Crown Court, where legal aid costs are higher.

During 1998, the Legal Aid Board announces the results of the first round of bidding for criminal legal aid contracts under the system first proposed in the Green Paper of 1995,[1] and passed into law in the Legal Aid Reform Act of 1997. (The Act was the last piece of legislation to be passed under the Conservative Government of John Major and Michael Heseltine, but won the broad endorsement of the then Labour Opposition leader, Tony Blair, and his legal affairs spokesperson, Paul Boateng, as being necessary in order to 'modernise' the legal aid system.) Contracts are awarded to half-a-dozen local criminal defence firms, but not to Firm X. Its 'bid', based on the average cost of its cases over the previous year, was considered to be too high, and there were also doubts about the firm's management and 'quality assurance' systems. There is no right of appeal against the refusal of a legal aid contract.

The firm is therefore instructed that it must cease to take on new legally-aided criminal defence cases from the beginning of the contracts awarded to the other firms in three months' time. Moreover, it is told that under the special rules applying to criminal legal aid, it will now be excluded from bidding for the separate contracts to be let for court and police station duty solicitor services. This is despite the fact that the firm has always had a policy of using fully-qualified solicitors familiar with court procedures as much as possible on police station work, as distinct from other firms in the area who make extensive use of unadmitted staff. Indeed, in some of these other firms, almost all police station work has been assigned for the last few years to 'accredited' police station representatives who have been specifically employed for this purpose and therefore never have any contact with the courts. In other firms, use has been made of a series of 'probationary' representatives taken on for short periods and then dismissed or moved to other work (e.g., sitting behind counsel in the Crown Court) when they have failed to obtain accreditation.[2]

In fact, even the three-month grace period allowed to the firm to wind up its criminal defence work proves illusory. As soon as the announcement of the legal aid contracts is made, Firm X is informed by its bank that its overdraft facilities have been withdrawn. Firm X therefore sends a 'customer care' letter

---

[1] Lord Chancellor's Department, *Legal Aid – Targeting Need: The future of publicly funded help in solving legal problems and disputes in England and Wales*, Cm 2854, London: HMSO, 1995 (hereinafter, 'the Green Paper').

[2] See Bridges, L. and Hodgson, J., 'Improving custodial legal advice', *Criminal Law Review*, 1995, p. 101.

to all of its existing clients informing them of the very real possibility that they will have to switch their cases to new solicitors.

Word spreads in the local black community that Firm X — *their* solicitors — is about to be closed down by the Legal Aid Board. There is an immediate outcry: petitions to the Lord Chancellor are signed, protest meetings organised, resolutions passed in the local council. There is even talk of organising a sit-in at the local magistrates' court on the first occasion when one of Firm X's former clients is forced to use another solicitor. (The last time there was a similar protest was a few years earlier when the local council, under threat to its budget from central government, had proposed to withdraw its grant from the local law centre. Then, many firms of local solicitors, including Firm X, joined in the protests, arguing that the council had a conflict of interest given that the law centre often assisted clients in taking legal action against it. Even the Legal Aid Board expressed disquiet. Faced with this opposition, just before new local elections, the council decided to maintain the law centre's grant, although at a somewhat lower level of funding.)

Members of the newly-appointed Regional Legal Services Committee quickly deny that they had any role to play in the contract letting process — their role is advisory only and limited to much wider issues of setting priorities between different types of legal aid and possible alternative services, especially in the field of 'social welfare law'. The Regional Legal Services Committee does pass a resolution demanding that the national Legal Aid Board send a representative to explain its contract decision to the local community at a meeting it has organised in the area.

At the meeting, several speakers endorse Firm X's high reputation and long years of devoted service to members of the black community in particular. The representatives of the Legal Aid Board — an accountant who has recently been appointed to the Legal Aid Board itself and the 'contracts manager' for the Area Office — provide a technical explanation of the contract letting process, denying that only the lowest cost bids were accepted and asserting that they also took account of assessments of the quality of service provided by the various firms in terms of their compliance with the Board's 'transaction criteria'[3] and other indicators of administrative performance. In the face of specific allegations of poor service received from some of the firms awarded contracts, the Legal Aid Board representatives refuse to discuss individual cases or firms, although they do hint that on the basis of an analysis of case outcomes done since the protests arose and on other 'soundings' taken (a local magistrate and a Crown Court judge are mentioned), Firm X's clients are said

---

[3] Sherr, A., Moorhead, R. and Paterson, A., *Transaction Criteria*, London: HMSO, 1992.

often to contest 'hopeless cases' and appear on average to receive longer and more frequent custodial sentences than those of other firms.

It is even suggested that, by forcing Firm X's clients to go to other solicitors, the contract system will end up giving them what, on any rational assessment, is likely to be a better service. A speaker from the floor responds to this in an impassioned speech, pointing out that the issue is not one of 'quality assurance systems' or 'outcome measures' but of who, in the highly politicised atmosphere of police–community relations in the area, young black people feel that they can trust to stand up and fight for their rights. The meeting ends in uproar.

Following this, the Regional Legal Services Committee passes a resolution requesting that the decision to deny Firm X a contract be reviewed. By the time this request reaches the Legal Aid Board, several letters have been sent by other solicitors' firms in the area threatening to take the Legal Aid Board to judicial review if it should accede to the request for a reconsideration of its contract decisions. On legal advice, the Legal Aid Board decides to take no further action. The Lord Chancellor's Department, in reply to Parliamentary Questions from the local black MP, denies any responsibility for the contract letting decision as this is a matter for the Legal Aid Board as an independent agency.

In the meantime, there is confusion in the local courts, as several of Firm X's former clients refuse to accept representation by other solicitors. Their legal aid is discharged on the grounds of their unreasonable behaviour and their cases proceed without representation. When one of these defendants is subsequently convicted and receives a custodial sentence, there are several offers made by solicitors outside the area to take the case to the European Court of Human Rights under a conditional fee agreement.

A retired solicitor, who previously practised in the area, writes to the local press, pointing out the similarity between the situation produced as a result of the legal aid contract letting and that which pertained within the locality back in the late 1960s. Then, when far fewer people received legal aid for defending themselves in magistrates' court, the work was confined to only a handful of solicitors, with allegations that they maintained their oligopolistic position through corrupt relationships with the local police and magistrates' court clerks.

The local oligopoly had been broken down only through the setting up of a magistrates' court duty solicitor scheme, first on a voluntary basis (and resisted by the local justices' clerk) and then, after the Legal Aid Act 1982, on a statutory basis, and by the gradual widening in the number of defendants receiving legal aid. Indeed, when the statutory duty solicitor scheme was set up, one of the cardinal principles built into its rules had been that client choice of solicitor had to be preserved. How paradoxical that the former oligopolistic system had now been restored, with all that implied about the denial of client choice, not through local corruption but under the new national statutory scheme, with all of its supposedly objective and rational criteria for judging quality of legal services and determining who should receive the sanction *of* the state to defend the citizen *against* the state.

II IDEOLOGY VERSUS PRAGMATIC REFORM — THE GREEN PAPER

Of course, it is not the intention behind the Green Paper,[4] *Legal Aid – Targeting Need*, to politicise the administration of criminal legal aid in the way described above, let alone to contribute to the increasing racial polarisation in our criminal justice system. But the fact that it can reasonably be foreseen as having precisely these outcomes is evidence of how poorly thought out and confused is much of the Green Paper's approach to legal aid reform.

The trouble with the Green Paper is that it attempts an uneasy marriage between several pragmatic initiatives taken over recent years to deal with problems of poor quality and rising costs within the legal aid system — franchising — standard fees — and ideologically-driven notions of supply-side cost control — competitive tendering and exclusive contracting. These last proposals can accurately be described as ideological in character precisely because they rest on an as yet unproven hypothesis that the dramatic rise in legal aid costs over the past ten to 15 years has been the product primarily of 'supplier-induced demand'. According to this hypothesis, it has been the legal profession — solicitors and barristers — who, in order to provide a vehicle for their own profits, have induced more and more people to undertake litigation and to seek legal aid for it. What is worse, neither the legal professionals nor their clients have the least interest in controlling legal aid costs, whether through limits on the types of cases they take on under legal aid or in terms of the amount or quality of service they provide in particular cases. As the state (usually referred to as 'taxpayers') is paying the bill, both case numbers and costs can be driven up relentlessly.[5]

On the face of it, this hypothesis has a good deal of plausibility in respect of criminal legal aid. As has been demonstrated elsewhere,[6] over the period from

---

[4] *Op. cit.*
[5] The purest explication of this hypothesis is to be found in Bevan, G., Holland, T. and Partington, M., *Organising Cost-Effective Access to Justice*, London: Social Market Foundation, 1994.
[6] Bridges, L., 'The professionalisation of criminal justice', *Legal Action*, August 1992, p. 7 and McConville, M., Hodgson, J., Bridges, L. and Pavlovic, A., *Standing Accused: The Organisation and Practices of Criminal Defence Lawyers in Britain*, Oxford: Clarendon Press, 1994, ch. 1. See also Goriely, T., 'The Development of Criminal Legal Aid in England and Wales', at chapter 2 of this volume.

the late 1960s to the early 1990s, legal aid has financed a major professional-isation of criminal legal proceedings, especially at magistrates' courts, and a rapid expansion both in criminal defence solicitors' firms and the numbers at the criminal Bar. In the 1970s, as the numbers of persons prosecuted for criminal offences grew, an increasing proportion of these defendants obtained legal representation through legal aid, a trend encouraged by the solicitors' profession through such measures as the setting up of magistrates' court duty solicitor schemes on a voluntary basis. By the 1980s, the growth in the numbers prosecuted at least for the more serious indictable/either-way offences levelled off, yet the numbers receiving legally-aided representation continued to increase.

Various attempts made throughout this period to restrict the growth of criminal legal aid, through such devices as circulars and guidelines issued to magistrates' courts, failed to stem the expansionary trend. Indeed, research published in the early 1990s[7] tended to confirm the haphazard and inconsistent application by different courts of the statutory criteria for granting criminal legal aid and the inadequate and often inaccurate information from solicitors on which such decisions could be based. All of this has contributed to the inability of the Lord Chancellor's Department to predict with any degree of accuracy future levels of expenditure on criminal legal aid. Neither has the problem always been one of under-estimation. In fact, after several years of over-spending on the projected budget in the late 1980s and early 1990s, it appears that the Lord Chancellor's Department allowed itself to be panicked by over-estimates of future criminal legal aid costs into introducing compen-sating cuts in eligibility for the Green Form Legal Advice and Assistance Scheme in 1993. In the event, criminal legal aid expenditure has in most recent years come in under-budget, although this has not produced any reversal by the Government in the cuts in eligibility for the Green Form.

Yet, despite all the evidence of a seemingly unrelenting expansion in criminal legal aid, the hypothesis of 'supplier-induced demand' is inadequate and simplistic.[8] Even the Green Paper acknowledges that in this field, unlike 'most other forms of legal aid, demand is determined by the state'.[9] Certainly, it appears to have been a decline in the number of persons arrested and charged by the police and subsequently prosecuted by the Crown Prosecution Service that has contributed to the reduced rate of growth in criminal legal aid over

---

[7] The research is discussed in Wall, D. S., 'Keyholders to Criminal Justice? Solicitors and Applications for Legal Aid' and Young, R., 'Will Widgery Do?: Court Clerks, Discretion, and the Determination of Legal Aid Applications', at chapters 6 and 7 of this volume respectively.

[8] A point developed by Samuel, E., 'Criminal Legal Aid Expenditure: Supplier or System Driven? The Case of Scotland', at chapter 10 of this volume.

[9] Green Paper, *op. cit.*, p. 30, para. 4.40.

recent years. But supply-side theorists also tend to ignore the more specific state interests that lie behind the expenditure of public funds on criminal legal aid.

At one level, criminal legal aid clearly plays a role in legitimating the criminal justice system, which itself has expanded in the face of the various disorders attendant on late industrial and post-industrial society.[10] Again, the Green Paper notes this function when it states that those faced with criminal charges 'have no choice but to defend themselves against the power of the state ranged against them in the form of the prosecuting authorities'.[11] A particular example of the legitimating role of criminal legal aid is to be found in its extension to cover custodial legal advice under the Police and Criminal Evidence Act 1984, legislation which otherwise had the effect of greatly extending and codifying the powers of the police over the citizen.[12] The creation of a statutory right to legal advice for those held in police custody and a universal entitlement to legal aid for this purpose was portrayed at the time as a measure to 'balance' new police powers of detention and questioning of suspects. The Tory Government's acceptance of this need for political balance led directly to a major increase in the overall costs of criminal legal aid, so that today the provision of custodial legal advice accounts for some £70m out of a total expenditure of £450m per annum in this field. Moreover, once the linkage between legal aid provision and extended police powers had been established in this way, its contribution to driving up legal aid expenditure seems likely to be perpetuated. The recent limitation in suspects' 'right to silence' under the Criminal Justice and Public Order Act 1994 can therefore be predicted to produce a further surge in demand for custodial legal advice.[13]

At another level, immediate control over the supply of criminal legal aid currently rests with local magistrates' courts, who are responsible for the initial decision whether or not particular defendants will be granted legal aid orders for representation. Yet, courts have their own bureaucratic interest in ensuring high levels of legal representation, as this assists in the administrative processing of their own case-loads. In this sense, courts are both the 'consumers' and 'suppliers' of legal aid, albeit at one remove from the financial consequences of their decisions in this area. This division of functions, between the courts who decide on the grant of criminal legal aid, on the one hand, and the Legal Aid Board and (for Crown Court cases) the Lord Chancellor's Department who hold the responsibility for funding, on the other, is what lies

---

[10] For similar observations in the context of Ireland, see Cousins, M., 'At the Heart of the Legal: The Role of Legal Aid in Legitimating Criminal Justice', at chapter 5 of this volume.

[11] Green Paper, *op. cit.*, p. 30, para. 4.40.

[12] Bridges, L. and Bunyan, T., 'Britain's new urban policing strategy', *Journal of Law and Society*, 1983, vol. 10, p. 85.

[13] Bridges, L., 'The silence about what it will all cost', *Parliamentary Briefing*, February/March 1994, p. 10.

at the root of the inadequate financial management and planning that has characterised criminal legal aid and has led directly to the Comptroller and Auditor-General's decision to qualify the Lord Chancellor's Department's accounts for each of the past four years.

In this context, it is perhaps surprising that the Government so readily rejected proposals, drawn up by the Legal Aid Board in 1993, to transfer decision-making responsibility for the granting of criminal legal aid away from magistrates' courts and to the Board itself.[14] These proposals would have required automatic 'early cover' legal aid for all defendants charged with indictable/either-way offences up to the point of entering pleas in the magistrates' court, with the decision on any further extensions of legal aid being made by the Legal Aid Board on the basis of submissions by solicitors. By the time this proposal was put forward, however, steps had already been instituted to bring individual case costs under control through the introduction of a system of standard fees for magistrates' court criminal legal aid. At the time of its introduction, this measure attracted widespread criticism and prophesies of doom within the legal profession, as likely to reduce standards of criminal defence work to an even lower level of routinised service and to drive the more conscientious practitioners out of this field of activity altogether.[15]

In the event, it appears that the solicitors' profession has adjusted with relative equanimity to the introduction of standard fees for criminal legal aid. This is partly due to the fact that, when planning the scheme, the Lord Chancellor's Department failed to take account of the gap that has traditionally existed between the number of criminal legal aid orders issued each year by magistrates' courts and the lower number of magistrates' court criminal legal aid claims submitted by solicitors for payment to the Legal Aid Board. The levels of standard fee to be paid under the scheme were calculated on the basis of different 'bands' of average costs paid out in relation to each *claim* presented to the Legal Aid Board.[16] On the other hand, rules were belatedly drawn up so as to entitle solicitors to payment of a standard fee in relation to each criminal legal aid *order* issued by a magistrates' court. As explained by the Legal Aid Board, the result has been 'an increase in the ratio of bills paid to offences' and in 'a number of sets of proceedings where two or more ... standard fees have

---

[14] Legal Aid Board, *The Legal Aid Board's Advice to the Lord Chancellor on the Implications of its Taking over Responsibility for Criminal Legal Aid in the Magistrates' Courts*, London: Legal Aid Board, 1993.

[15] See McConville et al., *op. cit.*, p. 270, and Law Society, *Memorandum on the Future of Criminal Legal Aid: Evidence to the Royal Commission on Criminal Justice*, London: Law Society, 1992.

[16] See Price Waterhouse, *Lord Chancellor's Department: Advice and Survey on Criminal Legal Aid in Magistrates' Courts, Report*, London: Price Waterhouse, 1992.

been claimed where previously one ... bill would have been submitted'.[17] Put more simply, solicitors have been able to present more claims in relation to the overall volume of defendants assisted than was previously the case.[18]

III FROM AN OPEN TO A CONTROLLED MARKET FOR LEGAL SERVICES

The real significance of standard fees may be in paving the way for the shift, now planned under the Green Paper proposals, completely away from the case-by-case funding of criminal legal aid and toward what has been called 'block contracts', under which particular firms of solicitors would be contracted to undertake a specified volume of legal aid cases within a given field for a particular overall price. The adoption of contracting as envisaged in the Green Paper will, of course, imply much more than an extension of the standard fee system. After all, standard fees seek only to introduce an element of prior control over the costs expended on individual cases in place of the previous, cumbersome system of detailed, *ex post facto* assessments of the work claimed by solicitors and barristers. Standard fees do not affect the overall volume of defendants who may receive legal aid, or the number of solicitors' firms who may undertake legally-aided cases.

Indeed, ever since its inception the current legal aid scheme has operated on the basis of an open market for legal services, under which the client might choose any solicitor through whom to seek assistance, and all legal practitioners had the opportunity to participate in legally-aided work. Currently, over 6,000 out of the 11,000 solicitors' offices receiving legal aid payment each year undertake at least some criminal cases. Within this total, there are probably about 1,000 offices that handle around three-fifths of the criminal legal aid case-load, but this still leaves 40 per cent of assisted defendants dependent on the services of a much wider group of solicitors. The Green Paper proposes to replace this open market system with what will amount to a state-regulated cartel of providers in each locale and field of legal work, operating within the tight constraints both of fixed budgets and controls over the numbers of cases they will be able to take on in any given period. There are several elements of this proposed reform programme that need to be considered.

---

[17] Legal Aid Board, *Annual Report 1994-95*, HC 526, London: HMSO, 1995, para. 2.2, p. 70.
[18] It also appears that some costs previously claimed under criminal legal aid bills have now been transferred to claims under the Green Form Legal Advice and Assistance Scheme. See further, Gray, A., Fenn, P. and Rickman, N., 'Controlling Lawyers' Costs Through Standard Fees: An Economic Analysis', at chapter 9 of this volume.

To begin with, while accepting the principle that no criminal case 'that would otherwise qualify could be refused legal aid for lack of money',[19] the Green Paper still leans heavily in favour of subjecting overall spending on criminal legal aid to a pre-determined cash limit. The Green Paper at first acknowledges some of the complexities of cash-limiting criminal legal aid when it states that it will be:

> necessary to set the budget at a level that was likely to meet reasonable demand. The number of criminal cases and the distribution of their costs vary from year to year. There are a number of factors such as police clear-up rates and police cautioning policy which have an effect on the number of cases coming to trial. The role of the Crown Prosecution Service also has an impact. New laws, such as changes to the right to silence, might increase demand for legal aid.[20]

The Green Paper then somewhat wishfully asserts that 'there should be sufficient information to set the level for the predetermined budget in any one year to reflect demand' and that 'it should be possible to anticipate the effects of legislative and other policy changes'.[21]

In the next chapter, setting out how such a cash limit would actually be administered, the Green Paper reverts to a much cruder basis of calculation 'on the basis of historic expenditure patterns since these are likely to reflect the pattern of need'.[22] In particular, it is claimed that within the present arrangements for allocating criminal legal aid 'there is no evidence that there is current demand that is not being met' and that while 'volume is variable over a period of time, the current distribution describes the pattern of distribution the Government will want to maintain in the future and provides a model for allocating funds between the different Areas of England and Wales'.[23]

Given the difficulties that have been encountered in the past in predicting levels of expenditure in relation to criminal legal aid and the more specific error made in introducing standard fees on the basis of historic levels of expenditure, it is not clear why an overall cash limit derived from similar methods should command public confidence. And while it is true to say that 'current demand'

---

[19] Green Paper, *op. cit.*, p. 30, para. 4.41.
[20] *Ibid.*, p. 31, para. 4.44.
[21] *Ibid.*
[22] *Ibid.*, p. 34, para. 5.7.
[23] *Ibid.*, p. 35, para. 5.9.

is (largely)[24] being met, it is quite another thing to assert that demand necessarily reflects 'need' at present, let alone into the future. For example, the level of demand for custodial legal advice (at least up to April 1995 when the restrictions on suspects' right to silence came into force) probably encompassed only somewhere between a third and two-fifths of the eligible population; the majority of arrested suspects were still not requesting legal advice while in custody despite this service being available under legal aid free of charge.[25] The Green Paper provides no explanation of why it is considered that all of these suspects not currently 'demanding' legal advice do not in fact 'need' it.

Equally, had a cash limit for this service for the current year been set purely on the basis of historic expenditure, no provision would have been made for the increase in demand likely to arise as the result of the imposition of limits on the right to silence,[26] or for the improvements in service that seem to be required to meet the standards now being promulgated by the Legal Aid Board and the Law Society through the training and accreditation scheme for police station advisers, which seem to demand considerable additional adviser time spent in police stations.[27] Neither is this the only area of criminal legal aid services where there is evidence of the need for better standards possibly implying additional costs. Research has shown that the standards of legal representation, particularly in the preparation stages, provided under criminal legal aid both by solicitors in magistrates' courts and by barristers in the Crown Court, leave considerable room for improvement.[28]

The Green Paper proposals for imposing a cash limit on criminal legal aid therefore display a certain degree of naivety and self-contradiction. Perhaps too much should not be made of this, since in practice any such cash limit will probably need to include a substantial reserve fund to cater for unpredictable surges in the criminal case-load. In this sense, the already looming political row over the issue of cash-limiting legal aid may prove to be of little more than symbolic significance, certainly as far as the criminal legal aid budget is concerned. On the other hand, it is not obvious what a cash limit containing a substantial reserve will achieve in terms of imposing financial discipline on

[24] Around one in 20 of applications for legal aid in the magistrates' courts are refused: Young, *op. cit.* In addition, not all of those who request legal advice when detained in the police station actually receive any: Sanders, A., 'Access to Justice in the Police Station: An Elusive Dream?', at chapter 12 of this volume.
[25] See Sanders, *op. cit.*
[26] See Bridges, *op. cit.* (1994).
[27] Bridges and Hodgson, *op. cit.*
[28] See McConville et al., *op. cit.*, and Bridges, L., 'The Royal Commission's Approach to Criminal Defence Services – A Case of Professional Incompetence', in McConville, M. and Bridges, L. (eds), *Criminal Justice in Crisis*, Aldershot: Edward Elgar, 1994.

those administering or delivering legal aid services. It could, in fact, have the opposite effect, with the reserve funds providing a target for the legal profession as a whole and for individual practitioners to seek to reach by taking on additional cases.

Potentially of far greater significance in the longer term will be the limitations that the type of competitive, exclusive contract system envisaged in the Green Paper will exert over the number of solicitors able to provide criminal defence services, and the control this will enable the state to exert in regulating local markets and even the practices of individual firms. It is important to note that the problem in this respect does not lie with the concept of the bulk purchase of legal aid services under contracts, but rather with the Green Paper's insistence that only a restricted number of contracted firms within each locality will be allowed to provide legal aid services following a process of competitive tendering. With the advent of standard fees, it would be a relatively simple step to introduce longer-term contracts for the bulk purchase of legal aid services with at least the larger providers, and such a system could have distinct advantages both for the Legal Aid Board and the solicitors' firms themselves in providing a mechanism for improved budgetary and service planning. Indeed, without the element of competitive tendering, it would be possible to negotiate tailor-made contracts with each firm covering all of their criminal legal aid work, based on their past involvement in police station and court duty solicitor schemes and magistrates' and Crown Court representation.

At the same time, the provision of criminal legal aid need not be confined exclusively to contracted suppliers; the contract system could be run in parallel with a continuing system of case-by-case funding under standard fees for non-contracted firms. In this respect, much of the administrative burden of decisions on granting legal aid in individual cases could be removed by 'deeming' certain categories of offence or defendants as automatically eligible and delegating this non-discretionary decision-making to solicitors. This proposal, first put forward under the name of 'early cover' in connection with the idea of transferring decisions on the grant of criminal legal aid from magistrates' courts to the Legal Aid Board, is again canvassed in the Green Paper.[29] But the Green Paper itself is less enthusiastic about the Legal Aid Board becoming involved in making decisions on the grant of criminal legal aid, even in the minority of cases (e.g., those involving summary offences) where the decision would remain discretionary. Instead, the Green Paper proposes that such decisions be given over entirely to solicitors operating under fixed-priced contracts, subject to 'incentives and quality controls ... to ensure

---

[29] *Op. cit.*, p. 74, paras 10.16–10.17.

that the application of the [interest of justice or other similar] test was done sensibly and reasonably' and to subsequent auditing of performance.[30] Although this is portrayed as providing solicitors with 'flexibility' in operating under fixed price contracts, it would in effect be passing the buck to them for withholding legal representation or other forms of assistance from persons facing criminal charges; and it would create a clear conflict of interests between the solicitor, who would have a financial incentive to limit the provision of services in order to enhance profits, and the criminal defendant.

The Green Paper suggests that the total number of solicitors' firms undertaking all forms of legal aid work under the contract system would be reduced to just 3,000, about a quarter of the present total. In other fields, this reduction in solicitors able to provide legal aid services would be balanced to some extent by the introduction of more non-solicitor agencies. But the Green Paper specifically rules this out in the field of criminal defence work, even in areas such as custodial legal advice where it could be envisaged that community-based voluntary agencies might become involved as an alternative to private solicitors.[31] Instead, as a special restrictive practice applying only to criminal legal aid, contracts for police station and court duty solicitor work would be limited to those firms already holding them for criminal court representation.[32] On the other hand, not all firms with contracts to provide court representation would be required to undertake police station or court duty solicitor work. Although the Green Paper suggests that suspects or defendants could still use the services of solicitors without contracts for obtaining custodial legal advice, they would be able to do so only without the benefit of legal aid.[33] In practice, therefore, the market for duty solicitor services is likely to be restricted to an even smaller number of firms than that for criminal representation in magistrates' courts, and it can be anticipated that over time the firms involved in duty solicitor work would develop a local monopoly of service in this field.

The overall effect of the Green Paper proposals would therefore be not only greatly to restrict clients' choice of the legal representatives to defend them against the state, but also to concentrate criminal defence work within a much smaller number of providers within any locality. Indeed, it is difficult to see how a system of contracting, with all that this implies in terms of pre-contract tendering and negotiation and subsequent monitoring and auditing of compliance with contract conditions, would be administratively feasible without restrictive practices designed to bring about such market concentration. The

---

[30] *Ibid.*, p. 73, para. 10.13.
[31] For a discussion of this possibility, see McConville et al., *op. cit.*, pp. 294–8.
[32] Green Paper, *op. cit.*, p. 70, para. 10.3.
[33] *Ibid.*, p. 71, para. 10.5.

situation will be further complicated by the fact that, in order to introduce competitive tendering, it will be necessary to divide criminal defence work into different blocks covering, for example, court representation, court duty solicitor, and police station duty solicitor services. Separate contracts would have to be let and subsequently monitored in relation to each of these services, rather than having one tailor-made contract to cover the combination of criminal defence work a firm hopes to provide based on past practices, as would be possible under a non-competitive and non-exclusive system of block funding.

Under the proposed system, any firm seeking a contract would be required to meet the Legal Aid Board's standards for franchising, which have only recently been introduced on a voluntary and non-exclusive basis. This is presented as a means of guaranteeing minimum standards of quality, although in fact there is no firm evidence as yet that franchising does guarantee quality in individual case-work. Rather, it may simply contribute to a standardisation of case-work within and across different firms. The Green Paper suggests that firms may wish to offer higher quality services than are demanded by franchising and that so long as they 'met value for money criteria, they would be more likely to win contracts'.[34] But it is just as likely that, when combined with price competition through competitive tendering, the result would be to drive standards down to a lowest common denominator, especially where the budget is subject to an overall cash limit based on historic levels of expenditure.

It is this standardisation of criminal legal aid work that is perhaps the most worrying feature of the proposed system. It is certainly difficult to see what role there would be within it for the 'niche' firm specialising in defending particular types of case or sections of the community. At present, such firms have a capacity to develop their practices within the 'open market' system for allocating legal aid, for example taking on cases within their field of expertise across a large number of courts, or even different areas of the country. So long as they can meet the 'interests of justice' test in order to obtain legal aid in the first instance, and subsequently operate within the constraints of national standard fees, it makes little difference what political or social values solicitors (or barristers) bring to their work at present. Franchising already seeks to extend the Legal Aid Board's control over solicitors' firms into areas of practice management and standards, and this system of regulation would be likely to be extended further under a contract system.[35] The Green Paper warns against the potential for direct political interference that would be implicit in a contract

---

[34] *Ibid.*, p. 42, para. 6.15.
[35] The sociological implications of such control are explored by Sommerlad, H., 'Criminal Legal Aid Reforms and the Restructuring of Legal Professionalism', at chapter 14 of this volume.

system,[36] but the more serious risk may be in terms of indirect bias of a system where the firm with unorthodox ideas and practices would find that it simply did not fit in with the supposedly rational criteria of allocation.

Lastly, it is worth considering the administrative burden that a fully-developed contract system might impose. Given that criminal representation is based at present around magistrates' courts and their 'feeder' police stations, it is likely that an estimate would have to be made for each court area of the number of cases in which representation would have to be provided over the contract period at different level of services. These might be divided into the different categories of standard fees covering guilty pleas, trials, and committals in magistrates' courts, with similar divisions for Crown Court work. There would also need to be similar estimates for court and police station duty solicitor work. So, take a typical medium-sized court area where it is estimated that, over a three-year contract period, 15,000 defendants will require representation in the local magistrates' courts, 3,000 representation in the Crown Court, 6,000 the services of a court duty solicitor, and 20,000 legal advice in the police station. Firms might be asked to tender initially for the number of magistrates' court and Crown Court cases they would hope to take on. Presumably, some minimum number of cases would be specified in order to constitute a valid tender. It would also be necessary to specify a maximum number of cases to be allocated to any one firm so as to preserve some element of client choice and to cater for conflicts of interests. It might be decided, for instance, that no firm should be allowed to control more than 30 per cent of the criminal case-load in an area. In the example cited above, therefore, firms could be invited to tender for between a minimum of 150 cases initially starting in the magistrates' court and a maximum of 4,500 spread over the three-year period.

In the type of area described above, even if some of the firms with only very small case-loads were to drop out of the bidding process, it might be anticipated on the basis of current levels of solicitor participation in criminal legal aid that as many as 30 or 40 firms would wish to make bids for criminal defence contracts. Indeed, some individual firms could put in several bids incorporating different unit prices depending on the volume of cases eventually awarded. Faced with the task of evaluating this range of bids, it is difficult to imagine that any detailed investigation of quality standards could be carried out. Far more likely that the bids would be assessed by computer to provide the 'best price' solution, with limited follow-up enquiries to ensure that the minimum

---

[36] *Op. cit.*, p. 34, para. 5.6, where it states that the system of allocation of funds would be 'intended to prevent any suggestion of political bias at local level where, for example, it might be suggested that public funds had been withheld because someone wished to apply for the judicial review of a Government decision'.

standards required by franchising are met. A 'best price' system of evaluation would tend to favour the larger bidders. In the end, contracts might be let to a dozen or fewer firms, each with varying quotas of different categories of case to be completed within the contract period for a price. The whole process would then have to be gone through separately for local court and police station duty solicitor services.

This would cover only one set of courts out of possibly a hundred or more court areas throughout the country. In the end, criminal legal aid alone, including court and police station duty solicitor services, might require the evaluation of as many as 10,000 separate bids and the negotiation and subsequent monitoring of something in the region of 3,000 or 4,000 contracts across the country as a whole. Far from simplifying the machinery of legal aid, this type of contract system could produce an administrative nightmare. This may indeed prove a more telling objection to the Green Paper with the present Government than many of the others outlined above.

IV CONCLUSION

Fortunately, there is an alternative, less ideologically-driven, path to reform open to this or another Government. The introduction of standard fees covering much of criminal work has already produced apparent administrative savings both for the Legal Aid Board and probably for many solicitors, and should result in improved predictability of the overall criminal legal aid budget. There is scope for developing contracts for the bulk purchase of legal aid services from the larger providers on a non-competitive and non-exclusive basis. The idea of deeming substantial categories of defendants charged with a more serious offence automatically eligible for legal aid on grounds of merits holds out the promise of further administrative savings, whether or not it is combined with a transfer of decisions on the grant of criminal legal aid in other cases away from magistrates' courts. Above all, it is necessary to address the issue of quality of service across the full range of criminal legal aid, perhaps not so much through franchising as by further developing programmes of specialist training and accreditation such as that now in operation for police station advisers. None of these reforms depends on being part of the type of price competitive and highly regulated system of allocating legal aid exclusively through contracts that has been put forward in the Green Paper and which should now be rejected for all the risks it poses of restricted access and choice, poorer and more standardised quality of service, and potential political interference in the provision of criminal defence services.

14

Criminal Legal Aid Reforms and the Restructuring of Legal Professionalism

Hilary Sommerlad*

I INTRODUCTION

This chapter explores the impact of criminal legal aid reforms upon the concept of legal professionalism. Under these reforms, ideological and practical aspirations towards universal entitlement to high quality legally-aided services are being replaced by a system in which the state uses a range of direct and indirect devices to limit access to justice to those it accuses of crime. In the process, the legal profession's ideological and practical relationships with the state and with its own clients are being fundamentally recast.

Recent government initiatives to reform legal aid, such as franchising and the proposals outlined in the 1995 Green Paper,[1] have profound implications for the structure of the legal profession and the delivery of legal services. When considered with other recent professional, social and ideological changes, these developments can be seen as representing a major paradigm shift,[2] particularly for solicitors. The dominant agent of change is 'the new managerialism'. This complex of ideas and practices is presented simply as a technical innovation in the delivery of services, but it is also an ideological change, an element in the

---

* The author would like to acknowledge all the support given by the Policy Research Unit at Leeds Metropolitan University and the generous responses of all the solicitors who participated.
[1] Lord Chancellor's Department, *Legal Aid – Targeting Need: The future of publicly funded help in solving legal problems and disputes in England and Wales*, Cm 2854, London: HMSO, 1995 (hereinafter the 'Green Paper').
[2] Glasser, C., 'The Legal Profession in the 1990s – Images of Change', *Legal Studies*, 1990, vol. 10, p. 1.

current Government's re-conceptualisation of the 'nation', of citizenship, and of democratic forms of government.[3]

Why should reforms which appear primarily to be concerned with the organisation, distribution and pricing of 'legal work' be seen as so significant? It will be argued in this chapter that the essence of the classical view that solicitors held both of themselves and of their function is predicated on their control over their work, their professional autonomy. The ideology and (to a lesser extent) practice of the profession have been rooted in universalist notions of service and access to justice. As a result, the transformation of the delivery of 'justice' into a disaggregated assortment of 'skills' and 'services' has obvious implications for the profession and for its notion of service. It also has corresponding implications for the sustaining self-image of practitioners, for the experience of those who are now designated as 'customers' or 'consumers' of the 'services', and consequently for the very notion of access to justice itself.

The classical paradigm was of course developed in harness with a class-based system of justice, and the credibility of the universal service ethic is challenged not only by its ideological function of disguising the unequal distribution of power and goods, but also by the empirical fact of the poor service offered to poor clients.[4] However, it is argued here that the idea of impartiality had to contain some validity if it were to provide any degree of legitimation, and, correspondingly, that the principle of universal service retained a core role in the identity of the profession as 'client-centred'. The current reforms, on the other hand, are likely to institutionalise the worst aspects of traditional practice under the guise of 'ensuring quality'. The historical process of the loss of professional control over the character of 'legal' work has consequences, therefore, not just for practitioners, but for the wider conception of justice too.

Although the discussion which supports this argument is largely theoretical, it is informed by an analysis of documentary evidence and by interviews with a small sample of legal aid practitioners from a range of firms in the North and West Yorkshire areas.[5]

---

[3] This transformation has been associated with other changes in the legal system, see Lacey, N., 'Government as Manager, Citizen as Consumer: The Case of the Criminal Justice Act 1991', *Modern Law Review*, 1994, vol. 57, p. 534, and has also been associated with the colonisation of large areas of the public sector by the notion of 'consumerism': Barron, A. and Scott, C., 'The Citizen's Charter Programme', *Modern Law Review*, 1992, vol. 55, p. 526.

[4] The best evidence for this is supplied by the research carried out between 1988 and 1992 by McConville and colleagues (McConville, M., Hodgson, J., Bridges, L., and Pavlovic, A., *Standing Accused*, Oxford: Clarendon Press, 1994).

[5] Structured interviews were conducted with 20 firms who were chosen because they represented a balance of the firms typified by McConville et al., *op. cit.*, pp. 18–20, as the 'classical' the 'managerial' and the 'political'. The bulk of the data relating to change is drawn from the 'classical' and 'political' firms, as they are the ones most affected by the impending changes.

The structure of the chapter is as follows: we begin by examining the tensions that exist within the classical paradigm of legal professionalism; we then analyse the way in which the Government's programme of legal aid reforms is restructuring the profession and its relationships with its clients. In conclusion, it is argued that this programme will produce a stratified and degraded system of justice.

II THE CLASSICAL PARADIGM OF LEGAL PROFESSIONALISM AND ITS EROSION

The classical paradigm[6] of legal professionalism was embodied in the notion that the professions occupied a niche above the class struggle as embodiments of civic morality. Their privileged position, expressed in the grant of self-regulation and financial rewards, was based on occupational monopoly. This was justified by the possession of specific characteristics, namely, a long and specialised training in an esoteric body of knowledge and a code of distinctive ethics, which then produced an autonomous practitioner devoted to the service of the community.

The Weberian critique[7] exposed important internal contradictions in this paradigm. For example, it was crucial to the legitimacy of the professional project that lawyers' ability to command high rewards in the market place and consequent high social status should be viewed as derived from free and fair competition and acknowledgement of merit. In reality, the profession both retained and adopted many aristocratic values and attributes,[8] and, as Larson has shown, was crucially dependent on state support. Her history of the professions demonstrates that they *won* autonomy; far from being independent of the class structure, the project was a middle-class one aimed at 'gaining status through work', which was achieved by obtaining 'state protection and state enforced penalties against unlicensed competitors ... producers of services whose training and entry into the market they had not controlled'.[9]

Thus, legal professionalism was in reality never wholly disengaged from the class struggle;[10] it was also a 'crucially important motif of governance in

---

[6] Articulated in functionalist 'trait theory', originally by Durkheim, E., *Professional Ethics and Civic Morals*, London: Routledge and Kegan Paul, 1957; more recently by Millerson, E., *The Qualifying Associations: a Study in Professionalism*, London: Routledge and Kegan Paul, 1964; and Barber, B., 'Some Problems in the Sociology of the Professions', *Daedalus*, 1963, vol. 92, no. 4, p. 669.

[7] Johnson, T. J., *Professions and Power*, London: Macmillan, 1972; Larson, M. S., *The Rise of Professionalism – A Sociological Analysis*, Berkeley: University of California Press, 1977, p. 220.

[8] Duman, D., 'The Creation and Diffusion of a Professional Ideology in Nineteenth Century England', *Journal of Social History*, 1979, vol. 27, pp. 113–38.

[9] Larson, *op. cit.*, pp. 5–14.

[10] Larson, *op. cit.*

capitalist societies'.[11] Furthermore, the political character of modern law is masked by its administration by 'an identifiable high status group who "objectively" apply recognised (seemingly universal) standards with no ulterior motive other than the determination and application of these standards in the public interest'.[12] Consequently, it could be argued that there was a correspondence between the flaws in the claims of the profession to a universal service ethic and the flaws in the claims of the law to be universally and equitably applicable.

However, the fact that the universalist claims of the system and the profession were flawed does not mean they should be dismissed out of hand. The successful capture of the privilege of professional autonomy through the idealisation and mystification of the profession's knowledge base and its ethical code allowed the professional a degree of independence in the justice system. This independence, in addition to its ideological significance, also created an ethical space within which it was and is possible to give that claimed independence and altruism some reality, and further acted as a guarantor for the ideology of justice and the rule of law. The legal profession has had a key role, both as gatekeeper to the justice system, and as mediator between public values and legal expression: 'Attorneys mediate between the established normative order guaranteed by the state, and diverse interests and developments in society.'[13]

It is therefore argued that for the rhetoric of impartiality to function as a form of legitimation at all, it was essential that, both for the profession and the justice system, it should have some substance: as Thompson argues,[14] it is from that very rhetoric that radical critique is often fashioned.[15] Consequently, the rhetoric or the classical 'ideal type' is significant in two ways: first, it represents a benchmark by which to identify historical change in the profession, so that while professional practice may by no means ever have conformed universally to the ideals of the service ethic, self-governance and technical expertise, the degree of approximation to these ideals and their distribution between different sectors, is a crucial means of plotting the trajectory of the professional project. Secondly, social action theorists like Weber remind us that ideologies and beliefs have significance, indeed a material reality, for actors, no matter how riven these ideologies are by internal contradiction. So, while the critics of trait

---

[11] Dhavan, R., 'Legal Education as Restrictive Practice: a Sceptical View', in Twining, W., Kibble, N. and Dhavan, R., *Access to Legal Education and the Legal Profession*, London: Butterworths, 1989, pp. 273, 277.

[12] *Ibid.*, at p. 297.

[13] Rueschemeyer, D., *Lawyers and Their Society: a Comparative Study of the Legal Profession in Germany and the United States*, Cambridge, Mass. : Harvard University Press, 1973, p. 173.

[14] Thompson, E.P., *Whigs and Hunters*, Harmondsworth: Penguin, 1977, pp. 264–5.

[15] After all, it is by its own standards that the system is found wanting by its critics.

theory may expose practices which challenge the realisation of professional ethics in professional practice, this does not undermine the claim of trait theory to have identified the value rationality[16] underlying professional practice. This value rationality also translates into individual practice through its development as an element of the disposition of individual practitioners, or what Bourdieu describes as their *habitus*.[17] The intimate form of the 'classical practice', and the central role in that practice of the autonomous solicitor, served to nurture that disposition.[18]

So while the idealisation of lawyers as professionals rather than as business people is the profession's business plan, and, as Freidson observed, rests on 'untried and untested propositions',[19] its success as a market strategy as well as a legitimating device, both required and allowed it to have some substance. However, the balance between rhetoric and reality is a very fine one, particularly between the claim to altruistic service and the pursuit of profit. As one interviewee remarked, 'It's always been a balancing act between being a professional and running a business'. Consequently the trajectory of the professional project is characterised by persistent debates over the compatibility of the professional and business ethic.[20]

The tension between profit and service has, over the past ten to 15 years, been most often rehearsed in the context of advertising, competition and the growth of corporate law firms. The germ of the conflict, however, lay within the classical practice as well, originating in the benefits obtained by a classical division of labour — as expounded here by the pioneer of the rationalisation of mental labour:

> The master manufacturer, by dividing the work to be executed into different processes, and requiring different degrees of skill or of force, can purchase exactly that precise quantity of both which is necessary for each process; whereas, if the whole work were executed by one workman, that person must possess sufficient skill to perform the most difficult, and sufficient strength

---

[16] See Weber, M., *The Theory of Social and Economic Organisation*, New York: The Free Press, 1964, p. 115.

[17] Bourdieu, P., *Outline of a Theory of Practice*, Cambridge: CUP, 1977, p. 80.

[18] As the description of the 'type' of the classical practice in the work of some of the sterner critics of criminal legal aid practice tends to confirm: McConville et al., *op. cit.*, p. 18.

[19] Freidson, E., *Profession of Medicine: A Study of the Sociology of Applied Knowledge*, New York: Dodd and Mead, 1970.

[20] For instance, see Napley, D., 'The Ethics of the Professions', *Law Society's Gazette*, 20 March 1985, vol. 82, p. 818; and Mungham, G. and Thomas, P., 'Solicitors and Clients: Altruism or Self-interest?', in Dingwall, R. and Lewis, P. (eds), *The Sociology of the Professions*, London: Macmillan, 1983.

to execute the most laborious, of the operations into which the work is divided.[21]

The claims of classical practices that clients were provided with continuous service were undermined by their use of unqualified clerks for the very work for which a monopoly was justified by reason of its complexity and its sole susceptibility to the technical expertise of professionals.[22] The other related problem with the classical paradigm was the fact that, until the advent of legal aid, the profession seldom concerned itself with those who did not have the means to compete in the market for their services. Generalised access to legal services was evidently limited until at least 1949.[23] Factors such as class, income and the cultural congruence between participants in the system also clearly modified the notion of universal service.

The increased availability of legal help consequent on legal aid did not, however, resolve these tensions. Instead, it may be seen as hastening the erosion of the professional paradigm. In particular, state funding lessened professional control over the character and organisation of their work, thereby impairing its unitary character, and represented a challenge to the direct relationship with the client. Post-war changes in socio-political culture generated other processes which dissolved these key aspects of the profession, partly because they put the rhetoric of the traditional paradigm to the test, and partly because the development of a direct relationship with the state raised the possibility of managerial control over the legal aid sector.[24] These changes included the near universalisation of legal services[25] and the opening up of education to more social groups, leading in turn to the erosion of old notions of status and deference and, correspondingly, to a new consumer conscious-ness.

For Johnson,[26] the profession's defining characteristic of control is achieved by the heterogeneity of the clientele *vis-à-vis* the homogeneity of the profession. However, with the establishment of legal aid, the heterogeneity of

---

[21] Babbage, C., *On the Economy of Machinery and Manufactures*, London: C. Knight, 1832, pp. 175–6.

[22] For instance, see Joseph, M., *The Conveyancing Fraud*, 2nd ed., Woolwich: Michael Joseph, 1989.

[23] See Goriely, T., 'Rushcliffe Fifty Years On: the Changing Role of Civil Legal Aid within the Welfare state', *Journal of Law and Society*, 1994, vol. 21, p. 545 and, by the same author, 'The Development of Criminal Legal Aid in England and Wales', at chapter 2 of this volume.

[24] Freidson, E., 'The Theory of Professions: State of the Art', in Dingwall and Lewis, *op. cit.*, n. 20 and Rueschemeyer, *op. cit.*, n. 13, date this challenge from the 1960s, but in fact the process has its origins in the immediate post-war period.

[25] Eligibility on income grounds covered 80% of the population when the Legal Aid Scheme was established in 1950: Legal Action Group, *A Strategy for Justice*, London: LAG, 1992, p. 4.

[26] *Op. cit.*

lawyers' clientele increased to an extent which resulted in competing views of the role of law[27] and threatened the homogeneity of the profession, in that it contributed to the emergence of a group of radical lawyers critical of the traditional professional model. At the same time, proximity with lawyers resulted in a decline in deference on the part of a large proportion of the new clientele.[28] According to Mungham and Thomas, 'the new clients have seen the profession at work and they are not pleased'.[29]

On the other hand, the fact was that for legal aid lawyers the real client was the state rather than the recipient of advice and assistance. The lower status and income of legal aid recipients meant, despite protestations to the contrary,[30] that they were considered by many practitioners to be less worthy of respect than the middle-class consumers who had previously constituted the overwhelming majority of solicitors' private clients. This became particularly clear in the emergent field of criminal law, which, prior to the development of legal aid, was not serviced by the legal profession other than on a voluntary basis. Even then, it was largely neglected until the decline in conveyancing work.[31] As it developed, it became stigmatised as dirty, low status work — a clear reflection of the connection between the status of the client and the lawyer.[32] Furthermore, the class basis of the legal profession and the shared legal culture with other sections of the criminal legal system challenged central aspects of the traditional paradigm such as neutrality, the integrity of the client/lawyer relationship, and the uniformity and individualisation of the service owed to the client.[33]

The decline in public esteem and the threat to paradigmatic unity was intensified by other developments. For instance, the illusion of practitioner independence was undermined by state funding, and finally stripped bare by the removal of the administration of legal aid from the Law Society with the Legal Aid Act 1988.[34] In their ideologically weakened state, legal aid lawyers made an obvious target when welfarism came under attack and demands were

---

[27] *Ibid.*

[28] Rueschemeyer, D., 'Professional Autonomy and the Social Control of Expertise' in Dingwall and Lewis, *op. cit.*, n. 20, p. 38 at p. 40.

[29] Mungham and Thomas, *op. cit.*, p. 131 at p. 132.

[30] For instance, Burton, A., 'The Demise of Criminal Legal Aid', *New Law Journal*, 1994, vol. 144, p. 1491.

[31] See Mungham and Thomas, *op. cit.*, pp. 140–41, on the origins of this decline in the 1970s housing slump, and the ending of scale fees (though clearly the removal of the conveyancing monopoly in the Administration of Justice Act 1985 was the point of no return).

[32] Portwood, D. and Fielding, A., 'Privilege and Professions', *Sociological Review*, 1981, vol. 29, p. 749; Galanter, M., 'Mega-Law and Mega-Lawyering in the Contemporary United States', in Dingwall and Lewis, *op. cit.*, p. 152.

[33] See McConville et al., *op. cit.*

[34] Legal Action Group, *op. cit.*, p. 11.

made for cuts in public spending. At the same time, the decline in status and the corresponding de-mystification of much of the lawyer's work and code of ethics generated academic and radical critiques. In his review of the profession's claim to self-control, Rueschemeyer notes that there are various alternative forms of control, one of which is the:

> case of a lack of effective control. Especially if the recipients of expert services are economically, socially and politically weak, we find both in history and in contemporary modern societies many instances where clients are protected neither by their own control resources — a strong market position or organisational means of control — nor by professional self-restraint nor by effective third-party interventions.[35]

Much of the literature on solicitors' criminal legal aid work illustrates just such an abuse of practitioner autonomy and a betrayal of the service ideal.[36] Thus a variety of factors have coalesced to produce a questioning of the basic tenets of the classical professional paradigm and, as a corollary, demands to control and regulate the legal aid practitioner's work. Hence, when the Legal Aid Act 1988 placed the administration of legal aid in the hands of a Legal Aid Board, it was determined that the profession's direct influence on the Board should be minimal. However, even this form of external control is now considered insufficient: the stance of the Green Paper[37] makes it evident that the monitoring of paperwork submitted by autonomous practitioners is now regarded by the Government as inadequate in kind as well as volume. There is a close parallel here with Braverman's discussion of the innovation that F. W. Taylor[38] made in developing the idea of management control from 'general control' to precise control over the labour process:

> Workers who are controlled only by general orders and discipline are not adequately controlled, because they retain their grip on the actual processes of labour. So long as they control the labour process itself they will thwart efforts to realise to the full the potential inherent in their labour power. To change this situation, control over the labour process must pass into the

---

[35] In Dingwall and Lewis, *op. cit.*, at p. 48.
[36] See, for instance, McConville et al., *op. cit.*; Sanders, A., Bridges, L., Mulvaney, A. and Crozier, G., *Advice and Assistance at Police Stations and the 24 Hour Duty Solicitor Scheme*, London: Lord Chancellor's Department, 1989; Bridges, L., 'Guilty Pleas and the Politics of Research', *Legal Action*, April 1993, p. 9 and Sanders, A., 'Access to Justice in the Police Station: An Elusive Dream?', at chapter 12 of this volume.
[37] *Op. cit.*
[38] Taylor, F. W., *The Principles of Scientific Management*, New York: Harper and Row, 1911.

hands of management, not only in the formal sense, but by the control and dictation of each step of the process, including its mode of performance.[39]

In the case of the legal profession, obtaining management control involves controlling the diagnostic relationship between practitioner and client, and a clarification of the indeterminate nature of legal skills. Professionalism as an ideology places great weight on the 'need for occupational and individual independence as a precondition of fulfilling obligations to the consumer', and this independence is related to the 'emphasis laid upon the diagnostic relationship . . . it is only in an *unfettered* person to person relationship with the consumer that expert diagnosis can take place and be successfully followed through' (emphasis added).[40] Larson argues that this relationship is supported by the distinctive claim of professionals to be exercising unique judgment in response to unique human experiences and problems, and that

typically, professions maintain indeterminate and untestable cognitive areas in order to assert collectively the uniqueness of individual capacities. Collectively, they solicit trust in individual professionals and individual freedom from external controls.[41]

The processes whereby managerial control is being introduced through franchising and block contract mechanisms, ostensibly concerned with 'quality of service', will be explored below.

The opening out of the legal profession has also been accompanied by a decrease in the possibility of realising the ideal of the classical profession, that of the free, self-employed practitioner.[42] This development must be attributed both to the increased numbers entering the profession and to the lower income status of many of these new practitioners. Other factors include the decline of traditional sources of income, and technological developments which have increased the capital costs of establishing a practice. The decline of the 'mastership' ideal is again a result and symbol of the decline in the lawyer's status; the emergence of a trend towards bigger firms with solicitors as employees, and the establishment of mechanised, routinised working patterns relate to both the proletarianisation of the practitioner and the degradation of

[39] Braverman, H., *Labour and Monopoly Capital*, New York: Monthly Review Press, 1976, p. 100.
[40] Johnson, *op. cit.*, p. 57.
[41] Larson, *op. cit.*, p. 41.
[42] Although the number of sole practitioners is still increasing (Law Society, *Annual Statistical Report*, London: Law Society, 1994, p. 4), the consensus of this author's sample was that sole practices were becoming harder to set up and sustain. See also Devonald, D., 'An Endangered Species', *The Gazette*, 29 June 1994, vol. 91, no.25, p. 2.

their skills. McConville et al.'s work[43] reveals the extent to which these managerial style practices depart from the ideal of individualised, handcrafted service proposed by 'leaders' of the profession[44] and frequently produce instead a poor, discontinuous service.

A further effect of the expansion in legal services, coinciding with the expansion in higher education in the 1960s, was to weaken the mechanisms of social closure. Johnson's description of a profession as a 'gentleman's club' which disguised its ties to power structures, exemplified both the traditional class background of lawyers and the subtle nature of their links with powerful elites. These did indeed enable them to operate as a club without the necessity of clear rules which outsiders would have required. Thus the so-called distinctive code of ethics was largely characterised by an indeterminacy similar to that claimed in practitioners' working practices and was rooted more in the concept of gentlemanly conduct than in precise rules. As a result, Napley was able to comment with approbation in 1977 that the middle classes were the backbone of the profession for recruitment purposes.[45] The social solidity and cohesion of the profession was a major component in its justification of self-regulation. Thus, according to Lord Hailsham in 1971:

> In order to protect the public from the charlatan or the quack, entry into the profession must be guarded, its standards policed and its rules of practice defined in the first instance by the profession itself.... The ground rules of completion [qualification] are designed for the interests of the public and not for the interests of the profession alone.[46]

Lastly, many of the changes discussed above have found expression in the new approach to solicitors' training. Larson[47] noted the relationship between elite status and knowledge of the whole field. This omnicompetence endows all practitioners with semi-charismatic authority, as they are set apart by their total grasp of an esoteric body of knowledge which allows them to perform the role described by Cain as 'conceptive ideologist'.[48] Such a role and the expertise on which it is based relates in turn to the claim to indeterminacy.[49]

---

[43] *Op. cit.*
[44] For example, Napley, D., *The Technique of Persuasion*, London: Sweet and Maxwell, 1975.
[45] Cited in Mungham and Thomas, *op. cit.*, p. 151.
[46] Quoted by Mungham and Thomas, *op. cit.*, p. 135.
[47] Larson, *op. cit.*, p. 231.
[48] Cain, M., 'The General Practice Lawyer and the Client: Towards a Radical Conception', in Dingwall and Lewis, *op. cit.*, p. 106.
[49] Jamous, H. and Peloille, B., 'Professions or Self-Perpetuating Systems? Changes in the French University-hospital System', in Jackson, J. A., (ed.), *Professions and Professionalisation*, Cambridge: CUP, 1970, p. 111.

Practitioners' monopoly of knowledge gives them a unique status as mediators between the law and everyday experience, and this in turn requires them alone to determine the length of time needed to deal with each individual problem. As Larson notes: 'The secrecy and mystery which surround the creative process maximise the self-governance conceded to experts.'[50] Furthermore, such processes are portrayed as utterly detached from social and political considerations; the law is concerned with universal, transcendent, neutral values. This perspective is the basis for education in black letter law and the corresponding approach which characterised the traditional vocational solicitors' training. The replacement of the latter by the skills-based Legal Practice Course in 1993 forms part of the transformation of the 'lawyer as priest' into the 'lawyer as technician', and is part of the wider processes alluded to above which are contributing to the managerialisation of lawyers' practices.

The rifts in the structure of the profession have been plain to see for some time. The typification developed by McConville et al.[51] is of analytical use here. 'Classical' solicitor-centred practices adhere to the ideology, if not always the practice, of continuous service, such that qualified lawyers are 'deeply involved in every aspect of the case', deal 'with clients personally' and know 'their lives as well as their cases intimately'.[52] The 'managerial' firm bears the characteristics already discussed, principally routinisation and the heavy use of unqualified staff, and represents a threat to the classical model of firm in terms of its potential to monopolise business, particularly as the bias of current proposals for funding legal aid is towards such firms.[53] The 'political' firm opposes managerialism on the grounds of its effect on 'client-centredness', and associates 'quality' with commitment to clients rather than procedures.[54]

In addition to these divisions, the rapid increase in entry to the profession has introduced participants — women, ethnic minority solicitors and upwardly mobile males — who do not fit the classic model of the 'gentleman professional', and whose generally limited opportunities for progression indicate the prospect of a segmented and stratified profession.[55] The fault lines engendered by this process of change are demonstrated by the 1995 presidential elections for the Law Society, won by a candidate whose programme included retrenching professional authority by restricting entry and who was widely

---

[50] Larson, *op. cit.*, p. 235.
[51] *Op. cit.*
[52] *Ibid.*, p. 18.
[53] See Smith, R., 'Survival of the Biggest', *Legal Aid News*, August 1994, p. 9.
[54] McConville et al., *op. cit.*, p. 20. See also Bridges, L., 'The Reform of Criminal Legal Aid', at chapter 13 of this volume.
[55] Sommerlad, H., 'The Myth of Feminisation: Women and Cultural Change in the Legal Profession', *International Journal of the Legal Profession*, 1994, vol. 1, p. 31.

perceived as the candidate opposed to managerialism and the interventionist stance of the Lord Chancellor's Department.[56] The novelty of a contested election, combined with the fact that the candidate backed by the Law Society was defeated, provides a metaphor for the paradigmatic crisis engulfing the profession.

III   THE IMPACT OF THE NEW MANAGERIALISM UPON PROFESSIONAL AUTONOMY

Practitioner autonomy was portrayed above as the founding characteristic of the traditional legal paradigm. Flowing from it is the notion of impartiality, which in turn confers the role of social mediator. In practical terms it is expressed in the solicitor's self-employed status, which results in the freedom to engage in adversarial contest with the state on behalf of the client. It also permits complete control over professional time, so that it is possible to deliver the service individually tailored to the client which is required in the interests of justice. Thus Johnson has argued that professionalism as an ideology places great weight on the 'need for occupational and individual independence as a precondition of fulfilling [its] obligations'.[57] That, in brief, was the value rationality of the profession's claim to independence and self-regulation which, in turn, helped legitimate the legal system. Standard fees, franchising and the Green Paper proposals cast doubt on its continued viability: in the words of an interviewee, 'the idea behind franchising is that solicitors can't be trusted, so they must be monitored — it undermines the profession'.[58]

It is important to emphasise that the immediate importance of these initiatives is ideological. It could convincingly be argued that the practical impact may be minimal, and that if the changes were so drastic, opposition to them would be more widespread.[59] The responses from this author's interviews indicated that practitioners were aware of the practical implications of government policy, but felt resigned to the inexorability of the change, particularly as the rhetoric of 'quality' rendered opposition difficult. As one sole practitioner specialising in criminal legal aid work put it:

---

[56] The impact of the Lord Chancellor's policies on legal aid are explored below.

[57] *Op. cit.*, p. 57.

[58] A practitioner, late-30s, working in a small town for a medium-sized, traditional firm with a good reputation for service to clients (interview 11).

[59] Discussions at a recent conference on legal aid appeared to demonstrate little division of opinion between franchise holders and non-franchise holders, and there was support for a 'sensible block contract system', provided there was a method 'for judging the quality of the work that solicitors did': 'A Climate of Change', *The Gazette*, 28 June 1995, vol. 92, no. 25, p. 17.

Why did I apply for a franchise? What choice did I have? I wanted to get in at the ground floor ... at the moment it's voluntary, but it will certainly become exclusive ... which is of course the point of the Green Paper.[60]

Franchising has been described in the following way: 'it sets up a "preferred supplier" relationship with firms of solicitors and other legal service providers in which the quality of work carried out is assured to the clients.'[61] The franchise researchers acknowledge that it represents an attack on self-regulation, but justify this through the link with quality:

The LAB's [Legal Aid Board] new franchising scheme ... has management of costs as a concern, but the professional aim is broader; it is to ensure a 'value for money' service through the accreditation of Legal Aid practices that meet standards for quality. This presages systematic and routine scrutiny of the quality of lawyers' work and legal organisations on a scale not seen before. Franchising may represent an entirely new conceptualisation of legal service delivery which is a hybrid of public service and private practice models.[62]

At first sight, the franchising scheme appears to represent an interesting anomaly in the New Right's agenda of privatisation, in that a sector which was private (despite its receipt of public funds) is now to be subject to central, if disguised, control. However, the scheme is characterised by what Stewart and Walsh have identified as the main features of the New Right's approach to the management of public services. These include the imposition of contractual or semi-contractual relations and their control through external regulation and inspection (the key notion being audit rather than accountability); a disengagement of the management and political processes; the transformation of the client into a customer and the creation of a market or quasi-market which, in turn, supports the notion of customer control.[63]

In reality, the loss of practitioner control signalled by these mechanisms directly relates to increased state control; the supposed purchaser of services, the client, is in fact represented by the principal stakeholder in franchising agreements, namely the Legal Aid Board, which in turn works within

[60] Sole practitioner in his 50s specialising in criminal legal aid (interview 4).
[61] Sherr, A., Moorhead, R. and Paterson, A., 'Transaction Criteria: Back to the Future', *Legal Action*, April 1993, p. 7.
[62] Sherr, A., Moorhead, R. and Paterson, A., 'Assessing the Quality of Legal Work: Measuring Process', *International Journal of the Legal Profession*, 1994, vol. 1, no. 2, p. 135.
[63] Stewart, G. and Walsh, K., 'Change in the Management of Public Services', *Public Administration*, 1992, vol. 70, p. 499.

parameters laid down by the Government.[64] Furthermore, given clients' generally partial knowledge, heterogeneity and individualisation,[65] the idea of consumer control remains illusory, and, as is argued by one practitioner, 'the customer with choice is the state not the client'.[66] Indeed client choice will be drastically reduced by the decrease in 'suppliers' of legal aid. In any event, the clients themselves are objects rather than subjects; they are the product. This is a point made clear by one of the prophets of the new managerialism. Dirks advises practitioners, in his manual *Making Legal Aid Pay*, that 'Efficiency and effective costing can best be judged by the number of clients that the firm can produce in the working day'.[67]

In his work on commercial franchises, Felstead argues that 'franchisees occupy a position best described as "controlled self-employment"' and that 'despite being formally autonomous, franchisees are bound to franchisors by a number of contractual clauses'.[68] In support of this analysis he cites various operational controls commonly found in franchise contracts: stress on uniformity of product so that the promise of quality inherent in the trademark retains credibility in a mass market; the ability of the franchisor unilaterally to modify the contract; and provisions for regular monitoring of the franchisee.[69] Similarly, Fuller and Smith's study of management techniques designed to achieve quality in service and retail industries shows the way in which allegedly autonomous worker participation schemes tend to mask rigid forms of management control:

> Employers have continued to seek ways to circumscribe or limit the autonomy of interactive service workers that borrow heavily from and extend traditional management paradigms ... based on 'low trust' relations.[70]

These analyses appear pertinent to the situation that legal aid lawyers will find themselves in under the block contract arrangement, and Felstead's description is apposite to the situation of the franchised supplier. As one practitioner put it,

---

[64] A recent President of the Law Society claimed that the Legal Aid Board's (LAB) 'much vaunted independence from the Government was a myth'. Quoted in Gilvarry, E., 'Elly hits out at franchise chaos', *The Gazette*, 27 April 1994, vol. 91, no. 16, p. 8.

[65] Johnson, *op. cit.*, p. 53.

[66] Montague, B., 'It's Legal Aid, Jim, but not as we know it', *Solicitors Journal*, 26 May 1995, vol. 139, p. 494.

[67] Dirks, J., *Making Legal Aid Pay*, London: Sweet & Maxwell, 1994, p. 5.

[68] Felstead, A., 'The Social Organisation of the Franchise: a Case of Controlled Self-Employment', *Journal of Work, Employment and Society*, 1991, vol. 5, p. 37 at p. 39.

[69] *Ibid.*, pp. 44–5.

[70] Fuller, L. and Smith, V., 'Consumers' Reports: Management by Customers in a Changing Economy', *Journal of Work, Employment and Society*, 1991, vol. 5, p. 1 at p. 14.

'if your firm is franchised they then have all the power and you're an agency rather than an independent firm'.[71]

The mechanism of external control and audit of files based on externally imposed systems has already been noted as widely characteristic of public sector reform. While the appearance of independence is maintained through the contractual mechanism, practitioner autonomy will be eroded in a variety of ways.

On the one hand, both franchising and the proposals for contracting will achieve, for the state, authority without responsibility. The state will be able to set budgets and determine priorities, yet it is the practitioner who, as an agent of the state with responsibility without authority, must adhere to and implement such decisions. Hence rationing decisions can be presented, not as the responsibility of the state, but as the product of either technical judgments, or the consequence of poor resource management at the level of delegated responsibility. A franchised practitioner has therefore expressed the following concerns about the relationship which will be established by the Green Paper proposals:

> ... spending limits and overall priorities will be imposed by government ... However it is the solicitors and advice agencies who will have the responsibility for determining at the level of the individual case, within the strict requirements of their block contracts, who will be helped. ... In making such decisions the solicitor will act not on behalf of the client but as an agent of the Board.[72]

In this process, the Lord Chancellor's Department will be endeavouring to destroy the notion that there will be any link between the level of central resources and local decisions.[73] Consequently, the individual practitioners or practices, while apparently maintaining autonomy, will be obliged to translate the calculative rationality which lies behind a cash-limited rationing system into their own relationships with clients.

This calculative rationality is based on a cost-benefit model, though with a particular asymmetrical emphasis. As with most applications of the model to areas of social policy, the costs are easy to identify, while the benefits, the 'quality' element in the contracting and monitoring process, are problematic, and are generally articulated only in terms of the easily measurable, such as the

---

[71] Partner in traditional small-town practice in his early 40s (interview 6).

[72] Montague, *op. cit.*, p. 494.

[73] One commentator described the Lord Chancellor's attempts to square this circle at the 1995 Legal Aid Conference as 'a cash limited scheme, where the money never ran out': Hayes, J., 'A Climate of Change', *The Gazette*, 28 June 1995, vol. 92, no. 25, p. 17.

procedural mechanisms used for file management. The result will be that practitioners will find it hard to justify to themselves or to the Board benefits which are not directly observable, while being forced to confront the issue of cost on a continual basis throughout the progression of any case. As one practitioner argued about the impact of standard fees:

> Financially, you can't take individual actions for clients any more — you must deal with them in a mechanised way. For example, you can't write lots of letters designed for a particular person because of a guilty plea because you're going to get the £140 fee whatever you do. The theory is that you can jump to the higher band but that's set at such a higher level that you don't get there easily ... if it's what appears to an outsider as a reasonably simple case even though of devastating consequence to the client, it will be held that form of client care is unjustified.[74]

In this way, autonomy is also undermined by covert means. Given that it is proposed, for instance, that 'contracts would encourage suppliers to consider the most effective, efficient and economical ways of resolving problems' and that 'compliance with the contract terms would be determined primarily by monitoring and auditing',[75] the ability of practitioners to choose whether or not to process clients in the way urged by those in favour of the new managerialism will be severely curtailed. In fact, franchising has already established a relationship of precise control between the state and the lawyer because the pressure to conform will be economically irresistible. That this outcome is possible is acknowledged by the franchise researchers. Thus one of the new powers that franchisees will obtain, which apparently contradicts the argument that they are losing autonomy, is the power to grant some forms of legal aid. However, this power is to be subjected to monitoring to ensure that 'the franchisee's decision-making is of a similar "standard" to the Board's ... The danger is that the lawyer is encouraged to be conservative on the legal aid applications ...'.[76] This likelihood is increased by the fact that if too many grants are subsequently vetoed by the Board, the lawyers's franchise may be endangered.

The covert destruction of autonomy is also achieved by the monitoring of firms' unit costs; thus, 'If average costs per case are higher than other firms in the area then an explanation will be sought from the firm'.[77] Again, it is

---

[74] Former partner in a 'political' practice, in mid-40s, now an associate in a small to medium-sized 'classical' practice in the process of transition to managerialism (interview 2).

[75] Lord Chancellor's Department, *op. cit.*, pp. 25–6.

[76] Sherr et al., *op. cit.* (1994), p. 138.

[77] *Ibid.*

acknowledged that this could be problematic: 'The concern must be that this is used as a means to drive down expenditure on cases at the expense of quality ... a desire to push firms towards a specific level of average costs could push down quality.'[78] However, having identified this as a problem, the franchise researchers fail to provide a solution, and there therefore remains a scenario of instrumentalism by stealth, through a persistent downward push on the freedom to provide individualised, quality service. Consequently, one practitioner has noted that aspects of the franchising criteria erode

the discretion which solicitors should retain about the way that they deal with their clients ... what emerges is the worrying possibility that an inflexible system is being created which will restrict more ambitious practices without ensuring that overall standards will rise.[79]

The most controversial device by which practitioner discretion will be restricted is through the transaction criteria. These 'set out in a checklist form the essential points of information, advice and action which would be expected to be evidenced on a file',[80] and purport to assess the quality of practitioners' advice and assistance to clients. The difficulties of producing an accurate and effective measure of the indeterminate core of the professional's work is acknowledged by the franchise researchers: 'the quality standard defined by transaction criteria is fundamentally limited to processes observable from a file by assessors confined to utilise minimum discretion through the checklist mechanism'.[81] There was consensus too amongst interviewees that the criteria were incapable of truly measuring quality; for instance:

some firms who will comply with standard transaction criteria may still give poor advice, fail to communicate to clients a clear understanding of the situation and be terrible at representing them in court — but they will have the appearance of offering quality service.[82]

But despite their limited power to assess the worth of practitioners' work, the transaction criteria are likely to contribute to the pressure on firms to routinise and standardise their work. For Smith they appear to have been drafted with the aim of reducing 'professional discretion to a minimum in the

---

[78] *Ibid.*
[79] Harman, S., 'Franchising: the preliminary audit experience', *Legal Action*, January 1994, p. 9 at p. 10.
[80] Sherr et al., *op. cit.* (1994), p. 145.
[81] *Ibid.*, p. 155.
[82] Interview 4, see n. 60.

search for objective standards',[83] while an applicant for a legal aid franchise expresses anxiety that

> insistence on complying with rigidly interpreted criteria, coupled with the aim to control case costs, is likely to limit practitioners' ability to spend time on dealing creatively and appropriately with complex cases. This standardisation will inevitably result in us losing power and professional discretion about the best way to deal with our individual clients.[84]

It must be stressed again, of course, that loss of practitioner autonomy is already a growing feature of the profession as an increasing number of solicitors have an employed rather than self-employed status. The control over their labour process by such solicitors is therefore already circumscribed. This is especially so in the new managerial-style firms where the approach tends to be that documented by McConville et al.[85] and advocated by one of the protagonists of the industrialisation of legal practice in the following way: 'what is required are the management methods which reduce the time taken to complete the client file'.[86]

This latter tendency is further accelerated by the growing numbers of practice amalgamations which are taking place in response to the exposure to market forces. Thus one interviewee explained that the small general practice of which he was a partner had recently merged with a bigger firm in a neighbouring town 'for commercial reasons; we needed to be bigger, to make economies of scale, to have more specialists'. Despite being an equity partner he had clearly lost a great deal of autonomy, and regretted this:

> . . . in the old days I just sat here, worked hard and billed out . . . I would do anything that came through the door . . . but there's a definite way of working in big firms which tends to ignore the needs of individuals. Everything is geared up to maximising profits . . . the clients are reduced to being widgets . . . and it's all about time sheets and targets.[87]

It is clear that the concentration of firms will be further hastened by the franchising and contracting initiatives, despite the Green Paper's assertion that there 'is no reason why smaller organisations and sole practitioners should not

---

[83] Smith, R., 'Transaction Criteria: the Face of the Future', *Legal Action*, February 1993, p. 11.
[84] Harman, *op. cit.*
[85] *Op. cit.*
[86] Dirks, J., *Making Legal Aid Pay*, London: Waterlow, 1989, p. 83.
[87] Equity partner from a small-town practice, in his 50s (interview 14).

be able to obtain contracts as well as larger firms'.[88] As one interviewee observed, 'franchising and the Green Paper proposals are designed for the larger firms — because they're all about mass production and specialisation';[89] and in the words of a general practitioner from a 'political' practice, 'the firms who will get the contracts will clearly get them on the basis of cost — that is if they can do the work cheaply, and you can only do that if you cut corners — have a sausage machine approach'.[90]

It is evident that integral to the loss of autonomy is the development of a refined division of labour. As a respondent from another 'political' firm observed, 'we're beginning to recognise that you can only make money out of legal aid by having central control over work, and through specialisation and deskilling people'.[91] The necessity for specialisation was recognised by the overwhelming majority of the respondents, from all varieties of firm. It might be thought that the process of specialisation would, if anything, increase the level of, and premium on, expertise. Instead, it appears that specialisation is seen as a necessary precursor to routinisation and 'speed-up', rather than in terms of the development of expertise.

It needs to be acknowledged, of course, that the competitive pressures in non-legal aid practice are producing similar results, with similar reservations about quality.[92] However, there are serious implications in the routinisation of criminal legal aid work and the standardisation, for example, of the 'guilty plea', as has been graphically demonstrated by the work of McConville et al.[93] The tendency in the stratified system of working outlined above is that the pricing is seen to determine the character of the work — it will become routine because of the standard fee applied, not because of the circumstances of the individual case. This was seen as an already developing trend by several of the criminal legal aid specialists, referring, of course, to other practices — generally the larger ones. Most respondents, however, acknowledged that there was a danger that any practitioner could be driven to the same conclusion:

Lawyers are learning to use standard fees system and do very little for it. Because in fact £140 for a guilty plea — if you can do it all in one hearing

---

[88] Lord Chancellor's Department, *op. cit.*, p. ix.
[89] Sole practitioner, in his 50s (interview 3): a point echoed by several of the respondents.
[90] An associate (in his late 40s) in a two-partner general practice in a small town (interview 1).
[91] Associate in her late 30s (interview 8).
[92] Consider, for example, the views of this 'traditional' sole practitioner, working largely in non-contentious commercial work: 'The whole set-up today knocks all the law and expertise out of it, we're just reduced to filling in standard forms, fitting work into compartments – like products in a box. But this approach can't cope with complexities – for instance standard forms and precedents don't cover private tenants' water rights. . . On basic work I do, I run it like a production line' (interview 7).
[93] *Op. cit.*, see, in particular, at p. 210.

— then it's quite profitable. So I see lawyers having quick discussions with their clients in court — on the hard chairs — instead of lengthy discussions in the office.[94]

Another acute difficulty raised by the specialised division of labour encouraged by the legal aid reforms concerns the discontinuity of service in a context where continuity is crucial. For instance, the transaction criteria on case preparation in magistrates' courts assume that this work will generally be done by personnel other than those who will conduct the advocacy. Yet as a Law Centre employment specialist argued, 'only the litigator can really see the whole problem ... I am therefore very concerned by the prospect of Citizens' Advice Bureaux giving out initial advice and assistance; it should be the litigator who gives advice at the start of the case, and throughout'.[95] This is supported by McConville et al.'s emphasis on the deleterious effects of discontinuous service, and in particular of the delegation to non-solicitor staff of the preliminary tasks of criminal legal aid, especially assisting suspects in police stations, which they argue 'requires ... the skills of an experienced criminal defence solicitor'.[96]

Let us be clear about the significance of this discussion in terms of access to justice. The loss of professional autonomy implicit in franchising, standard fees, block contracts, and other legal aid reforms will promote and entrench deskilling, discontinuous service and a mechanised approach whereby the client will be processed rather than represented. Adversarialism, involving the testing of the prosecution case and the construction of a defence to throw reasonable doubt upon that case, will become something to which only the wealthy have access.

IV CONCLUSION

In this chapter it has been argued that the decline in professional autonomy is leading to the development of what many interviewees described as 'sausage machine practices', thus legitimating a restricted form of access to justice for poorer clients. The changes will cause legal professionalism to depart from the ideals of altruistic service and the promotion of access to justice which have helped to underpin the rule of law.

The sociological literature on the legal profession clearly indicates the absurdity of the notion that there ever was a 'golden age' when universalist ideas of service and access to justice governed the day-to-day practice of all

---

[94] Interview 2 (see n. 74).
[95] Interview 21.
[96] *Op. cit.*, p. 287.

solicitors. However, this author does argue that these universalist notions have been of crucial importance in maintaining some of the forms and practices which have helped to give them substance, for example practitioner independence and the notions of equality and individuation of service. It is also argued that while the replacement of the classical paradigm by one imbued with the ethic of scientific managerialism is formulated in a neutral discourse of improved working systems and client choice, in reality it is predicated on a proletarianisation of the producer and a degradation of the product.

The franchising enterprise rests on the notion of differentiated pricing for differentiated qualities of service.[97] Thus Sherr et al. argue that 'legal services may be provided along a continuum of levels',[98] in support of which they quote Garth: 'Poverty lawyers must practise a kind of law that emphasises "mass delivery" and maximum impact of legal services instead of uniform, high quality "mega-lawyering" along corporate lines.'[99] Such differentiation stems from and contributes to the Conservative Government's reconstitution of citizenship and hence of the nation. We are now witnessing the implementation of Thatcher's famous denial of the existence of society and the reconstruction of the nation in terms of 'legal individualism based on economic rights, contract and legal remedies'.[100] Such a conceptualisation represents an overthrow of the inclusionary and egalitarian vision which informed both the rhetoric and some of the practice of welfarism and the delivery of legally-aided services, and replaces it with a variable notion of citizenship based on variable entitlements.

This reconfiguration of citizenship, while presented in the discourse of social empowerment, is in fact selective; although its discourse of rights is characterised by an absence of socio-economic context, in fact the socio-economic status of the citizen is of overriding significance. Thus, although legal aid clients will continue to include those excluded from other aspects of citizenship (such as the homeless), and although the discourse of the legal aid programme of reform is formally inclusive and empowering, in reality the politics of exclusion and disempowerment are its foundation. It will serve to create, through a transformation of the profession, a stratified system of justice which will restrict access and downgrade the level of service in the multiple ways explored above.

---

[97] Sherr et al., *op. cit.* (1994).
[98] Sherr et al., *op. cit.* (1994), p. 141.
[99] *Ibid.*
[100] Cooper, D., 'The Citizen's Charter and Radical Democracy', *Social and Legal Studies*, 1993, vol. 2, p. 150.

15

Alternatives to Prosecution: Access to, or Exits from, Criminal Justice?

Adam Crawford

I INTRODUCTION

In order to situate the present debates on criminal legal aid within a wider context of access to justice, this chapter will outline and assess the growing 'alternatives' to criminal prosecution in England and Wales, their use and potential. It begins by mapping out the various 'alternatives' available, their possibilities and limitations and the manner in which they connect with wider policy debates. It goes on to consider the involvement of lawyers in diversionary schemes and their implications for legally-aided services. The premise of this chapter is that law as a social system is shaped by 'institutional supply' rather than demand: by, the infrastructure of legal services, the nature of the procedural framework, the costs and availability of legal aid, the ease with which the courts work, the existence of inducements to avoid litigation and the availability of accessible 'alternatives'. Thus the greater availability of 'alternatives' to prosecution will impact directly — although in complex and sometimes unpredictable ways — upon the administration and delivery of criminal legal aid and legal representation.

Given this complex interrelationship between 'alternatives' and the formal criminal justice process, this chapter will question the extent to which diversionary initiatives can realistically guarantee the voluntariness, agency and voice to the parties, which is central to their normative appeal and value. The extent to which they involve an abandonment, or a dilution, of the procedural protections of the formal criminal prosecution process is evaluated. Against this background it will be argued that the increasing 'managerialism' within the criminal justice system which prioritises efficiency, effectiveness, economy and the smooth management of increasing case-loads, has contradictory effects upon our conceptualisation of justice. Diversion schemes, while offering opportunities for 'alternative' and normatively driven (often reparative) conceptions of justice, also deny and delimit such considerations, in so far as they reflect and are forced to prioritise an administrative and managerialist ethic.

II DIVERSION FROM CRIMINAL PROSECUTION: THE 'ALTERNATIVES'[1]

There exists a variety of avenues open to the police and/or Crown Prosecution Service (CPS) which may impact upon, or result in, criminal litigation avoidance. Taken together, these developments constitute what one commentator has called 'a practice in search of a theory',[2] rather than a series of well-formulated and coherently implemented policies. This combined 'movement' has found support from diverse interests with often conflicting motivations. Forms of 'alternative dispute resolution' (ADR) and diversion have met with enthusiasm from different quarters — both within professional and community groups and across the political spectrum[3] — in the various beliefs that they will reduce the stigma and labelling of (particularly young) offenders; increase justice; cut court costs and delays to the parties and to the Government; cut court workloads; reduce the complexity and formality of the law for the parties, thus encouraging their participation and involvement; ensure 'better' (longer-lasting) settlements of disputes and reduce reoffending rates; and encourage a more socially constructive approach to disputing. The present Government has joined in the currently fashionable calls for the realisation of more 'alternative' means of resolving disputes outside of the

---

[1] It should become clear to the reader that it is not assumed here that diversion schemes necessarily divert or constitute real alternatives, i.e., that they only involve populations destined for prosecution rather than drawing in new populations. Although the exact proportions of those not genuinely diverted are difficult to estimate, Klein's seminal warning should be heeded: 'diversion means to turn away from and one cannot turn someone away from something to which he was not already heading' (Klein, M.W., 'Deinstitutionalization and Diversion of Juvenile Offenders: A Litany of Impediments', in Morris, N. and Tonry, M. (eds), *Crime and Justice: An Annual Review of Research*, Chicago: University of Chicago, 1979, vol. 1, p. 145 at p. 153).

[2] Matthews, R., *Informal Justice?*, London: Sage, 1988, p. 2.

[3] This growing interest in 'alternatives' to court-based processing of cases is not something that is to be found only within the Government but is shared by all established political parties. The Labour Party, in February 1995, published its own proposals for improving the justice system, in which 'promoting alternative dispute resolution' is seen as a fundamental means of meeting the twin demands of the spiralling cost of legal aid and access to justice: see Labour Party, *Access to Justice: A Consultation Paper on Labour's Proposals for Improving the Justice System*, London: Labour Party, 1995.

courts. In the recently published Green Paper on Legal Aid,[4] the Government's stated aim of improving access to justice is to be met, in part, by encouraging ADR which avoids the use of lawyers and courts.

The diversion of (potential) offenders from the criminal justice system before reaching the court can take place at various stages in the process and at different levels of (in)formality. At one extreme stands a decision by the police to drop a case by taking 'no further action'. Given the nature of discretion within the police, this may take place in the informal setting of the street or the home, where an incident has occurred, at the instigation of an individual officer or more formally, in consultation with colleagues in the police station or other relevant agencies. The police may prefer to 'move a suspect on', to 'turn a blind eye', or they may not define an event as sufficiently serious or noteworthy to warrant their time and effort to pursue the matter further.[5] Research suggests that 'no further action' is used in two principal ways: first, where there is an impediment or obstacle to further prosecution and the police are unable to proceed; and, secondly, as a disposal in its own right where the police choose not to proceed.[6]

As 'informal' and discretionary measures have become increasingly formalised and extended, we can now identify a number of specified forms of action which lie between 'no further action' and prosecution through the criminal courts. These include:

(a) an 'informal' warning or caution, administered by the police;

(b) a 'formal' — in that it is recorded — police caution at the discretion of the police or on referral from the CPS;

(c) related to (b) although slightly different in its impact upon the offender, the use of 'caution plus' schemes, whereby conditions are attached to the issuing and acceptance of a formal caution;

(d) the use of mediation and reparation services, which may or may not be part of a 'caution plus' scheme; and

(e) finally, the use (and potential) of fixed fines.

---

[4] Lord Chancellor's Department, *Legal Aid – Targeting Need: The future of publicly funded help in solving legal problems and disputes in England and Wales*, Cm 2854, London: HMSO, 1995, paras 1.1 and 1.5.
[5] See Skolnick, J., *Justice Without Trial*, New York: Wiley, 1966; Smith, D. A. and Visher, C. A., 'Street-Level Justice: Situational Determinants of Police Arrest Decisions', *Social Problems*, 1981, vol. 29, p. 2; and Kemp, C., Norris, C. and Fielding, N., *Negotiating Nothing: Police Disputes and the Law*, Aldershot: Avebury, 1992.
[6] Wilkinson, C. and Evans, R., 'Police Cautioning of Juveniles: The Impact of Home Office Circular 14/1985', *Criminal Law Review*, 1990, pp. 165, 168.

Alternatives to Prosecution: Access to, or Exits from, Criminal Justice?

(i) Cautioning

The power to caution is not to be found in legislation, neither is there currently any legislative framework regulating the practice of cautioning, although the recent Royal Commission recommended that a statutory framework governing cautioning should be established.[7] In theory the police make the decision to caution an offender in accordance with Home Office guidelines. The police have always had the discretion to caution rather than to prosecute suspects, but the practice has become increasingly formalised over recent years. The central difference between an informal and a formal caution is that an informal caution should not be recorded as a caution in the criminal statistics, neither may it be cited in subsequent court proceedings.

The very process of identifying and classifying informal cautions has brought about their formalisation, to the extent that we can now talk about 'genuinely informal' cautions as distinct from 'formal informal' cautions. The former occur at the pre-report stage when no formal part of the prosecution process has begun, while the latter occur after a suspect has been reported.[8] The latest Home Office guidance has sought to reverse its earlier attempt to formalise informal cautions through the establishment of criteria which differentiate them,[9] declaring this earlier advice to be 'confusing and not to be recommended'.[10] Yet the practice is likely to continue.

Encouraged by Home Office circulars 14/1985 and 59/1990, and in accordance with developments elsewhere in criminal justice,[11] increasing emphasis has been placed upon diversionary decisions being made in liaison with other relevant organisations — notably juvenile justice workers — often with competing ideologies, policies and practices.[12] Consultation arrangements frequently take the form of multi-agency panels or bureaux, the use and practice of which remain considerably variable. In juvenile matters some panels have sought to influence not only individual cases, but also broader cautioning policies. More exceptional and successful examples have been able to 'in effect

---

[7] Royal Commission on Criminal Justice, *Report*, Cm 2263, London: HMSO, 1993.
[8] Wilkinson and Evans, *op. cit.*, pp. 167–8.
[9] Home Office guidance had previously defined the conditions for an informal caution as the same as for a formal caution, but in circumstances where 'a formal caution is considered inappropriate' (Home Office, *Circular 59/1990*, Annex C, para. 3). The guidance went on to suggest that informal cautions did not require the same criteria for administration as those set out in the National Standards for (formal) cautioning.
[10] Home Office, *Circular 18/1994*, para. 13.
[11] Crawford, A. and Jones, M., 'Inter-Agency Co-operation and Community-Based Crime Prevention', *British Journal of Criminology*, 1995, vol. 35, p. 17.
[12] Pratt, J., 'Corporatism: The Third Model of Juvenile Justice', *British Journal of Criminology*, 1989, vol. 29, p. 236; and Crawford, A., 'The Partnership Approach to Community Crime Prevention: Corporatism at the Local Level?', *Social and Legal Studies*, 1994, vol. 3, p. 497.

316

act as independent diversion agencies',[13] most notably the Northamptonshire Juvenile Bureau.[14] Yet these conditions are not universal and it is clear that the police remain the dominant party within the multi-agency decision-making process.[15] Nevertheless, the existence of multi-agency panels and broader inter-agency liaison has added another dynamic in the local formalisation of cautioning practice.

In the past decade this formalisation has gone hand in hand with an increasingly liberal use of cautioning, initially in relation to juveniles but more recently extended to include the adult population. In 1971, the number of persons cautioned was 77,300. By 1993, this figure had risen to 311,300, more than a four-fold increase on the 1971 figures and nearly double the number cautioned ten years earlier.[16] The majority of cautions are given to juveniles. This does not mean, however, that they concern necessarily trivial offences. The recent Royal Commission noted that more than 96,000 of the 279,000 cautions issued in 1991 involved adults who had admitted offences for which they could have been tried in the higher criminal (Crown) court, if prosecuted.[17] According to the latest Home Office guidelines, a caution should be administered only where evidence of the offender's guilt exists which is sufficient to support a realistic prospect of conviction and where a suspect admits the alleged offence and fully understands the significance of a caution (in the case of juveniles a parent or guardian should be present and understand its implications). Although a formal caution does not amount to a criminal conviction, it is recorded and it may be brought to the attention of a court if it is relevant to the offence under consideration.

Research shows that the practice of cautioning is highly diverse.[18] Despite various attempts by the Home Office to standardise the practice — through the use of regularly updated central guidelines; National Standards applicable to juveniles and adults alike; and recording and monitoring on a force-wide basis — a considerable degree of differential usage persists both within and between

[13] Blagg, H. and Smith, D., *Crime, Penal Policy and Social Work*, Harlow: Longman, 1989, pp. 105–6.
[14] See Davis, G., Boucherat, J. and Watson, D., 'Pre-Court Decision-Making in Juvenile Justice', *British Journal of Criminology*, 1989, vol. 29, p. 219.
[15] See Blagg, H., Pearson, G., Sampson, A., Smith, D. and Stubbs, P., 'Inter-Agency Co-operation: Rhetoric and Reality', in Hope, T. and Shaw, M. (eds), *Communities and Crime Reduction*, London: HMSO, 1988.
[16] Home Office, *Criminal Statistics England and Wales 1993*, Cm 2680, London: HMSO, 1994, p. 90.
[17] Royal Commission on Criminal Justice, *op. cit.*, p. 82.
[18] Giller, H. and Tutt, N., 'Police Cautioning of Juveniles: The Continuing Practice of Diversity', *Criminal Law Review*, 1987, p. 367; and Evans, R. and Wilkinson, C., 'Variations in Police Cautioning Policy and Practice in England and Wales', *Howard Journal of Criminal Justice*, 1990, vol. 29, p. 155.

forces.[19] The latest statistics show that considerable fluctuations and force-wide discrepancies have not been eliminated. For example, the 1993 cautioning rate for indictable offences for male youths (10-17 years of age) ranged from 55 per cent in West Yorkshire to 86 per cent in Kent.[20]

The latest Home Office circular represents a marked change in central policy direction on the use of cautions. The new tougher line aims to encourage greater consistency in the use of cautions and to 'discourage their use in inappropriate cases, for example for offences which are triable on indictment only'.[21] The circular states that cautions should not be administered to an offender in circumstances where there can be no reasonable expectation that this will curb his or her offending. More than one caution should be considered only where the subsequent offence is trivial, or where there has been a sufficient lapse of time since the first caution to suggest that it had some effect. Multiple cautions, it is argued:

> ... brings cautioning into disrepute; cautions should not be administered to an offender in circumstances where there can be no reasonable expectation that this will curb his offending. It is only in exceptional circumstances that more than one caution should be considered.[22]

The consequences of this latest shift in policy will serve to limit the use of cautions, at least in the short term, particularly among the adult population. As a direct result, we will most probably see an increased resort to criminal litigation. One commentator has speculated that the youth courts may witness an increase of one-third in the number of cases.[23] The latest statistics show that in the year 1993 the total number of persons cautioned declined by some 10,000 on the previous year's figures. What is more telling, from the statistics, is that the fall occurred in the last quarter of 1993, clearly reflecting the impact that the issuing of the draft Home Office circular, in October 1993, had on police policy.[24] Evans suggests that a further implication will be the drastic reduction in the work of juvenile panels and bureaux, which will result in practical difficulties in implementing the new guidelines.[25] For, while juvenile justice workers are unlikely to want to give up their involvement in multi-agency

---

[19] Evans, R., 'Comparing Young Adult and Juvenile Cautioning in the Metropolitan Police District', *Criminal Law Review*, 1993, p. 572.

[20] Home Office, *op. cit.* (1994), p. 94.

[21] Home Office, *Circular 18/1994*, para. 3.

[22] *Ibid.*, para. 8.

[23] Evans, R., 'Cautioning: Counting the Cost of Retrenchment', *Criminal Law Review*, 1994, pp. 566, 575.

[24] Home Office, *op. cit.* (1994), p. 92.

[25] Evans, *op. cit.* (1994), p. 574.

consultation, particularly given their commitment to the liberal use of cautioning, 'neither is it easy to imagine that the police will unilaterally or instantly withdraw from these arrangements'.[26] This leaves a potentially contradictory position, which if anything is likely to increase local variations as forces are required to renegotiate, while linked into wider multi-agency relations, how and to what extent they comply with circular 18/1994.

(ii) Caution plus

Increasingly, in the last few years a number of voluntary and statutory agencies have been experimenting with what are referred to as 'caution plus' schemes, in which some form of additional element is made a requirement of the caution. The 'plus' aspect may be counselling for alcohol/drug abuse, some other therapeutic regime or referral to mediation. The development of 'caution plus' schemes has been *ad hoc* and highly localised. While participation in such schemes is not mandatory for the police, many forces have cooperated with other agencies in implementing 'caution plus' schemes. It is these agencies, most notably the probation service, who resource and fund the schemes.

The attraction of 'caution plus' for many is that the non-interventionism of the caution is replaced by some form of limited 'benign' intervention. Many practitioners emphasise that 'caution plus' is an attachment to, rather than a condition of, a caution and that therefore, in theory at least, a decision to caution should be made independently of, and prior to, any agreement between offender and agencies as to participation in a specific scheme.[27] The importance of this emphasis is to highlight and preserve (at least as an ideal) the voluntariness of participation (a theme we return to later).

Both the House of Commons Home Affairs Committee[28] and the recent Royal Commission[29] have encouraged the expansion of cautioning and have welcomed 'caution plus' programmes. The Home Office has adopted a more guarded approach, warning that 'caution plus needs further evaluation before a decision can be made on its future'.[30] It goes on to advise police forces participating in 'caution plus' schemes to 'monitor the results'[31] and reminds them that the 'decision to caution is in *all* cases one for the police, and although

---

[26] *Ibid.*

[27] Evans and Wilkinson, *op. cit.*, p. 169.

[28] House of Commons Home Affairs Select Committee (1989–90), *Fourth Report: Crown Prosecution Service*, London: HMSO, 1990.

[29] Royal Commission on Criminal Justice, *op. cit.*

[30] Home Office, *Circular 18/1994*, para. 14.

[31] *Ibid.*, para. 14.

it is open to them to seek the advice of multi-agency panels, this should not be done as a matter of course'.[32]

(iii) Mediation and reparation

The recent history of criminal mediation and reparation in the UK is a diverse one, and is also one beset by conceptual obfuscation. Mediation is generally accepted by those working in the field as a process within which dispute negotiation may occur. It is a method of communication by which negotiations between the opposing parties ('face-to-face' or through the mediator as a 'go-between') are brought about by a third party who attempts to help the parties reach their own solutions to their problems.[33] The mediator acts as an intermediary — a conduit in communication — but has no authority to make a decision or to force a settlement. Nevertheless, the mediator has a powerfully influential role in the process. Ideally it is consent-based, participatory and forward-looking in which the parties arrive at mutually agreed settlements as to reparation.[34] And yet within the concept of mediation the questions of who initiates the process[35] and its relationship with the existing formal criminal court, remain deliberately open-ended. Both these elements may of themselves influence and contaminate the 'pure' process. Further, mediation is, in theory, neither unencumbered by, nor tied to, the attainment of any specific outcome — i.e., reparation. Such outcomes may be desirable, but the mediator has no 'socially legitimate authority to render a decision'.[36] Consequently, the mediator faces a central dilemma, 'to settle a case without imposing a decision'.[37] Many of the ongoing concerns about mediation and reparation spring directly from these tensions.

In the 1970s a small number of victim/offender mediation and reparation schemes were established as a result of concern and awareness that victims were denied any basic rights of involvement — to have a say or to be listened to — in their own criminal dispute. Christie described this as the theft of a victim's conflict, not only by the state but also by professionals, in which

---

[32] *Ibid.*, para. 3.

[33] See Eckhoff, T., 'The Mediator, the Judge and the Administrator in Conflict-Resolution', *Acta Sociologica*, 1966, vol. 10, p. 158; and Roberts, S., 'Mediation in Family Disputes', *Modern Law Review*, 1983, vol. 46, pp. 537, 545 at p. 545.

[34] See Zehr, H., *Changing Lenses; A New Focus for Criminal Justice*, Scottdale, PA: Herald Press, 1990, and Wright, M., *Justice for Victims and Offenders*, Buckingham: Open University Press, 1991.

[35] Davis, G., Boucherat, J. and Watson, D., *A Preliminary Study of Victim Offender Mediation and Reparation Schemes in England and Wales*, Research and Planning Unit Paper, No. 42, London: Home Office, 1987, p. 5.

[36] Silbey, S. and Merry, S., 'Mediator Settlement Strategies', *Law and Policy*, 1986, vol. 8, p. 7.

[37] *Ibid.*

offenders also lose out.[38] However, many of these early victim/offender mediation and reparation schemes were set up with the explicit aim of diversion from the courts as part of 'caution plus' schemes. The Forum for Initiatives in Reparation and Mediation (FIRM) was established in 1984 to act as an umbrella organisation (now Mediation UK). In 1985 the Home Office funded, to the sum of £200,000 over two years, four pilot victim/offender mediation and reparation projects in Coventry, Leeds, Wolverhampton and Cumbria. These schemes were the subject of considerable evaluation and scrutiny, an important element of which was commissioned by the Home Office. However, the Home Office's sudden enthusiasm for the idea of reparation was short-lived. Funding for the initial schemes was withdrawn at the end of the pilot period and the publication of the 'official' research report, which was sympathetic to the ideal of mediation and reparation while acknowledging some of its shortfalls in practice, was significantly delayed. It was published only in 1990, by which time the Home Office appeared to have lost interest in the subject.[39] Davis explains this 'inglorious episode of criminal justice policy making' as the product of a significant lack of liaison within the Home Office, between the policy division and the Research and Planning Unit.[40] The former's principal interest lay in developing cost-effective means of disposing of petty and low tariff offenders outside of the criminal courts.[41] In contrast, the Research and Planning Unit's involvement, according to Davis, revolved around the pivotal role of Tony Marshall,[42] the principal researcher on the project, who was more interested in the normative aims of mediation: its therapeutic and expiatory potential; its claims to interpersonal accountability; and its capacity for relational and restorative justice.

Many of the research findings were critical of the way in which, in practice, the needs of victims were often subordinated to the aims of diverting offenders from custody or mitigating their subsequent court sentence.[43] In addition, it was found that there was little or no interest in effecting material reparation.[44] In their struggle for legitimacy these early local schemes suffered from a deliberate arm's length approach adopted by Victim Support[45] and the National

---

[38] Christie, N., 'Conflicts as Property', *British Journal of Criminology*, 1977, vol. 17, p. 1.

[39] See Marshall, T. and Merry, S., *Crime and Accountability*, London: HMSO, 1990.

[40] Davis, G., *Making Amends: Mediation and Reparation in Criminal Justice*, London: Routledge, 1992.

[41] Home Office, *Reparation: A Discussion Document*, London: Home Office, 1986.

[42] Marshall went on to become Director of FIRM.

[43] See Davis, G., Boucherat, J. and Watson, D., 'Reparation in the Service of Diversion: the Subordination of a Good Idea', *The Howard Journal of Criminal Justice*, 1988, vol. 27, p. 127; Young, R., 'Reparation as Mitigation', *Criminal Law Review*, 1989, p. 463; and Davis, *op. cit.*

[44] Davis, G., 'Reparation in the UK: Dominant Themes and Neglected Themes', in Messmer, H. and Otto, H.-U. (eds), *Restorative Justice on Trial*, Kluwer: Dordrecht, 1992.

[45] Reeves, H., *The Victim and Reparation*, London: Victim Support, 1984.

Association of Probation Officers,[46] as well as difficulties in securing cooperation with the police.[47] With the withdrawal of support by the Home Office, an unofficial orthodoxy in policy-making and academic circles began to take hold. This ran along the lines that the 'new deal for victims' launched with great publicity by the Home Office in 1985 — of which victim/offender mediation and reparation had been seen as a key element — had become a 'new deal for offenders'.

In the intervening years, and on the back of more favourable research findings,[48] the schemes that have survived and weathered the changing winds of policy have done much to answer their critics. The currently operating schemes (about 25) exist on local funding, principally through the probation service, which is itself a source of debate given its traditional offender-orientation. The referral points and the aims of the schemes continue to differ widely, but most schemes operate at the cautioning stage, or after conviction but prior to sentencing.[49] Mediation UK has done much to coordinate practice, principally through guidelines on training and standards and the dissemination of 'good practice'.[50]

Today's schemes differ from their predecessors in that they have learnt many of the lessons of the 1980s experiments. They have become more acutely aware of, and attempt to meet, the needs of victims; they have developed better links with Victim Support;[51] set up advisory or management committees which draw together the involvement and support of other relevant agencies (with the associated increased legitimacy that this image of independence brings); placed greater emphasis on mediation as a process rather than the attainment of

---

[46] NAPO, *Policy Document on Reparation*, London: NAPO, 1985.

[47] See Davis et al., *op. cit.* (1987) and Marshall and Merry, *op. cit.*

[48] Dignan, J., *Repairing the Damage: An Evaluation of an Experimental Adult Reparation Scheme in Kettering*, Sheffield: Centre for Criminological and Legal Research, University of Sheffield, 1990.

[49] Wright, M., 'Victims, Mediation and Criminal Justice', *Criminal Law Review*, 1995, pp. 187, 190.

[50] This in turn has led to the perception that we are witnessing a reformalisation and reprofessionalisation of mediation as a means of dispute resolution which runs counter to the informalising and deprofessionalising aspirations of the early proponents. This has certainly been the view of many American commentators, see for example Sarat, A., 'The New Formalism in Disputing and Dispute Processing', *Law and Society Review*, 1988, vol. 21, p. 695.

[51] Similarly, Victim Support has adopted a more positive stance towards mediation, both locally and nationally: see, for example, Victim Support, Victim Support, Reparation and Mediation, Policy Document, London: Victim Support, 1990, and Reynolds, T., 'Victims' Needs and Experiences', in Martin, C. (ed.), *Resolving Crime in the Community: Mediation in Criminal Justice*, Report of a Conference organised by the ISTD and London Victim-Offender Mediation Network, London: ISTD, 1995.

specific outcomes (be they reparation, diversion or mitigation); and sought to establish and develop guidelines for ethical practice.[52]

In many senses we are now witnessing a second wave of victim/offender mediation services reflected by renewed growth and interest. In West Yorkshire, for example, the provision of mediation and reparation services has been extended throughout the region, which is now covered by five schemes and aims to provide a universal service thus, in part, meeting the concerns as to differential access and uneven coverage of mediation.[53] Some schemes have deliberately developed in ways which seek to avoid contamination by the criminal justice process by attracting referrals regardless of whether they are attached to diversion; refusing to be bound by court timetables; and refusing to provide any significant information to the courts.[54] This is more akin to the 'separatist' model advocated by Marshall in which mediation and reparation is seen as voluntary and extra-legal.[55] One problem with this approach is that it supplements the work of the court and the offender may end up receiving a double punishment in the form of both a court sentence and reparation. In addition, absolute independence from the existing institutions of crime control is not only an unachievable ideal, but also is one which is likely to consign such schemes to a peripheral role with little influence on the existing process and which will impact upon few people. Other commentators prefer an 'integrationist' strategy, whereby mediation and reparation are firmly located within the practice of the court, but not simply as a way of dispensing with minor cases.[56] It is only through material ties with the formal criminal justice system that mediation and reparation can realistically seek to influence and 'civilise' it. To this end some schemes are now reviewing and reconsidering their traditional unwillingness to get involved in the possibility of 'reparation orders' attached to probation as a sentence of the court. Under such arrangements, assessment for mediation alone would be a condition of a probation order, rather than the successful completion of reparation itself, in order to preserve voluntariness. In such a scenario the pitfalls and dangers into which the early initiatives fell reappear and place an even greater requirement upon practitioners to limit normative contamination. This requires less ambiguity of

---

[52] See for example, Quill, D. and Wynne, J. (eds), *Victim & Offender Mediation Handbook*, Leeds: Save the Children/West Yorkshire Probation Service, 1993.
[53] West Yorkshire Probation Service, *Victim/Offender Mediation Reparation Policy*, Wakefield: WYPS, 1994.
[54] For example, the Bradford scheme, see Leda Group, *Bradford Mediation and Reparation: April '93–April '94*, Hebden Bridge: Leda Group, 1994.
[55] Marshall and Merry, *op. cit.*; and Marshall, T. 'Informal Justice: The British Experience', in Matthews, *op. cit.*
[56] For example Davis, *op. cit.* (1992).

purpose, greater coherence of aims and the development of clear strategies around those prioritised objectives which acknowledge and try to reconcile the tensions between reparation and diversion; restoration and punishment;[57] and the attraction and applicability of mediation as an end in itself. The uncertainty, however, is whether the objectives prioritised by practitioners will be congruous with those prioritised by policy-makers.

Neighbourhood mediation

Some victim/offender schemes also offer mediation for neighbourhood 'disputes'.[58] In addition, there is a growing number of specific neighbourhood mediation services currently operating in the UK (some 40–50 schemes).[59] Neighbourhood disputes differ in that they are potentially criminal or civil disputes at the boundaries of the law. Schemes take referrals directly from individuals and from a variety of agencies (including local authority housing departments) who may for various reasons seek to give greater expression to the 'dispute' element in some 'crimes' — usually where there are pre-existing social relationships — and to downplay the 'criminal' element. This conceptually ambiguous distinction between crimes and disputes offers a further means of reducing criminal litigation, through the 'civilianisation' of criminal disputes.

Here, potentially criminal cases are redefined as civil disputes and dealt with by means of civil negotiation in the shadow of the courts. The attraction of neighbourhood mediation, once a conflict has been defined as a dispute rather than as a crime, perversely often lies in the more extensive procedural and financial restrictions upon access to civil justice.[60] The boundaries between civil and criminal disputes are not clearly delineated but blurred and fuzzy. There tends to be a working assumption that disputes involving parties with interpersonal relations are more suitable for civil mediation, regardless of the seriousness of the dispute itself or of the blameworthiness of either of the parties. However, this dominant understanding of interpersonal relations is by

---

[57] Lucia Zedner has very usefully begun to think through the contours and implications of this particular debate, see Zedner, L., 'Reparation and Retribution: Are They Reconcilable?', *Modern Law Review*, 1994, vol. 57, p. 228.

[58] For example, the Sandwell scheme: see Young, R., 'Neighbourhood Dispute Mediation: Theory and Practice', *Civil Justice Quarterly*, 1989, p. 319.

[59] Mediation UK, *Directory of Mediation and Conflict Resolution Services*, Bristol: Mediation UK, 1994.

[60] Crawford, A., 'Alternatives to Courts and Judges in the City', in Bell, J. and Garapon, A. (eds), *Comparative Western European Judicial Cultures*, forthcoming.

and large very narrow, restricted to those with spatial connections, either by living together or by living next to each other. This tends to ignore the fact that other, more nuanced forms of interdependencies exist in the contemporary world,[61] as well as decades of feminist research which has shown that most crime is familiar or familial[62] and, if not, is nevertheless highly localised, albeit further afield than the next-door neighbour.[63] On one level, this would seem to amount to a good argument for the majority of crimes to be treated by means of civil mediation. However, the principal danger of such schemes is that they selectively restrict access to the law as a consequence of agencies redefining 'events' as non-criminal. The recent history of the policing of domestic violence highlights these problems most acutely.[64] Similarly, the legal profession may wish to dump unprofitable (criminal or civil) cases onto such schemes, particularly in a context of shifting legal aid eligibility. Against this background the question of what constitutes an appropriate case for neighbourhood mediation is both complex and one upon which there is no consensus. In this context we need to be sensitive to the extent to which the processing of a dispute transforms it into a suitable subject matter by picking out what it chooses to treat as the salient features of a case for its purpose.

The future of mediation and reparation in criminal disputes   Mediation and reparation is still in its infancy. However, it has developed an established place on the international criminal policy agenda, as witnessed by its prominent inclusion within the 1995 UN Conference on Crime Prevention. There continues to be an expansion of experiments in North America and across Europe.[65] Further, lessons from other countries, particularly in relation to

---

[61] Braithwaite, J., *Crime, Shame and Reintegration*, Cambridge: CUP, 1989.
[62] Stanko, E.A., 'When Precaution is Normal: A Feminist Critique of Prevention', in Gelsthorpe, L. and Morris, A. (eds), *Feminist Perspectives in Criminology*, Milton Keynes: Open University Press, 1990.
[63] See Jones, T., MacLean, B. and Young, J., *The Islington Crime Survey*, Aldershot: Gower, 1986; and Crawford, A., Jones, T., Woodhouse, T. and Young, J., *The Second Islington Crime Survey*, Enfield: Centre for Criminology, Middlesex Polytechnic, 1990.
[64] Edwards, S., *Policing 'Domestic' Violence*, London: Sage, 1989.
[65] See Umbreit, M. and Coates, R. B., 'Cross-Site Analysis of Victim-Offender Mediation in Four States', *Crime and Delinquency*, 1993, vol. 39, p. 565; Messmer and Otto, *op. cit.*; and Bonafé-Schmitt, J.-P., *La Médiation: Une Justice Douce*, Paris: Syros-Alternatives, 1992.

young people, in New Zealand,[66] Germany[67] and Norway,[68] show the potential (and pitfalls) of placing mediation and reparation schemes on a legislative footing. At a national level, despite the limited number of mediation and reparation schemes and their relatively small case-loads, their attraction for policy-makers remains evident. Perversely the fluctuations and 'U' turns in cautioning policy have opened up new spaces for mediation and reparation to fill and exploit. While the practice of cautioning is unlikely to go away, the present Government's unease with simple cautioning appeals to more intensive and interventionist forms of disposal short of prosecution. Leading academics and practitioners have come to advocate mediation and reparation as a part of 'caution plus' schemes as representing the ideal, or at least the best available, means of meeting many of the normative and administrative failings of the present (court-based) criminal justice process. Like others, David Faulkner, a former leading civil servant in the Home Office, has recently called upon the Government to (re)consider the options available through mediation and reparation.[69] The original concerns which attracted the Government to mediation and reparation in the mid-1980s — the cost of criminal prosecutions, the belief that mediation may provide a cheaper means of disposing with certain criminal cases, and the problematic role of victims — have not diminished. However, the research evidence is ambivalent as to whether mediation offers real cost savings.[70] The danger is that if a centrally driven expansion in mediation and reparation were to occur, the administrative and cost considerations would dominate over any normative and reparative potential.

---

[66] The Children, Young Persons and Their Families Act 1989 established a system of Family Group Conferencing (FGC) in New Zealand, in which offenders, their extended family, victims, their supporters, police, social worker (in certain cases) and significant others if requested, meet at a conference convened and facilitated by a youth justice coordinator to mediate the conflict. See Maxwell, G. M. and Morris, A., *Family, Victims and Culture: Youth Justice in New Zealand*, Wellington: University of Wellington, 1993; Morris, A., Maxwell, G. M. and Robertson, J. P., 'Giving Victims a Voice: A New Zealand Experiment', *Howard Journal of Criminal Justice*, 1993, vol. 32, p. 304; and Alder, C. and Wundersitz, J. (eds), *Family Conferencing and Juvenile Justice*, Canberra: Australian Institute of Criminology, 1994.

[67] The Juvenile Court Act 1990 established a legislative framework for mediation in Germany. See Kerner, H-J., Marks, E. and Schreckling, J., 'Implementation and Acceptance of Victim-offender Mediation Programs in the Federal Republic of Germany: A Survey of Criminal Justice Institutions', in Messmer and Otto, *op. cit.*, p. 29.

[68] A law passed in April 1991, in Norway, extended the Conflict Resolution Boards (which had been set up in 1983 as an experiment) to cover all municipalities in Norway and place them within a legislative framework. See Royal Norwegian Ministry of Justice and Police, *Municipal Mediation Boards: An Alternative to Prosecution*, Oslo: Ministry of Justice and Police, 1993; and for a more critical review Nergard, T. B., 'Solving Conflicts Outside the Court System: Experiences with the Conflict Resolution Boards in Norway', *British Journal of Criminology*, 1993, vol. 33, p. 81.

[69] Faulkner, D., 'Relational Justice: A Dynamic for Reform', in Burnside, J. and Baker, N. (eds), *Relational Justice: Repairing the Breach*, Winchester: Waterside Press, 1994, p. 173. See the endorsements by Lord Woolf in the Foreword.

[70] Marshall and Merry, *op. cit.*

However, the other important benefit of mediation and reparation attached to 'caution plus' schemes relates to the role of the victim. Victims are not disadvantaged in the same way as they are through 'simple' cautioning, where the possibility of financial compensation is precluded. A common criticism of 'simple' diversion is that it is often perceived by victims, and those who seek to champion them, as serving the interests of the criminal justice system and the offender while ignoring victims' own needs. Further, mediation can provide important information for victims that they would otherwise be denied, about the offence, the offender and their processing through the criminal justice system. Mediation, therefore, can (and does) draw support from, and connect with (although not unproblematically), increasing concerns in relation to the rights, needs and treatment of victims.[71] In this way it is in accord with the rhetoric of the Government's Victim's Charter, if not its practice.[72] Indeed, some of the pioneering mediation schemes, like the Leeds service, have developed their work to include the provision of pre-release enquiry reports in relation to life sentence prisoners. Mediators interview, give a voice and provide information to, the relatives and families of victims of life prisoners in the run up to their release on licence. This work, on behalf of the probation service, is undertaken in fulfilment of probation's requirements under the Victim's Charter.[73]

Lessons from family mediation Salutary lessons can be learnt from an examination of the debates and issues raised by the place and role of mediation in civil justice matters, particularly divorce proceedings. While the nature of the interests at stake between the parties differs substantially across the different legal contexts, many of the same dilemmas arise as a result of the often confused and conflicting aims of mediation and the dissonance between the rhetoric of mediation and the reality of mediation practice.

Unlike mediation in the criminal justice field, in matrimonial matters mediation has mushroomed in Britain in the last 15 years, to the point that the present Government has come to recognise mediation as a central ingredient in the divorce process. In April 1995, the Lord Chancellor's Department published a White Paper which outlines the Government's proposals in this

---

[71] See Meirs, D., 'The Responsibilities and Rights of Victims of Crime', *Modern Law Review*, 1992, p. 482; Maguire, M., 'The Needs and Rights of Victims of Crime' in Tonry, M. (ed.), *Crime and Justice: A Review of Research*, Chicago: University of Chicago Press, 1991, vol. 14, p. 363; and Mawby, R. and Walklate, S., *Critical Victimology*, London: Sage, 1994.
[72] Home Office, *Victim's Charter: A Statement of the Rights of Victims of Crime*, London: Home Office, 1990.
[73] Johnston, P., *The Victim's Charter (1990) and the Release of Life Prisoners: Implications for Probation Service Practice, Values and Management*, Wakefield: West Yorkshire Probation Service, 1995.

field.[74] It is clear from the White Paper that the Government sees mediation as fulfilling a number of objectives. First, it is seen as a means of better 'managing and reducing conflict' within the adversarial process.[75] However, an equally, if not more, important objective is the reduction of the cost to the state. It is proposed that the new system involving mediation 'should therefore be structured in such a way that total costs borne by the taxpayer... will not exceed those which would have been borne by the Legal Aid Fund under the present system'.[76]

The Government's proposals will introduce a system whereby mediation itself will not be compulsory. However, an initial interview, which will aim to encourage 'couples to consider family mediation rather than arm's length negotiations through lawyers or litigation', will be 'a pre-condition of commencing the divorce process'.[77] Thus structural 'subtle coercive pressures',[78] as well as informal inducements, to mediate will tie it, in practice if not in theory, to the demands and dominant ideologies of the formal process. The Government has accepted that assistance with the cost of mediation will be available under the same eligibility criteria as for the provision of legal services under the legal aid scheme.[79] The funding will be through a franchised system of local mediation services whose quality will be regulated by the Legal Aid Board in a manner similar to the franchising of other legal services.[80] Despite initial cautious research findings as to the benefits of mediation in relation to cost,[81] the Government is convinced that the new scheme will result in cost savings.

Returning our gaze to the criminal justice field, there is a number of lessons that we can draw from the experience in family matters. First, it would appear that in the Government's proposals cost considerations have been accorded

---

[74] Lord Chancellor's Department, *Looking to the Future: Mediation and the Ground for Divorce*, Cm 2799, London: HMSO, 1995.

[75] *Ibid.*, para. 7.4.

[76] *Ibid.*, para. 6.27.

[77] *Ibid.*, paras 7.6–7.7. More recently, Lord Mackay has restated that, under the legislative scheme announced in the Queen's Speech in November 1995, 'people will not be forced to mediate' (*The Times*, 8 November 1995). However, the proposals contain a presumption in favour of mediation which means it should be considered in all but the most urgent cases before litigation begins. Further, in what has been seen as a concession to the legal professions, the Lord Chancellor has questioned the nature of the full arrangements for the initial information session. Various options will be tried out in a pilot study.

[78] Tomasic, R., 'Mediation as an Alternative to Adjudication', in Tomasic, R. and Feeley, M. (eds), *Neighborhood Justice*, New York: Longmans, 1982, p. 227.

[79] Lord Chancellor's Department, *Looking to the Future*, *op. cit.*, para. 2.37.

[80] *Ibid.*, paras 6.24–6.26.

[81] Conciliation Project Unit, *Report to the Lord Chancellor's Department on the Costs and Effectiveness of Conciliation in England and Wales*, Newcastle: Conciliation Project Unit, 1989, paras 20.4-20.5.

primacy. Mediation is essentially viewed as a means of reducing the legal aid budget by reducing lawyer involvement in the process.[82] Secondly, by tying mediation to the court process and the availability of legal aid, the framework creates clear 'incentives' and 'coercive sticks' which will undermine the sacred cow of voluntariness. Lastly, the conceptual separation of process and outcome appears to have been abandoned as outcome pressures have been prioritised over process aims. These insights highlight some of the potential directions in which victim/offender mediation and reparation, particularly in its relation to cautioning, may be pulled in the future.

However, we need to sound a note of warning regarding the lessons that can be drawn from civil legal matters. There are significant differences between civil and criminal justice. Settlement out of court is a major and essential feature of civil justice systems. While civil litigation is associated with final adjudication, for the parties this often represents a means to an end, rather than an end in itself. Much that regularly occurs in the name of civil litigation takes place in 'the shadow of the court'. The fact is that the great majority of civil cases never reach authoritative judgment and are 'settled' through negotiation. Yet the implications are not the same for criminal justice, particularly given its important symbolic presence, as a representation of state sovereignty and collective conscience through the expression of social disapprobation. The symbolic and normative value of criminal justice should not be underestimated, and is recognised and enshrined within the principles (if not the practice) of some European systems by the notion of mandatory prosecution which symbolically re-emphasises the intrinsic link between uniformity and justice.[83]

(iv) Administrative fines

A further suggestion for reducing criminal litigation is the introduction of a system of administrative fines. Currently in England and Wales, fixed fines exist as an alternative for the police only in relation to a range of minor motoring offences, such as the fixed penalty fine under the Road Traffic Offenders Act 1988 (Part III and sch. 3). A total of 5,676,000 fixed penalty notices were issued in England and Wales in 1991.[84] The CPS has no power to

---

[82] The extent to which the latter will occur is debatable as many solicitors are now training as mediators.

[83] For example, the Federal Republic of Germany, see Leigh, L. H. and Zedner, L., *A Report on the Administration of Criminal Justice in Pre-Trial Phase in France and Germany*, Royal Commission on Criminal Justice Research Study No.1, London: HMSO, 1992.

[84] In comparison, there were only 885,000 prosecutions in that year for summary motoring offences.

offer to 'transact' or 'compound' offences on payment of a penalty.[85] The Royal Commission on Criminal Justice, however, recommended that the CPS should be allowed to levy fines directly on offenders, with their agreement, as an alternative to prosecution. It suggested that prosecutors should have a choice between a range of fines and/or be able to make direct compensation payments to the victim.[86] This type of prosecutor fine is common in continental jurisdictions — for example, The Netherlands, Sweden, and France — and was recently introduced into Scotland, where it is known as the 'fiscal fine' because it is issued by the procurator fiscal (the local public prosecutor in Scotland).[87] It is used for more serious crimes — like theft and minor assaults — than mere regulatory offences. The advantage of the prosecutor fine, like mediation and reparation, is that it can meet some of the demands of victims through compensation, although the extent to which the victim is given a voice is limited, particularly in the Scottish model.[88]

Having outlined the various alternatives to prosecution available and their potential, let us now consider some of the vexed issues which surround diversion from prosecution.

III THE ROLE OF STATE-FUNDED LEGAL AID

In chapter 3 of this book, Andrew Ashworth argues that four central principles directly connect the necessity of legal aid and assistance to the fundamental right not to be wrongly convicted. These he identifies as:

(a) the complexity and technicality of the process;

(b) the differential power relations (access to resources) between the accused and the state in the guise of the police and prosecution;

(c) the adverse consequences of conviction for the individual; and

(d) the principle of equality before the law.

---

[85] In Scotland, in contrast, such a power exists in respect of minor criminal offences under s. 56 of the Criminal Justice (Scotland) Act 1987. In 1990 the CPS suggested, in evidence to the Parliamentary Home Affairs Committee, that the Government should introduce a scheme of cautioning offenders which included the imposition of a penalty by the prosecutor similar to the Scottish system. While the Committee agreed with the principle, it felt that such a power might more properly be exercised by the police. The Government, however, rejected this latter proposal on the ground that the police did not want to become involved in sentencing.

[86] Royal Commission on Criminal Justice, op. cit., para. 63.

[87] See Duff, P. and Meechan, K., 'The Prosecutor Fine', Criminal Law Review, 1992, p. 22, and Duff, P., 'The Prosecutor Fine', Oxford Journal of Legal Studies, 1994, vol. 14, p. 565.

[88] In contrast the Dutch system accords greater voice to the victim. Most notably, if the victim is dissatisfied with the lack of prosecution the victim may apply to the Appeal Court to have the prosecutor's decision set aside. For further details on the differences between the Scottish and Dutch systems, see Duff, op. cit., p. 573.

Let us briefly consider the application and relevance of these principles within the context of alternatives to prosecution rather than court-based adjudication which is Ashworth's focus. Here, the concern is that non court-based alternatives, in which legal aid is not available, may result in considerable numbers of low visibility miscarriages of justice. However, at first glance it is only the second of Ashworth's principles — differential power relations — which retains its full poignancy in relation to alternatives to prosecution.

First, in relation to technicality and complexity, diversionary processes are patently less formal, standing in marked contrast to the formality of the court-based process, partly one might argue, because of the absence of lawyers. However, we should not become blinded by claims to informality. The practice is often quite different. Suspects may easily be confused by novel procedures which professionals operating within them take for granted. A suspect may not be fully aware of the implications of a given decision, including, for instance, an acceptance of guilt as part of a caution and its ramifications. Further, there is the enduring danger that such new initiatives can go through a process of re-formalisation and re-professionalisation in which novel technicalities and jargon emerge alongside new professional, or para-professional, groups. To some extent, this has been the experience of many American schemes.[89] And yet the answer may not necessarily lie in legal representation but in the greater communication and assurance of comprehension, on the part of the suspect, of the nature of the process, its significance and its implications. Nevertheless, the principle of access to legal advice has most leverage in relation to decisions by suspects to accept a caution. For at this point the highly complex legal issues surrounding the determination of guilt (and associated notions of intention) are in question. A person may easily accept a caution for something for which they were not in fact legally guilty, without due regard to the establishment of guilt or the subsequent implications of a caution. This is particularly the case given the alienating environment in which cautioning often takes place[90] and/or if the individual was involved in some way in the incident under consideration although not necessarily guilty of the specific offence for which he or she is under suspicion. Access to legal advice is rendered all the more important in this context given the fact that, unlike pre-trial investigations, there is no direct subsequent open opportunity or forum at which to challenge the validity of any statements made or their voluntariness.

Ashworth's third principle, the 'consequences of conviction', is clearly not as relevant in the context of alternatives to prosecution. Diversionary processes are neither directly concerned with establishing conviction, in that they can

---

[89] Sarat, *op. cit.*, n. 50, p. 695.
[90] Lee, M., 'Pre-court Diversion and Youth Justice', in Levi, M., Maguire, M. and Noaks, L. (eds), *Contemporary Issues in Criminology*, Cardiff: University of Wales Press, 1995.

hide behind the prior acknowledgement of guilt by the suspect, nor are their consequences as severe as those of courts. Neither the passing of a sentence, as such, nor the loss of liberty are key features of alternatives to prosecution. However, stigma, blame and censure are central aspects of the practice of cautioning[91] and the ideal of mediation.[92] While diversionary processes tend to deal with minor cases and the consequences are less severe, it is all too easy to get lost in the 'ideology of triviality' which may shroud low-level miscarriages of justice.[93] For if a case is serious enough to evoke and involve the criminal law then in principle it may equally be retorted that suspects, at all stages of the process, should be granted state-funded legal advice if they are unable to pay for it themselves.

Ashworth's fourth principle of 'equality before the law', can be avoided and addressed if legal advice and representation is denied to all parties so that even those able to pay from their own resources are barred from doing so, thus equalising the situation of the wealthy and the poor suspect. Consequently, the person of insufficient means as well as the wealthy suspect would formally be in the same position as a consequence of a 'levelling down of the playing field'.

It is the logic of Ashworth's second principle — inequality of resources — from which promoters of diversionary schemes, untouched by state-funded legal aid, cannot escape. It is the fact that the decision as to whether to accept guilt and proceed to a diversionary alternative is devolved to the suspect in isolation, without recourse to legal assistance and up against the awesome power of the police and prosecution, that most offends the principles of justice with which Ashworth is concerned. However, there appears to be an important debate of principle which springs out of the preceding discussion, which revolves around the — more than semantic — distinction between legal advice and legal representation. In the context of alternatives to prosecution the former remains a fundamental element in satisfying the principles of justice, while the latter may not. Technical and substantive legal advice may help empower the individual in his or her decision-making. Legal representation is likely both to distort the non-adjudicatory process itself and to disempower individuals, in that lawyers in managing clients' disputes appropriate them.[94] Principles aside, the reality of contemporary politics dictates that expediency rather than ethics will prevail. And, as this author has sought to show, the very attraction, and

---

[91] *Ibid.*

[92] Even if – as followers of Braithwaite, *op. cit.*, might argue – it involves forms of 'reintegrative shaming'.

[93] McBarnet, D., *Conviction: Law, the State and the Construction of Justice*, London: Macmillan, 1983, pp. 143–7.

[94] Christie, *op. cit.*

consequent development, of alternatives to prosecution is rooted in the fact that they circumvent the costly traditional processes of state-funded legal aid.

IV THE INVOLVEMENT OF LAWYERS

All forms of dispute processing are based upon a central 'triadic relationship',[95] in which a third party is called upon to resolve the dispute between the conflicting parties. In criminal matters the state appropriates the place of the victim on the basis that the conflict — in Durkheimian phraseology — is deemed to strike at the heart of the 'collective conscience'.[96] Yet this 'triadic relationship' is an inherently unstable one. There exists always the threat that the triad will break down and turn into a relationship of two against one. This danger is most acute in criminal matters, where the boundary between the state as party to the dispute and the state as a neutral third-party arbitrator is particularly blurred and where the power differentials between the parties are so immense. The best way of guaranteeing 'equality of arms' and the preservation of the triadic structure, it is often assumed, is by the insistence upon a neutral arbiter immersed in a legal culture of equal rights and due process and by according the parties legal representation.

Nevertheless, the nature of the roles and ambitions of lawyers and their participation within alternatives to the formal court-based processes are problematic. It is questionable whether it is wise to involve within such processes, or seek mediators from among, lawyers whose traditions and organisational culture are rooted in partisan advisory and representative roles. Rights-based forms of representation may run counter to the logic of interest-based negotiation. Thus, we need to ask to what extent the involvement of lawyers will increase the likelihood that alternatives to prosecution will become subordinated to the essential requirements of the formal process and reproduce its failings — i.e., the processing of large numbers of cases through the 'construction of conviction'[97] — without fully according sufficient weight to its more desirable attributes, i.e., the attempt to maintain an equality of arms.

It is often presumed that the lack of legal representation disadvantages many disputants, particularly if they are the relatively weaker party. While this is very often true in forms of adjudication, it is not necessarily the case for all forms of dispute processing. Crucially it depends upon the third party's role, ambition and their ability to facilitate communication and comprehension. The demands for legal representation in all forms of dispute processing also raise vexed

---

[95] Shapiro, M., *Courts: a Comparative and Political Analysis*, Chicago: Chicago University Press, 1981, p. 1.
[96] Durkheim, E., *The Division of Labour in Society*, New York: Free Press, 1964, p. 73.
[97] McBarnet, *op. cit.*

questions as to how far to extend representationalism. Should victims likewise be accorded access to legal advice and representation? Further, there are clear dangers in the assumption that lawyers, experienced in adversarial litigation and immersed in a culture which celebrates adjudication, can move unproblematically, with a minimum of retraining, into mediatory roles or even act as advisers within an interest-based mediatory process. Roberts has made this point forcefully:

> As active, dominant professionals, accustomed to occupying partisan advisory and representative roles, lawyers should recognise that they may have great difficulty in adapting to the posture of impartial facilitator of other people's decision-making.[98]

This often occurs at the expense of party participation and the more therapeutic and forward-looking concerns which often constitute the original *raison d'être* of many diversionary initiatives.

And yet the antithesis of the professional legal 'management' of disputes through representation, the ideal of 'party control', embodies its own contradictions and unresolved dilemmas in criminal matters. First, who are the parties? For if victims are to return to reclaim their conflicts — an aim that victim/offender mediation purports to meet — then what role does the state occupy within the 'triadic relationship'? Secondly, there appears to be an inevitable tension between the idea of 'party control' and the imposition of a 'triadic relationship' upon what is, after all, reconceived as a bilateral exchange. If full 'party control' were desirable and attainable, it would most likely occur much further away from the long shadows of the court, in genuinely (private) informal social settings. In essence, what is really at issue here is the nature of third-party conflict management, whether it is facilitatory or directive and coercive. The extent to which third-party involvement empowers (rather than disempowers) the parties actively to participate in the disputing process lies at the heart of 'party control'. However, the levers and incentives used by mediators to facilitate such participation and 'sense of control' often verge on undermining the very notion of voluntariness and agency which are fundamental to the core aims of mediation and diversionary processes.[99]

---

[98] Roberts, S., 'Mediation in the Lawyers' Embrace', *Modern Law Review*, 1992, vol. 55, p. 258 at p. 261.
[99] Silbey and Merry, *op. cit.*

V THE ROLE OF THE CROWN PROSECUTION SERVICE

Debates about the scope of future developments in diversion from prosecution soon return to, and revolve around, the nature of the role and ambitions of the CPS. In England and Wales the discretion to prosecute historically has rested almost exclusively with the police, both at various organisational levels and at different times in the early stages of a case.[100] This has placed the police in the dual role of investigators of the crime and the initial prosecutors, a tension which has resulted in what one commentator has called 'prosecution momentum'.[101] This relationship has militated against any consistent policy in favour of diversion from prosecution. The Prosecution of Offences Act 1985 established the CPS as an independent check on prosecutions. It sought to separate the investigator's role from what the Royal Commission on Criminal Procedure 1981 deemed to be the lawyer's role of evaluating the merits of prosecution. Section 10 of the Prosecution of Offences Act 1985 and the Code for Crown Prosecutors issued thereunder give the CPS considerable discretion as to whether or not to proceed with a prosecution[102] and, if a prosecution is to be brought, as to the nature of the charge(s) and the mode of trial. The statutory Code sets out two tests with reference to which the CPS determines whether to continue or discontinue prosecution. The first is an evidential sufficiency test, i.e., whether the case is supported by admissible, substantial and reliable evidence of a quality which offers a 'realistic prospect of conviction'.[103] The second test refers to whether prosecution is in the 'public interest'. The Code reminds Crown Prosecutors that 'the stigma of a conviction can cause very serious harm to the prospects of a youth offender or a young adult'.[104] It also goes on to direct them to 'look at the alternatives to prosecution when they consider the public interest. Crown Prosecutors should tell the police if they think that a caution would be more suitable than a prosecution'.[105]

---

[100] A small number of less commonly prosecuted offences require the consent of either the Attorney-General or the Director of Public Prosecutions before prosecution can proceed.

[101] Sanders, A., 'The Limits to Diversion from Prosecution', *British Journal of Criminology*, 1988, vol. 28, p. 513.

[102] A decision which must be kept under constant review as the case progresses. The CPS recently introduced a first set of national 'Charging Standards for Criminal Offences', which lays out factors relevant to the choice of charge in relation to offences against the person. The aim of the standards is to provide greater uniformity of approach between the police and CPS – see Editorial, *Criminal Law Review*, 1994, p. 777.

[103] Crown Prosecution Service, *The Code for Crown Prosecutors*, London: CPS, 1994, para. 5.1. Sanders has referred to this as 'the fifty one per cent rule' in which the 'winnability' of the case is seen as a central criterion as to whether to proceed (Sanders, A., 'Constructing the Case for the Prosecution', *Journal of Law and Society*, 1987, vol. 14, p. 229). For a discussion of this latest code see Ashworth, A. and Fionda, J., 'The New Code for Crown Prosecutors', *Criminal Law Review*, 1994, p. 894.

[104] Crown Prosecution Service, *op. cit.*, para. 6.8.

[105] *Ibid.*, para. 6.9.

The CPS has no investigative role, unlike prosecution departments in some other countries. Therefore, it remains dependent upon the investigative role of the police for information and evidence.[106] While it may legally discontinue any prosecution initiated by the police, the CPS's diversionary powers are limited by the momentum which results from the initial police construction of a case. Sanders argues that the nature of 'case construction' — which suggests that prosecution is both expedient and desirable — will remain largely unchallenged, as a result of the structural reliance of the CPS upon the police for information combined with the CPS's contradictory position as case vetter (a supposedly inquisitorial function) and case prosecutor (a supposedly accusatorial function).[107] This view is endorsed by Gelsthorpe and Giller's empirical research into the work of the CPS. They found that Crown Prosecutors 'use the same conceptual categories' as the police 'in their decisions to divert or refer to court'.[108] They go on to conclude: 'For those recommended for prosecution the police ''construction'' of the cases provides the basis for Crown Prosecution Service assessment and review.'[109]

Crown Prosecutors may advise the police that a caution, rather than prosecution, is appropriate, but at present the police are not obliged to accept such advice, although the Royal Commission on Criminal Justice recommended that the CPS should be enabled to require the police to administer a caution in lieu of prosecution (provided that the defendant consents). This would increase the ability of the CPS to promote diversion without having to 'abandon' cases altogether through discontinuance, as at present. The Commission recognised that taking 'no further action' may not always be a desirable alternative to prosecution and wished to provide the CPS with a compromise option, albeit indirectly through the agency of the police.[110]

One model of future development would be to increase the role of the CPS along continental lines. This, it is argued, would ensure greater uniformity of decision-making than do existing local police arrangements. [111]

Currently, in England and Wales it is possible for the prosecutor or the court to discontinue a case, but not to defer a case in its early stages and recommend

---

[106] Gelsthorpe, L. and Giller, H., 'More Justice for Juveniles: Does More Mean Better?', *Criminal Law Review*, 1990, pp. 153, 161.
[107] Sanders, A., *op. cit.* (1988), and see McConville, M., Sanders, A. and Leng, R., *The Case for the Prosecution*, London: Routledge, 1991, ch. 7.
[108] Gelsthorpe and Giller, *op. cit.*, pp. 161–2.
[109] *Ibid.*, p. 162.
[110] Royal Commission on Criminal Justice, *op. cit.*, para. 50.
[111] Leigh and Zedner, *op. cit.*

mediation.[112] In Scotland, in contrast, the procurator fiscal may defer cases for mediation provided that they are deemed to be of sufficient seriousness to merit prosecution. It is on this basis that the Scottish Association for the Care and Resettlement of Offenders (SACRO) Reparation and Mediation Project operates. [113] It has been suggested that the CPS could be given a similar role in England to facilitate and extend the space for, and availability of, mediation.[114]

VI THE VOICE OF THE VICTIM

The appropriate involvement of the victim in the criminal justice process is both a vexed problem and one that cannot be wished away or ignored. The victim's interests may stand in stark conflict with the public interest, the offender's rights and notions of justice.[115] Nevertheless, victims need to be accorded a degree of agency and voice.

The appropriate space for this to occur, in order better to reconcile these tensions, needs to be located at an arm's length from what is a highly punitive and stigmatising criminal court-based process. The dangers of incorporating the victim into the adversarial court-based process of sentencing and punishment are immense. They have begun to be expressed in relation to the Australasian and American experiences of victim impact statements, whereby the impact of the crime on a victim is taken into account in the proceedings. [116] In England and Wales, in contrast, the Code for Crown Prosecutors, in elaborating the appropriate criteria upon which public interest considerations should be made, makes very clear that Crown Prosecutors must always think 'very carefully' about the interests of the victim as an 'important factor when deciding where the public interest lies'.[117] What is a very real current concern is that the diversion or discontinuance of prosecution by the police, CPS or other executive body, may fail to meet the needs and demands of victims. [118] What is more problematic is that research has highlighted the reluctance of the

---

[112] Though under s. 23 of the Prosecution of Offences Act 1985 the accused may demand that the prosecution be continued.

[113] Warner, S., *Making Amends: Justice for Victims and Offenders*, Aldershot: Avebury, 1992, pp. 5–8.

[114] Dignan, J., 'Repairing the Damage: Can Reparation be Made to Work in the Service of Diversion?', *British Journal of Criminology*, 1992, vol. 32, p. 453.

[115] See Ashworth, A., 'Punishment and Compensation: Victims, Offenders and the State', *Oxford Journal of Legal Studies*, 1986, vol. 6, p. 86, and Zedner, *op. cit.*

[116] Ashworth, A., 'Victim Impact Statements and Sentencing', *Criminal Law Review*, 1993, p. 498.

[117] Crown Prosecution Service, *op. cit.*, para. 6.7.

[118] In 1994 the CPS decided not to prosecute 159,803 cases, which constitutes nearly a 50% increase on the 1987 figure of 108,000.

police to prosecute in certain types of cases, particularly cases involving accusations of rape, racial motive and 'domestic violence'.[119]

Despite a growing victims' 'movement', in which victims' 'needs' and 'rights' increasingly are recognised as having been for too long disregarded by the criminal justice system,[120] and the Government's Victim's Charter,[121] considerable dissatisfaction is still felt by many victims of crime. Some victims, despite their criticisms of the legal system, have turned to it as their potential remedy in the form of either civil actions for damages or private prosecutions. Although there are no clear figures on the number of private prosecutions, lawyers suggest that while the number of cases of neighbours bringing petty disputes to the criminal courts has declined, there is a comparatively new phenomenon of private prosecution of serious cases.[122] The cost of private prosecutions, given the lack of legal aid, means that this kind of remedy will only ever be within the reach of certain groups of people.

VII   THE PROBLEM OF 'NET WIDENING'

A central and much debated problem at the heart of diversion is the issue of net widening. Given the formalisation of informal processes, the risk is that new populations are being drawn into the criminal justice system rather than being diverted away from it. The problem remains to what extent diversion is used as an alternative to genuinely informal processes, or as an alternative to screening out by the police or prosecution service ('no further action', informal caution or other discontinuance), but not as an alternative to prosecution.[123] Rather than seeing the various developments outlined in this chapter as alternatives *to* processing criminal disputes, perhaps we need to consider the extent to which they are part of a much larger framework which supplements and assists the formal criminal court in its work. In other words they may better be understood as alternative methods *of* processing criminal disputes.

---

[119] Edwards, *op. cit.* (1989). This problem has increasingly become acknowledged by some police forces and the Home Office. Recently, specialist domestic violence units have been set up within police forces – encouraged by a Home Office circular 60/90 – separate from routine policing so as to counter the traditional (de)construction of such cases. Nevertheless, their success remains questionable (see Home Office, *Policing Domestic Violence in the 1990s*, Research Study 139, London: HMSO, 1995).

[120] See Mawby, R., 'Victims' Needs or Victims' Rights: Alternative Approaches to Policy Making', in Maguire, M. and Ponting, J. (eds), *Victims of Crime: A New Deal?*, Milton Keynes: Open University Press, 1988, and Meirs, *op. cit.*

[121] Home Office, *op. cit.* (1990).

[122] Cohen, N. and Victor, P., 'Do-It-Yourself Justice', *Independent on Sunday*, 30 April 1995. The private prosecution of the alleged murderers of Stephen Lawrence is a notable case in point.

[123] Cohen, S., *Visions of Social Control*, Cambridge: Polity, 1985, p. 52, and Pratt, J., 'Diversion from the Juvenile Court', *British Journal of Criminology*, 1986, vol. 26, p. 212.

Much has been written on the possible impact of net widening, and numerous empirical studies have attempted to quantify the extent to which it occurs within existing systems.[124] What is clear is that the dangers of net widening are real. Nevertheless, they have tended to be overstated.[125] Implicit in much of the literature is the assumption that net widening is inherently 'a bad thing' in all circumstances. It often fails to acknowledge the need to recognise that some forms of intervention and social control are more benign and desirable than others. Rather than rejecting diversion outright as an impossible aim, there is a pressing need to construct and provide rigorous criteria for distinguishing and choosing between the more malign and benign forms of social intervention that diversion schemes herald.

VIII EXITS FROM, OR ACCESS TO, JUSTICE?

There is a number of further questions which need to be considered in any evaluation of diversionary initiatives. The first is whether these methods of processing criminal disputes involve an abandonment or a dilution of legality; and, if so, whether the loss of formal safeguards and procedural protections of the formal court is a price worth paying? Secondly, are we witnessing a shift in the framework for negotiating the meaning of particular events, from a language of claims and rights typical of legal discourse to a language grounded in the shared interests, mutual experiences and inter-dependencies of the parties? What are the implications of any such shift, particularly for the voluntariness of the parties?

A legitimate concern of many commentators is that forms of diversion represent means of disposing of cases which circumvent the (costly) procedural safeguards of the legal form, due process and professional representation. The principal fear, as suggested earlier, is that power imbalances between the parties will remain unchecked. In a criminal justice context this is particularly worrying given the awesome power differentials between the individual (potentially young) suspect and the state as represented by the police/CPS. It is argued by some supporters of mediation that one way to address this power imbalance (at least after guilt has been established) is to return the conflict to the parties themselves. While this appears to remove the obvious presence of

---

[124] See McMahon, M., 'Net-Widening: Vagaries in the Use of a Concept', *British Journal of Criminology*, 1990, vol. 30, p. 245, and Duff, P., 'The Prosecutor Fine and Social Control', *British Journal of Criminology*, 1993, vol. 33, p. 481.

[125] McMahon, *op. cit.*; and Matthews, R., 'Decarceration and Social Control: Fantasies and Realities', *International Journal of the Sociology of Law*, 1987, vol. 15, p. 39. Also see Cohen's recognition of the shortfalls of his own earlier position in Cohen, S., 'The Critical Discourse on "Social Control": Notes on the Concept as a Hammer', *International Journal of the Sociology of Law*, 1989, vol. 17, p. 347.

the state as one of the conflicting parties, social power imbalances remain an important consideration. The mediator is placed in the delicate position of acting simultaneously as the guardian against power imbalances within the process, which may require him or her to intervene on behalf of one of the parties; the guarantor of procedural safeguards and personal safety; the symbolic representative of the 'moral community'; and the facilitator of an agreed settlement. These roles do not sit together easily or unproblematically.

In addition, the emphasis on forms of negotiation of the parties' common interests — as in mediation — rather than on their legal entitlements as the basis for settlement, runs counter to ideals embodied in notions of legality. It raises the danger of individualised justice, as well as the concern that, in the absence of adequate legal safeguards and direct appeal to the formal court, differential social power relations between the parties remain unchecked and will influence eventual settlements. Diversion, as opposed to prosecution, assumes that decisions which would otherwise have been made by the court can and should be made by an administrative authority. The concern is that we appear to be witnessing a process in which legal definitions and due process are giving way to decision-making by administrative and professional bodies.

And yet, implicit in many of these critiques is an uncritical assumption that:

(a) the formal criminal justice system is in accordance with notions of legality;

(b) professional representation is always in the interests of the parties; and

(c) a rights-based approach to negotiation is desirable in all cases.

After all, the principal finding of years of socio-legal research into criminal justice processes has consistently revealed that the courts and legal profession are primarily concerned with the processing and management of large numbers of cases. [126] Given the critiques of legal processes and legal representation, we have to ask whether this shift from rights-based negotiation to interest-based negotiation is inherently negative. Rather, what is needed is the regulation of the negative aspects of many existing administrative decision-making bodies, their discretionary and secretive nature and lack of openness, accountability and reviewability.

Diversionary processes are premised upon a concept of voluntary participation. The nature of the interests and social networks which structure and are

---

[126] See McConville, M., Hodgson, L., Bridges, L. and Pavlovic, A., *Standing Accused*, Oxford: Clarendon Press, 1994; Sanders, A., Bridges, L., Mulvaney, A. and Crozier, G., *Advice and Assistance at Police Stations and the 24 Hour Duty Solicitor Scheme*, London: Lord Chancellor's Department, 1989; and Sanders, A. and Young, R., *Criminal Justice*, London: Butterworths, 1994, ch. 6 and 7.

embedded in a dispute are thus central to an interest-based approach to negotiation. There is a greater incentive to settle where close-knit social networks link the two disputing parties; escape from a local social system and avoidance of a dispute are costly; the parties must deal with one another in the future, or there are expectations of a future to the relationship; the cost of substituting the relationship is high; and the availability of avoidance of court is culturally acceptable and socially possible.[127] The therapeutic and socially constructive aspects of interest-based negotiation and conflict resolution are unlikely to be realised if some, or all, of the parties to the conflict are coerced into the process.[128] Given the complex interrelationship between forms of diversion and the court process, it is questionable whether they can ever be truly voluntary. The considerable incentives, 'subtle coercive pressures' and inducements to participate in diversionary schemes (for victims as well as offenders) run counter to the notion of 'voluntariness'. There are dangers that decisions by suspects in their acceptance of guilt in relation to a particular charge will be influenced by the availability of alternatives to prosecution, particularly within the broader context of a criminal justice system which increasingly is willing to recognise formal plea bargaining.[129] The general tone of criminal justice in trying to reduce the case-load on the courts through incentives, can also be read as creating penalties for those who choose to go to trial. The further danger is that not only do incentives and inducements undermine voluntariness, but they also can become pressures and penalties. The dilemma remains that legal oversight of diversionary schemes like mediation and reparation may be required in order to ensure that individualised justice does not trample upon the rights of any given individuals. However, at the same time the nature of such oversight may well undermine any genuinely interest-based and relational approach to conflicts.

IX MANAGERIALIST AND NORMATIVE AIMS: AN UNRESOLV-ABLE CONFLICT?

A final concern that has been alluded to throughout this chapter, relates to the question of whether an antagonism exists between the administrative and the normative aims of particular forms of diversion. To what extent do the former serve to undermine the latter? Some commentators have highlighted the structural pressures within an accusatorial criminal justice system which

---

[127] Merry, S.E., 'Defining "Success" in the Neighborhood Justice Movement', in Tomasic and Feeley, *op. cit.*, p. 177.

[128] Silbey and Merry, *op. cit.*, p. 13, suggest that coercion of some form is an essential prerequisite of mediator settlement strategies.

[129] Royal Commission on Criminal Justice, *op. cit.*, pp. 110–14.

facilitate and encourage prosecution and severely delimit any diversionary potential.[130] While such pressures are real, they should not be over-stated. First, we should not lose sight of the fact that the criminal justice process is not a unified or coherent whole, but rather comprises a variety of agencies with differing ideologies, interests and traditions.[131] Secondly, there are clear dangers in characterising and classifying any legal process in overly neat terminology, such as 'accusatorial' as against 'inquisitorial' systems (or functions). Comparative studies show that there are no ideal or pure systems to be found empirically and that the rhetoric of law and legal systems rarely matches the practice.[132] Lastly, there are contradictory political pressures exerted upon criminal justice agencies which prioritise the efficient and cost-effective management of cases. Such pressures may run counter to the retributive prosecution of cases with which the accusatorial system is traditionally associated.

The administrative ethos of 'new public management' in criminal justice may have been relatively late in coming — in comparison with other public services — but its impact, although largely neglected by most commentators, is nevertheless extensive.[133] We are witnessing what some commentators have referred to as the growth of an 'essentially bureaucratic-administrative law-enforcement system',[134] in which institutionally derived managerial goals rather than normatively or socially derived ones, have become dominant.[135] The growing emphasis on the efficient management of criminal justice places greater import on the system-like qualities of criminal justice. Criminal justice is increasingly viewed as requiring 'smoothing' through the removal and/or elimination of 'friction', 'duplication', 'bottlenecks',[136] all of which is in accordance with the increased use of pre-trial diversion, 'fast-track' prosecution and early case assessment to weed out minor offences.[137] These developments are not unique to England and Wales but resonate across Europe

---

[130] Sanders, op. cit. (1987) and McConville et al., op. cit. (1991).
[131] See Crawford, A., 'Social Values and Managerial Goals: Police and Probation Officers' Experiences and Views of Inter-Agency Co-operation', Policing and Society, 1994, vol. 4, p. 323.
[132] See Leigh and Zedner, op. cit. and Crawford (forthcoming), op. cit.
[133] Among those commentators who have identified the impact of new public management on criminal justice, the most developed and insightful are Reiner, R., 'Fin de Siècle Blues: the Police Face the Millennium', Political Quarterly, 1992, vol. 63, p. 37; and Lacey, N., 'Government as Manager, Citizen as Consumer: The Case of the Criminal Justice Act 1991', Modern Law Review, 1994, vol. 57, p. 534.
[134] Bottoms, A. E., 'Neglected Features of Contemporary Penal Systems', in Garland, D. and Young, P. (eds), The Power To Punish, London: Heinemann, 1983, p. 186.
[135] Garland, D., Punishment and Modern Society, Oxford: Clarendon Press, 1990, p. 184.
[136] See Moxon, D. (ed.), Managing Criminal Justice: A Collection of Papers, London: HMSO, 1985.
[137] See Feeley, M. and Simon, J., 'Actuarial Justice: the Emerging New Criminal Law', in Nelken, D. (ed.), The Futures of Criminology, London: Sage, 1994.

and North America.[138] As Feeley and Simon suggest, the new iconography of criminal justice is 'the flow chart of systems analysis'.[139] This growing intra-organisational 'bureaucratic' focus of the three 'Es' — efficiency, effectiveness, and economy — hierarchical control and an emphasis on management-by-outcomes, means that forms of diversion remain attractive options.

This begs the question to what extent administrative priorities serve to undermine the normative (most notably reparative) potential of diversionary schemes. The danger of such an eventuality is augmented by the very fact that many such schemes seek to meet multiple normative and administrative aims, including the promotion of attitude change in offenders, greater involvement of the victim in the process of justice, cutting of cost to the public purse, reduction in court congestion, promotion of restorative justice, and destig-matisation. Perversely, while multiple aims enable diversionary schemes to draw upon a wide and diverse audience for support, they also constitute their Achilles heel. In seeking to meet the divergent aims that they proclaim, these schemes — particularly mediation and reparation — are pulled in different, and often competing, directions as they attempt to satisfy the divergent demands of their different constituents. Given the managerialist appeal of diversion and the administrative ethic from which it draws much of its support, the difficulty — for those committed to extending mediation/diversion because of its reparative appeal — is to ensure that its normative potential is not undermined by the need to dispose of large numbers of cases as quickly and as cheaply as possible. Otherwise, mediation and other normatively driven forms of diversion will merely provide prosecutors, lawyers and judges with a means of disposing of 'junk cases': the inconvenient, unprofitable and time-consuming. The fear remains that outcome pressures, in an increasingly managerial age, will undermine normative process-oriented goals.

X CONCLUSION

The net widening literature rightly warns us of two concerns.[140] First, it highlights the means by which the proliferation of new diversionary schemes and 'alternatives' to the court may act not to undermine the formal court process and its adjudicative/punitive procedures, but on the contrary to rejuvenate and re-legitimate those processes. Secondly, in doing so it may

---

[138] See the collection of articles in van Dijk, J. (ed.), *Criminal Law in Action: An Overview of Current Issues in Western Societies*, Deventer: Kluwer, 1986, particularly those by Blumstein, Steenhuis and Peters.
[139] Feeley and Simon, *op. cit.*, p. 188.
[140] See Cohen, *op. cit.* (1985).

produce a two-tiered or multi-tiered system in which the degree of formal legality and the extent of legal advice and assistance is determined not by any intrinsic normative quality but by extraneous considerations, like cost, efficiency and convenience. This has extensive implications for the provision and delivery of criminal legal aid in England and Wales.

The specific form that future developments will take remains uncertain. However, it has been the aim of this chapter to raise wider issues, all too often ignored within debates on criminal legal aid. Ultimately, the nature and extent of alternatives to prosecution will reshape the institutional supply of criminal justice and the avoidance of litigation, lawyers and legal aid.

Lastly, the managerialist appeal of forms of diversion is unlikely to disappear. If anything, it is likely to grow more intense in coming years. The uncertainty is the extent to which this appeal can, and will, serve to undermine their reparative and normative potential. The current reality is that priority is too often given to administrative requirements in which moral and ethical arguments are subordinated to the demands of 'smooth management' — although called upon from time to time as rhetorical devices to legitimate developments. The danger, then, is that even the most normatively driven experiments in restorative justice, as diversion from prosecution, may come to constitute exits from, rather than access to, justice.

Bibliography

Note: Full references for all sources used in this book are provided in the footnotes to each individual chapter. A bibliography is provided for ease of reference and as a resource for those with an interest in access to criminal justice and criminal legal aid. Only items referred to in this book are listed here, but some of the more dated or minor references have not been included.

Abel, R., 'Law without Politics: Legal Aid under Advanced Capitalism', *UCLA Law Review*, 1985, vol. 32, p. 474.

Abel, R., *The Legal Profession in England and Wales*, Oxford: Basil Blackwell, 1988.

Abel, R., 'Between Market and State: The Legal Profession in Turmoil', *Modern Law Review*, 1989, vol. 52, p. 285.

Abel-Smith, B. and Stevens, R., *Lawyers and the Courts*, London: Heinemann, 1967.

Alder, C. and Wundersitz, J. (eds), *Family Conferencing and Juvenile Justice*, Canberra: Australian Institute of Criminology, 1994.

Armstrong, S., 'Labor's Legal Aid Scheme: The Light That Failed', in Scotton, R., and Ferber, H. (eds), *Public Expenditure and Social Policy in Australia Vol. 2*, Melbourne: Longman Cheshire, 1979.

Armstrong, S., 'The Objective and the Reality: Legal Aid in Australia 1984', *Labor Forum*, 1985, vol. 6, p. 6.

Ashworth, A., 'Punishment and Compensation: Victims, Offenders and the State', *Oxford Journal of Legal Studies*, 1986, vol. 6, p. 86.

Ashworth, A., 'Victim Impact Statements and Sentencing', *Criminal Law Review*, 1993, p. 498.

Ashworth, A., *The Criminal Process: an Evaluative Study*, Oxford: Oxford University Press, 1994.

Bibliography

Ashworth, A., *Principles of Criminal Law*, 2nd ed., Oxford: Oxford University Press, 1995.

Ashworth, A., *The English Criminal Process: a Review of Empirical Research*, Centre for Criminological Research, University of Oxford, 1984.

Ashworth, A. and Fionda, J., 'The New Code for Crown Prosecutors', *Criminal Law Review*, 1994, p. 894.

Astor, H., 'The Unrepresented Defendant Revisited: a Consideration of the Role of the Clerk in Magistrates' Courts', *Journal of Law and Society*, 1986, vol. 13, p. 225.

Australian Bureau of Statistics, 'Usage of Legal Services, New South Wales, October 1990', Canberra: ABS, 1991.

Babbage, C., *On the Economy of Machinery and Manufactures*, London: C. Knight 1832.

Baldwin, J., 'Legal Advice at the Police Station', *Criminal Law Review*, 1993, p. 371.

Baldwin, J., *The Role of Legal Representatives at the Police Station*, Royal Commission on Criminal Justice, Research Study No. 3, London: HMSO, 1993.

Baldwin, J., *Preparing the Record of Taped Interview*, Royal Commission on Criminal Justice Research Study No. 2, London: HMSO, 1992.

Baldwin J. and Hill S., *The Operation of the Green Form Scheme in England and Wales*, London: Lord Chancellor's Department, 1988.

Barber, B., 'Some Problems in the Sociology of the Professions', *Daedalus*, 1963, vol. 92, no. 4, p. 669.

Barron, A., and Scott, C., 'The Citizen's Charter Programme', *Modern Law Review*, 1992, vol. 55, p. 526.

Beattie, J.M., 'Crime and the Courts in Surrey 1736–1753', in Cockburn, J.S. (ed.), *Crime in England 1550–1800*, London: Methuen and Co., 1977.

Beddard, R., *Human Rights in Europe*, 3rd ed., Cambridge: Cambridge University Press, 1993.

Bell, J., 'Discretionary Decision-Making: A Jurisprudential View', in Hawkins, K. (ed.), *The Uses of Discretion*, Oxford: Clarendon Press, 1992.

Benson, Sir Henry, *Final Report of the Royal Commission on Legal Services in England and Wales*, Cm 7648, HMSO, 1979.

Berlin, I., *Four Essays on Liberty*, Oxford: Oxford University Press, 1979.

Bevan, G., Holland, T. and Partington, M., *Organising Cost Effective Access to Justice*, Memorandum No. 7, Social Market Foundation, July 1994.

Black, D., 'The Mobilization of Law', *Journal of Legal Studies*, 1973, vol. 2, p. 125.

Blagg, H. and Smith, D., *Crime, Penal Policy and Social Work*, Harlow: Longman, 1989.

346

Blagg, H., Pearson, G., Sampson, A., Smith, D. and Stubbs, P., 'Inter-Agency Co-operation: Rhetoric and Reality', in Hope, T. and Shaw, M. (eds), *Communities and Crime Reduction*, London: HMSO, 1988.

Blake, M., 'Legal Assistance for Servicemen', *American Bar Association Journal*, 1951, vol. 37, p. 9.

Blankenburg, E., 'Comparing Legal Aid Schemes in Europe', *Civil Justice Quarterly*, 1992, vol. 11, p. 106.

Bonafé-Schmitt, J.-P., *La Médiation: Une Justice Douce*, Paris: Syros-Alternatives, 1992.

Borrie, G.J. and Varcoe, J.R., *Legal Aid in Criminal Proceedings: A Regional Survey*, Birmingham: Institute of Judicial Administration, 1970.

Bottoms, A.E., 'Neglected Features of Contemporary Penal Systems', in Garland, D. and Young, P. (eds), *The Power To Punish*, London: Heinemann, 1983.

Bottoms, A.E. and McClean, J.D., *Defendants in the Criminal Process*, London: Routledge & Kegan Paul, 1976.

Bourdieu, P., *Outline of a Theory of Practice*, Cambridge: Cambridge University Press, 1977.

Braithwaite, J., *Crime, Shame and Reintegration*, Cambridge: Cambridge University Press, 1989.

Braverman, H., *Labour and Monopoly Capital*, New York: Monthly Review Press, 1976.

Bridges, L., 'The professionalisation of criminal justice', *Legal Action*, August 1992, p. 7.

Bridges, L., 'The Royal Commission's Approach to Criminal Defence Services – A Case of Professional Incompetence', in McConville, M. and Bridges, L. (eds), *Criminal Justice in Crisis*, Aldershot: Edward Elgar, 1994.

Bridges, L., 'The silence about what it will all cost', *Parliamentary Briefing*, February/March 1994, p. 10.

Bridges, L., 'Guilty Pleas and the Politics of Research', *Legal Action*, April 1993, p. 9.

Bridges, L. and Bunyan, T., 'Britain's new urban policing strategy', *Journal of Law and Society*, 1983, vol. 10, p. 85.

Bridges L., Sufrin, B., Whetton, J. and White, R., *Legal Services in Birmingham*, Birmingham: Birmingham University, 1975.

Bridges, L. and Hodgson, J., 'Improving custodial legal advice', *Criminal Law Review*, 1995, p. 101.

Brown, D., Ellis, T. and Larcombe, K., *Changing the Code: Police detention under the revised PACE Codes of Practice*, Home Office Research Study No. 129, London: HMSO, 1992.

347

Brownlee, I.D., Mulcahy, A. and Walker, C., 'Pre-Trial Reviews, Court Efficiency and Justice: A Study in Leeds and Bradford Magistrates' Courts', *The Howard Journal*, 1994, vol. 83, p. 109.

Burstein, P. and Monaghan, K., 'Equal Employment Opportunity and the Mobilization of Law', *Law and Society Review*, 1986, vol. 20, p. 355.

Burton, A., 'The Demise of Criminal Legal Aid', *New Law Journal*, 1994, vol. 144, p. 1491.

Cain, M., 'The Symbol Traders', in Cain, M. and Harrington, C.B. (eds), *Lawyers in a Postmodern World*, Buckingham: Open University Press, 1994.

Cain, M., 'The General Practice Lawyer and the Client: Towards a Radical Conception', in Dingwall, R. and Lewis, P. (eds), *The Sociology of the Professions*, London: Macmillan, 1983.

Cape, E., 'Defence services: What should defence lawyers do in police stations?', in McConville, M. and Bridges, L. (eds), *Criminal Justice in Crisis*, Aldershot: Edward Elgar, 1994.

Cappelletti, M., Gordley, J. and Johnson, E., *Toward Equal Justice*, Dobbs Ferry, New York: Oceana, 1975.

Carlen, P., *Magistrates' Justice*, London: Martin Robertson, 1976.

Carney, C., 'The Growth of Legal Aid in the Republic of Ireland', *Irish Jurist*, 1979, vol. XIV, pp. 61 and 211.

Cavadino, M., *Mental Health Law in Context*, Aldershot: Dartmouth, 1989.

Choo, A., *Abuse of Process and Judicial Stays of Criminal Proceedings*, Oxford: Oxford University Press, 1993.

Christie, N., 'Conflicts as Property', *British Journal of Criminology*, 1977, vol. 17, p. 1.

Cohen, S., *Visions of Social Control*, Cambridge: Polity Press, 1985.

Cohen, S., 'The Critical Discourse on "Social Control": Notes on the Concept as a Hammer', *International Journal of the Sociology of Law*, 1989, vol. 17, p. 347.

Conciliation Project Unit, *Report to the Lord Chancellor's Department on the Costs and Effectiveness of Conciliation in England and Wales*, Newcastle: Conciliation Project Unit, 1989.

Conseil d'État, *L'aide juridique pour un meilleur accès au droit et à la justice*, Paris: La documentation française, 1991.

Cooper, D., 'The Citizen's Charter and Radical Democracy', *Social and Legal Studies*, 1993, vol. 2, p. 150.

Cornish, W.R. and Clark G. de N., *Law and Society in England 1750–1950*, London: Sweet & Maxwell, 1989.

Cotterrell, R., *The Sociology of the Law*, London: Butterworths, 1992.

Cousins, M., 'Civil Legal Aid in France, Ireland, The Netherlands and the United Kingdom', *Civil Justice Quarterly*, 1993, vol. 12, p. 154.

Cousins, M., 'The Politics of Legal Aid – A Solution in Search of a Problem?', *Civil Justice Quarterly*, 1994, vol. 13, p. 111.

Craig, P., *Administrative Law*, 3rd ed., London: Sweet & Maxwell, 1994.

Cranston, R. and Adams, D., 'Legal Aid in Australia', *The Australian Law Journal*, 1972, vol. 46, p. 508.

Crawford, A., 'Access to Justice and Alternatives to Litigation in England and Wales', 1994, conference paper, Lille.

Crawford, A., 'The Partnership Approach to Community Crime Prevention: Corporatism at the Local Level?', *Social and Legal Studies*, 1994, vol. 3, p. 497.

Crawford, A., 'Social Values and Managerial Goals: Police and Probation Officers' Experiences and Views of Inter-Agency Co-operation', *Policing and Society*, 1994, vol. 4, p. 323.

Crawford, A. and Jones, M., 'Inter-Agency Co-operation and Community-Based Crime Prevention', *British Journal of Criminology*, 1995, vol. 35, p. 17.

Crawford, A., Jones, T., Woodhouse, T. and Young, J., *The Second Islington Crime Survey*, Enfield: Centre for Criminology, Middlesex Polytechnic, 1990.

Criminal Legal Aid Review Committee, *Report*, Prl. 9986, Dublin: Stationery Office, 1981.

Crown Prosecution Service, *The Code For Crown Prosecutors*, London: CPS, 1994.

Curran, B., *The Legal Needs of the Public*, Chicago: American Bar Foundation, 1977.

Davis, G., *Making Amends: Mediation and Reparation in Criminal Justice*, London: Routledge, 1992.

Davis, G., 'Reparation in the UK: Dominant Themes and Neglected Themes', in Messmer, H. and Otto, H.-U. (eds), *Restorative Justice on Trial*, Dordrecht: Kluwer, 1992.

Davis, G., Boucherat, J. and Watson, D., 'Pre-Court Decision-Making in Juvenile Justice', *British Journal of Criminology*, 1989, vol. 29, p. 219.

Davis, G., Boucherat, J. and Watson, D., *A Preliminary Study of Victim Offender Mediation and Reparation Schemes in England and Wales*, Research and Planning Unit Paper, No. 42, London: Home Office, 1987.

Davis, G., Boucherat, J. and Watson, D., 'Reparation in the Service of Diversion: the Subordination of a Good Idea', *The Howard Journal of Criminal Justice*, 1988, vol. 27, p. 127.

Davis, J., 'A Poor Man's System of Justice: the London Police Courts in the Second Half of the Nineteenth Century', *Historical Journal*, 1984, vol. 27, p. 309.

Dell, S., *Silent in Court*, London: Bell, 1971.

Derrida, J., *Force de loi*, Paris: Galilée, 1994.

Dhavan, R., 'Legal Education as Restrictive Practice: a Sceptical View', in Twining, W., Kibble, N. and Dhavan, R., *Access to Legal Education and the Legal Profession*, London: Butterworths, 1989.

Dias, C. and Paul, J., *Lawyers in the Third World*, Uppsala: Scandinavian Institute of African Studies, 1981.

Dias, C. and Paul, J., 'Developing Legal Resources for Participatory Organisations of the Rural Poor', *Third World Legal Studies, 1985*.

Dignan, J., *Repairing the Damage: An Evaluation of an Experimental Adult Reparation Scheme in Kettering*, Sheffield: Centre for Criminological and Legal Research, University of Sheffield, 1990.

Dignan, J., 'Repairing the Damage: Can Reparation be Made to Work in the Service of Diversion?', *British Journal of Criminology*, 1992, vol. 32, p. 453.

Dirks, J., *Making Legal Aid Pay*, London: Waterlow, 1989.

Dixon, D., 'Common Sense, Legal Advice, and the Right of Silence', *Public Law*, 1991, p. 233.

Dixon, D., 'Legal Regulation and Policing Practice', *Social and Legal Studies*, 1992, vol. 1, p. 515.

Duff, P., 'The Prosecutor Fine and Social Control', *British Journal of Criminology*, 1993, vol. 33, p. 481.

Duff, P., 'The Prosecutor Fine', *Oxford Journal of Legal Studies*, 1994, vol. 14, p. 565.

Duff, P. and Meechan, K., 'The Prosecutor Fine', *Criminal Law Review*, 1992, p. 22.

Duman, D., 'The Creation and Diffusion of a Professional Ideology in Nineteenth Century England', *Journal of Social History*, 1979, vol. 27, p. 113.

Durkheim, E., *Professional Ethics and Civic Morals*, London: Routledge & Kegan Paul, 1957.

Durkheim, E., *The Division of Labour in Society*, New York: Free Press, 1964.

Dworkin, G. 'The Progress and Future of Legal Aid in Civil Litigation', *Modern Law Review*, 1965, vol. 28, p. 432.

Dworkin, R.M., 'Principle, Policy, Procedure', in Tapper, C. (ed.), *Crime, Proof and Punishment*, London: Butterworths, 1981.

Eckhoff, T., 'The Mediator, the Judge and the Administrator in Conflict-Resolution', *Acta Sociologica*, 1966, vol. 10, p. 158.

Edwards, S., *Policing 'Domestic' Violence*, London: Sage, 1989.

Ehrlich, E., 'The Sociology of Law', *Harvard Law Review*, 1922, vol. 36, p. 130.

Emerson, R. and Paley, B., 'Organizational Horizons and Complaint-Filing', in Hawkins, K. (ed.), *The Uses of Discretion*, Oxford: Clarendon Press, 1992.

Esping-Andersen, G., *The Three Worlds of Welfare Capitalism*, Cambridge: Polity, 1990.

Evans, R., 'Comparing Young Adult and Juvenile Cautioning in the Metropolitan Police District', *Criminal Law Review*, 1993, p. 572.

Evans, R., 'Cautioning: Counting the Cost of Retrenchment', *Criminal Law Review*, 1994, p. 566.

Evans, R. and Wilkinson, C., 'Variations in Police Cautioning Policy and Practice in England and Wales', *Howard Journal of Criminal Justice*, 1990, vol. 29, p. 155.

Fairall, P., 'The Right not to be Tried Unfairly without Counsel: *Dietrich v The Queen*', *University of Western Australia Law Review*, 1992, vol. 22, p. 396.

Fallon, P. and Verry, D., *The Economics of Labour Markets*, Oxford: Philip Allan, 1988.

Faulkner, D., 'Relational Justice: A Dynamic for Reform', in Burnside, J. and Baker, N. (eds), *Relational Justice: Repairing the Breach*, Winchester: Waterside Press, 1994.

Feeley, M., *The Process is the Punishment*, New York: Sage, 1979.

Feeley, M. and Simon, J., 'Actuarial Justice: the Emerging New Criminal Law', in Nelken, D. (ed.), *The Futures of Criminology*, London: Sage, 1994.

Feldman, D., *Civil Liberties and Human Rights in England and Wales*, Oxford: Clarendon Press, 1993.

Felstead, A., 'The Social Organisation of the Franchise: a Case of Controlled Self-Employment', *Journal of Work, Employment and Society*, 1991, vol. 5, p. 37.

Fenwick, H., 'Curtailing the Right to Silence, Access to Legal Advice, and Section 78', *Criminal Law Review*, 1995, p. 132.

Finlay, Mr Justice, *First Report of the Committee on Legal Aid for the Poor*, Cm 2638, London: HMSO, 1926.

Finlay, Mr Justice, *Final Report of the Committee on Legal Aid for the Poor*, Cm 3016, London: HMSO, 1928.

Fleming, D., *The Mixed Model of Legal Aid in Australia*, Paper to the 'Legal Aid in the Post Welfare State Society Conference', Den Haag, The Netherlands, April 1994.

Foucault, M., *Discipline and Punish: The Birth of the Prison*, London: Allen Lane, 1977.

Freeman, M.D.A., *Lloyd's Introduction to Jurisprudence*, London, Sweet & Maxwell, 1994.

Freidson, E., *Profession of Medicine: A Study of the Sociology of Applied Knowledge*, New York: Dodd and Mead, 1970.

Freidson, E., 'The Theory of Professions: State of the Art', in Dingwall, R. and Lewis, P. (eds), *The Sociology of the Professions*, London: Macmillan, 1983.

Fuller, L. and Smith, V., 'Consumers' Reports: Management by Customers in a Changing Economy', *Journal of Work, Employment and Society*, 1991, vol. 5, p. 1.

Galanter, M., 'Mega-Law and Mega-Lawyering in the Contemporary United States', in Dingwall, R. and Lewis, P. (eds), *The Sociology of the Professions*, London: Macmillan, 1983.

Galligan, D., *Discretionary Powers: A Legal Study of Official Discretion*, Oxford: Clarendon Press, 1986.

Garfinkel, H., 'Conditions of Successful Degradation Ceremonies', *American Journal of Sociology*, 1956, vol. 61, p. 420.

Garland, D., *Punishment and Modern Society*, Oxford: Clarendon Press, 1990, p. 184.

Gatrell, V.A.C. and Hadden, T.B., 'Criminal Statistics and their Interpretation' in Wrigley, E.A. (ed.), *Nineteenth Century Society: Essays in the Use of Quantitative Methods for the Study of Social Data*, Cambridge: Cambridge University Press, 1972.

Gearty, C., 'The European Court of Human Rights and the Protection of Civil Liberties: an Overview', *Cambridge Law Journal*, 1993, vol. 52, p. 89.

Gelsthorpe, L. and Giller, H., 'More Justice for Juveniles: Does More Mean Better?', *Criminal Law Review*, 1990, p. 153.

Giles, M. and Lancaster, T., 'Political Transition, Social Development and Legal Mobilization in Spain', *American Political Science Review*, 1989, vol. 83, p. 817.

Giller, H. and Tutt, N., 'Police Cautioning of Juveniles: The Continuing Practice of Diversity', *Criminal Law Review*, 1987, p. 367.

Gilvarry, E., 'Elly hits out at franchise chaos', *The Gazette*, 27 April 1994, vol. 91, no. 16, p. 8.

Ginsberg, M., *On Justice In Society*, Harmondsworth: Pelican, 1965.

Glasser, C., 'The Legal Profession in the 1990s – Images of Change', *Legal Studies*, 1990, vol. 10, p. 1.

Gordon, G. H., *Scots Criminal Law*, Edinburgh: W. Green, 1992.

Goriely, T., 'Rushcliffe Fifty Years On: The Changing Role of Civil Legal Aid Within the Welfare State', *Journal of Law and Society*, 1994, vol. 21, p. 545.

Gray, A., 'The reform of legal aid', *Oxford Review of Economic Policy*, 1994, vol. 10, no. 1, p. 51.

Gray, A. and Fenn P., 'The rising cost of legally aided criminal cases', *New Law Journal*, 1991, vol. 141, p. 1622.

Gray, G., 'Identifying the Differences: The Development of Legal Aid Policy', in Alexander, M. and Galligan, B. (eds), *Comparative Political Studies: Australia and Canada*, Melbourne: Pittman, 1992.

Greer, S., 'Miscarriages of Justice Reconsidered', *Modern Law Review*, 1994, vol. 57, p. 58.

Gregory, H., *The Queensland Law Society Inc*, Brisbane: Queensland Law Society, 1991.

Halpern, D., *Entry into the Legal Professions*, London: Law Society, 1994.

Hamermesh, D. and Rees, A., *The Economics of Work and Pay*, New York: Harper & Row, 1988.

Hansen, O., 'What a Difference a Clerk Makes', *LAG Bulletin*, March 1982, p. 11.

Hansen, O., 'A Future for Legal Aid?,' *Journal of Law and Society*, 1992, vol. 19, p. 85.

Harkins, J.P., *Federal Legal Aid in Australia*, Canberra: Attorney-General's Department, 1976.

Harman, S., 'Franchising: the preliminary audit experience', *Legal Action*, January 1994, p. 9.

Harris, P., 'The Politics of Law Practice', in Grigg-Spall, I. and Ireland, P. (eds), *The Critical Lawyers' Handbook*, London: Pluto Press, 1992.

Hawker, G., 'The Rise and Fall of the Australian Legal Aid Office', in Encel, S., Wilenski, P. and Schaffer, B. (eds), *Decisions: Case Studies in Australian Public Policy*, Melbourne: Longman Cheshire, 1981.

Hawkins, K., 'The Use of Legal Discretion: Perspectives from Law and Social Science', in Hawkins, K. (ed.), *The Uses of Discretion*, Oxford: Clarendon Press, 1992.

Hay, D., 'Property, Authority and the Criminal Law' in Hay, D., Linebaugh P. and Thompson, E.P. (eds), *Albion's Fatal Tree: Crime And Society In Eighteenth-Century England*, London: Allen Lane, 1975.

Hayek, F.A., *Law, Legislation and Liberty*, London: Routledge & Kegan Paul, 1981.

Hodgson, J., 'No defence for the Royal Commission', in McConville, M. and Bridges, L. (eds), *Criminal Justice in Crisis*, Aldershot: Edward Elgar, 1994.

Holland, A., 'Access to justice', *New Law Journal*, 1995, vol. 145, p. 1256.

Home Office, *Victim's Charter: A Statement of the Rights of Victims of Crime*, London: Home Office, 1990.

Home Office, *Criminal Statistics England and Wales 1993*, Cm 2680, London: HMSO, 1994.

Home Office, *Code of Practice for the detention, treatment and questioning of persons by police officers*, London: HMSO, 1995.

353

Home Office, *Policing Domestic Violence in the 1990s*, Research Study No. 139, London: HMSO, 1995.

Home Office, *Reparation: A Discussion Document*, London: Home Office, 1986.

Hostettler, J., *The Politics of Criminal Law Reform in the Nineteenth Century*, Chichester: Barry Rose, 1992.

House of Commons Home Affairs Select Committee (1989–90), *Fourth Report: Crown Prosecution Service*, London: HMSO, 1990.

Hunt, A. and Wickham, G., *Foucault and Law*, London: Pluto Press, 1994.

Jackson, R.M., 'The Incidence of Jury Trial during the Past Century', *Modern Law Review*, 1937, vol. 1, p. 132.

Jamous, H. and Peloille, B., 'Professions or Self-Perpetuating Systems? Changes in the French University-hospital System', in Jackson, J.A. (ed.), *Professions and Professionalisation*, Cambridge: Cambridge University Press, 1970.

Jenkins, J., *Annual Statistical Report 1994*, London: Law Society, 1994.

Johnson, T.J., *Professions and Power*, London: Macmillan, 1972.

Johnston, P., *The Victim's Charter (1990) and the Release of Life Prisoners: Implications for Probation Service Practice, Values and Management*, Wakefield: West Yorkshire Probation Service, 1995.

Jones, T., MacLean, B. and Young, J., *The Islington Crime Survey*, Aldershot: Gower, 1986.

Joseph, M., *The Conveyancing Fraud*, 2nd ed., Woolwich: Michael Joseph, 1989.

JUSTICE, *The Unrepresented Defendant in the Magistrates' Courts*, London: Stevens and Sons, 1971.

Kemp, C., Norris, C. and Fielding, N., *Negotiating Nothing: Police Disputes and the Law*, Aldershot: Avebury, 1992.

Kempson, E., *Legal Advice and Assistance*, London: Policy Studies Institute, 1989.

Kerner, H.-J., Marks, E. and Schreckling, J., 'Implementation and Acceptance of Victim-offender Mediation Programs in the Federal Republic of Germany: A Survey of Criminal Justice Institutions', in Messmer, H. and Otto, H.-U. (eds), *Restorative Justice on Trial*, Dordrecht: Kluwer, 1992.

Kerner, K., *Defence Agents' Attitudes and Experiences of Criminal Legal Aid*, Edinburgh: Scottish Office Central Research Unit, 1993 (unpublished manuscript).

Kerner, K., *Specialism in Private Legal Practice*, Edinburgh: Scottish Office Central Research Unit, 1995.

Kessler, M., 'Legal Mobilisation for Social Reform: Power and the Politics of Agenda Setting', *Law and Society Review*, 1990, vol. 24, p. 121.

King, D. and Waldron, J., 'Citizenship, Social Citizenship and the Defence of Welfare Provision', *British Journal of Political Science*, 1988, vol. 18, p. 415.

King, M., *The Framework of Criminal Justice*, London: Croom Helm, 1981.

King, M., *Bail or Custody*, London: Cobden Trust 1971.

King, P., 'Decision-Makers and Decision-Making in the English Criminal Law 1750–1800', *Historical Journal*, 1984, vol. 27, p. 25.

Klein, M.W., 'Deinstitutionalization and Diversion of Juvenile Offenders: A Litany of Impediments', in Morris, N. and Tonry, M. (eds), *Crime and Justice: An Annual Review of Research, Vol. 1.*, Chicago: University of Chicago, 1979.

Kurland, P.B. and Waters, D.W.M., 'Public Prosecutions in England 1854–79: an Essay in English Legislative History', *Duke Law Journal*, 1959, p. 493.

Kymlicka, W. and Norman, W., 'Return of the Citizen: A Survey of Recent Work on Citizenship Theory', *Ethics*, 1994, vol. 104, p. 352.

Labour Party, *Access to Justice: A Consultation Paper on Labour's Proposals for Improving the Justice System*, London: Labour Party, 1995.

Lacey, N., *State Punishment: Political Principles and Community Values*, London: Routledge, 1988.

Lacey, N., 'Government as Manager, Citizen as Consumer: The Case of the Criminal Justice Act 1991', *Modern Law Review*, 1994, vol. 57, p. 534.

Lacey, N., 'Making Sense of Criminal Justice', in Lacey, N. (ed.), *Criminal Justice*, Oxford: Oxford University Press, 1994.

Langbein, J.H., 'Shaping the Eighteenth Century Criminal Trial: a view from the Ryder sources', *University of Chicago Law Review*, 1983, vol. 50, p. 1.

Larson, M.S., *The Rise of Professionalism – A Sociological Analysis*, Berkely: University of California Press, 1977.

Law Society, *Annual Statistical Report*, London: Law Society, 1994.

Law Society, *Advising a Suspect in the Police Station*, London: Law Society, 1991.

Law Society, *Memorandum on the Future of Criminal Legal Aid: Evidence to Royal Commission on Criminal Justice*, London: Law Society, 1992.

Law Society and LCAC, *Legal Aid: 38th Annual Reports of the Law Society and the Lord Chancellor's Advisory Committee (1987–1988)*, HC 134, London: HMSO, 1989.

Leda Group, *Bradford Mediation and Reparation: April '93–April '94*, Hebden Bridge: Leda Group, 1994.

Lee, M., 'Pre-court Diversion and Youth Justice', in Levi, M., Maguire, M. and Noaks, L. (eds), *Contemporary Issues in Criminology*, Cardiff: University of Wales Press, 1995.

Legal Aid Board, *Annual Report, 1993–4*, HC 435, London: HMSO, 1994.

Legal Aid Board, *Annual Report 1994–5*, HC 526, London: HMSO, 1995.

Legal Aid Board, *Legal Aid Handbook 1995*, London: Sweet & Maxwell, 1995.

Legal Aid Board, *A Practical Guide to Legal Aid*, London: Legal Aid Board, 1993.

Legal Aid Board, *The Legal Aid Board's Advice to the Lord Chancellor on the Implications of its Taking over Responsibility for Criminal Legal Aid in the Magistrates' Courts*, London: Legal Aid Board, 1993.

Legal Aid Board, Annual Report 1994–95, HC 526, London: HMSO, 1995.

Legal Action Group, *A Strategy for Justice*, London: LAG, 1992.

Leigh, L.H. and Zedner, L., *A Report on the Administration of Criminal Justice in Pre-Trial Phase in France and Germany*, Royal Commission on Criminal Justice Research Study No. 1, London: HMSO, 1992.

Lempert, R., 'Mobilizing Private Law: An Introductory Essay', *Law and Society*, 1976, vol. 11, p. 173.

Lempert, R., 'Discretion in a Behavioral Perspective: The Case of a Public Housing Eviction Board', in Hawkins, K. (ed.), *The Uses of Discretion*, Oxford: Clarendon Press, 1992.

Leng, R., *The Right to Silence in Police Interrogation: A Study of some of the Issues Underlying the Debate*, Royal Commission on Criminal Justice, Research Study No. 10, London: HMSO, 1993.

Leng, R., 'Losing Sight of the Defendant: The Government's Proposals on Pre-Trial Disclosure', *Criminal Law Review*, 1995.

Levenson, H., *The Price of Justice*, London: Cobden Trust, 1981.

Lord Chancellor's Department, *Report of a Survey of the Grant of Legal Aid in Magistrates' Courts*, 1983.

Lord Chancellor's Department, *Legal Aid Efficiency Scrutiny*, London: LCD, 1986.

Lord Chancellor's Department, *Legal Aid for the Apparently Wealthy: A Consultation Paper*, London: December 1994.

Lord Chancellor's Department, *Legal Aid – Targeting Need: The future of publicly funded help in solving legal problems and disputes in England and Wales*, Cm 2854, London: HMSO, 1995.

Lord Chancellor's Department, *Judicial Statistics 1994*, Cm 2891, London: HMSO, 1995.

Lord Chancellor's Department, *Looking to the Future: Mediation and the Ground for Divorce*, Cm 2799, London: HMSO, 1995.

Lord Chancellor's Department, Justices' Clerks Society, & Legal Aid Board, *Guidance on the Interests of Justice Test for the Grant of Criminal Legal Aid*, London: LCD, JCS & LAB, May 1994.

Lund, T.G., 'Legal Aid and Advice Scheme', *Solicitors' Journal*, 1948, vol. 92, pp. 716 and 728.

MacBride, S. (ed.), *Crime and Punishment*, Dublin: Ward River Press, 1982.

Machin, D., Ward, S. and Millar, A., *Applications for Criminal Legal Aid*, Edinburgh: Central Research Unit, 1994.

Maguire, M., 'Effects of the PACE Provisions on Detention and Questioning', *British Journal of Criminology*, 1988, vol. 28, p. 19.

Maguire, M., 'The Needs and Rights of Victims of Crime' in Tonry, M. (ed.), *Crime and Justice: A Review of Research, Vol. 14*, Chicago: University of Chicago Press, 1991.

Marshall, T., 'Informal Justice: The British Experience', in Matthews, R., *Informal Justice?*, London: Sage, 1988.

Marshall, T. and Merry, S., *Crime and Accountability*, London: HMSO, 1990.

Marshall, T.H., *Citizenship and Social Class and Other Essays*, London: Heinemann, 1950.

Mashaw, J., 'The Management Side of Due Process: Some Theoretical and Litigation Notes on the Assurance of Accuracy, Fairness and Timeliness in the Adjudication of Social Welfare Claims', *Cornell Law Review*, 1974, vol. 59, p. 772.

Matthews, R., 'Decarceration and Social Control: Fantasies and Realities', *International Journal of the Sociology of Law*, 1987, vol. 15, p. 39.

Matthews, R., *Informal Justice?*, London: Sage, 1988.

Mawby, R., 'Victims' Needs or Victims' Rights: Alternative Approaches to Policy Making', in Maguire, M. and Ponting, J. (eds), *Victims of Crime: A New Deal?*, Milton Keynes: Open University Press, 1988.

Mawby, R. and Walklate, S., *Critical Victimology*, London: Sage, 1994.

Maxwell, G.M. and Morris, A., *Family, Victims and Culture: Youth Justice in New Zealand*, Wellington: University of Wellington, 1993.

McBarnet, D., 'Pre-Trial Procedures and the Construction of Conviction' in Carlen, P. (ed.), *The Sociology of Law*, Keele: University of Keele, 1976.

McBarnet, D., *Conviction: Law, the State and the Construction of Justice*, London: Macmillan, 1983.

McBarnet, D., 'Two Tiers of Justice', in Lacey N. (ed.), *Criminal Justice*, Oxford: Oxford University Press, 1994.

McCabe, D., '"That part that laws of kings can cause or cure"': Crown Prosecution and Jury Trial at Longford Assizes, 1830–45', in Gillespie, R. and Moran, G. (eds), *Longford: Essays in County History*, Dublin: Lilliput, 1991.

McCann, M., 'Legal Reform and Social Reform Movements: Notes on Theory and its Application', *Studies in Law, Politics and Society*, 1991, vol. 11, p. 225.

McConville, M. and Mirsky, C., 'The State, the Legal Profession, and the Defence of the Poor', *Journal of Law and Society*, 1988, vol. 15, p. 342.

McConville, M., Sanders, A. and Leng, R., *The Case for the Prosecution*, London: Routledge, 1991.

McConville, M. and Hodgson, J., *Custodial Legal Advice and the Right to Silence*, Royal Commission on Criminal Justice, Research Study No. 16, London: HMSO, 1993.

McConville, M., Hodgson, J., Bridges, L. and Pavlovic, A., *Standing Accused: The Organisation and Practices of Criminal Defence Lawyers in Britain*, Oxford: Clarendon Press, 1994.

McConville, M. and Sanders, A., 'The Case for the Prosecution and Administrative Criminology', in Noaks, L., Levi, M. and Maguire, M. (eds), *Contemporary Issues in Criminology*, Cardiff: University of Wales Press, 1995.

McMahon, M., 'Net-Widening: Vagaries in the Use of a Concept', *British Journal of Criminology*, 1990, vol. 30, p. 121.

Mediation UK, *Directory of Mediation and Conflict Resolution Services*, Bristol: Mediation UK, 1994.

Meehan, E., Citizenship and the European Community, London: Sage, 1993.

Meirs, D., 'The Responsibilities and Rights of Victims of Crime', *Modern Law Review*, 1992, p. 482.

Merry, S.E., 'Defining "Success" in the Neighborhood Justice Movement', in Tomasic, R. and Feeley, M. (eds), *Neighborhood Justice*, New York: Longmans, 1982.

Millerson, E., *The Qualifying Associations: a Study in Professionalism*, London: Routledge & Kegan Paul, 1964.

Montague, B., 'It's legal aid, Jim, but not as we know it', *Solicitors' Journal*, 26 May 1995, vol. 139, p. 494.

Morris, A., Maxwell, G.M. and Robertson, J.P., 'Giving Victims a Voice: A New Zealand Experiment', *Howard Journal of Criminal Justice*, 1993, vol. 32, p. 304.

Moxon, D. (ed.), *Managing Criminal Justice: A Collection of Papers*, London: HMSO, 1985.

Mungham, G. and Thomas, P., 'Solicitors and Clients: Altruism or Self-interest?', in Dingwall, R. and Lewis, P. (eds), *The Sociology of the Professions*, London: Macmillan, 1983.

Napley, D., *The Technique of Persuasion*, London: Sweet & Maxwell, 1975.

Napley, D., 'The Ethics of the Professions', *Law Society's Gazette*, 20 March 1985, vol. 82, p. 818.

NAPO, *Policy Document on Reparation*, London: NAPO, 1985.

National Legal Aid Advisory Committee, *Legal Aid For The Australian Community*, Canberra: AGPS, 1990.

National Audit Office Report by the Comptroller and Auditor General, *The Administration of Legal Aid in England and Wales*, London: HMSO, 1992.

Nergard, T.B., 'Solving Conflicts Outside the Court System: Experiences with the Conflict Resolution Boards in Norway', *British Journal of Criminology*, 1993, vol. 33, p. 81.

Newburn, T., *Crime and Criminal Justice Policy*, London: Longman, 1994.

Nozick, R., *Anarchy, State and Utopia*, Oxford: Basil Blackwell, 1974.

Office of Legal Aid and Family Services, *Community Legal Centres: A Study of Four Centres in New South Wales and Victoria*, Canberra: OLAFS, 1991.

Oldfield, A., 'Citizenship: An Unnatural Practice', *Political Quarterly*, 1990, vol. 61, p. 177.

Paterson, A.A. and Bates, T.S.N., *The Legal System of Scotland: Cases and Materials*, Edinburgh: W. Green, 1993.

Philips, D., *Crime and Authority in Victorian England*, London: Croom Helm, 1977.

Philips, D., 'A New Engine of Power and Authority: the Institutionalization of Law-Enforcement in England 1780–1830', in Gatrell, V.A.C., Lenman, B. and Parker, G. (eds), *Crime and the Law: the Social History of Crime in Western Europe since 1500*, London: Europa Publications, 1980.

Portwood, D. and Fielding, A., 'Privilege and Professions', *Sociological Review*, 1981, vol. 29, p. 749.

Pratt, J., 'Diversion from the Juvenile Court', *British Journal of Criminology*, 1986, vol. 26, p. 212.

Pratt, J., 'Corporatism: The Third Model of Juvenile Justice', *British Journal of Criminology*, 1989, vol. 29, p. 236.

Price Waterhouse, *Lord Chancellor's Department: Advice and Survey on Criminal Legal Aid in Magistrates Courts Report*, London: Price Waterhouse, 1992.

Quill, D. and Wynne, J. (eds), *Victim & Offender Mediation Handbook*, Leeds: Save the Children/West Yorkshire Probation Service, 1993.

Radzinowicz, L. and Hood, R., *The Emergence of Penal Policy in Victorian and Edwardian England*, Oxford: Clarendon Press, 1990.

Raine, J. and Wilson, M., 'Organizational Culture and the Scheduling of Court Appearances', *Journal of Law and Society*, 1993, vol. 20, p. 237.

Rees, R., 'The Theory of Principal and Agent, Parts I and II', *Bulletin of Economic Research*, 1985, vol. 37, p. 3 and p. 77.

Reeves, H., *The Victim and Reparation*, London: Victim Support, 1984.

Regan, F., *Is It Time To Rethink Legal Aid? Beyond Lawyers and Money*, Paper to the Socio-Legal Studies Association Conference, Exeter, England, March 1993.

Regan, F., *Are There 'Mean' and 'Generous' Legal Aid Schemes?*, Paper to the 'Legal Aid in the Post Welfare State Society Conference', Den Haag, The Netherlands, April 1994.

359

Regan, F., 'Legal Resources Development in Uganda', *International Journal of the Sociology of Law*, 1994, vol. 22, p. 203.

Regan, F. and Fleming, D., 'International Perspectives on Legal Aid', *Alternative Law Journal*, 1994, vol. 19, p. 183.

Reiner, R., 'Fin de Siècle Blues: the Police Face the Millennium', *Political Quarterly*, 1992, vol. 63, p. 37.

Reynolds, T., 'Victims' Needs and Experiences', in Martin, C. (ed.), *Resolving Crime in the Community: Mediation in Criminal Justice*, Report of a Conference organised by the ISTD and London Victim-Offender Mediation Network, London: ISTD, 1995.

Roberts, D., 'Questioning the suspect: the solicitor's role', *Criminal Law Review*, 1993, p. 368.

Roberts, D., 'Legal Advice, the Unrepresented Suspect and the Courts', *Criminal Law Review*, 1995, p. 483.

Roberts, P. and Willmore, C., *The Role of Forensic Science Evidence in Criminal Proceedings*, Royal Commission on Criminal Justice Research Study No. 11, London: HMSO, 1993.

Roberts, S., 'Mediation in Family Disputes', *Modern Law Review*, 1983, vol. 46, p. 537.

Roberts, S., 'Mediation in the Lawyers' Embrace', *Modern Law Review*, 1992, vol. 55, p. 258.

Robertson, A.H. and Merrills, J., *Human Rights in Europe*, 2nd ed, Manchester: Manchester University Press, 1993.

Rock, P., *The Social World of an English Crown Court*, Oxford: Clarendon Press, 1993.

Ross, D., 'A Legal Assistance Scheme', *The Australian Law Journal*, 1948, vol. 22, p. 51.

Rottman, D., *The Criminal Justice System : Policy and Performance*, Dublin: National Economic and Social Council, 1985.

Royal Commission on Criminal Procedure, *Report*, Cm 8092, London: HMSO, 1981.

Royal Commission on Criminal Justice, *Report*, Cm 2263, London: HMSO, 1993.

Royal Commission on Legal Services, *Final Report: Volume Two – Surveys and Studies*, London: HMSO, 1979.

Royal Commission on Legal Services in Scotland, *Report*, Cm 7846, London: HMSO, 1980.

Royal Norwegian Ministry of Justice and Police, *Municipal Mediation Boards: An Alternative to Prosecution*, Oslo: Ministry of Justice and Police, 1993.

Rozenberg, J., *The Search for Justice*, London: Hodder & Stoughton, 1994.

Rueschemeyer, D., *Lawyers and Their Society: a Comparative Study of the Legal Profession in Germany and the United States*, Cambridge, Mass. : Harvard University Press, 1973.

Rueschemeyer, D., 'Professional Autonomy and the Social Control of Expertise', in Dingwall, R. and Lewis, P. (eds), *The Sociology of the Professions*, London: Macmillan, 1983.

Rushcliffe, Lord, *Report of the Committee on Legal Aid and Legal Advice in England and Wales*, Cm 6641, London: HMSO, 1945.

Ryan, E. and Magee, P., *The Irish Criminal Process*, Dublin: Mercier, 1983.

Sainsbury, R., 'Administrative Justice: Discretion and Procedure in Social Security Decision-making', in Hawkins, K. (ed.), *The Uses of Discretion*, Oxford: Clarendon Press, 1992.

Sanders, A., 'Constructing the Case for the Prosecution', *Journal of Law and Society*, 1987, vol. 14, p. 229.

Sanders, A., 'The Limits to Diversion from Prosecution', *British Journal of Criminology*, 1988, vol. 28, p. 513.

Sanders, A., Bridges, L., Mulvaney, A. and Crozier, G., *Advice and Assistance at Police Stations and the 24 Hour Duty Solicitor Scheme*, London: Lord Chancellor's Department, 1989.

Sanders, A. and Young, R., 'The Rule of Law, Due Process, and Pre-trial Criminal Justice', *Current Legal Problems*, 1994, p. 125.

Sanders, A. and Young, R., *Criminal Justice*, London: Butterworths, 1994.

Sanders, A. and Young, R., 'The Legal Wilderness of Police Interrogation', in *The Tom Sargant Memorial Lecture*, London: JUSTICE, 1994.

Sappington, D.E.M., 'Incentives in Principal-Agent Relationships', *Journal of Economic Perspectives*, 1991, vol. 5, p. 45.

Sarat, A., 'Access to Justice: Citizen Participation and the American Legal Order', in Lipson, L. and Wheeler, S. (eds), *Law and the Social Sciences*, New York: Russell Sage Foundation, 1986.

Sarat, A., 'The New Formalism in Disputing and Dispute Processing', *Law and Society Review*, 1988, vol. 21, p. 695.

Schneider, C. 'Discretion and Rules: A Lawyer's View', in Hawkins, K. (ed.), *The Uses of Discretion*, Oxford: Clarendon Press, 1992.

Scottish Legal Aid Board, *The Scottish Legal Aid Handbook 1992*, Edinburgh: Ritchie, 1992.

Scottish Legal Aid Board, *Annual Report 1994/5*, Edinburgh: Scottish Legal Aid Board, 1995.

Scottish Office, *Criminal Legal Aid Review: A Consultation Paper* (MAB00624.073), November 1993.

Scottish Office, *Firm and Fair*, White Paper (Dd 0287999 C10), Edinburgh: HMSO, June 1994.

Shapiro, M., *Courts: a Comparative and Political Analysis*, Chicago: Chicago University Press, 1981.

Shepherd, E., *Becoming Skilled: A Resource Book*, London: Law Society, 1994.

Sherr, A., Moorhead, R. and Paterson, A., *Transaction Criteria*, London: HMSO, 1992.

Sherr, A., Moorhead, R. and Paterson, A., 'Transaction criteria: back to the future', *Legal Action*, April 1993, p. 7.

Silberman, M., *The Civil Justice Process: A Sequential Model of the Mobilization of Law*, Orlando: Academic Press, 1985.

Silbey, S. and Merry, S., 'Mediator Settlement Strategies', *Law and Policy*, 1986, vol. 8, p. 7.

Skolnick, J., *Justice Without Trial*, New York: Wiley, 1966.

Smith, D.A. and Visher, C.A., 'Street-Level Justice: Situational Determinants of Police Arrest Decisions', *Social Problems*, 1981, vol. 29, p. 2.

Smith, R., 'Transaction criteria: the face of the future', *Legal Action*, February 1993, p. 9.

Smith, R., 'Survival of the Biggest', Legal Aid News, August 1994, p. 9.

Smith, R., 'Current Trends', in Smith, R. (ed.), *Shaping the Future: New Directions in Legal Services*, London: Legal Action Group, 1995.

Society of Labour Lawyers, *Justice for All*, London: Fabian Research Pamphlet No. 273, 1968.

Sommerlad, H., 'The Myth of Feminisation: Women and Cultural Change in the Legal Profession', *International Journal of the Legal Profession*, 1994, vol. 1, p. 31.

Spigelman, J., 'Poverty and the Law', *Australian and New Zealand Journal of Criminology*, 1969, vol. 2, p. 87

Stanko, E.A., 'When Precaution is Normal: A Feminist Critique of Prevention', in Gelsthorpe, L. and Morris, A. (eds), *Feminist Perspectives in Criminology*, Milton Keynes: Open University Press, 1990.

Stephen, J.F., *A History of the Criminal Law of England*, (vol. 1) London: Macmillan and Co., 1883.

Stephen, J.F., *A General View of the Criminal Law of England*, London: Macmillan and Co., 1890.

Stewart, G. and Walsh, K., 'Change in the Management of Public Services', *Public Administration*, 1992, vol. 70, p. 499.

Sudnow, D., 'Normal Crimes', *Social Problems*, 1965, vol. 12, p. 255.

Sackville, R., *Legal Aid in Australia*, Canberra: AGPS, 1975.

Taylor, F.W., *The Principles of Scientific Management*, New York: Harper and Row, 1911.

Thompson, E.P., *Whigs and Hunters*, Harmondsworth: Penguin, 1977.

Tomasic, R., 'Mediation as an Alternative to Adjudication', in Tomasic, R. and Feeley, M. (eds), *Neighborhood Justice*, New York: Longmans, 1982.

Travers, P. and Richardson, S., *Living Decently*, Melbourne, Oxford University Press, 1994.

Turner, B., 'Outline of a Theory of Citizenship', *Sociology*, 1990, vol. 24, p. 189.

Turner, B. (ed.), *Citizenship and Social Theory*, London: Sage, 1993.

Twining, W., *Theories of Evidence: Bentham and Wigmore*, London: Weidenfeld & Nicolson, 1985.

Tzannes, M., 'Strategies for the Selection of Students to Law Courses in the 21st Century: Issues and Options for Admissions Policy Makers', *The Law Teacher*, 1995, vol. 29, no. 1, p. 43.

Umbreit, M. and Coates, R.B., 'Cross-Site Analysis of Victim-Offender Mediation in Four States', *Crime and Delinquency*, 1993, vol. 39, p. 565.

United Nations Development Program, *Human Development Report*, New York: Oxford University Press, 1990.

van Dijk, P. and van Hoof, G.J.H., *Theory and Practice of the European Convention on Human Rights*, 2nd ed., Dordrecht: Kluwer, 1990.

van Dijk, J. (ed.), *Criminal Law in Action: An Overview of Current Issues in Western Societies*, Deventer: Kluwer, 1986.

Varian, H.R., *Intermediate Microeconomics: a modern approach*, 3rd ed., New York: Norton, 1993.

Victim Support, *Victim Support, Reparation and Mediation*, Policy Document, London: Victim Support, 1990.

Walker, C., 'Introduction', in Walker, C. and Starmer, K. (eds), *Justice in Error*, London: Blackstone Press, 1993.

Walker, D.M., *The Scottish Legal System*, Edinburgh: W. Green, 1992.

Wall, D.S., *Policy into Practice: The Impact of Changes in Policy upon Discretionary Decision Making in the Magistrates' Courts*, paper delivered to Socio-Legal Studies Association conference held in Leeds, England, 27 March 1995.

Wall, D.S. and Wood, A., 'An endangered species: The experienced criminal practitioner', *Solicitors' Journal*, 1992, vol. 136, p. 796.

Wall, D.S. and Wood, A., 'Buying time for the debate over criminal legal aid', *New Law Journal*, 1993, vol. 143, p. 324.

Wall, D.S. and Wood, A., *The Administration of Criminal Legal Aid in the Magistrates' Courts of England and Wales: Final Report*, Leeds: Centre for Criminal Justice Studies, 1994.

Warner, S., *Making Amends: Justice for Victims and Offenders*, Aldershot: Avebury, 1992.

Weber, M., *The Theory of Social and Economic Organisation*, New York: The Free Press, 1964.

West Yorkshire Probation Service, *Victim/Offender Mediation Reparation Policy*, Wakefield: WYPS, 1994.

White, R., 'The Distasteful Character of Litigation for Poor Persons', *Juridical Review*, 1975, vol. 3, p. 233.

Widgery, Mr Justice, *Report of the Departmental Committee on Legal Aid in Criminal Proceedings*, Cm 2934, London: HMSO, 1966.

Wilkinson, C. and Evans, R., 'Police Cautioning of Juveniles: The Impact of Home Office Circular 14/1985', *Criminal Law Review*, 1990, p. 165.

Wolchover, D. and Heaton-Armstrong, A., 'The Questioning Code Revamped', *Criminal Law Review*, 1991, p. 232.

Wright, M., *Justice for Victims and Offenders*, Buckingham: Open University Press, 1991.

Wright, M., 'Victims, Mediation and Criminal Justice', *Criminal Law Review*, 1995, p. 187.

Young, R., 'Neighbourhood Dispute Mediation: Theory and Practice', *Civil Justice Quarterly*, 1989, p. 319.

Young, R., 'Reparation as Mitigation', *Criminal Law Review*, 1989, p. 463.

Young, R., 'Court clerks, legal aid and the interests of justice', *New Law Journal*, 1992, vol. 142, p. 1264.

Young, R. and Sanders, A., 'A wise and sensible move?', *New Law Journal*, 1992, vol. 142. p. 1409.

Young, R., 'The Merits of Legal Aid in the Magistrates' Courts', *Criminal Law Review*, 1993, p. 336.

Young, R., Moloney, T. and Sanders, A., *In the Interests of Justice?: The Determination of Criminal Legal Aid Applications by Magistrates' Courts in England and Wales*, London: Legal Aid Board, 1992.

Young, R. and Sanders, A., 'Boxing in the defence: the Royal Commission, disclosure, and the lessons of research', *The Criminal Lawyer*, November 1994, No. 50, p. 3.

Zander, M., 'Unrepresented Defendants in the Criminal Courts', *Criminal Law Review*, 1969, p. 632.

Zander, M., 'A study of Bail/Custody Decisions in London Magistrates' Courts', *Criminal Law Review*, 1971, p. 191.

Zander, M., 'Unrepresented Defendants in Magistrates' Courts', *New Law Journal*, 1972, vol. 122, p. 1041.

Zander, M., 'Operation of the Bail Act in London Magistrates' Courts', *New Law Journal*, 1979, vol. 129, p. 108.

Zander, M., *Cases and Materials on the English Legal System*, 5th ed., London: Weidenfeld & Nicolson, 1988.

Zander, M. and Glasser, C., 'A Study in Representation', *New Law Journal*, 1967, vol. 117, p. 815.

Zdenkowski, G., 'Defending the Indigent Accused in Serious Cases: a Legal Right to Counsel?', *Criminal Law Journal*, 1994, vol. 18, p. 135.

Zedner, L., 'Reparation and Retribution: Are They Reconcilable?', *Modern Law Review*, 1994, vol. 57, p. 228.

Zehr, H., *Changing Lenses; A New Focus for Criminal Justice*, Scottdale, PA: Herald Press, 1990.

Zemans, F.K., 'Framework for Analysis of Legal Mobilization: A Decision-Making Model', *American Bar Foundation Research Journal*, 1982, p. 911.

Zemans, F.K., 'Legal Mobilization: The Neglected Role of Law in the Political System', *American Political Science Review*, 1983, vol. 77, p. 690.

Zuckerman, A.A.S., 'Miscarriages of Justice – A Root Treatment', *Criminal Law Review*, 1992, p. 323.

Index

Index

Index

Index

Index

Index